OS/360
JOB CONTROL LANGUAGE

Harry W. Cadow

International Business Machines Corporation

OS/360 JOB CONTROL LANGUAGE

Prentice-Hall, Inc.

Englewood Cliffs, New Jersey

13–642926–2

Library of Congress Catalog Card Card No.: 70–123089

Printed in the United States of America

Current printing (last digit):

10 9 8 7 6 5 4 3 2

PRENTICE-HALL INTERNATIONAL, INC., *London*
PRENTICE-HALL OF AUSTRALIA, PTY. LTD., *Sydney*
PRENTICE-HALL OF CANADA, LTD., *Toronto*
PRENTICE-HALL OF INDIA PRIVATE LIMITED, *New Delhi*
PRENTICE-HALL OF JAPAN, INC., *Tokyo*

PREFACE

The objective of this textbook is to explain WHY the System/360 Operating System and its *manager,* Job Control Language, are needed. The WHY's are exemplified in many cases, showing HOW to use the Operating System via Job Control. The selection and use of specific job control information for any given computer installation should however be based upon the latest reference manuals prepared by IBM. The Job Control Language (JCL) reference manual is the main document required. During the first part of 1969 IBM had made its eighth major revision to the Job Control reference manual (there have been an average of two major revisions a year). Hence, you should make it a point to acquire each revision as it is published.

This textbook is as resistant to obsolesence as possible. There will undoubtedly be improvements to the System/360 (S/360) computing system and new data processing techniques will be discovered and implemented; but these should have minimal effect on the currency of this text.

ACKNOWLEDGEMENT: Prentice-Hall, Inc., and the author are grateful to the IBM corporation for giving permission to use material copyrighted by IBM. The IBM copyrighted publications which the author wrote for IBM are:

System/360 Operating System Concepts for Operators (text) R20-4114
System/360 Operating System Concepts for Operators (illustrations) R20-4115
System/360 Operating System JCL for Operators (text) R20-4118
System/360 Operating System JCL for Operators (illustrations) R20-4119

CONTENTS

1 *COMPONENTS OF A COMPUTER* **1**

The computer is a data factory 1
Computing speeds—milliseconds, microseconds, and nanoseconds 4
The CPU 5
Computer storage (main storage) 9
Instruction components 18
CPU controls sequence of execution 26
Interruptions and masking 27
Storage protection 28
The interval timer 29
Summary 29

2 *INPUT/OUTPUT DEVICES, CONTROL UNITS, CHANNELS, AND RECORDING DATA* **33**

Typewriter 33
Punched cards and card readers 35
Printer 38
Hardware buffers 40
Other card readers, punches, and printers 41
Multiplexor channel 41
Slow-speed I/O device and channel summary 44
Data files—sets of data 44
Organization of data sets 45
Magnetic tape 47
Reading tape records into storage 53
Type of record lengths—fixed and variable 55
Processing records on tape 56
Selector channel—path for tape data 58
Frequency of processing data recorded on tape 58
Relationship between channels and CPU 59
I/O interruptions 60
Summary 61

3 *DISK STORAGE DEVICES* 65

The disk 66
Selector channel for disk 72
The cylinder concept of disk storage 72
Rotational delay and access time 73
Physical records on disk 73
Creating an index for sequentially organized records 75
Dircct organization 79
Other direct-access devices 80
Disk I/O operations 83
Problem program—I/O program relationship 84
Installation layout 84
Summary 85

4 *VARIETIES OF DATA PROCESSING* 89

Review of batch processing 89
Inquiry processing 90
Using terminals to transmit batches of data 95
Sending messages between terminals
via the computer 97
Real-time processing 97
Electronic sketch pad 98
Miscellaneous input devices 101
Addresses of I/O devices 103
Summary 104

5 *USING THE COMPUTER INSTALLATION* 107

A description of a "typical" institution 107
Programming the company's computers 110
Compiler Programs 110
A compiler program's I/O requirements 111
Submitting programs to be compiled
from terminals 112
Conversational programming 114
Managing the computer installation 115
Summary 115

6 *THE SYSTEM/360 OPERATING SYSTEM* 119

Factory managers 119
Operating system: Definition 120
Collection of programs in an operating system 120

Each installation generates its own operating system 121
The supervisor 121
The S/360 interrupt system 125
Program library 129
Subroutine libraries 131
Multiple data sets per volume: the VTOC 132
How the operating system gets programs (tasks) started (initiated) 134
Describing the I/O requirements and naming the program 134
System tasks 135
The reader and source statement cards 135
Definition of a job step 138
Definition of a job 138
Related job steps comprise a job 139
The job card 139
The job stream 140
Classifications of jobs 141
Multiple job streams 141
Production of output–output writer 144
Program production in an OS/360 installation 145
Uniprogramming 148
Organizing of main storage for multiprogramming 149
Sequential scheduler 151
Scheduling jobs for a multiprogramming operating system 152
Priority scheduler and job priorities 152
How the supervisors remember what's going on 152
Resources 153
The attach macro 155
Hierarchy relationships between system and problem program tasks 155
Reentrant, reusable and non-reusable programs 156
Resident SVC's 160
SVCLIB 160
Job control statements 161
Reducing the number of job control cards to be handled 162
Summary 162

7 *DATA MANAGEMENT* 167

Review of data 168
Review of media on which data is recorded 168
Review of I/O devices 169
Review of access methods 169
How the programmer communicates with the access methods 170
OS data-retrieval schemes 170
Types of entries in VTOC 174

Describing a data set and specifying access method information 179
Data control block 179
Changing access method requirements 180
Retrieving a specific generation of a data set 183
Operational factors concerning data management 189
Summary 198

8 *THE JOB STATEMENT* **203**

Review 203
The job statement format 203
Rules about job statements 203
Job accounting parameters 205
Programmer name 207
Message display 207
Termination conditions 209
Classification code of the job 210
Priority of the job 210
Output device on which messages are displayed 211
Amount of main storage required for a region (MVT) 211
Preventing a job from being initiated 212
Rollout/rollin (MVT) 212
Checkpoint/restart 213
Summary 215

9 *THE EXECUTE STATEMENT* **217**

Review 217
The execute statement format 217
Rules about the exec statement 217
Name of the program 219
Name of the procedure 219
Passing parameters to the program 220
Job step accounting information 221
Job step time limit 222
Amount of main storage required (MVT only) 222
Bypassing job steps 223
Rollout/rollin 224
Defining a restart 224
Summary 225

10 *THE DD STATEMENT* **227**

Review 227
Status and disposition of data sets (DISP) 227
Data set names 231

Specifying and requesting I/O units (UNIT=) 234
Identification of the volume 239
Requesting space on direct-access storage devices 242
Splitting data sets into smaller sets 245
Arranging data sets into a series 248
Optimizing channel usage 248
Identification of data sets on tape 249
Protecting the data set 250
Specifying data set attributes and access method requirements 251
Defining the character set for the printer 254
Informing the initiator to look for a program in a private library 254
Summary 255

11 ***PROCEDURES AND THEIR USE*** **259**

Review 259
Size of PROCLIB 259
Symbolic parameters 260
Rules for symbolic names 260
Substituting the actual value for the symbolic value 260
Defaults for actual values 261
The override technique 261
Reader and writer procedures 262
Sample catalogued procedures 266
Summary 271

Appendix I ***DEFINITION OF A PROGRAM*** **273**

Types of instructions in Figure A3 276
Data and constants 276
Debugging 278
Encoded instructions 278
Number of programming languages 279
Classifying programming language levels 281
The linkage editor 282

Appendix II ***NUMBERING & COUNTING SYSTEMS*** **285**

Number system base 287
Converting from one numbering system to another 289
Adding and subtracting HEX numbers 294

INDEX **297**

INTRODUCTION

Probably the most complex body of knowledge in existence today on the topic of computers and data processing is the Operating System (OS) for the IBM System/360. Many a previously accomplished data processing professional or technician has been overcome by the seemingly impossible task of learning the functions and capabilities of OS by reading the available publications. Learning these functions and capabilities is now greatly simplified; not only for the accomplished non-OS technician or professional but also for the beginning data processing student. Presented in one relatively small textbook are the fundamentals of data processing through the concepts of multiprogramming and the use of Job Control Language for OS/360.

This textbook is organized in such a way that it allows you to start anywhere based upon your level of data processing experience. If you have not yet acquired even a conversational background of basic programming terms, you should study Appendix I; if you lack the skill to convert between numbering systems used by the S/360, studying Appendix II will provide the skill. If you are not versed in the basic architecture of the S/360, start with Chapter 1; if you have but little knowledge of conventional input/output devices, read Chapter 2; if you are already familiar with the contents of Chapters 1 and 2, Direct Access Storage Devices and general data processing capabilities and terminology, start with Chapter 6.

Each of the eleven chapters concludes with a collection of summarizing statements, each of which concisely states a major topic or point developed in the text. This feature has two major advantages. The first is that it provides you with a checklist of what you may already know; that is, read the summary before reading the chapter . . . if you find the summary statements familiar, you don't have to read the narrative. The second advantage makes it possible for you to quickly refresh your memory weeks or even months after having read the text.

OS/360
JOB CONTROL LANGUAGE

…NTS OF A
…R

…? In the past two decades this question … in dozens of ways. An engineer's an-… it is an ordered collection of electronic … function it is to manipulate bits of data. … ot point to any fallacies in the defini-… ke the reader of the definition feel as … anything. A computer operator might … is a system of input and output devices, … g unit, and a storage unit. Again, the … ut it raises more questions. What is an … t is an output device? What is a storage … central processing unit? The purpose of … tell you what the components of a … hat you can make up your own defini-…

…R IS A
…Y

…ter" and "data processor" are generally … synonymous. Another synonym could … a factory." A data factory's objective is … rs from related facts by following a pro-… ers are generally referred to as the output and the facts are usually called the input. If a data factory were staffed by human beings, if the input and output were received and shipped in boxes and crates like conventional raw materials and processed goods, the operation might look as in Fig. 1.

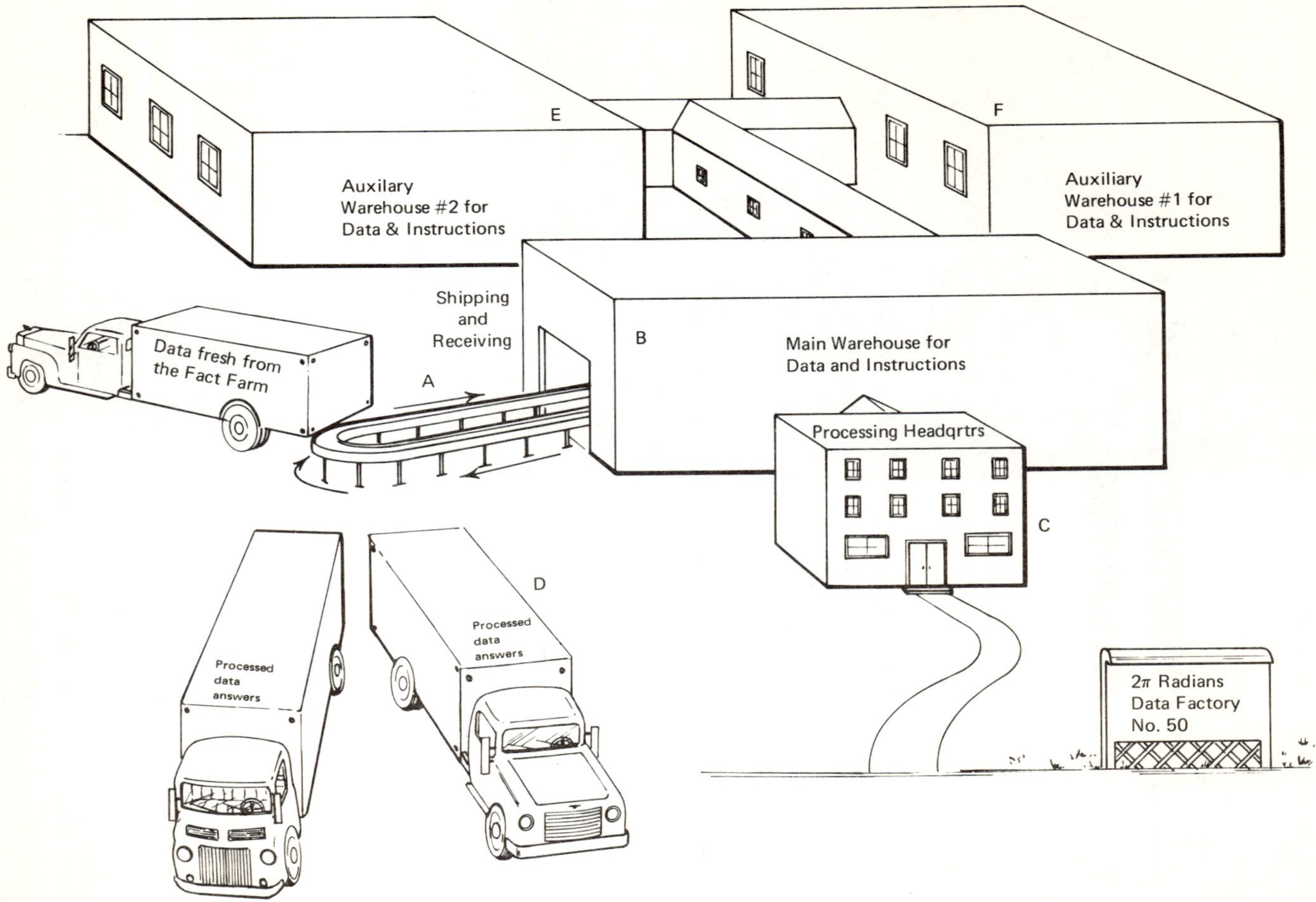

Fig. 1 Data factory.

Fresh input is delivered via a conveyor-belt system to the main warehouse, where it is stored, Ⓐ. The warehouse also contains the instructions used by the processing staff to process the data, Ⓑ. The processing department, Ⓒ, gets one instruction at a time from the warehouse. The instruction tells the processing department which operation it is to perform, where in the main warehouse the data can be found, and where in the main warehouse the processed data should be placed.

Output for visual inspection usually comes out via the same conveyor belt system in which the fresh data entered, Ⓓ. Each parcel of output is properly identified so that it will be picked up only by the proper recipient. The auxiliary warehouses Ⓔ and Ⓕ contain data and instructions which are in excess of the main warehouse's capacity. Very often, fresh facts (input) cannot be processed right away. Rather than slow down the delivery of the input it is allowed to enter main storage and then, under control of processing headquarters, it is transferred to an auxiliary warehouse.

Later, the input will be retrieved from the auxiliary warehouse and placed in the main warehouse, from which it can be retrieved for processing. In a similar fashion, the results produced by the processing department are often passed on to the auxiliary warehouses for later distribution. (The stockpiling of input or output data is not very much different from the stockpiling of raw materials by automobile manufacturers to assure continued production or the stockpiling of finished autos in anticipation of work slowdowns.)

Notice that there is no direct path from processing headquarters to the auxiliary warehouses (everything goes through the main warehouse). Notice also that the only way to transport data (and instructions) between the main warehouse and either the auxiliary warehouses or the objects at Ⓐ and Ⓓ is via a path through a tunnel or over a conveyor-belt system connected to the main warehouse.

Processing Speeds versus Shipping and Receiving Speeds

In a data factory there are often great discrepancies between processing speeds and input/output speeds. In many cases, the processing department can get at information in the main warehouse *one thousand* times faster than shipping and receiving bring it in or remove it.

Processing Speeds versus Speeds between Main and Auxiliary Warehouses

The discrepancy between processing speeds and the transfer speeds between main and auxiliary warehouses is not nearly as great. In general, the processing department can get at information in the main warehouse about five to fifty times faster than it can get at the information in the auxiliary warehouse.

Balancing the Speeds

Couldn't one simply increase the speeds of the slower objects? No, the relative speeds we mentioned above are about as high as they can reliably be made. The picture is not as bleak as it may seem, however. When the processing is very complex, the processing department may have to carry out thousands of instructions for every unit of input that arrives. Under these conditions, speeding up the delivery of fresh data would be of very little value. If the processing is either quite simple, or the percentage of relevant inputs quite low (that is, only one fourth or one fifth or less of the units of input is eligible for processing), speeding up the input delivery would be beneficial. Unfortunately, the speed of an input device in a data-processing factory is fixed during its creation. Hence it would always be either slow or fast, and the faster it is, the more one has to pay for it.

The alternative is to have the factory involved in several processes at the same time. In this way process X can be worked on while processes A, B, C, and so on, are waiting for fresh data or for their distribution area to empty (so that new output can be stored). When process X has to wait for something crucial to happen, the processing department selects one of the other tasks that is now ready. Of course, if none of the tasks (i.e., processes A, B, C, X, etc.) is ready, the processing department takes a break. Sooner or later (the sooner, the better) the processing department's siesta will be interrupted with the announcement that one of the tasks can be resumed.

COMPUTING SPEEDS—MILLISECONDS, MICROSECONDS, AND NANOSECONDS

The shortest time unit we use in our daily activity is the second. To give the impression that something is going to occur in a very short period of time we say, "I'll be with you in a second," or "It won't take me more than a couple of seconds to do this." In a computing system, the second is a very long period of time. Most input/output operations are expressed in a time framework of one thousandth of a second; small and relatively inexpensive central processing units (CPU's) carry out each operation in time units of one millionth of a second; the time units required for an operation of a large and powerful CPU are expressed in billionths of a second. Terms such as thousandths, millionths, and billionths are conversational jawbreakers—hence we use Latin and Greek prefixes: millisecond for one thousandth of a second, microsecond to signify one millionth of a second, and nanosecond to mean one billionth of a second.

The significance of such microscopic units of time (or maybe they're nanoscopic) is hard to comprehend. Let's make some comparisons to ease the comprehension. A millisecond is to a second as a second is to $16\frac{2}{3}$ minutes; a microsecond is to a second as a second is to about $11\frac{1}{2}$ days; a nanosecond is to a second as a second is to about $31\frac{1}{2}$ years. Another way to look at the relative units is as follows. One milliyear consists of 8 hours and 45 minutes, a microyear is 31.5 seconds long, and a nanocentury has only 3.15 seconds. [Remembering the comparisons in this paragraph won't increase the probability that you'll become a computer expert one iota (even smaller than a nano); they are presented so that you'll have some relative idea of a computer's phenomenal speeds.]

A computer's speed can also be emphasized by comparing it to the speed of light. Electricity travels at the speed of light, about 186,000 miles per second. This is about equivalent to 1,000 feet per microsecond, or 1 foot per nanosecond, or one hundredth of an inch per picosecond (trillionths of a second).

The first part of the text will acquaint you with the IBM System/360 (S/360), which is the base of the operating system to be studied. While studying this first part you should obtain a fundamental knowledge of some components of the S/360 computer and how these components interact.

THE CPU

In the description of the factory we talked about several components. The following list equates the names of the components as we described them and their comparable names in data-processing terminology:

Processing Department	Central Processing Unit (CPU)
Auxiliary Warehouses	High-Speed Input/Output Devices
Conveyor Belt and Tunnels	Channels
Main Warehouse	Main Storage
Fresh Data Trucks	Slow-Speed Input
Answer Trucks	Slow-Speed Output
Data Factory (everything above)	Computer (everything above)

People often ask the question, "Is the electronic computer something like an automatic adding machine or desk calculator?" The traditional answer is, "Absolutely not!!!—the computer is a sophisticated electronic device capable of performing complex mathematical operations at ultrahigh speeds." It is unfortunate that this answer is so common and popular. It gives the impression that only Ph.D.'s with an I.Q. of 150 or higher are capable of using it. It would be much better to say, "Although the electronic computer can trace its ancestry to the desk calculator, its capabilities exceed those of the desk calculator" (just as modern man's technical capabilities exceed those of Neanderthal man). The electronic computer can perform a desk calculator's job. A desk calculator is capable of performing arithmetic operations through the use of mechanical components—The computer uses electronic components for doing arithmetic. The desk calculator performs only when a human being depresses the buttons of the keyboard (for entering data, for doing arithmetic, for printing output). The electronic computer performs when it is electronically activated by a coded instruction (for entering recorded data, for doing arithmetic, for recording output). One could say that a computer performs only when it receives the electronic equivalent of a human being's depression of the buttons on a keyboard.

Shown in Fig. 2 is a picture of the S/360 CPU. The function of the CPU is to carry out the operations that have been built into the electronic circuitry of the computer. As you read the following partial list of the basic operations of which the S/360 is capable, try to envision small labeled boxes each containing a separate set of electronic circuits for each operation.

1. The arithmetic operations
   - Addition
   - Subtraction
   - Multiplication
   - Division
2. The testing and branching operations
   - Comparisons
   - Detection of conditions
   - Zero result
   - Nonzero result
   - Equal to (two values are equal)
   - Less than (value *A* less than value *B*)
   - Greater than (value *A* greater than value *B*)
   - Positive result
   - Negative result
   - Unequal (two values are different)
   - Branching
3. Input and output operations (I/O operations), that is, getting data to be processed into the computer and processed data out of the computer
   - Start an input or output operation (see note below)
   - Test the condition of an input or output device
   - Halt an input or output operation
   - Test the condition of the channel

Note. Specific I/O operations in the S/360, such as reading and writing, to and from the I/O devices are executed by the *channel.* The CPU actually starts the I/O operations in that it gives the channel permission to execute. (Channel operations are described later.)

4. Miscellaneous operations
   - Translating character strings
   - Truncating character strings (chopping off the right end)
   - Lengthening character strings (adding zeros to the right end)
   - Converting between number systems (decimal to binary and vice versa)

Fig. 2 Front and side view of S/360, Model 40.

This partial list will suffice for now. The important point for you to remember is that the number of operations a CPU can perform with its electronic circuits is fairly limited.

CPU Setup

An undisciplined CPU with its limited number of operations is of very little use. The electronic circuits of the CPU (if they are to do anything either useless or useful) must somehow be "set up" or disciplined. That is, the sequence of operations it is to perform must be spelled out (or, as we usually say, it must be programmed), and then this sequence must be accessible to the CPU. For example, if the computer is to calculate the potential value of an initial investment (say $100.00) with a compound interest (say 5 percent) for a certain period (say 10 years) one might spell out the sequence of operations (using a programming language) in the following way:

Statement No.	OPERATION (Written in English)
1	Set principal equal to $100.00
2	Set principal and interest factor equal to 1.05
3	Set periods equal to 10 years
4	Multiply principal times interest and principal factor
5	Round off the product
6	Set product equal to principal
7	Subtract 1 from number of periods
8	If number of periods >0, branch to operation at statement 4
9	Halt
10	Principal
11	Interest and principal factor
12	Periods

There is no doubt about it—the above is a sequence of operations (i.e., program) one could compile into an execution language and then have the CPU calculate the value of the 10-year investment.

The CPU Understands Machine Language

If the CPU is to perform these operations they must be in *execution language* or, as it is usually referred to, *machine language form.* That is, even though the sequence of operations shown above is correct, they must be first translated into a coded form that the CPU can "understand," usually referred to as machine language form. To illustrate, the machine language form of the above 12 statements might appear as follows (*note*: This is the machine language for a fictitious computer):

```
R5  450  100
R5  460  105
```

```
R5 470 010
MP 450 460
AJ 450 002
R6 450 002
SB 470 001
BN 004 470
ST 450 000
10000
105
10
```

A few paragraphs back we said that the program must be accessible to the CPU. By this we mean that the program (in machine language form) must be in a place from which the CPU can retrieve, in the proper sequence, each instruction. The place where the program (and where the data it processes) must be for the CPU to retrieve one instruction at a time will be discussed next.

COMPUTER STORAGE (MAIN STORAGE)

The place where both the instructions and data to be processed are kept (for accessibility to the CPU) is called the computer's storage unit or main storage, or just storage. (In the data-factory parable this is called the main warehouse.) Whatever it's called, it is one of the major components of a computing system. Figure 3 schematically illustrates the relationship between CPU and storage. Storage units come in assorted sizes—the size can range from 8,000 positions to 4 million positions. To understand what is meant by a *position of storage,* you will have to know something about the physical characteristics of storage.

Magnetic Cores

The storage of the S/360 computer is comprised of a collection of small magnetic cores. Like anything magnetic, a core may be in either of two states; whereas an active electro bar magnet has either a north–south polarity or a south–north polarity (depending upon the direction of the electricity), a magnetic core has either clockwise polarity or counterclockwise polarity (Fig. 4). Hence the polarity of a single core can be used to represent one of two things. If the core is magnetized clockwise it represents one thing; if it is magnetized counterclockwise it represents another thing. In the computer, we want the polarity of these cores to represent characters that are numeric, alphabetic, or special. Since one core can represent only two different characters, cores have to be used in combinations to represent numerical and alphabetic characters and special symbols (see Fig. 5).

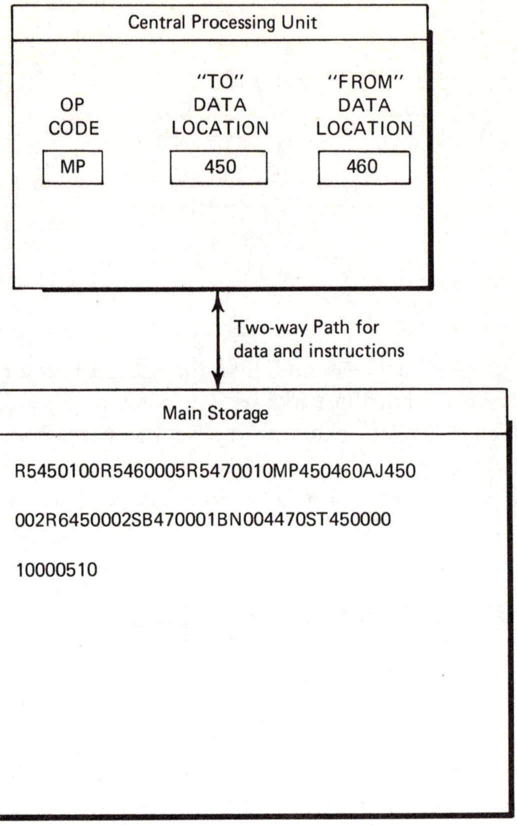

Fig. 3 Relationship of CPU and main storage.

Core Combinations

The number of combinations possible with any given quantity of cores is very predictable. For example, one core allows 2 combinations, two cores allow 4 combinations, three cores allow 8 combinations, four cores allow 16 combinations, eight cores allow 256 combinations, and so on. These relationships can be better illustrated by the following table:

No. of Cores	No. of Combinations
1	2
2	4
3	8
4	16
5	32
6	64
7	128
8	256

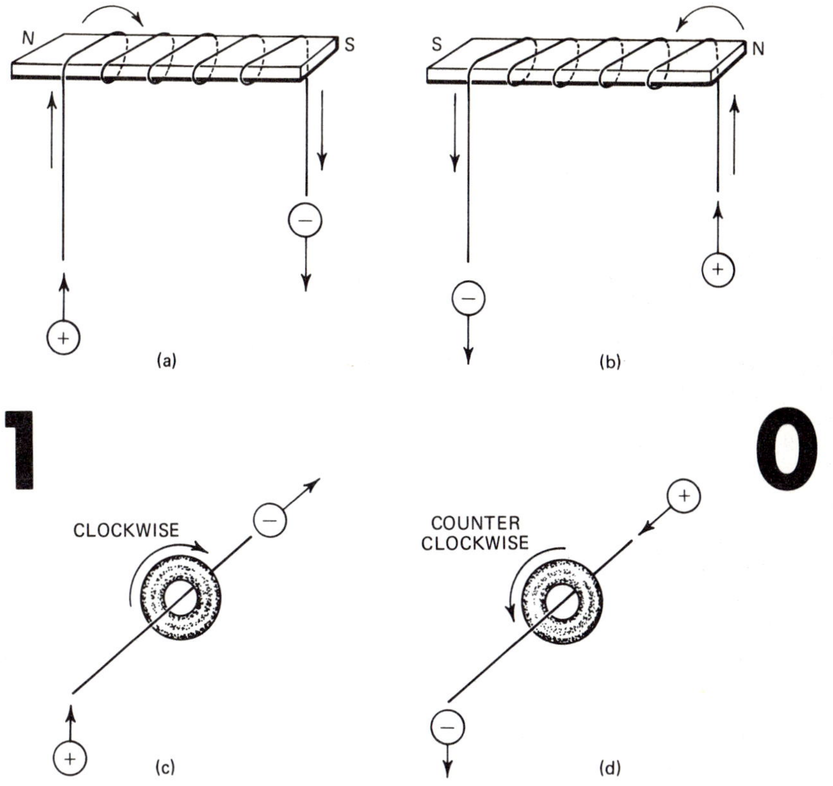

The polarity of a single magnet, either bar shaped or doughnut shaped, is traditionally represented by 0's (zeros) and 1's (ones). For example, the NS polarity of a bar magnet and the clockwise polarity of a core may be represented by a 1; likewise, the SN polarity of a bar magnet and the counterclockwise polarity of a core may be represented by a 0.

It really doesn't matter which polarity is represented by a 0 or 1 as long as all of the engineers of each computer agree on which is which.

Fig. 4 Bar and core magnetism.

The Byte

In the S/360, each collection of eight cores comprises a unit of storage called a *byte*. Hence each byte of storage can, at any instant, have one of 256 combinations. Now, the standard character and symbol set of most languages used for human speech is comprised of something less than 256 different items (e.g., in English there are 26 capital letters, 26 lowercase letters, 10 digits, etc.). Thus it seems that one byte (consisting of eight cores, or bits) can represent any of the standard characters or symbols of the English language. (Anything that can represent either of two different things is often referred to as a *bit*. Hence it is

Polarity Combinations of Six Cores	Character Represented by this Combination
000001	1
000010	2
000011	3
000100	4
000101	5
000110	6
000111	7
001000	8
001001	9
001010	0
001011	#
001100	@
010001	/
010010	S
010011	T
010100	U
100000	—
100001	J
100010	K
100011	L
110000	&
110001	A
110010	B
110011	C

This partial list of the polarity combinations of 6 cores and the characters each combination represents, is the code structure used by many computers prior to the System/360.

Fig. 5 Polarity combinations of 6 cores.

customary for people to say that one byte consists of eight bits, rather than saying that a byte consists of eight cores, or eight bar magnets, etc.)

The Extended Binary Coded Decimal Interchange Code

When graphic symbols are represented by some pattern of bits, that pattern of bits is called a code. Prior to the S/360, most computers had six bits in one unit of core storage (as shown in Fig. 5). When the S/360 was designed (with its unit of core storage, i.e., eight bits) the number of graphic symbols that could be represented was greatly extended. Hence the pattern of the eight bits to represent the graphic symbols is called *extended binary coded decimal* (EBCD). EBCD is an interchange code (interchangeable so that the code would be inter-

① Decimal	② Hexadecimal	③ System/360 8-bit Code	④
0	00	0000 0000	
1	01	0000 0001	
2	02	0000 0010	
3	03	0000 0011	
4	04	0000 0100	
5	05	0000 0101	
6	06	0000 0110	
7	07	0000 0111	
8	08	0000 1000	
9	09	0000 1001	
10	0A	0000 1010	
11	0B	0000 1011	
12	0C	0000 1100	
13	0D	0000 1101	
14	0E	0000 1110	
15	0F	0000 1111	
16	10	0001 0000	
17	11	0001 0001	
18	12	0001 0010	
19	13	0001 0011	
20	14	0001 0100	
21	15	0001 0101	
22	16	0001 0110	
23	17	0001 0111	
24	18	0001 1000	
25	19	0001 1001	
26	1A	0001 1010	
27	1B	0001 1011	
28	1C	0001 1100	
29	1D	0001 1101	
30	1E	0001 1110	
31	1F	0001 1111	
32	20	0010 0000	
33	21	0010 0001	
34	22	0010 0010	
35	23	0010 0011	
36	24	0010 0100	
37	25	0010 0101	
38	26	0010 0110	
39	27	0010 0111	
40	28	0010 1000	
41	29	0010 1001	
42	2A	0010 1010	
43	2B	0010 1011	
44	2C	0010 1100	
45	2D	0010 1101	
46	2E	0010 1110	
47	2F	0010 1111	
48	30	0011 0000	
49	31	0011 0001	
50	32	0011 0010	
51	33	0011 0011	
52	34	0011 0100	
53	35	0011 0101	
54	36	0011 0110	
55	37	0011 0111	
56	38	0011 1000	
57	39	0011 1001	
58	3A	0011 1010	
59	3B	0011 1011	
60	3C	0011 1100	
61	3D	0011 1101	
62	3E	0011 1110	
63	3F	0011 1111	

① Decimal	② Hexadecimal	③ System/360 8-bit Code	④
64	40	0100 0000	SP
65	41	0100 0001	
66	42	0100 0010	
67	43	0100 0011	
68	44	0100 0100	
69	45	0100 0101	
70	46	0100 0110	
71	47	0100 0111	
72	48	0100 1000	
73	49	0100 1001	
74	4A	0100 1010	¢
75	4B	0100 1011	.
76	4C	0100 1100	<
77	4D	0100 1101	(
78	4E	0100 1110	+
79	4F	0100 1111	|
80	50	0101 0000	&
81	51	0101 0001	
82	52	0101 0010	
83	53	0101 0011	
84	54	0101 0100	
85	55	0101 0101	
86	56	0101 0110	
87	57	0101 0111	
88	58	0101 1000	
89	59	0101 1001	
90	5A	0101 1010	!
91	5B	0101 1011	$
92	5C	0101 1100	*
93	5D	0101 1101	)
94	5E	0101 1110	;
95	5F	0101 1111	¬
96	60	0110 0000	-
97	61	0110 0001	/
98	62	0110 0010	
99	63	0110 0011	
100	64	0110 0100	
101	65	0110 0101	
102	66	0110 0110	
103	67	0110 0111	
104	68	0110 1000	
105	69	0110 1001	
106	6A	0110 1010	
107	6B	0110 1011	,
108	6C	0110 1100	%
109	6D	0110 1101	_
110	6E	0110 1110	>
111	6F	0110 1111	?
112	70	0111 0000	
113	71	0111 0001	
114	72	0111 0010	
115	73	0111 0011	
116	74	0111 0100	
117	75	0111 0101	
118	76	0111 0110	
119	77	0111 0111	
120	78	0111 1000	
121	79	0111 1001	
122	7A	0111 1010	:
123	7B	0111 1011	#
124	7C	0111 1100	@
125	7D	0111 1101	'
126	7E	0111 1110	=
127	7F	0111 1111	"

① Decimal	② Hexadecimal	③ System/360 8-bit Code	④
128	80	1000 0000	
129	81	1000 0001	a
130	82	1000 0010	b
131	83	1000 0011	c
132	84	1000 0100	d
133	85	1000 0101	e
134	86	1000 0110	f
135	87	1000 0111	g
136	88	1000 1000	h
137	89	1000 1001	i
138	8A	1000 1010	
139	8B	1000 1011	
140	8C	1000 1100	
141	8D	1000 1101	
142	8E	1000 1110	
143	8F	1000 1111	
144	90	1001 0000	
145	91	1001 0001	j
146	92	1001 0010	k
147	93	1001 0011	l
148	94	1001 0100	m
149	95	1001 0101	n
150	96	1001 0110	o
151	97	1001 0111	p
152	98	1001 1000	q
153	99	1001 1001	r
154	9A	1001 1010	
155	9B	1001 1011	
156	9C	1001 1100	
157	9D	1001 1101	
158	9E	1001 1110	
159	9F	1001 1111	
160	A0	1010 0000	
161	A1	1010 0001	
162	A2	1010 0010	s
163	A3	1010 0011	t
164	A4	1010 0100	u
165	A5	1010 0101	v
166	A6	1010 0110	w
167	A7	1010 0111	x
168	A8	1010 1000	y
169	A9	1010 1001	z
170	AA	1010 1010	
171	AB	1010 1011	
172	AC	1010 1100	
173	AD	1010 1101	
174	AE	1010 1110	
175	AF	1010 1111	
176	B0	1011 0000	
177	B1	1011 0001	
178	B2	1011 0010	
179	B3	1011 0011	
180	B4	1011 0100	
181	B5	1011 0101	
182	B6	1011 0110	
183	B7	1011 0111	
184	B8	1011 1000	
185	B9	1011 1001	
186	BA	1011 1010	
187	BB	1011 1011	
188	BC	1011 1100	
189	BD	1011 1101	
190	BE	1011 1110	
191	BF	1011 1111	

① Decimal	② Hexadecimal	③ System/360 8-bit Code	④
192	C0	1100 0000	
193	C1	1100 0001	A
194	C2	1100 0010	B
195	C3	1100 0011	C
196	C4	1100 0100	D
197	C5	1100 0101	E
198	C6	1100 0110	F
199	C7	1100 0111	G
200	C8	1100 1000	H
201	C9	1100 1001	I
202	CA	1100 1010	
203	CB	1100 1011	
204	CC	1100 1100	
205	CD	1100 1101	
206	CE	1100 1110	
207	CF	1100 1111	
208	D0	1101 0000	
209	D1	1101 0001	J
210	D2	1101 0010	K
211	D3	1101 0011	L
212	D4	1101 0100	M
213	D5	1101 0101	N
214	D6	1101 0110	O
215	D7	1101 0111	P
216	D8	1101 1000	Q
217	D9	1101 1001	R
218	DA	1101 1010	
219	DB	1101 1011	
220	DC	1101 1100	
221	DD	1101 1101	
222	DE	1101 1110	
223	DF	1101 1111	
224	E0	1110 0000	
225	E1	1110 0001	
226	E2	1110 0010	S
227	E3	1110 0011	T
228	E4	1110 0100	U
229	E5	1110 0101	V
230	E6	1110 0110	W
231	E7	1110 0111	X
232	E8	1110 1000	Y
233	E9	1110 1001	Z
234	EA	1110 1010	
235	EB	1110 1011	
236	EC	1110 1100	
237	ED	1110 1101	
238	EE	1110 1110	
239	EF	1110 1111	
240	F0	1111 0000	0
241	F1	1111 0001	1
242	F2	1111 0010	2
243	F3	1111 0011	3
244	F4	1111 0100	4
245	F5	1111 0101	5
246	F6	1111 0110	6
247	F7	1111 0111	7
248	F8	1111 1000	8
249	F9	1111 1001	9
250	FA	1111 1010	
251	FB	1111 1011	
252	FC	1111 1100	
253	FD	1111 1101	
254	FE	1111 1110	
255	FF	1111 1111	

This figure shows how the 256 combinations of any one byte are used to represent:

1. The byte's decimal value
2. The byte's hex value
3. The byte's binary value (the S/360 8-bit code)
4. The graphic symbol (as the byte could appear on the typewriter, printer, or visual display device)

Fig. 6 256 combinations per byte.

changeable with other computers), or IC. The term EBCD was then appended with the IC. Hence the eight-bit code is now referred to as EBCDIC (pronounced ebb sea dick). Figure 6 shows the 256 combinations possible with an eight-bit byte and those combinations which have a corresponding graphic symbol. When the contents of a byte (eight bits) is transferred to a printer or typewriter, all eight bits are used to determine which graphic symbol is to print. For example, if the byte's pattern is *01011011* and the byte's contents is transmitted to a keyboard, a $ (dollar sign) would print. (Appendix II discusses the binary number system and its relationships to the decimal and hexadecimal numbering systems.)

The Half-Byte and the Hexadecimal Value

One of the ways of categorizing the types of data-processing information is to say that it is either numeric or nonnumeric. (What are some examples of each? Proper names, mailing addresses, and the names of colors are examples of non-numeric information. Social security numbers, weekly salaries, number of size 46 suits to manufacture, and the tensile strengths of ferrous alloys are examples of numeric information.)

All of you who have been able to read this textbook up to this point know that it doesn't take an eight-bit byte to represent one numeric character (*decimal* numeric character, that is—0, 1, 2, 3, 4, 5, 6, 7, 8, 9). As a matter of fact, it takes something between three and four bits to represent the 10 combinations required for the 10 decimal numeric characters.

Question Set 1

1. Three bits allow how many combinations?
2. Four bits allow how many combinations?
3. What is the least number of bits required to represent the 10 decimal characters?

Since most of the data processing in our modern world deals with numeric information, the 10 combinations needed to represent the 10 decimal digits can be accommodated with four bits, that is, half a byte. Even in this *half-byte,* however, one uses only $62\frac{1}{2}$ percent ($\frac{10}{16}$) of the combinations available in a half-byte (four bits).

Hex Representation Makes Efficient Use of Core

Naturally the designers of S/360 wanted to eliminate this poor utilization of four bits. So as an alternative to the decimal system they built the hexadecimal (meaning 16) number system into the S/360. The hexadecimal number system (as is shown in Appendix II) has 16 characters, whereas the decimal number system has only 10 characters. One advantage of the hexadecimal system is that each use of a half-byte (four bits) can be used to represent one of 16 different characters (whereas the decimal system allows only one of 10 characters to be represented by four bits).

Whether a byte represents one EBCDIC character or two numeric characters is up to the programmer. As you know, when the contents of a byte is transferred to a printing device, all eight bits are used to select one EBCDIC character that is to print. If the programmer has been using a byte to represent two hex values, he must translate the contents of each half-byte (one hex character) into its full-byte EBCDIC equivalent before he requests a printing operation (see Fig. 7).

What is the significance of this discussion of the hexadecimal representation?

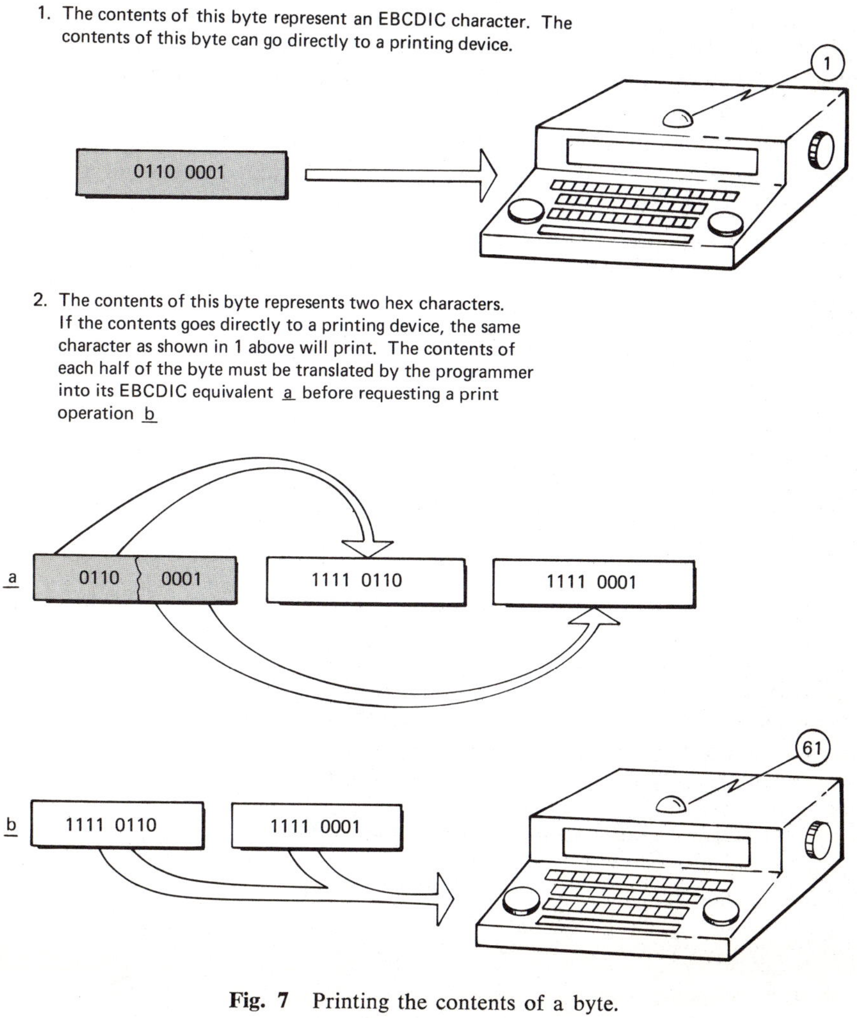

Fig. 7 Printing the contents of a byte.

Most important is that one byte of S/360 storage can represent two characters of the hexadecimal number system. Another advantage of the hexadecimal system is its close kinship to the binary system. For example, the byte-size binary—equivalent of $143_{(10)}$ is 10001111. Finding the hexadecimal equivalent merely requires translating each four-bit group: 10001111 is equivalent to 8F.

You may have been wondering about the dreadfully tedious job it would be for a person to convert decimal numbers to hexadecimal numbers just so the S/360 can be more efficient. There is no need for concern, however. As was stated earlier, two of the operations of a S/360 are the conversion of decimal to binary and the conversion of binary to decimal.

Other Units of Storage

The main unit of storage in the S/360 (as we have seen) is the byte. It is made up of eight data bits. To represent hexadecimal values a byte can be subdivided into half-bytes.

Another unit of storage consists of four bytes. This quantity is generally referred to as a *word.* That is, a word of S/360 storage consists of four bytes. Two other units of storage have been derived from the word; these are the *half-word* and the *double-word* (see Fig. 8).

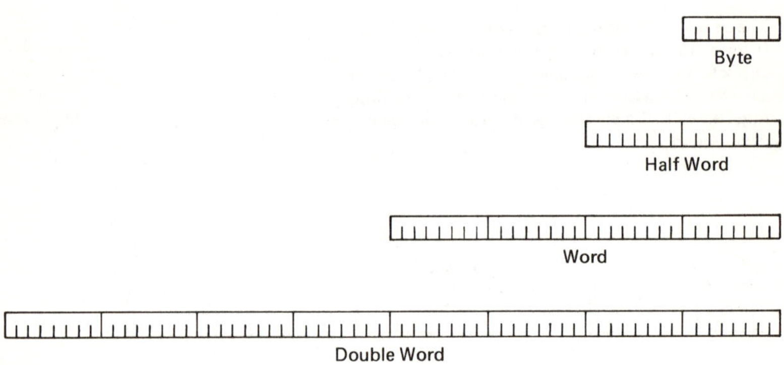

The binary capacity of the byte is equivalent to 2^8 or 256

The binary capacity of the half-word is equivalent to 2^{16} or 65536

The binary capacity of the word is equivalent to 2^{32} or 4,294,967,296

The binary capacity of the double word is equivalent to 2^{64} or 2,305,843,009, 213,693,952

Fig. 8 Capacity of storage components.

Question Set 2

1. How many bits in a half-word?

2. How many bytes in a double-word?

3. How many hexadecimal characters can be accommodated in a half-word?

4. How many hexadecimal characters can be accommodated in a double-word?

Identifying Storage Positions

Storage in the S/360 can be described as consisting of a continuous and finite string of bytes. Since each byte occupies a position relative to the beginning of the storage string, each byte can be identified by its location relative to the beginning of the string. The numerical value of a location is called an *address*. Figure 9 shows various substrings of addresses (decimal) in a S/360 with 8,192 storage positions.

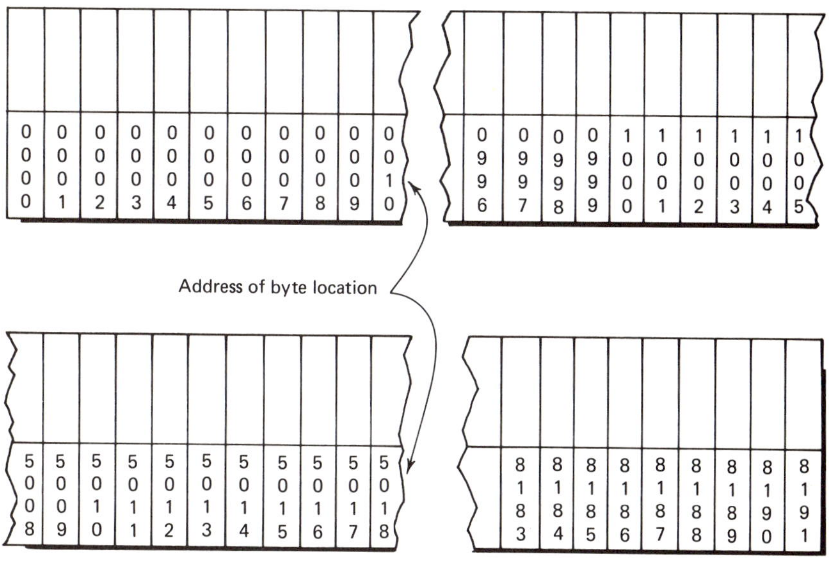

Fig. 9 Decimal addresses of storage.

Sizes of Storage Units

We said earlier that S/360's come with an assortment of storage sizes. Figure 10 shows the basic increments between sizes of storage units and the storage-size class letter associated with the quantity. This class letter is often used when referring to a S/360 of a particular size. For example, a G40 means a Model 40 with 131,072 positions of core storage and a J65 signifies a Model 65 with 1,048,576 bytes of core.

Capacity (bytes)	System Model					
8,192	C30					
16,384	D30	D40				
32,768	E30	E40				
65,536	F30	F40	F50			
131,072		G40	G50	G65		
262,144		H40	H50	H65	H75	
524,288			I50	I65	I75	I85
1,048,576				J65	J75	J85
2,097,152						K85
4,194,304						L85

System/360 models and the number of storage positions a model may have. Certain combinations of basic storage positions are also possible.

Fig. 10 Storage unit sizes.

Storage Hierarchy

Certain models of the System/360 can have their core storage capacity increased by attaching special core storage units. These are usually referred to as high-capacity storage. The speed with which information is available from high-capacity storage is about four times slower than regular core storage. High-capacity storage is often used for storing data with a low use frequency. To distinguish between the two speeds of core storage, the regular core storage is called *hierarchy 0* (zero) and the slower, high-capacity storage is called *hierarchy 1*.

Relationships between CPU and Storage

As you now know, the CPU executes instructions. To be accessible to the CPU, the instructions must be in storage. The data that an instruction processes must also be in storage.

Once the instructions are in storage, the CPU can start executing them. The CPU retrieves instructions from successive storage locations unless there is a branch operation. What if the operation being executed by the CPU concerns data? If the operation concerns data, the data is retrieved from storage by the CPU and manipulated according to the operation. Only after the data has been operated upon does the CPU retrieve the next instruction.

INSTRUCTION COMPONENTS

Each machine language instruction of which the S/360 is capable consists of two main parts. These parts are the operation code and the operand.

Operation Code

The *operation code* (expressed in hexadecimal) tells the CPU what operation to perform. For example, 1A and FA are operation codes which tell the CPU to add two quantities; 91 is an operation code which tells the CPU to test the pattern of bits in a byte; D5 is the operation code to compare two fields of data. In each of these examples we see that the operation code is concerned with data to be operated upon. These operation codes do not, however, specify where the data to be operated upon is located. To tell the CPU where the data is located requires one or more *operands.*

Operands

The *operands* (expressed in hexadecimal) in a machine language instruction tell the CPU where the data for the operation code is located. This may mean where it's coming from, or where it's going to, or both. Each operand specifies the address of the data being operated upon. In the S/360 each operand may consist of as many as three parts.

BASE ADDRESS

The first part we shall consider is called the *base address.* The use of a base address for data processing is pretty much like the use of a base camp for mountain climbers. That is, all distances stated in the climbing of a particular mountain are relative to the base camp (see Fig. 11). Storage locations referred to in an operand are relative to a base address. With regard to Fig. 11, the base camp could have been anywhere as long as the ultimate distance toward the mountain from the base camp is not more than 50 miles (50 miles is the limit of the hikometer). Also, there could be several other hiking clubs from Beginkor, each with its own destination and base camp (Fig. 12).

The base addressing scheme for the S/360 is very similar in concept to the base distance in the mountain-climbing illustration. That is, the base address is the distance in *bytes* from the beginning of core.

DISPLACEMENT

The base address is always used in conjunction with the second part of an operand, which is referred to as the *displacement.* The displacement is the distance in bytes from the *base address.* The displacement can have a maximum decimal value of 4,095 (or a hexadecimal value of FFF). Hence we say that the displacement specifies how far from the reference point (i.e., base address) the data under consideration is located. Figure 13 shows the relationship among several base addresses and their related displacements. When the CPU is executing

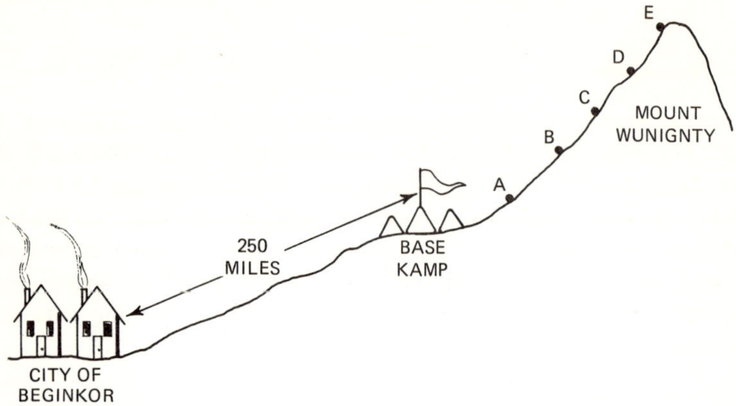

This illustration shows that the base camp for the mountain climbers of SEASEKT is 250 miles from the city of BEGINKOR. The distances (or linear displacements) of each of the locations A thru E are relative to the Base camp. To determine these distances, the climbers have a hikometer which can record up to 50 miles. Therefore, when someone says "We have recorded 17 miles to Point B" he means that he is 17 miles from base camp. Then, to determine the total distance from BEGINKOR to Point B, one adds the linear displacement from the base camp to the distance the base camp is from the city (250 + 17 = 267).

Fig. 11 Base camp location and linear displacement.

an instruction that requires data from storage, the CPU adds the displacement to the base address to determine the storage location of the data.

Registers—High-Speed Storage Devices

BASE ADDRESSES IN REGISTERS

The base address we've just been talking about must be in a high-speed storage device called a *general register* before it can be useful. A general register is called a *high-speed storage device* because whatever information it contains is available to the CPU quicker than if it had been in core storage. For example, in the Model 50, it takes the CPU 2 microseconds (μsec) to get four bytes of information from core storage but only 0.5 μsec to get it from a general register. How much of this high-speed storage can be placed into a computer? Relative to core storage size, general register storage is quite small. That is, in any model of the S/360, there are only 16 of these general-purpose registers and each one has a capacity of one word or four bytes. Each general register has an address—this address is a single, hexadecimal character and the range of register addresses is from 0 to F. Although general registers are *storage* devices, they are part of the CPU and not part of main storage.

Now back to the base address, the general register, the operation code, the displacement, and an example of how these are arranged in a S/360 machine

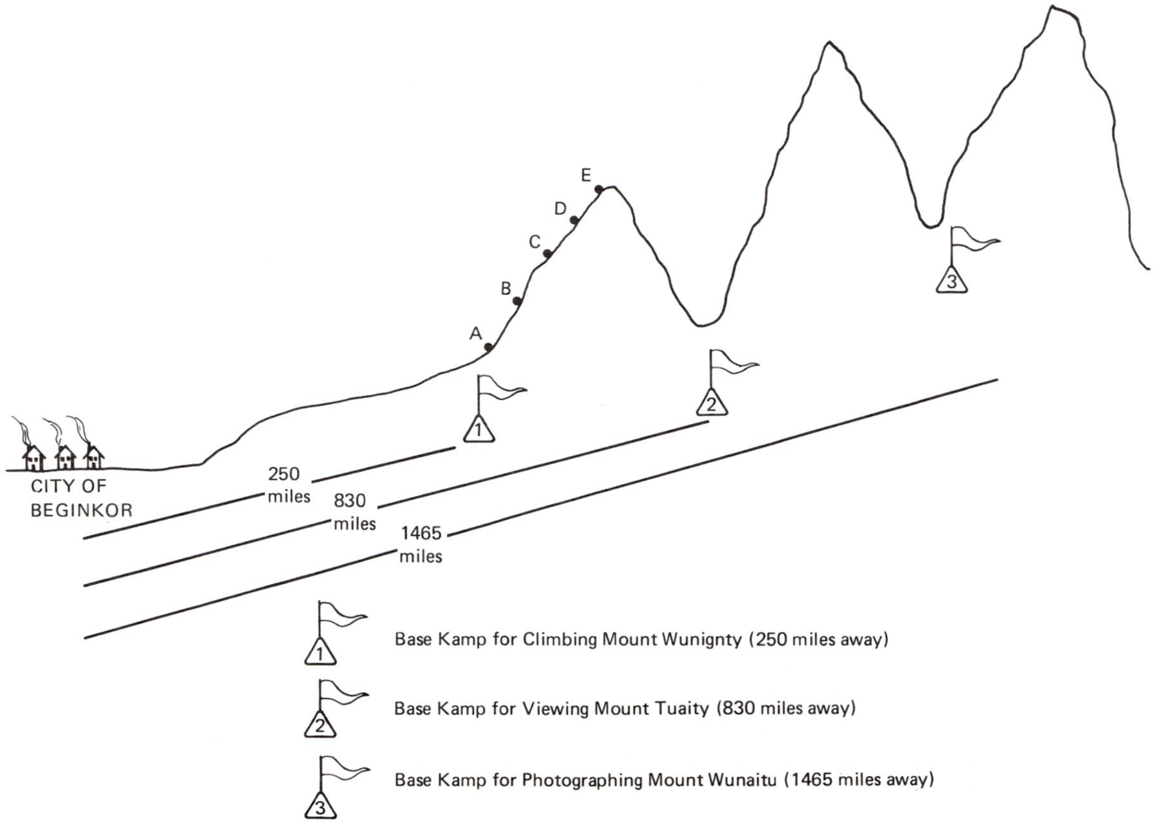

Fig. 12 Multiple base camps.

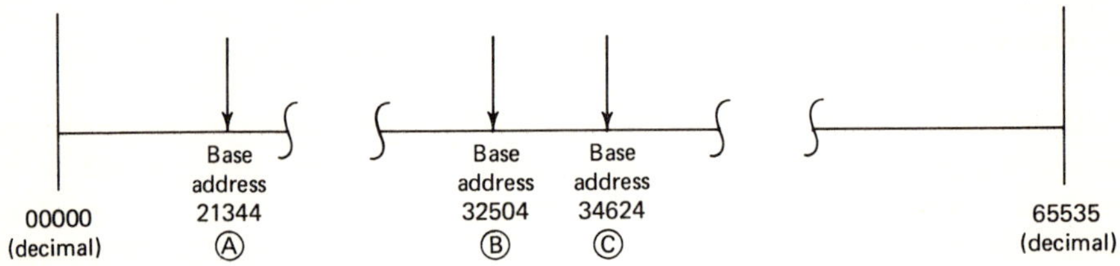

Here are three locations to be regarded as base addresses. (Any location can be chosen but usually the address for a base location is evenly divisible by 8.) Each base address can be used with a positive displacement. A displacement can have a positive value up to 4,095 bytes. The range of locations referrable by the base address at Ⓐ are 21344 to 25439. Determine the ranges addressable with Ⓑ & Ⓒ. Note that there are certain locations common to Ⓑ and Ⓒ.

Fig. 13 Base storage addresses and displacements.

language instruction. Let's give the verbal definition of an instruction. (*Note:* The displacement and base address are written in hexadecimal.) Move to that storage location whose address is to be determined with a base of 3D78 and a displacement of *16*, the data which comes from the storage location whose address is determined with a base of *3D78* and a displacement of *32*.

One of the first things to determine is which of the 16 general registers is to contain the base address. We'll assume it to be general register 9. (Any general register except zero may be used for a base address.) Another thing to know is the operation code (op code, for short), which in this case is D2. The last thing that must be known is how many bytes (in excess of one) there are to be moved. Now we can write the instruction in machine language form, as illustrated in Fig. 14.

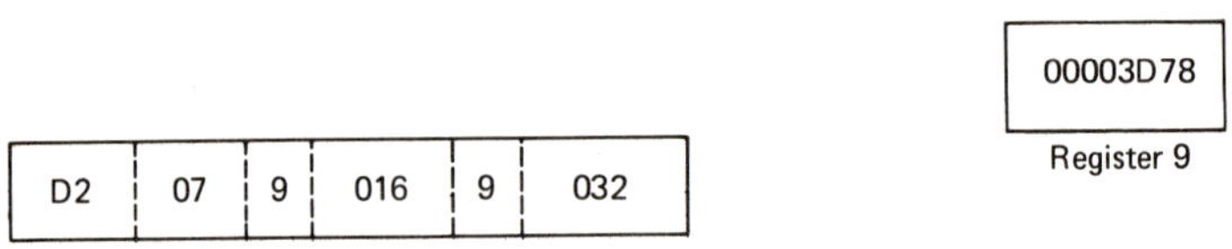

Format of machine language instruction for moving eight characters from one set of storage locations to another.

This illustrates the machine language version for accomplishing the following:

Move (D2) seven (07) plus one characters

TO the location whose address is the sum of a base register's (9) contents, and a displacement (016)

FROM the location whose address is the sum of a base register's (9) contents and a displacement (032)

Fig. 14 Machine language instruction.

OTHER USES OF GENERAL REGISTERS

In addition to using the general registers for base address, programmers use them for binary arithmetic functions, making comparisons between values and parameter passing. What is *parameter passing*? Let's answer it this way. The responsibility of writing a particular program is often given to several programmers, with each programmer responsible for one or more progam parts. Information that each programmer produces is often required by another. To *pass* information for another programmer's use, the information should be placed into a general register (i.e., if it requires no more than four bytes). If a programmer has many pieces of information to pass to another, he can store them in some contiguous storage locations used by his program and then place the storage *address* of the first piece of information into a general register. Of course, all the programmers must agree on the register and they must be aware of what is in the general register (i.e., an actual piece of information or the *address* of a list of contiguous pieces of information). It is now time to explain what parameter passing is. The people who design computers and write the operating systems programs prefer the term *parameter* to the phrase pieces of information. Hence the programmers are said to pass parameters or pass the address of a parameter list.

Addressing a Field of Data

Since most of the fields of data that a programmer deals with are longer than one byte, you may be wondering if the programmer has to specify the address of each byte. Fortunately, for the programmer the answer is *No!* All that he must specify is the address of the leftmost byte of the field. From now on, whenever the term *address* is used in conjunction with the locating of data we shall mean the address of the leftmost byte.

Instructions Come in Different Sizes

STORAGE-TO-STORAGE INSTRUCTIONS

The S/360 machine language instruction you were shown in Fig. 14 is an example of a *storage-to-storage instruction.* That is, the data being processed comes *from* one set of storage locations and goes *to* another set of storage locations. Storage-to-storage instructions are made up of *12* hexadecimal characters of *6* bytes or *3* half-words. Every S/360 storage-to-storage instruction consists of

2 hex characters for operation code
2 hex characters for length
1 hex character for specifying the *register* containing the data's destination base address

3 hex characters for specifying the displacement of the destination
1 hex character for specifying the register containing the source data's base
3 hex characters for specifying the source data's displacement

STORAGE-TO-REGISTER INSTRUCTIONS

The S/360 can also execute instructions that move data between storage and registers and vice versa. Since only one displacement, one base address, and no length is required for this type of instruction, it can be made up of eight hexadecimal characters or four bytes or two half-words. For example, the instruction to "load register 5 with the contents of location C200" (register 10 or A, used as the base register, contains C1E8 and the displacement is 18) is

```
58     5      0     A       018
|      |      |     |        |
|      |      |     |       displacement
|      |      |     base  register
|      |      zero—This position specifies a
|      |           register also. When it is
|      |           a zero, it has no effect
|      |           on the instruction.
|      register to receive data from storage
op code for load register
```

In this diagram we state that the third field of the instruction specifies a register—and when the register is zero, its contents have no effect on the instruction. This leads one to surmise: If it were a register other than zero its contents might affect the instruction. This is a good guess because it is true.

INDEXING

The way that the contents of a second, nonzero register affects the execution of a storage-to-register instruction is as follows. The CPU, in determining the address of the data, adds together the displacement, the contents of the base address register, and the contents of this other register. Why would anyone want to have that done? As you know, the instructions of a program are executed over and over—and one of the things a programmer wants to make sure of is that the storage address (i.e., the contents of the base register and the displacement) is going to be the same for each execution. There are, however, many programming occasions when it is necessary to adjust the storage address. In order to leave the displacement and the contents of the base register unaltered, the architects of S/360 allowed for the use of a second register in the storage-to-register instructions; the contents of this second register (as long as it isn't register zero) is used to adjust or index the sum of the base register's contents and the displacement. This second register is called the *index register*. Now then, if a storage address in a given instruction can vary from one execution to the next, it will be the contents of the index register that is adjusted and not the displacement or the base register's contents. Indexing is very popular when summing up a whole string of numbers. One needs only to increment the index register with a value equal to the length of each number before executing the add instruction again. (Just remember to reset the index register before summing up each string.)

REGISTER-TO-REGISTER INSTRUCTIONS

As you have probably guessed, there are instructions for moving data between registers. Since these instructions require one byte for the op code, *one half-byte* for the TO register and *one half-byte* for the FROM register, the entire instruction requires only two bytes, or *one half-word*. For example, the instruction to "add to the contents of register 7, the contents from register 12" is

```
1A7C
|||
||register containing factor 1
|register containing factor 2 and eventual sum
op code to add together 2 register's contents
```

Question Set 3

1. Why is it unnecessary for a register-to-storage or a storage-to-register instruction to have the length of the data specified?
2. There are three parts to an operand in a storage-to-register instruction. Name the three parts.
3. The following are operands of a storage-to-register (or vice versa) instruction. Shown to their right are the contents of some registers. You are to state the storage address formed by these operands (in hexadecimal).

Example	Base	Index	Displacement
1	4	3	123
2	5	3	21F
3	3	4	123 (How does this compare with example 1?)
4	2	1	000
5	5	0	ABC
6	0	2	FAD
7	0	0	000
8	0	0	FFF

Reg Contents
Reg 0 00000400
Reg 1 00001000
Reg 2 00002000
Reg 3 00004000
Reg 4 00008000
Reg 5 00000050

CPU CONTROLS SEQUENCE OF EXECUTION

Some rather popular descriptions of a computer program have been likened to a clothes-washing or dish-washing machine. It is said that both computer and automatic washers are programmed; to this extent, the analogy holds. There is one immense difference, however: The sequence of executing instructions in a computer can depend upon *conditions* that may change from one instruction to the next. The sequence of executing washing machine instructions never varies. (Some washing machines do have as many as a dozen washing patterns, but once the pattern is selected, it takes the same sequence as the last time the pattern was selected.) In other words, once a washing machine is started it will complete its program even when there is no water, no clothes, and no soap.

The Program Status Word

The component of the CPU which is responsible for choosing the next instruction to be executed is called the *program status word* (PSW). The PSW is comprised of 64 bits, the equivalent of a double-word. Although one would be justified in calling it the "program status double-word," it has been agreed to refer to it as though it were a single word.

One of the main functions of the PSW is to inform the CPU where the next instruction to be executed is located. Another major function is to retain the status of the program. One factor that contributes to the status of a program is the *condition* caused by the most recently executed condition-causing instruction. Examples of condition-causing instructions are ADD, SUBTRACT, and so on, and COMPARE.

When one of these instructions is executed, any one of two, three, or four side effects may occur. The result of an arithmetic instruction may be less than zero, equal to zero, greater than zero, or too large for the area where the result is being developed; the result of a compare instruction may be high, equal, or low. These characteristics of the results are called *conditions*. A condition is retained in the PSW in the form of a two-bit code (two bits can represent four different conditions).

Although instructions are normally executed in the same order as they exist in storage, the sequence will be changed after the CPU executes a *conditional branch* instruction (i.e., if the condition being checked exists). If the condition being tested does not exist, there will be no branch, and the instruction immediately following the conditional branch will be fetched next.

INTERRUPTIONS AND MASKING

You have learned that the execution of a program proceeds in a sequential order unless a branch instruction is executed. Now we are going to tell you about a major exception. If, during the execution of a program, certain unplanned or unpredictable events occur, the program's use of the CPU is interrupted. Some unplanned and unpredictable events that result in an interruption are: "loss" of a data bit in its movement within the electronic circuitry of the CPU; the attempt to access data from a storage address that is greater than the highest address of the computer's storage; developing an arithmetic result that requires more storage positions than were allotted by the problem programmer; the detection of an invalid character in a decimal field during an arithmetic operation. The interruption process is implemented by *replacing* the PSW that was in control just prior to the event, with a new PSW. In the address portion of the new PSW will be the location of an instruction; this instruction will be the first in another program which analyzes the specific cause of the interruption and then, if possible, provides some remedial action. If the remedial action is successful, the interrupt handling program will give CPU control back to the interrupted program by replacing the old PSW. There are five major types of interrupts (each type is discussed in greater depth in Chapter 6). Each interrupt type is associated with a unique new PSW which replaces the current PSW. The new PSWs are located in predetermined storage locations. Just prior to being replaced by the appropriate new PSW, the current PSW is placed into a predetermined storage location.

Is there anything that can be done to prevent an interrupt from occurring, especially if the event that causes it can be predicted? Yes! Certain bits of the PSW have been designated to reflect interruptability. For example, if a certain bit within the PSW that is in control of the CPU (the current PSW) has been set to 0 (zero), a corresponding type of interrupt will be ignored. On the other hand, if the certain bit of the current PSW is set to 1, the corresponding type of interrupt is allowed. The *pattern* of bits in the PSW that controls interruptability is called a *mask*. Hence an interrupt is said to be *masked off* if its corresponding bit is set to zero (0).

Not all types of interruptions can be masked off. That is, there are no bits in the PSW that correspond to these types of interrupt causing events; these events always cause an interrupt. Those interrupts that can be masked off are in one of two categories: interrupts that can be completely forgotten, and interrupts that can be temporarily ignored. If the mask is set off for the former (completely forgotten), it's as though the interrupt never occurred. If the mask is set off for the latter (temporarily ignored), the interrupt lies dormant until the corresponding mask bit in the current PSW is changed or until the current PSW is replaced with a new PSW containing a mask that allows the interrupt to be recognized.

Interrupt handling programs can be very complex; some of them require many man-months of effort to write, debug, and test. So that each problem programmer does not have to expend so much time writing his own interrupt handling programs, they are provided by IBM.

The setting of interrupt masks and the replacing of the old PSW (the one that lost control of the CPU at the time of interruption) are accomplished by special instructions in the interrupt program. These special instructions are classified as privileged. That is, only certain types of programmers are allowed to use them. Conversely, other types of programmers are not allowed to use them. In general, the programmers who are forbidden to use privileged instructions are the problem programmers. Think of what might happen if a problem programmer could load his own PSWs—he could mask off all interrupts making it impossible to alert the computer about certain interrupt causing events.

To *prevent* the problem programmer from issuing privileged instructions, the S/360 can be placed into the *problem state.* Placing the S/360 into a given state is accomplished when loading the PSW. That is, when the current PSW is replaced by a new PSW, the new PSW will have had a special bit set to 0 (zero). As long as the special bit is 0, the privileged instructions can be executed. However, when the special bit is 1 (in the problem state) and a privileged instruction is "executed," an unmaskable interruption occurs. The interrupt handling program detects that a privileged instruction was attempted and causes the problem program to end.

STORAGE PROTECTION

In the discussion of the data factory you were told that several processes or tasks can be worked on concurrently. In a computing system, it is possible to have several programs in storage at the same time. Each program uses the CPU exclusively until the occurrence of some event causes it to be interrupted. Many of these interrupts occur so that a different program can use the CPU for a while. Each of these programs and the data they are processing are vulnerable to destruction from the other programs unless there is a *protection* feature. In the S/360, blocks of 2,048 bytes can be "locked up" with a program key (there are a total of 16 different keys). Each program can access only the contents of storage locations for which it has the proper key. The storage key is part of the PSW. Just prior to giving a program the control of the CPU (a program gets control of the CPU by having its PSW made the current one), the appropriate key is inserted into the program's PSW.

THE INTERVAL TIMER

One of the features of the S/360 computer is an electronic timer. The timer is the electronic equivalent of a stop watch. They differ in that the capacity of most stop watches is one hour; the capacity of the electronic timer is about $15\frac{1}{2}$ hours. The timer is used to measure the amount of time a program uses the CPU, to interrupt a program when its interval of time has expired, to print the time of day on reports or on the computer's typewriter, and so on.

SUMMARY

1. Three major components of a computer are
   a. CPU
   b. main storage
   c. input/output devices and channels
2. The CPU executes one instruction at a time.
3. An instruction is made up of an operation code and one or more operands.
4. Operands are made up of one or more of the following:
   a. a base address
   b. a displacement
   c. an index value
5. Main storage is comprised of magnetic cores.
6. A magnetic core is called a bit.
7. Eight bits make a byte.
8. Each byte has an address.
9. One byte can represent an EBCDIC symbol.
10. A half-byte contains four bits.
11. A half-byte can accommodate one hex value or one decimal value.
12. Four bytes make up one word.
13. A half-word and a double-word are units of storage.
14. A register contains four bytes (one word).
15. There are 16 registers in a S/360.
16. To be executed by the CPU, an instruction must be
    a. in machine language form
    b. in main storage
17. Data to be processed by an instruction must be in storage.
18. Three of the main types of S/360 instructions are
    a. storage-to-storage

   b. register-to-storage and storage-to-register
   c. register-to-register
19. Registers can be used for
   a. binary arithmetic calculations
   b. containing base addresses
   c. containing index values
   d. passing parameters
20. The displacement value cannot exceed FFF (hex).
21. The PSW (program status word) contains the location of the next instruction to be executed by the CPU.
22. A condition code, which reflects the outcome of certain condition-causing instructions, is kept in the PSW.
23. If the condition (being tested by a conditional branch instruction) exists, the PSW will contain the address of the instruction to be branched to.
24. If the condition does not exist, the PSW will contain the address of the next sequential instruction.
25. The units of time used in data processing and their equivalents are as follows:
   a. millisecond = one thousandth of a second
   b. microsecond = one millionth of a second
   c. nanosecond = one billionth of a second
26. Regular core storage is referred to as hierarchy 0 and slower, high-capacity storage is referred to as hierarchy 1.
27. The PSW which controls the sequence of a program's execution is called the current PSW.
28. The current PSW is part of the S/360 electronic circuitry. It is not in core storage.
29. A program's use of the CPU is interrupted when a certain unplanned or unpredictable event occurs.
30. There are five major types of interrupts. Each interrupt type is associated with a unique replacement PSW.
31. The current PSW is replaced by the appropriate new PSW when an interruption occurs. The new PSWs are located in predetermined storage locations.
32. Just prior to being replaced by the appropriate new PSW, the current PSW is placed into a predetermined storage location.
33. Certain types of interrupt causing events can be ignored by having the appropriate mask bit in the PSW set to 0 (zero).
34. Masks cause certain types of interrupt causing events to be permanently ignored while others will be temporarily ignored. When the mask is turned on, the temporarily ignored event will cause an interrupt.
35. Blocks of 2,048 bytes of storage can be locked with one of 16 different storage protection keys. For a program to gain access to locked-up stor-

age, the key portion of its PSW must have been set to the same key identification that locked it.

36. The Interval Timer is used to measure CPU time, to provide the time of day, and to interrupt a program when its interval of CPU time has expired.
37. Setting masks and replacing displaced PSW's are accomplished by privileged instructions. Problem programmers may not use privileged instructions; if they do, an unmaskable interrupt occurs. The interrupt handling program then causes the problem program to end.

SUGGESTED READING ASSIGNMENT

IBM System/360 Principles of Operation (A22-6821)

The table of contents of the IBM System/360 Principles of Operation Manual is divided into sections, major topics, and minor topics. Listed below are the topics of various levels you should make an effort to read before proceeding to Chapter 2. Read only those topics listed; they are the only ones Chapter 1 has prepared you for. When the minor topics of a major topic are not listed, read all the minor topics.

System Structure

- Main Storage
- Central Processing Unit
- Arithmetic and Logical Unit
- Program Execution
  - Instruction Format
  - Address Generation
  - Sequential Instruction Execution
  - Branching
  - Program Status Word
  - Interruption (first four paragraphs)
- Byte-Oriented Operand Feature (first two paragraphs)
- Protection Features
- Timer Feature

2 *INPUT/OUTPUT DEVICES, CONTROL UNITS, CHANNELS, AND RECORDING DATA*

In this chapter you will read about the mechanical devices that provide input to the computing system and record the output of a program. You will also read about the equipment that transports the data between the main storage unit and the input devices and about the equipment that controls the actions of each input and output device.

TYPEWRITER

The simplest mechanical device for entering data into the S/360 is probably the typewriter (see Fig. 15). To enter data into the main storage of the computer, all the operator has to do is the following:

1. Type a line of information using the typewriter keys. (This causes the electronic counterpart of each typed character or space to enter a holding area called a *buffer*.)
2. Visually inspect what he has typed. If he approves, he'll do 3a, if not 3b.
3. a. Depresses a key or keys. (This transmits to storage the contents of the buffer which is holding the electronic representation of the typed line.) See Fig. 16.

   b. Depresses a key or keys different from 3a. (This says, in effect, "Disregard the line just typed.") See Fig. 17.

Fig. 15 IBM 1052.

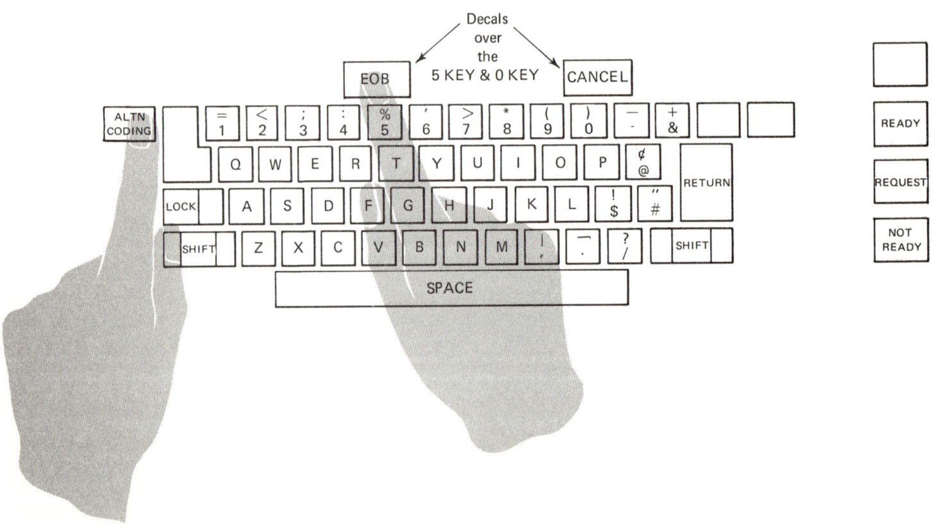

Fig. 16 Entering a typed line. Depressing these two keys enters a typed line of information into the computer's storage.

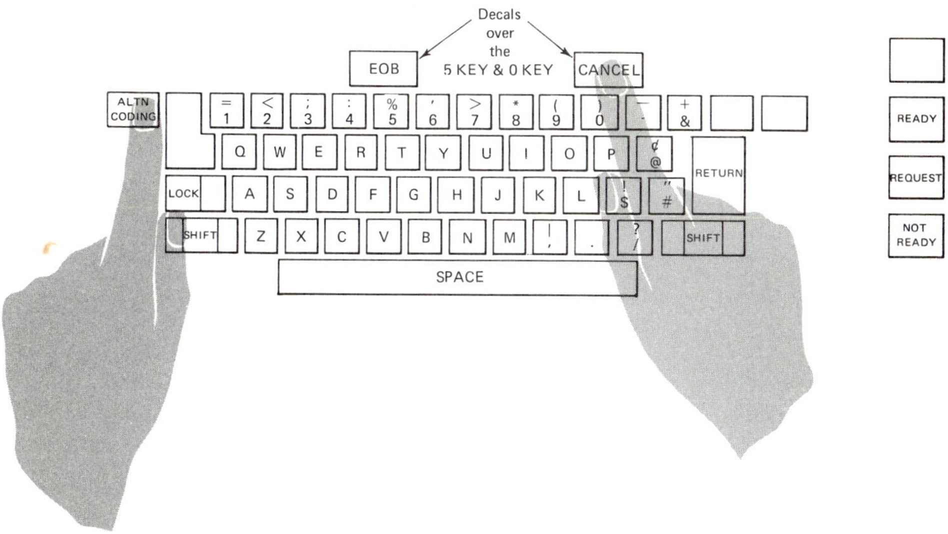

Fig. 17 Disregarding the typed line. Depressing these 2 keys causes a line of type to be disregarded.

As far as large volumes of data are concerned (not necessarily small volumes), the typewriter is probably the slowest, least efficient, and most expensive way of entering data into the computer's main storage. That this is true was evident to the very first computer designers.

PUNCHED CARDS AND CARD READERS

One of the most popular means for entering data into main storage of a S/360 is by way of a punched card. A punched card is really nothing more than a different way of representing a line of information (as long as the line of information accommodates no more than 80 characters).

Codes for Punched Cards

Whereas each byte of S/360 storage consists of 8 rows, each column of an IBM punched card consists of 12 rows (see Fig. 18). Why are the number of rows in a card different than the number of rows in a byte? The card was designed many years before very much thought was given to the design of a commercial computer. The card was designed for use with electromechanical data-processing machines which could only read a simple code. Shown in Fig. 19 is the code structure of the

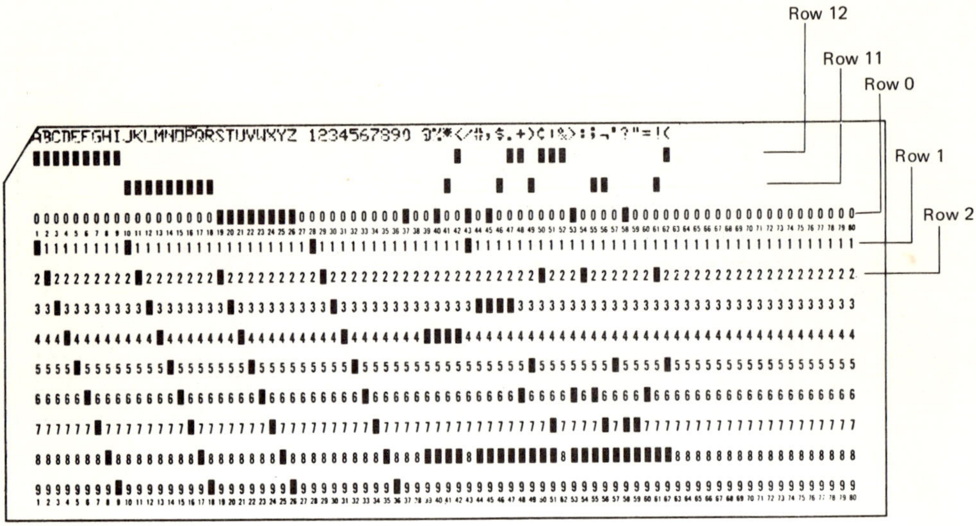

Fig. 18 Punched card and selected code. One card can accommodate up to 80 characters of information.

numeric, alphabetic, and a few special characters. When a card is read by a computer in normal fashion, the data that is punched in the card is converted into the equivalent EBCDIC representation. This conversion process is performed automatically by the S/360 hardware.

Note. The number of hole combinations in a card is 2^{12}, or 4,096. This is 3,840 more combinations than is possible in a byte (i.e., 2^8, or 256). The mechanical devices that read the card check for invalid hole combinations; if an invalid combination is detected, the computing system is alerted.

Card Punch (Keypunch)

The data-processing machine for creating the original punch card document is called the card punch. (Most people refer to it as the keypunch, because the machine has a keyboard very similar to that of a typewriter.) Figure 20 shows a keypunch operator preparing punch card documents from a program written by a data-processing student.

Card Reader

The main input device for reading punch cards into the S/360 is the IBM 2540 Card Read punch (see Fig. 21). The data from each of the card's eighty columns is transferred into a special storage area of a component called a *control unit* (see Fig. 22). The data is kept in this special storage area until the main storage of the computer is ready to receive it. To read a card, the computer must issue a

Character	Rows Punched	Character	Rows Punched
0	0	¢	12-2-8
1	1	.	12-3-8
2	2	<	12-4-8
3	3	(	12-5-8
4	4	+	12-6-8
5	5	|	12-7-8
6	6	&	12
7	7	!	11-2-8
8	8	$	11-3-8
9	9	*	11-4-8
–	–	)	11-5-8
A	12-1	;	11-6-8
B	12-2	>	11-7-8
C	12-3	–	• 11
D	12-4	/	0-1
E	12-5	,	0-3-8
F	12-6	%	0-4-8
G	12-7	–	• 0-5-8
H	12-8	>	0-6-8
I	12-9	?	0-7-8
J	11-1	:	2-8
K	11-2	#	3-8
L	11-3	@	4-8
M	11-4	'	5-8
N	11-5	=	6-8
O	11-6	"	7-8
P	11-7		
Q	11-8		
R	11-9		
S	0-2		
T	0-3		
U	0-4		
V	0-5		
W	0-6		
X	0-7		
Y	0-8		
Z	0-9		

This shows in tabular form, the rows of a column punched for the characters shown in Figure 18. The dash (–) and the underscore (_) are not in the card.

Fig. 19 Code structure for punched-card characters.

READ command. It is when the command is executed that the card is transported past the reading mechanism.

Card Punch (Automatic)

The results calculated by the computer are often recorded permanently. One of the more popular ways of recording results is to place the results into punch cards. The other end of the card reader shown in Fig. 21 is a card punch. Each

Fig. 20 Keypunch and operator.

column of a card to be punched receives its information from the control unit. In turn, the control unit receives its data from the main storage unit of the computer. To punch a card, the computer must issue a PUNCH command.

PRINTER

Output from a computer in the form of punched cards is very hard for human beings to read. If the output is to be referred to visually, the output should be printed. The main printing device of the S/360 is the IBM 1403 Printer (see Fig. 23). Whereas the 2540 Card Reader *puts* data into the IBM 2821 Control Unit, the 1403 Printer *gets* its data from the 2821 Control Unit. That is, the control unit receives data from main storage; as soon as the control unit has received the data for the line of information to be printed, it releases the data to the printer.

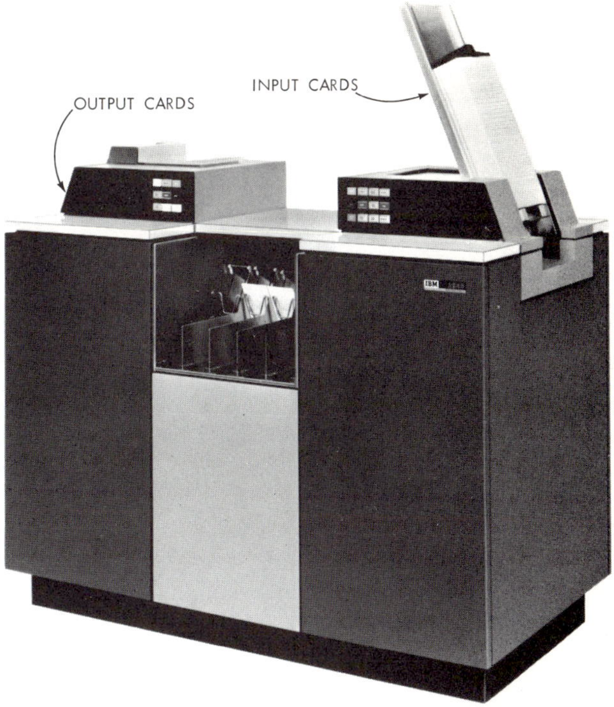

Fig. 21 IBM 2540 Card Read punch.

Fig. 22 The IBM 2821 Control Unit.

Fig. 23 IBM 1403 Printer, Model N1.

HARDWARE BUFFERS

The storage areas in the control unit for assembling data that has been read from a card, or is to be punched into a card, or is to be printed, are called *hardware buffers*. A hardware buffer can be likened to a person's piggy bank. Each time the saver has a coin, he doesn't go to his savings bank and deposit it—he puts it in his piggy bank. When the piggy bank is full, he empties it and takes the contents to the savings bank. By the same token, when he becomes a spender, he doesn't go to the savings bank and draw out an amount after each purchase—he withdraws a sufficient amount, puts it into his lamby bank (the opposite of piggy bank), and after each purchase removes the appropriate amount from it. These banks and the hardware buffers function as intermediate holding areas or staging areas.

Without these hardware buffers, the computing system would become much slower or more expensive. For example, if main storage were connected directly to a card reader, there would be either 80 transmission lines between card reader and main storage (very expensive and still slow) or one transmission line that polls each column in sequence (not very expensive but very slow), like going to the bank with each coin. Hence the concept and implementation of the hardware buffer.

OTHER CARD READERS, PUNCHES, AND PRINTERS

Some of you who are reading this text may have readers, punches, and printers other than the ones just described. Shown in Fig. 24 are some of these other devices. Figure 24 states that some of the devices are unbuffered. This means that only one character at a time goes to the punching mechanism or comes from the card reader. This is certainly a much slower procedure than having the device receive or provide the 80 characters for punching or 80 characters for reading simultaneously. For many installations this is of little concern. The lower cost of the unbuffered device offsets its slower speed.

MULTIPLEXOR CHANNEL

Figure 25 is a schematic of the complete path between an I/O device and core storage. Although Fig. 25 shows one 2821 Control Unit attached to the multiplexor channel, it is permissible to have several such control units attached. The significance of this last remark is that the multiplexor channel is the main path between a host of "slow" I/O devices and main storage, and that many of these I/O devices can be active at the same time. You may now ask the question: If so many I/O devices can be active at the same time, how does one avoid the obvious confusion of what device provided or gets which character? Confusion avoidance is one of the *built-in* responsibilities of the multiplexor channel. The multiplexor channel handles data to and from various devices on an *interleaved* basis. For example, if an input record is coming from a card reader and output records are going to a punch and printer, the multiplexor channel may take a few bytes from the reader, then send a few bytes to the printer, then a few bytes to the punch, then a few bytes to the reader again. The multiplexor channel remembers which device each byte is going to or is coming from. It is as though each byte were tagged with its source or destination.

Another responsibility of the multiplexor channel is to issue the commands that control the printers, card readers, card punches, and other devices which haven't been mentioned yet. That is, the multiplexor channel executes the commands for reading a card, for printing on paper, for skipping the paper form on the printer, for punching the card, and so on. The commands are kept in main storage and are called channel command words (CCW's).

Although the CPU executes the instruction to allow an I/O operation to start, it is the multiplexor channel which executes CCW's (channel command words) to activate the I/O devices. Here's how it works. The CPU executes the Start

(a)

(b)

(c)

(d)

Fig. 24 Other I/O devices: (a) IBM 2501 Card Reader; (b) IBM 2520 Card Read punch, Model B1; (c) IBM 1442 Card Read punch; (d) IBM 1443 Printer.

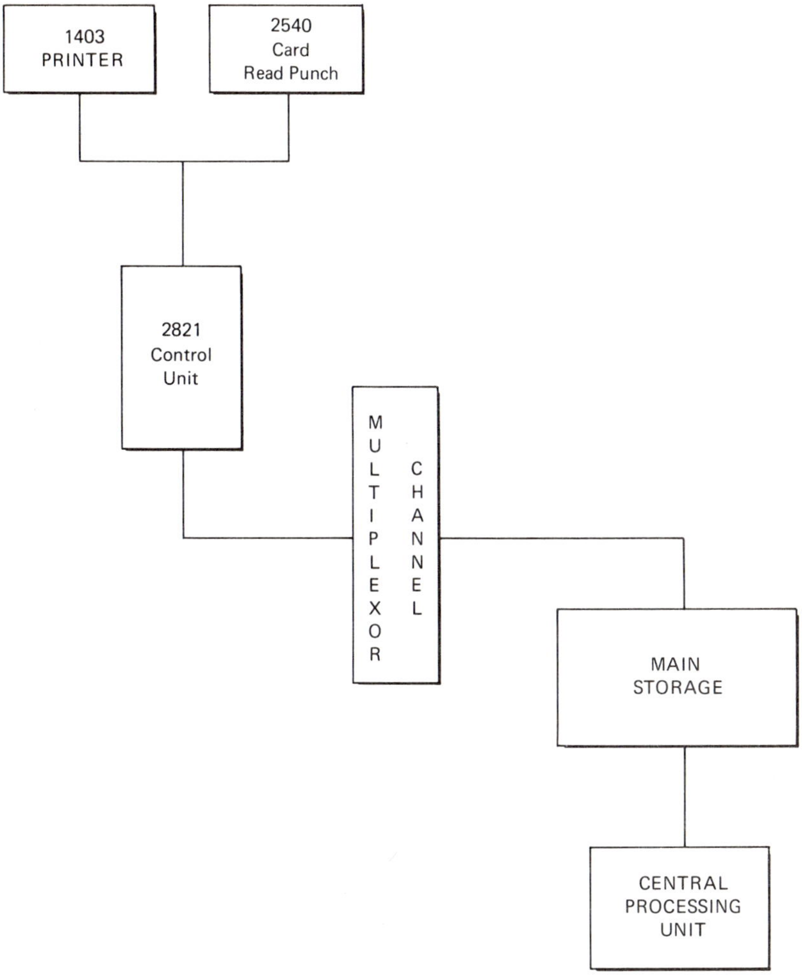

Fig. 25 Small-system schematic.

Input/Output (SIO) instruction. Part of the SIO instruction identifies the input or output unit to be started. As soon as the CPU realizes that an SIO instruction is being executed, the CPU informs the multiplexor channel where in storage it can find its CCW's. Then as soon as the multiplexor starts executing its CCW's, the CPU resumes executing instructions.

SLOW-SPEED I/O DEVICE AND CHANNEL SUMMARY

The data to and from the slow-speed input devices goes through the multiplexor channel. Relating back to the data factory of Chapter 1, the slow-speed I/O devices are like delivery trucks that load and unload at a relatively slow conveyor belt (multiplexor channel). Each box of data entering main storage is properly identified so that the truck (input device) from which it comes will be known. Likewise, each box of data leaving (output) main storage is tagged so that it will be placed on the proper truck (output device).

DATA FILES—SETS OF DATA

A great deal of the data recorded by industry, government, educational institutions, and the like has to be continually referred to; it must also be continually updated. If all the data required by a high school (for example) were in punched card form, the data could neither be retrieved quickly for referral nor be very quickly updated. (It could be retrieved and it could be updated, but not quickly. Retrieval and updating of data files in punched card form can easily become a matter of *hours* or even *days.*)

Before you "discover" the data-recording devices and data-organization techniques developed to overcome the time problem, we must first define three terms—a record, a field, and a data set.

Record and Field

A *record* can best be described as "all the information needed about a certain object." What is an example of an object? A college student is an example of an object. What is some of the information that might be needed about this student?

1. Name
2. Student number
3. Home address
4. Parents' name and address
5. Name of high school and grades obtained
6. Address on campus
7. Number of semesters matriculating
8. Grades of courses taken

9. Car registration number and make of car

•

•

•

20. Extracurricular interests

For each student the college might keep a list of the above items. In data-processing terms, the *list* is referred to as a record. Each of the items in the record (list) is referred to as a *field*. Regarding the above information, then, we might say that each student record consists of 20 fields.

Note. A field is never omitted, even though there may not be any information to record. For example, if a student has no car, field 9 might contain X's to signify that he has no car.

Data Set

The collection of records of all the students is called a set of data or, more properly, a *data set*. In the administrative offices of the college, these records might simply be called the "student data set."

Now that you have seen an example of a data set, let's define the general term. A data set is a collection of records that contains data about objects of a similar type. Some other examples of data sets are the following:

1. Drivers licensed in a state
2. Cars registered in a state
3. Payers of property tax in a county
4. Customers of a department store
5. Customers of a public utility
6. Subscribers to a magazine or newspaper
7. Holders of life insurance policies
8. Holders of casualty insurance policies
9. Credit card customers of a gasoline distributor

ORGANIZATION OF DATA SETS

No matter what kind of material a data set is recorded upon ($8\frac{1}{2}$- by 11-inch forms, 4- by 6-inch index cards, punched cards, microfilm, etc.), it is necessary to have a scheme of organizing the records if any of them is ever to be retrieved in an orderly fashion. For example, the names in the white pages of a telephone directory are printed in alphabetic sequence. That is, the alphabetic value of a name in the directory determines where it can be found. (No one looks for a last name beginning with G in the portion of the directory where the last names beginning with S are printed.)

The organization of records for data processing is just as important as the organization of names in a phone book. There is one big difference, however. When data records are to be processed by a computer, they should all have identifiers (names) of the same length. (If this were true for the process of looking up names in a phone book, every surname would be the same length. Fortunately, this is not necessary.) The reason for the equal-length identifier for items to be data processed is that it makes the processing much less expensive. That is, if the computer can assume that the length of the identifier never varies, it won't be necessary for the computer to first check each identifier for its beginning and end and then determine how long it is. There are, however, some data-processing applications in which there is no alternative.

The "Number"

The simple solution to the identifier-length problem is to give everything a *number*. (Some of these "numbers" may contain any letter of the alphabet and special symbols as well as the traditional digit.) That is why even small companies and schools assign a number to each employee or student. If some of the information in the employee's or student's record is required, the keeper of the files doesn't say "What's your name?" Instead he usually asks, "What's your man number?" or "What's your credit card number?" Assigning a number to each object about which data is to be recorded makes it very easy to keep the records orderly and organized. No matter what the conversational name of the object is, the position of the object's record in the data set can be quickly ascertained (by examining its number).

Sequential Organization

When records are stored in either alphabetic or numerical sequence, we say that the organization of the data set is sequential, hence the term *sequential organization*.

Devices for Containing a Large-Volume Data Set

For each of the nine data sets mentioned earlier, there are many that have 250,000 or more records. In each case the amount of data required for each record could easily exceed 250 characters. A punched card can accommodate only 80 characters, so four cards would be required to contain data about one record. This means 1 million cards for a data set containing 250,000 records. Not only is rapid retrieval and updating of such a volume of data virtually impossible, it is expensive to store. For example, if one file drawer can accommodate 2,000 cards, it would take 500 drawers to store a file of 250,000 records (where each record consists of four cards).

To relieve the problem of rapid retrieval and updating, data-processing engineers have developed two main types of I/O recording media and related devices. The first of these types is magnetic tape. (The second type is generally referred to as direct access and will be described later.)

MAGNETIC TAPE

The *magnetic tape* used for recording data is about ½-inch wide and is thinner than this paper. A standard reel contains 2,400 feet, or 28,800 inches, of magnetic tape (see Fig. 26). Depending upon the specific device on which the tape is to be used, there are either six or eight rows for recording data. In addition to the data bits, there is an additional bit (called the parity bit), which is used to check the integrity of the entire byte.

The technique for checking each byte is quite simple. The CPU determines how many of the data bits have been set to 1; if the number of 1 bits is odd, the

Fig. 26 A magnetic tape reel with 2400 feet of tape. The reel is 10½ inches in diameter.

CPU makes the parity bit a 0. Hence, each byte always has an odd number of bits.

How does this technique ensure the integrity of the byte? When an instruction is processing data, each byte goes through a great many electronic devices within the CPU. As reliable as these electronic devices are, there is a known probability of losing one of the byte's bits. (Let's say, for illustrative purposes, that this probability is 1 in 10^{12}, or 1 in 1 trillion.) If a bit is lost, the CPU in counting the remaining bits would detect an even number of bits. As soon as this is discovered, the CPU would be alerted that a machine check has occurred. The program in which the machine check had occurred could then be retried a certain number of times or stopped immediately. (There is, of course, a probability of losing two bits at a time, thus maintaining an odd bit count. The probability of this occurring is so much smaller that it hardly needs consideration. Besides, if it occurred, who would know it?) Hence data-processing people generally talk of seven-track tape (six rows or tracks for data and one for parity) or a nine-track tape (eight rows or tracks for data and one for parity.)

Nine-Track Tape

Data can be recorded on nine-track tape in exactly the same way that it is represented in core storage. That is, since one byte of core storage consists of the same number of bit positions as nine-track tape, any combination of bits in a byte can be directly recorded on nine-track tape. Likewise, any combination of bits on nine-track tape can be read into one byte of core storage.

Seven-Track Tape

Since there are only 6 bits for recording data on a seven-track tape, one column can represent only 2^6 (64) different characters [the eight bits for recording data on a nine-track tape can represent 2^8 (256) different characters]. How does one go about recording a byte of data on seven-track (six data bits) tape? Fortunately, the mechanism for doing this is automatic; the S/360 hardware is capable of converting and translating between seven- and nine-track data recording. [The S/360 takes three bytes (24 bits) and reorganizes them into four patterns of six bytes each. When this tape becomes input, the S/360 must be instructed to perform the reverse conversion.] The important fact to remember is that one needs more seven-track tape to record the same information that is on nine-track tape. This means that more tape has to be read or written when seven-track tape is used instead of nine-track tape.

Capacity of Magnetic Tape

The amount of data that can be stored on magnetic tape depends to a great extent upon the tape reading/writing device that is available. Some devices can use tape on which 1,600 characters have been recorded per inch. Think of what this means when compared with the size and capacity of a punched card. If we recorded 1,600 bytes per inch (bpi), it means that in 1 inch of tape we could record as much data as in 20 punched cards.

Speed of Magnetic Tape Reading and Writing

The devices that read and write magnetic tape have tape velocities varying from 18¾ inches per second (ips) to 200 ips. To determine how many bytes can be transmitted between a tape device and main storage, it is necessary to find the product of the density and speed. Hence even the slowest tape would transmit at the rate of 3,750 characters per second (18.75 ips × 200 bpi). By contrast, one of the more popular card readers can read 1,000 cards (80 characters per card) in a minute or 80,000 characters per minute. On a per-second basis this comes out to be about 1,333 characters. Even the slowest tape device is almost three times as fast.

Tape Units

There are three main devices that read magnetic tape for the S/360. These are the IBM 2401 Magnetic Tape Unit, which comes in six main models (see Fig. 27); the IBM 2415 Magnetic Tape Unit, which also comes in six models (see Fig. 28); and the IBM 2420 Magnetic Tape Unit (see Fig. 29).

Tape Control Units

Any data that goes from a magnetic tape to main storage (or vice versa) must go through a control unit. The purpose of the tape control unit is to "condition" the data being received or sent by the tape unit. The control unit also controls such operations as rewinding a reel of tape, backspacing one or more records, and erasing one or more records.

Format and Organization of Records on Tape

Almost without exception, records on tape are organized sequentially. One can always be certain that for a given record its predecessor has an identifier of lower value and its successor has one of higher value. Records on tape can be of almost any length one wishes to make them. Very seldom, however, does one require more than 1,000 positions for recording all the facts about a specific thing.

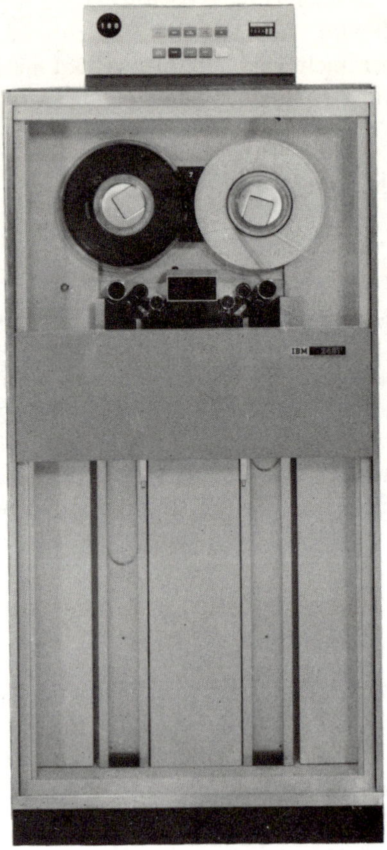

Characteristics	IBM 2401 Model 1	Model 2	Model 3	Model 4	Model 5	Model 6
Data Rate (bytes per second)	30,000	60,000	90,000	60,000	120,000	180,000
Tape Speed (inches per second)	37.5	75	112.5	37.5	75	112.5
Standard Density (bytes per inch)	800	800	800	1600	1600	1600
Nominal Interblock Gap (inches)	.6	.6	.6	.6	.6	.6
Nominal Interblock Gap Time (milliseconds)	16	8	5.3	16	8	5.3
Rewind Time (minutes) including reloading	3	1.4	1	3	1.4	1
Rewind and Unload Time (minutes)	2.2	1.5	1.1	2.2	1.5	1.1
Tape Width (inches)	.5	.5	.5	.5	.5	.5
Standard Number of Tracks	7 or 9	7 or 9	7 or 9	9	9	9

Fig. 27 IBM 2401 Magnetic Tape Unit. The amount of time required to mount and thread a reel of tape is about 20 seconds.

(There are exceptions, of course—some medical records consist of thousands of characters.)

How does one differentiate between the end of one record on tape from the beginning of the next? Since a reel of tape must remain as one continuous ribbon,

Characteristic	IBM 2415 Models 1-3	IBM 2415 Models 4-6
Data Rate (bytes per second)	15,000	30,000
Tape Speed (inches per second)	18.75	18.75
Standard Density (bytes per inch)	800	1600
Nominal Interblock Gap (inches)	.6	.6
Nominal Interblock Gap Time (milliseconds)	32	32
Rewind Time (minutes) including reloading	4	4
Rewind and Unload Time (minutes)	4	4
Tape Width (inches)	.5	.5
Standard Number of Tracks	7 or 9	9

Fig. 28 IBM 2415 Magnetic Tape Unit and Control Model 1. The amount of time required to mount and thread a reel of tape is about 20 seconds.

one cannot cut the tape into pieces (where each piece is a record). The alternative is to leave a certain amount of space between records. In data-processing circles, this space is known as the *inter-record gap* (IRG). How is the IRG made? After the specified number of characters has been written, the writing mechanism completely magnetizes several tenths of an inch of tape. This distinguishes the end of one record from the beginning of the next. When a tape unit is commanded to read the record, the magnetic tape is moved past the reading mechanism until the IRG is detected. A distinction of which you should be aware concerns what is recorded in an IRG and the recording of blank characters. A blank character is

Fig. 29 IBM 2420 Magnetic Tape Unit Model 7 with automatic threading. The tape is in a dust-free cartridge.

represented on nine-track tape by the following arrangement of bits (including parity)

001000000

On seven-track tape, a blank is represented as

1000000

On both seven- and nine-track tape, the IRG is completely magnetized.

READING TAPE RECORDS INTO STORAGE

Each time the tape unit receives a command to READ, the data between two IRG's is fed past the reading mechanism. Where does all this information go? It depends on some other information given. That is, the disposition of the data read between two IRG's can range from all of it entering storage to none of it entering storage.

One of the components of a READ command is a *count* of the number of characters that is to enter storage. If the count is equal to or greater than the number of characters between two IRG's, the entry of data into storage stops when the count has been satisfied; the rest of the data that is read (up to the IRG) goes nowhere.

Unblocked Records

When only one data record exists between IRG's, the records are unblocked. In this case, it is necessary to issue one read command to the tape unit for each record to be read. Using the unblocked record technique could be an example of inefficient use of tape. For example, suppose that the records on tape are nothing more than card images (i.e., 80 characters of information). If the recording density is 800 bpi it means that each record requires only 0.1 inch and the IRG between records is 0.6 inch (see Fig. 30). The ratio of nothing to data is 6:1, or,

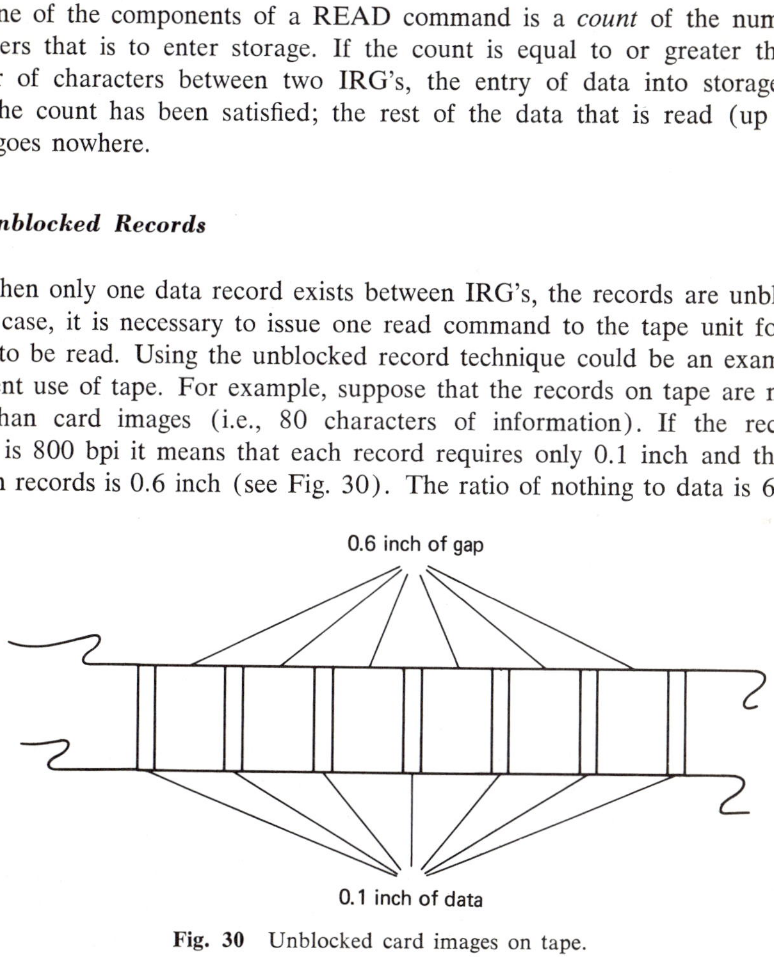

Fig. 30 Unblocked card images on tape.

stated another way, each 2,400-foot reel of tape contains about 340 feet of data and 2,060 feet of nothing.

Blocked Records

The "waste" of unused tape can be overcome by recording a large number of records between IRG's. The technique for doing this is as follows. The desired number of unblocked records are read one at a time into adjacent main storage areas. After the desired number of records has been read into main storage, a write command is issued. The number of bytes to be written would be the sum of the number of bytes in all the records. The program to block 20 card images might consist of the following logic:

1. Read a card into location 5000
2. Read a card into location 5080
3. Read a card into location 5160

•

•

•

19. Read a card into location 6440
20. Read a card into location 6520
21. Write a 1,600-character record on tape (start with location 5000)
22. Branch to instruction 1

The tape that results from the above program makes better use of the available space. That is, for each 0.6 inch required for an IRG, there are 2.0 inches of data. The solution of blocked tapes presents a new problem, however (i.e., when blocked records become input for processing). Each time that a tape read command is issued, 20 records enter storage. The problem the programmer faces is: Which record is the one to be processed next? The third one, the seventh one, the seventeenth one? You will find out later how this problem is easily overcome.

Logical and Physical Records

Some of you may have already discovered the inconsistency with which the term "record" has been used. That is, one can take two or more data records, block them together, and write them out as one record on tape. If one now says he is going to process a record, what is he talking about? The characters between two IRG's or the characters of one of the data records?

To help solve this problem, data-processing people use two terms to distinguish the two concepts. The term for describing all the data about one object is *logical record.* The term used for describing all the characters between two interrecord gaps is *physical record.* When logical records are unblocked, one physical record consists of one logical record. When logical records are blocked, one physical record consists of two or more logical records.

Strange as it may seem, one physical record could consist of less than one logical record. Although this condition doesn't occur too often when using magnetic tape, it occurs quite frequently when using punched cards. If four cards are required to contain all the information about an insurance policy, four physical records make up one logical record.

TYPE OF RECORD LENGTHS— FIXED AND VARIABLE

The simplest type of record *length* is fixed. This merely means that every record in a data set contains the same number of characters. (Although the number of informational characters varies per record, each record is "made" the same length by adding the correct number of *blanks*.) In many cases the fixed-length record is just what a particular data-processing installation needs. There are, however, many cases where the use of fixed records can be very wasteful. Consider, for example, an insurance policy that might be either standard or include dozens of extra coverages. Now the insurance company's data processing analyst has to decide whether to use fixed-length records or variable-length records. If he chooses the fixed-length record, all records must be long enough to accommodate the maximum amount of data that can be associated with a record. This would not be a bad choice if 80 to 90 percent of the records could utilize all the space. On the other hand, if only 10 to 20 percent of the records could use all the space, it would mean that 90 to 80 percent of the records contained fill-in blanks.

Variable-Length Records

Using the variable-length philosophy, each record requires only the amount of space equal to the number of characters in the record. (Well, almost; two or three additional positions are prefixed to the records for recording the length.) The program to determine the length of each variable-length record and then to block them might consist of the following logic. (The storage area into which these records of unknown length are to be read must be long enough to accommodate the longest record.)

1. Read a record into location N.
2. Count the number of bytes in the record.
3. Add 3 to the count value and prefix it to the record (i.e., the sum of the count value plus 3).
4. Add the value of the count, plus 3, to N in the first instruction (i.e., the sum of the count value plus 3).

5. Accumulate all the *count-plus-3* sums.
6. If the accumulation is less than "X," go to the first instruction; otherwise, go to the next instruction (X is a guide, not a limit).
7. Prefix the accumulated value plus 3 to the length recorded for the first record.
8. Write a record whose length is equal to the accumulated value plus 3.

Figure 31 illustrates blocked and unblocked variable-length records.

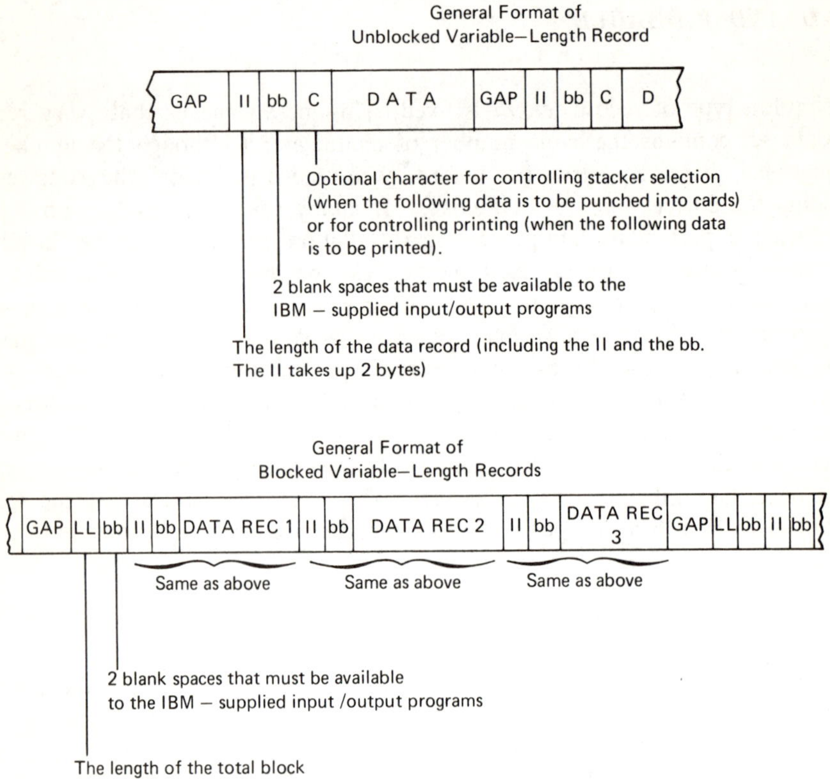

Fig. 31 General format of unblocked and blocked variable-length records.

PROCESSING RECORDS ON TAPE

A question you might like to have answered is: How often is the data of a half-million-record data set on tape processed? The answer to this might be very general —not too often. Let's find out what "Not too often" means. To assist the discussion, we shall describe a manual processing system for updating the white pages of the Manhattan telephone directory.

The 1968–1969 Manhattan telephone directory has about 1,800 pages with 400 names per page. Let's say that there exists, at the phone company's headquarters, one master copy of this immense data set. We shall also assume that in one day there is an average of four transactions per page to be made, transactions that reflect change of address (the people moved but are keeping the same number), a name has changed (to or from a state of marriage, shortening or lengthening a surname), a number has been disconnected, a new subscriber has had his phone installed. Each transaction is written on a 3- by 5-inch index card. The question now is: How does the updating clerk perform his function of noting the transactions on the proper page and line? One way would be to take each transaction record as it comes in, look at the last name, turn to the proper page, and make the change. Sometimes very few pages would have to be turned when the next transaction is to be noted, but most of the time there will be a lot of page flipping. It wouldn't take any time at all before most of the pages are so badly worn and frayed that a new master data set (phone directory) would have to be created.

There is very little that can be done about reducing the number of transactions, but there is one thing that can be done to cut down on the time. It is this. Wait until all the transactions for a 24-hour period have been gathered. (These transactions records may have been written on 3- by 5-inch index cards.) After they have been gathered, sort them into alphabetic sequence by name and then give them to the updating clerk. The clerk now looks at the name on the first transaction record and checks to see if it is on the first page of the directory. If it's not on this page, it may be a new number (which he'll enter), or else it's on a subsequent page; the clerk is smart enough to know which. Using this technique, the clerk moves in only one direction through the data set (phone book), from front to back.

When a computing system is used in a similar fashion we call it *batch processing*. That is, a quantity of transaction records is collected and sorted. Then they are brought to the computing room in one batch. When batched and sorted transaction records are processed in conjunction with a master data set on tape that is organized sequentially, it is called *sequential processing*. Even when tape (in contrast to cards) is used for recording large master data sets, batch processing can take a long time (several hours is no exaggeration). Hence the answer, "Not too often" to the question at the beginning of the section means "Not more than once a day."

Recreating Master Files (Master Data Sets)

The technique that the updating clerk uses for making additions and deletions has one very annoying by-product: The updated master data set is very messy, even after the first processing cycle. If the Manhattan phone directory were recorded on magnetic tape, it would be virtually impossible to make additions to the *very same tape*. Even if just one new record were to be inserted between two existing records, *all* the existing records that are higher in alphabetic value than the new one would have to be moved to provide space for the new one. Therefore, whenever data sets have been recorded on tape and the data set is being processed, you will see at least two tape units being used. One tape unit contains the tape with the existing data set; the second tape unit contains a tape upon which will be written the master data set in its updated form. When the updating job is through, there will be two copies of the master data set; one reflects the current status with all changes received to date included, the other one reflects the status as it was the day before. (*Note:* Ancestral data sets are never discarded until there is almost absolute certainty that more recent data sets are 100 percent accurate. Ancestral data sets are often referred to for settling disputes.) Sometimes a third tape unit is used. Many data-processing installations transcribe the transaction records onto tape before the update job is executed.

SELECTOR CHANNEL—PATH FOR TAPE DATA

Earlier you saw that the multiplexor channel is the computing system's component in charge of executing I/O commands for card punches, card readers, printers, and so on. It is possible to use the multiplexor channel for tape commands. When this is the case, however, the multiplexor channel must be dedicated to the tape unit for the length of time it takes to transmit the physical record. This means that while the characters to or from tape are traveling through the multiplexor channel, no other I/O devices should be using it. The architects of the S/360 designed the *selector channel* to handle the high speeds of character transmission between tape units and main storage. Although the selector channel is dedicated for the length of time it takes to transmit a physical record, it does not have all the expensive circuitry needed by the multiplexor (to keep track of I/O devices sharing the multiplexor). It is a selector channel which usually gets the responsibility for executing the I/O commands that control the reading, writing, backspacing, skipping, erasing, and rewinding of tape. Figure 32 schematically illustrates a S/360 with one multiplexor channel and one selector channel to which is attached one tape control unit and some associated tape drives.

FREQUENCY OF PROCESSING DATA RECORDED ON TAPE

What are some frequencies of processing data recorded on tape? Many companies, bureaus, state and local governments, schools, and so on, record on tape those

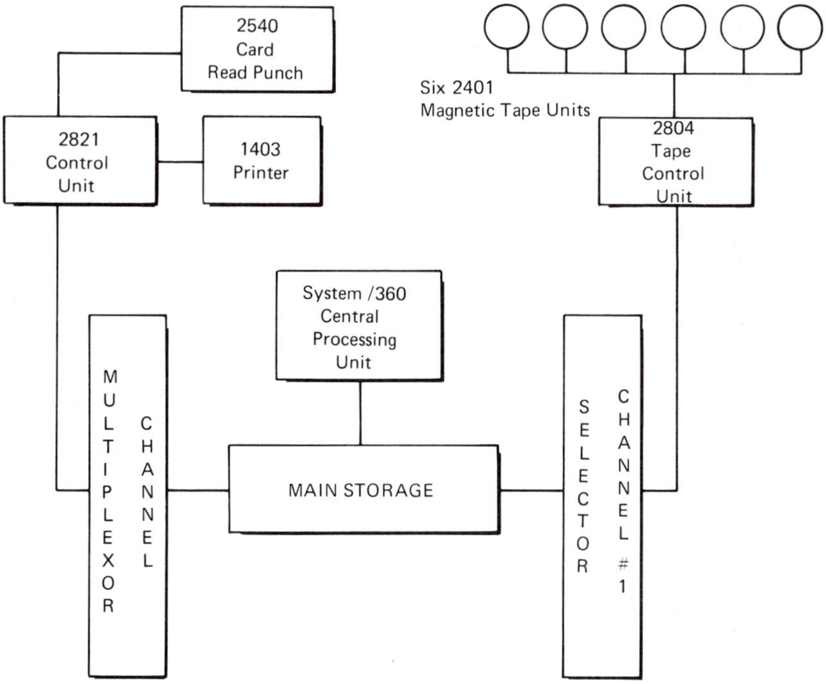

Fig. 32 Schematic of S/360 with one multiplexor channel and one selector channel.

data sets which need to be processed on a periodic basis. You have been told that this period is seldom less than one day (24 hours) and may be as infrequent as monthly, quarterly, or even annually. Very seldom do these companies record on tape those data sets whose records must be retrieved in a matter of a few seconds. Records that must be retrieved in a few seconds must be stored on a device appropriately called *direct-access storage devices,* the subject of Chapter 3.

RELATIONSHIP BETWEEN CHANNELS AND CPU

It may have already occurred to you that unless there is some hierarchy of controls, chaos is very possible when the channels and the CPU are executing their respective commands and instructions at the same time. There is, of course, control! As was said earlier, before a channel can execute a command, the CPU must have executed an instruction called Start I/O (SIO). However, before the SIO instruction is issued, some set-up instructions must be executed. The set up consists of determining the address in storage of the command (or chain of commands) that the channel is to execute. This location's address must then be placed in a special location in main storage. This special location is called the Channel Address Word (CAW). Then, when the SIO instruction is executed, the channel obtains the *address* of the first channel command word (CCW) from the Channel Address Word. Using this address, the channel then obtains the first CCW and executes it. As soon as the channel begins executing its channel program (one or more related CCW's) events start taking place in the I/O device, the control unit, and the channel. The nature of these events is recorded in a special storage area called the Channel Status Word (CSW). (Whereas the CPU's current PSW consists of electronic circuitry, the channel's CSW is in main storage.) The most common events are the successful completion by the channel, control unit, and I/O device. Other events concern activities that may require remedial action. Thus you see that a channel is subservient to the CPU.

I/O INTERRUPTIONS

Whenever an I/O operation terminates (either successfully or unsuccessfully), the program using the CPU is interrupted; this is called an I/O interruption. That is, the current PSW is replaced, in this case by the new I/O PSW. (Of course, before the current PSW is replaced, a copy of its contents is placed in the special storage area called the *Old I/O PSW.*) The new I/O PSW directs the CPU to an interrupt handling program which determines the exact nature of the interrupt; this program conducts its analysis with information from such sources as the old I/O PSW and the CSW. If the interrupt had been caused by an unsuccessful operation, the interrupt handling program may try some remedial action. If the operation had been successful, the program sets up the CAW in preparation for the next I/O operation.

Not all of the information about an unsuccessful I/O operation is recorded in the CSW; the detailed information is kept in special electronic circuits of the I/O device or its control unit. If the program analyzing the unsuccessful I/O operation requires this detailed information, the channel is made to execute a SENSE command. When the channel executes the SENSE CCW, the detailed information is sent (in the form of bit patterns called sense bytes) from the I/O device or its control unit to main storage.

Both the I/O interrupt handling programs and the programs to start and conduct I/O operations are very complex. To write these programs for all of the I/O devices in an installation could take a programmer many months. To make it unnecessary for each problem programmer to spend all this time, the I/O interrupt handling programs and the programs to start and conduct I/O operations are provided by IBM.

SUMMARY

1. A punched card's characteristics include the following:
   a. It can accommodate 80 EBCDIC characters.
   b. An EBCDIC character is represented by a hole or combination of holes in the 12 rows of a card.
2. The main card reader for the S/360 is the IBM 2540.
3. The main card punch for the S/360 is the IBM 2540.
4. The main printer for the S/360 is the IBM 1403.
5. The 2540 Card Reader/Punch and the 1403 Printer are attached to a control unit which contains buffers for these I/O devices.
6. Unbuffered I/O card punches and readers and printers are slower than buffered ones.
7. Slow I/O devices send data to and receive data from main storage via a multiplexor channel.
8. The multiplexor channel is responsible for issuing the commands to the card readers, punches, and printers.
9. All the information recorded about a certain object is called a record.
10. Each item of information in a record is called a field.
11. A collection of records all dealing with the same class of objects is called a data set.
12. Large volumes of data can be recorded on magnetic tape.
13. One reel of magnetic tape is 2,400 feet (28,800 inches) long.
14. The recording density of magnetic tape can vary from 200 to 1,600 characters per inch.
15. Magnetic tape can be read or written at speeds varying from 18.75 to 200 ips.
16. Data sets on tape are usually organized sequentially.
17. Any data that goes between magnetic tape and main storage must go through a control unit.
18. All the data about one object is called a logical record.
19. A physical record on tape consists of all the characters between two IRG's.
20. Records are unblocked when one physical record consists of one logical record.
21. Records are blocked when one physical record consists of more than one logical record.
22. A data set consists of fixed-length records when all the records are of the same length.
23. A data set consists of variable-length records when the records are not all of the same length.

24. One of the fields of a variable-length record must state how long the record is.
25. Sequential processing of a master file requires that the transaction records also be in sequence.
26. An input tape is never written upon. Data sets that are being updated are written upon an output tape.
27. Data being transmitted between main storage and magnetic tape travels over a selector channel.
28. Records of data sets that are recorded on tape are usually retrieved once a day or less often.
29. The SIO instruction causes the channel to obtain from the CAW the address of the first CCW the channel is to execute.
30. The status of an I/O operation is recorded in the CSW (Channel Status Word). The CSW is located in main storage.
31. The termination of an I/O operation causes an I/O interruption. When this happens, the current PSW is replaced by the new I/O PSW.
32. The new I/O PSW directs the CPU to a program which determines the exact nature of the interrupt.
33. Detailed information about an unsuccessful I/O operation can be obtained by the channel when it executes the SENSE command. The execution of the SENSE command brings detailed information from the I/O device to main storage. The detailed information is called sense bytes.
34. Interruption handling programs and programs to start and conduct the I/O operations of all I/O devices are supplied by IBM.

SUGGESTED READING ASSIGNMENTS

IBM System/360 Principles of Operation (A22-6821)

Listed below are the section names, major topics and subtopics we suggest you read. Please read only what is suggested.

<u>Input/Output Operations</u>

Attachment of Input/Output Devices
- Input/Output Devices
- Control Units
- Channels
- System Operation
- Compatibility of Operation

Execution of Input/Output Operations
- Blocking of Data
- Channel Address Word
- Channel Command Word
- Command Code
- Definition of Storage Area
- Chaining
- Skipping

3 DISK STORAGE DEVICES

When one compares the speed of reading data from a popular IBM card reader with the speed of reading data from the fastest tape unit, one is usually very impressed with the ratio (1,333 characters per second from the IBM 2540 Card Reader and 320,000 characters per second from the IBM 2420 Tape Unit); this is a ratio of about 1:255. The question often asked is, Who needs to go faster?

The answer to this question often actually disregards the question. That is, it is not so much a question of going faster but, rather, how quickly a certain record of information can be retrieved. For example, suppose someone wanted to inquire about the information that is recorded in a certain record; suppose further that this record was right in the middle of a 2,400-foot reel of tape. To locate this record, even on the 2420, might take as much as several *minutes.* This would be unacceptable unless one were willing to wait this long. Now let's make the situation even worse.

Many commercial and governmental institutions require dozens of reels of tape for a data set. If inquiries are submitted to obtain information in a record that is not in the reel in the tape unit, one tape reel must be dismounted and the proper one mounted. This manual activity could easily add another minute to the retrieval time for the desired information.

Not only is retrieval time for any specific record slow, it is very expensive. For example, let's say that the tape drive costs $1,000 per month and that it takes, on the average, 4 minutes to retrieve the record with the needed information. There are 176 *working* hours, or 10,560 *working* minutes, in a month (on which the $1,000 cost is based). This means that there can be about 2,500 retrievals (maximum) a month for information. The computer cost per retrieval is therefore at least 40 cents, a cost no company could afford.

To greatly reduce both the time and cost of retrieval, data-processing engineers have designed two related items. One is a type of I/O device from which data can be quickly retrieved (when the data is organized in a certain way). The second item is the organization schemes for storing the data. The I/O devices will now be described.

THE DISK

A disk with which you are all familiar is a phonograph record. The phonograph record contains one continuous track which starts at the outer edge and spirals inward. The primary contents of a phonograph record is "data" that produces an audible sound when "read" by a needle. Most phonograph records contain permanent data. That is, one is not generally able to erase a Mozart concerto and then record an Ives "symphony."

The disk used in data processing is quite different from the phonograph record. It is thin and it has tracks, but the tracks are quite different. That is, they are not spirals. Instead, each disk surface has tracks consisting of concentric circles (something like an archery or rifle target). One particular model of a data-processing disk contains 203 of these concentric tracks (see Fig. 33).

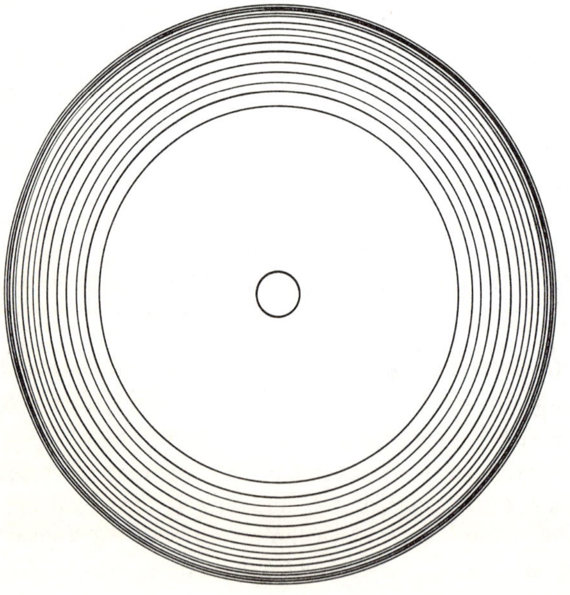

Fig. 33 A data processing disk with concentric tracks.

Another difference is that the surfaces (both top and bottom) of a data-processing disk consist of material that is easily magnetized. This means that data can be recorded on a track in the form of magnetized bits. Although the data can be read an almost-infinite number of times without being destroyed, it is possible, with a WRITE command, to first erase the existing data and then record new information.

A similarity between phonograph disk and a data-processing disk is that they both rotate around a shaft or spindle. However, the fastest common phonograph disk rotates at 78 revolutions per minute (rpm), whereas a data-processing disk rotates at over 2,000 rpm.

The Reading and Writing Mechanism for Disk

Most of the phonographs you have seen have a needle attached to a single arm. This arm reads only the data from the disk surface that is facing up. If you want to hear what's on the bottom side, you must move the arm away, turn the disk over, and reposition the arm. In data processing, each disk surface on which data is recorded has its own arm. Hence, if a disk has data recorded on its top and bottom surface, there will be two arms. In most cases it is really a split arm: one part of the split arm for reading the top surface and the other part for reading the bottom (see Fig. 34). If you wish to become a good data-processing terminologist you will not say split arm but *access arm*. Why *access* arm? Because the purpose of the arm is to get at, or access, the data to be read or written on the disk's track.

Fig. 34 Split arm for reading/writing either top or bottom tracks.

Motion of the Access Arm

In a phonograph record there is no effort involved in moving the access arm from the outside of the disk to the inside. This is because the spiral nature of the grooves moves the arm toward the center (except when a scratch is encountered). In the case of a data-processing disk, the in-and-out motion of the access arm must be accomplished by some controllable mechanism. It is not possible for the access arm to hop from one track to another on its own accord. Hence the access arm is attached to what is known as an *access mechanism*. The access mechanism is moved to the proper track by having the selector channel issue a command, telling it where to go.

The Disk Pack

The objective of a disk surface is to be able to store as much data as possible. Although a disk can store a lot of data (you'll see later how much), in many cases it's not enough. There are several solutions to this problem, and most of the solutions have been implemented in one way or another. The one we wish to mention now is the invention of the disk pack. A disk pack is nothing more than a shaft inserted through the center of a certain number of disks. How is the access arm going to function now? If the individual disks were touching each other it would be quite difficult to get the access arm between them; hence the disks are separated (see Fig. 35).

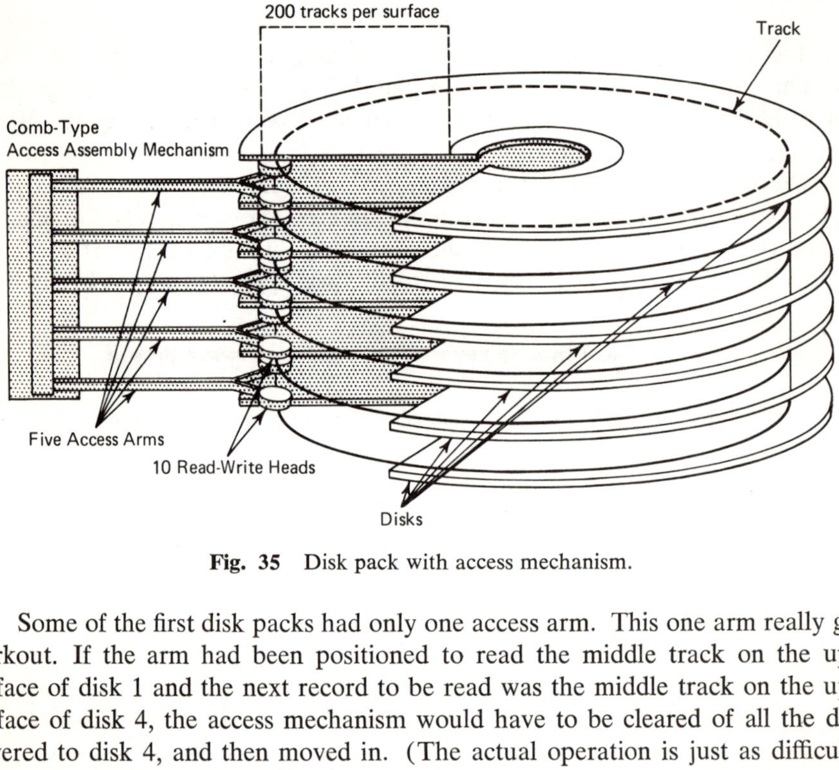

Fig. 35 Disk pack with access mechanism.

Some of the first disk packs had only one access arm. This one arm really got a workout. If the arm had been positioned to read the middle track on the upper surface of disk 1 and the next record to be read was the middle track on the upper surface of disk 4, the access mechanism would have to be cleared of all the disks, lowered to disk 4, and then moved in. (The actual operation is just as difficult as reading the sentence that describes it.)

Any mechanical motion that includes a number of stops and starts (as does the repositioning of a single access arm) takes a lot of time and produces much wear and tear. How can this time consuming, wearing/tearing motion be eliminated? The answer is to provide each disk with its own arm, combine all the access arms into one unit, and control the unit of arms with one access mechanism (see Fig. 35).

Capacity of Disk Packs

IBM has several varieties of disk packs, each of which is to be used with a different I/O device. Some of the packs are removable. That is, an operator can dismount one pack and replace it with another. Some "packs" are not removable, hence they are not removed.

- IBM 1316 (pronounced thirteen sixteen) Disk Pack (removable)
  This pack has 2,000 tracks with a capacity of 3,625 bytes per track, or 7,250,000 bytes
- IBM 2316 (pronounced twenty-three sixteen) Disk Pack (removable)
  This pack has 4,000 tracks with a capacity of 7,294 bytes per track, or 29,176,000 bytes
- IBM 2302 (pronounced twenty-three oh two) Disk Storage (not removable)
  One module of these disks has 23K tracks with a capacity of 5K bytes per track, or 112,790,000 bytes (K stands for thousand).

I/O Devices for Disks

The I/O device that can accommodate the 1316 Disk Pack is the IBM 2311 (usually pronounced twenty-three eleven).

The I/O device for reading and writing data on a 2316 disk pack is the IBM 2314 (twenty-three fourteen).

The I/O device that accommodates the unremovable disk storage "pack," the IBM 2302 (twenty-three oh two), does not exist as a separate entity. The I/O device and the pack are regarded as an integral unit.

Figure 36 shows the I/O devices and the disks that reside on them.

Transmission Speed of Data from Disk Devices

The maximum speed with which data flows between main storage and the three disk devices (assuming that the beginning of the record has moved under the reading mechanism) is as follows:

- 2311—156,000 bytes per second
- 2314—312,000 bytes per second
- 2302—156,000 bytes per second

Fig. 36 Disk drives and disk packs: (a) IBM 2311; (b) IBM 2302.

(c)

Fig. 36—*Cont.* IBM 2314 disk drive and disk pack.

Control Units for Disk Devices

Each disk device has a control unit associated with it. These are as follows:

- 2311—IBM 2841 Control Unit
- 2314—the control unit for the 2314 does not exist as a separate entity; it is "built into" the 2314
- 2302—IBM 2841 Control Unit

As in the case of the tape control units, the control units for disks oversee such activities as seeking a record, reading a record, and writing a record. *Seeking* is a process that positions the access mechanism over the appropriate record. (While an access mechanism is seeking, the selector channel can be used for executing other commands.) After a seek has successfully completed, the selector channel can issue the READ or WRITE command.

SELECTOR CHANNEL FOR DISK

The same selector channel that is attached to the tape control units can be attached to the disk control units. However, only one device, either tape unit or disk unit, can be transmitting or receiving data at one time. When an installation requires the simultaneous transmission of data to or from several tapes and disks, it will require several selector channels.

THE CYLINDER CONCEPT OF DISK STORAGE

Earlier you learned that a 1316 Disk Pack consists of 2,000 tracks. These 2,000 tracks are on 10 of the 12 surfaces of a six-disk pack. (Although there are 12 surfaces, the top surface of the top disk and the bottom surface of the bottom disk are not used—they are too vulnerable to scratches.)

There are two logical ways for determining the order of 2,000 tracks. One way is to start with track 0 of surface 0 and then proceed through all the tracks of that surface before going to the first track of the next surface. Then proceed through all the tracks of surface 1 before going to the first track of surface 2, and so on. There is one major disadvantage of ordering the tracks this way. Everytime it is necessary to access the data from the "next" sequential track, the access arms must physically move. This physical motion requires a certain amount of time, called *access time*. (Access time is defined in the next section.) The alternative is to start with the outermost track of surface 0, then proceed to the outermost track of surface 1, then to the outermost track of surface 2, and so on. Since each of the vertically related tracks has its own reading mechanism, the reading mechanism doesn't have to move when reading from track to track. Instead, the progression of reading from track to track is done *electronically*. Electronic switching is many times faster than physical motion. Only after the outermost track of surface 9 has been dealt with will it be necessary to move the access mechanism. After moving the access mechanism one track inward, 10 more tracks can be read in sequence before moving the access mechanism again.

Since 10 tracks (one on each surface) can be read without moving the access mechanism, we say that the 10 circular tracks stacked one above the other make up a "cylinder." Using the cylinder concept in designing a disk device makes it possible to initiate one operation and have 10 tracks read or written. (On the 2311 this amounts to 36,250 bytes—of course one may choose to read or write much less.) Even if the data is stored sequentially on disk (as it is on tape), having to move the access mechanism only once for every 10 tracks of data has its advantages. However, the primary objective of the disk designers was to permit data records to be recorded other than sequentially.

ROTATIONAL DELAY AND ACCESS TIME

We have already given the transmission speeds of data between storage and various disk devices after the starting point on the track had been located. How long does it take to find the starting point? It depends on how much the disk must rotate before the starting point on the track comes under the access arm. If the starting point is 359° (in case you've forgotten, there are 360° in a circle) away from the access arm, the disk must make an almost complete rotation. If the starting point is a few degrees away from the access arm, the reading or writing operation can commence quite quickly. However long it takes, this quantity of time is referred to as *rotational delay.*

Another consideration is: How far, in or out, must the access mechanism move before it's positioned within the proper cylinder? It would certainly take longer for the access mechanism to move the arms across 150 cylinders than it would for 2 cylinders (it takes no time at all if it doesn't have to move). The amount of time required to position the access arms if they have to be moved is called access time. The following table summarizes the rotational delay and access time for the three disk drives, the 2311, the 2314, and the 2302.

Disk	Rotational	Rotational Delay	Access Time,† msec *		
Drive	Speed, rpm	Average, msec *	Minimum	Av.	Maximum
2311	2,400	12.5	25	75	135
2314	2,400	12.5	25	75	135
2302	1,800	17.0	50	165	180

* An msec is one millisecond or one thousandth of a second.

† If the access arm doesn't have to move, access time is zero.

PHYSICAL RECORDS ON DISK

On tape we saw that a physical record consists of all the characters between two successive IRG's. (This is true for both fixed-length and variable-length records.) With disks, the idea of a physical record is somewhat different. Each track may have one or more physical records. The beginning of each physical record is indicated by an *address marker.* Following the address marker is a short gap which, in turn, is followed by the physical record's identification. The identification consists of a magnetic recording of such information as

1. The cylinder number within the pack (first, second, etc.)
2. The track number within the cylinder (first, second, third, etc.).
3. The record number within the track (first, second, third, fourth, etc.).
4. The number of bytes in the physical record (for fixed lengths as well as variable lengths).

If a physical record consists of 3,625 bytes, each track of a 1316 Disk Pack can accommodate one physical record. Hence there will be only one address marker and one identification. If a physical record consists of 118 characters, the 1316 track has a capacity of 20 physical records. There will then be 20 address markers (each followed by a short gap) and 20 identifications. The number of physical records on a track depends upon the length of the physical records when they were written. The physical records' data follows the area in the track where the identification has been recorded (there is also an intervening gap).

The Key

Although the magnetically recorded identification of a physical record on disk consists of such information as its order within the track (first record, second record, etc.), the identification does not contain the *key* of the record (an example of a key is an employee number, a student number, a part number, or a suit/dress code).

When data is recorded on tape, the field containing the key is embedded within each logical record. This is also true when a logical record is recorded on disk. In addition, the key may (it is not mandatory) be recorded separately just prior to the record itself (possible only on disk). Of course, if there is more than one logical record per physical record, the key should be a "copy" of the key from the highest logical record in the block. The same technique is used in many manual filing systems; on the front of each drawer of the file cabinets is the number of the highest record in the drawer. When one is looking for a specific record, he must first find out which drawer it is in. By scanning, in sequence, the numbers on the drawers, the clerk knows he has found the proper drawer when the number on the drawer is equal to or greater than the number of the record he is looking for. When the key is also recorded separately on disk, the length of the key becomes part of the identification.

1. The cylinder number within the pack
2. The track number within the cylinder
3. The record number within the track
4. The length of the key
5. The length of the physical record

Figure 37 is a schematic of a track (when projected as a straight line) for records without externally recorded keys and with external keys. The advantage of also

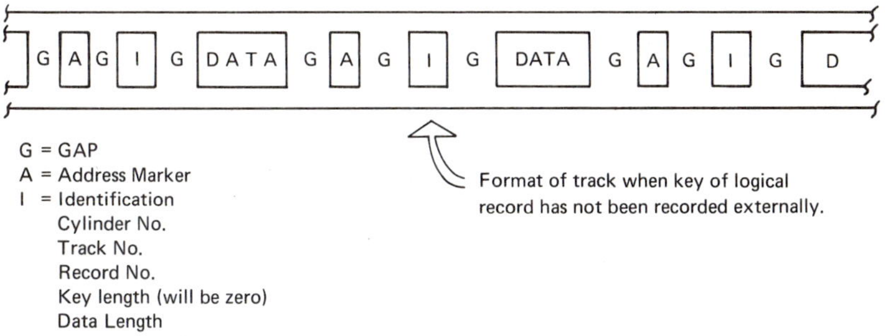

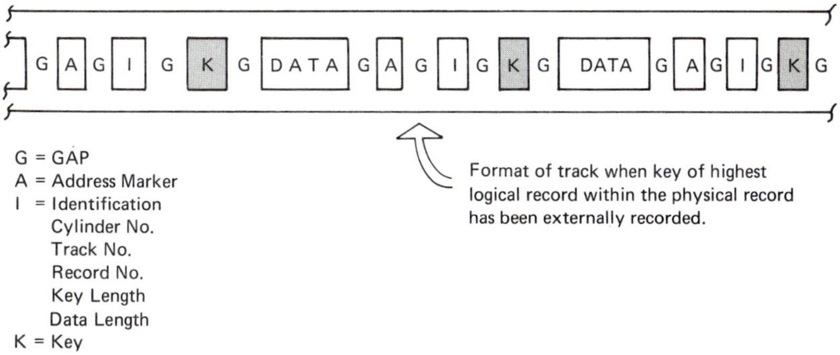

Fig. 37 Formats of DASD tracks.

recording the key separately is that the channel can be used to determine when the appropriate key has been located. (That is, the record doesn't have to be read into storage.) When the key exists only within the logical record, it is necessary to read the record into main storage and then have the CPU determine the appropriateness of the key.

CREATING AN INDEX FOR SEQUENTIALLY ORGANIZED RECORDS

Although sequential processing of sequentially organized files is the most popular type of data processing and organization, it has serious limitations for many applications. Let's consider a credit card company (with 50,000 subscribers) one of whose objectives is to answer any inquiry about a subscriber's record within 12 to 18 seconds. If all the subscribers' records were organized in the ordinary sequential manner on 1316 Disk Packs, it could take an average of almost 1 minute

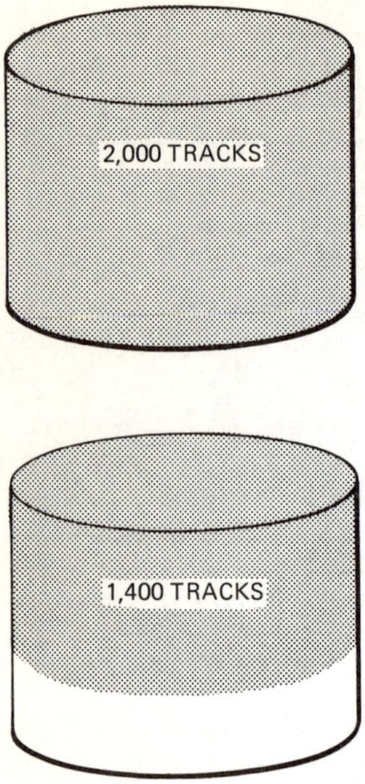

To store all of the credit card subscriber's records on disk storage requires 340 cylinders (or 3400 tracks). Therefore, on the average it would be necessary to scan 1,700 tracks. This would require in the order of one minute.

Fig. 38 Disk storage requirements for 50,000 records.

to get the answer to the inquiry (see Fig. 38). Since this doesn't meet the time criteria, one must devise a scheme to improve performance. One scheme that has been developed is to get all the records in sequence (the same as before), store them on a direct-access storage device such as a 2311, and determine the highest credit number on each track. As each highest number and the address of the track on which it resides is determined, both are recorded onto another track (we'll call this information the *track index*). See Fig. 39.

TRK 0	0017835	0017964	0018043	0018376	0018785	0018996	DATA
TRK 1	0019009	0019376	0019584	0019736	0020015	0020713	DATA
TRK 2	0021038	0021334	0021748	0022013	0022349	0022358	DATA
TRK 3							DATA
TRK 4							DATA
TRK 5							DATA
TRK 6							DATA
TRK 7							DATA
TRK 8	0034341	0034511	0034988	0035115	0035296	0035420	DATA
TRK 9	0018996-0	0020713-1	0022358-2		0035420-8		INDEX

Schematic of ten tracks (one cylinder) projected in a straight line. The values shown recorded on the tracks represent credit–card numbers. Note that tracks 0-8 are for data records and that track 9 contains the index information.

Fig. 39 Relationship of index to records.

The way this credit card data set has been designed will require about 3,400 tracks for recording the information for all subscribers (this means two disk packs). From this can be deduced the requirement for 3,400 track indexes. If each of these track indexes is such that 9 indexes can be recorded on one track (i.e., one track per cylinder devoted to index), the 3,400 track indexes would require 370 tracks (see Fig. 40). Now let's see how much of an advantage it is to find a credit card subscriber's record with the track index. Since there are 370 index tracks, the average number of tracks (of the index) to be looked at is 185. By then the track address that contains the record will have been obtained. So, instead of looking at an average of 1,700 tracks to find a record (using *plain* sequential organization), one has only to look at 186 tracks on the average (using *indexed* sequential organization).

To decrease even further the amount of time required to find a given credit card subscriber's record, one could take the highest index from each of the 370 index tracks and record them. (This would take about 10 additional tracks.) To retrieve a record would require looking at an average of 7 tracks (5 cylinder index tracks + 1 track index track + 1 record track). See Fig. 41.

As you can see, the indexed sequential technique is not free. For one thing, 370 extra tracks to hold the track index and 10 tracks for the cylinder index are required. In addition, there must be special processing just to create the index.

Another consideration is the "stability" of the customers. That is, do many subscribers withdraw in a relatively short period of time? Are there lots of new subscribers? If the answer to these questions is "yes," there isn't much stability.

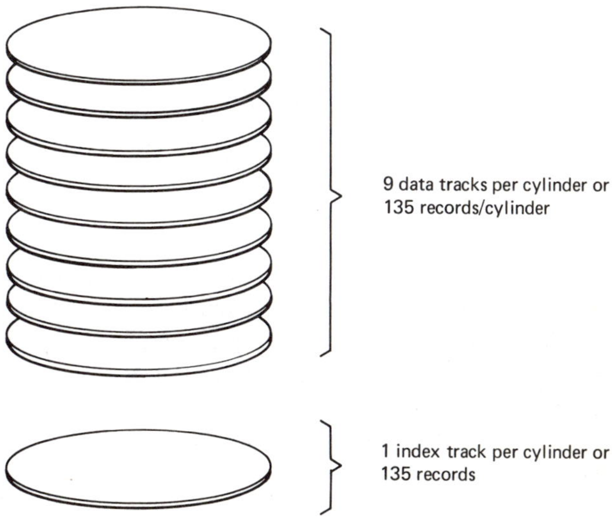

Since 135 records require 1 index track, 50,000 records require $\frac{50,000}{135}$ = 370 tracks

Fig. 40 Index track requirements.

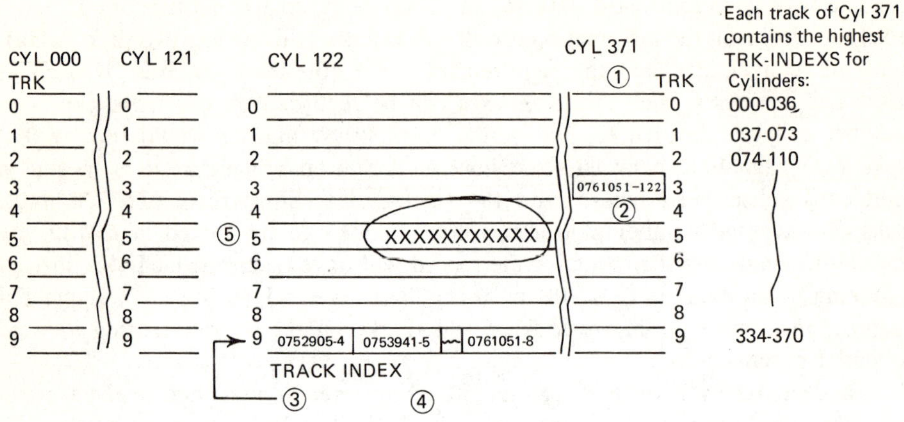

A. Given

1. A request for the subscribers record whose credit-card number is 0753821. (This record is located on cylinder 122, track 5 together with 8 other records.)

2. The following "highest" credit-card numbers on specific tracks and cylinders.

CYLINDER	TRACK	HIGHEST CC#
122	8	0761051
	≀	
	5	0753941
	4	0752905
	≀	
121	8	0732914

3. Recorded on track 3 of cylinder 371 is the fact that the highest credit-card number on cylinder 122 is "0761051".

B. Describe the sequence of events to locate record 0753821.

1. The number 075381 is compared with each value on cylinder 371 (starting with track 0) until a number higher than or equal to itself is found.
2. When the equal or higher value is found, the suffix is used to point out the cylinder with the requested number.
3. The number 0753821 is compared with each value of track 9 on cylinder 122 until a number higher than or equal to itself is found.
4. When the equal or higher value is found, the suffix is used to point out the track with the requested number (in this example, it is track 5).
5. The number 0753821 is compared with each credit-card number on track 5.
6. When an equal value is found the record is brought into core storage.

Fig. 41 Procedure for locating an indexed record.

When a data set is unstable, it must be recreated rather frequently so that the deletions and additions will be part of the automatic data-processing procedure. Although frequent recreation of an indexed sequential file requires considerable time, there may be no alternative.

For you to decide whether "sequential" or "indexed sequential" is better will require a great deal of research into the uses for which the considered data set is to be subjected. Basically you can say that if the records of your data set are to be processed sequentially once a day (or less frequently) with no requirement for inquiry, use sequential organization. However, if you require sequential processing and in addition must make inquiries requiring quick responses, use indexed sequential organization.

DIRECT ORGANIZATION

An even quicker way than indexed sequential for locating a specific record is to use an organization method called *DIRECT*. In its *purest* form, DIRECT organization means that the record's identification number key is the same as the address of a unit of space on a direct-access device. For example, if a direct-access volume has 2,000 tracks (or 200 cylinders with 10 tracks per cylinder) with a capacity of 10 records per track, its address might be of the form

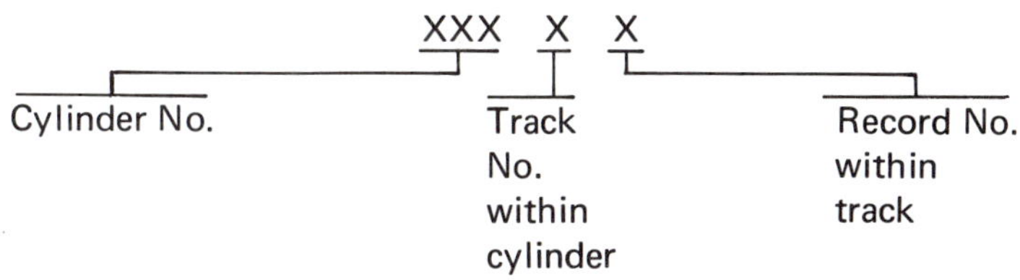

and the range of these addresses would be 00000 to 19999, providing 20,000 different addresses.

Let's get back to the credit card subscribers. (To simplify the rest of the discussion, we'll consider only the first 20,000 of the 50,000 subscribers. In this way, each subscriber's number would be within the range of 00000 to 19999 and they could all fit on one disk pack.) Let's apply the inquiry problem using the DIRECT organization scheme. When a request for information comes to the data-processing center, the inquirer enters the subscriber's number and immediately the appropriate cylinder, track, and record number are selected, making the information available.

It certainly is a great technique! Why, then, doesn't everybody use it? One reason is that it restricts everyone to his selection of what he can use for the key of the record (record identification numbers). Many companies like to have keys *mean* something. For example, the credit card company might wish to have the first two digits of the key refer to the state in which the subscriber lives, the next two represent a city within the state, the fifth digit the income bracket of the subscriber, and the last two digits the subscriber's trade or profession. The credit card company may wish to do this so that merely by looking at a subscriber's credit card number, it can obtain most of the information it needs. If each subscriber's number was identical to an address of a direct-access storage device, the entire record would have to be made visible just to determine some of the subscriber's basic characteristics.

Does this mean that DIRECT organization is of value only to the *theoretical* data-processing man? The answer is an emphatic No! Data-processing mathematicians have devised means of letting a company choose almost any record identification number scheme they want and then, using mathematical techniques, transform the record identification number into a disk storage address. (Since the record identification number can be referred to as a key, the process of computing the disk address from the key is called *key transformation.*)

Again, somebody asks a question: If key transformation and direct organization is so great, why doesn't everybody who has disk packs use it? Its major drawback is that it can't be used very efficiently for sequential processing. Although the *transaction* records might be sorted in sequence by key number, the disk addresses to which the keys are transformed might be scattered all over. That is, sequentially numbered records might be several cylinders away from each other or they might even be on another disk pack. (To go from track 1 to track 2 on cylinder 5 could take as little as 25 milliseconds. However, to go from track 1 on cylinder 5 to track 2 on cylinder 130 could take at least 100 milliseconds.) We see again that a great deal of research must be done before the type of record organization is selected.

OTHER DIRECT-ACCESS DEVICES

The requirements for storing data on direct-access devices by various commercial, industrial, governmental, and educational institutions are just as diverse as the products they make or services they provide. For example, a manufacturer of sporting goods equipment may have a data-processing application where large capacity is of little concern to him; rather, his main concern is a combination of fast access time and fast transmission time for a rather small volume of data. On the other hand, an insurance company may require a very large capacity, say 3 billion bytes. Although such a requirement could be met with 414 IBM 2311's or 104 IBM 2314's (i.e., 13 units each containing eight 2314's), such a solution might be too expensive. (Tape would be much less expensive, of course, but there would be the problem of reasonable retrieval time.) To meet the requirement for high-speed and small-volume direct-access devices, data-processing engineers have developed the *drum.* The *data cell drive* was designed to meet the requirement for a direct-access device of very large volume and low cost. We shall describe the drum first.

Drum Storage

The shape of a data-processing drum is very similar to the shape of a field drum used by marching bands (see Fig. 42). There are two drums that can be used with a S/360. Each of these drums is one cylinder (like an aluminum can). The single cylinder of each drum has 800 tracks. Each track has its own access

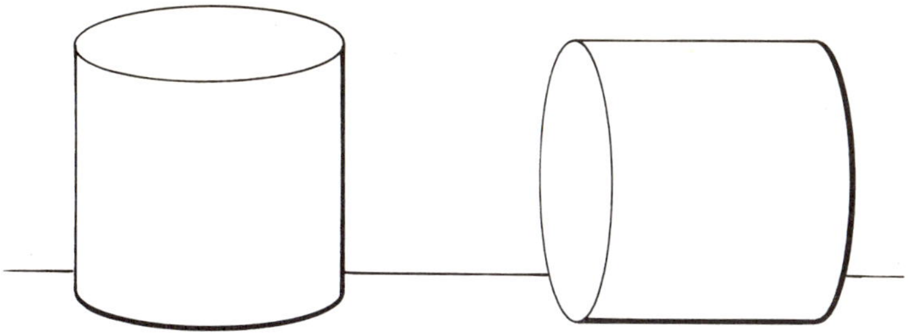

Fig. 42 Vertical and horizontal drum shapes.

arm. The table below shows the bytes per track, the transmission speed, and the capacity of the IBM 2301 (twenty-three oh one) and the 2303 (twenty-three oh three) Drums.

Drum	Bytes per Track	Transmission Speed, bps	Drum Capacity, Million bytes
2301	5,121	1,200,000	4.1
2303	4,892	312,500	3.9

Even more significant than the transmission speed is the matter of rotational delay and access time. Since there is one arm for each track of the drum, there is no access time. The average rotational delay of both drums is 8.6 milliseconds.

Data Cell Storage

To meet the requirements for economically storing very large volumes of data, engineers developed the IBM 2321 (twenty-three twenty-one) Data Cell Drive. Each drive has a capacity of 400 million bytes. (An insurance company with 1 million policies, each requiring 350 bytes, could store its entire master policy data set on one 2321.) Eight of these 2321's may be attached to a 2841 Control Unit. If this is done, there is a capacity of 3.2 billion bytes. One track of a 2321 can accommodate 2,000 bytes and there are 20 tracks per cylinder. Instead of using disks, the 2321 uses strips on which the data is recorded (Fig. 43). One 2321 has a total of 2,000 strips. Ten strips make up a subcell and there are 20 subcells per cell (200 strips per cell). A complete 2321 has 10 cells (2,000 strips), which is called an *array* (Fig. 44). When the 2321 determines which strip

Fig. 43 2321 strip. Each strip has 100 tracks; each track can record 2000 bytes.

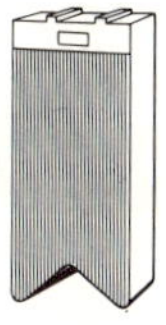

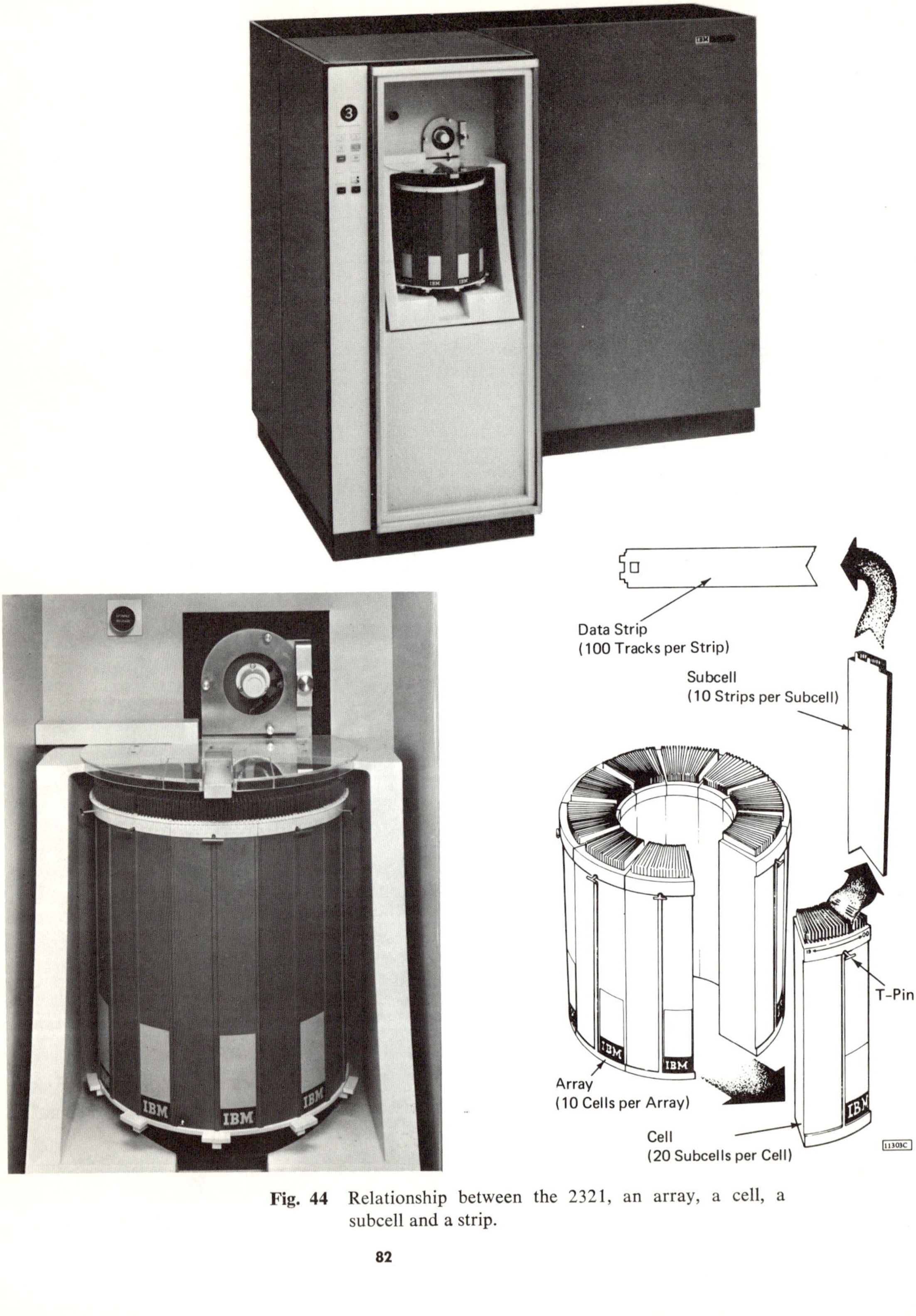

Fig. 44 Relationship between the 2321, an array, a cell, a subcell and a strip.

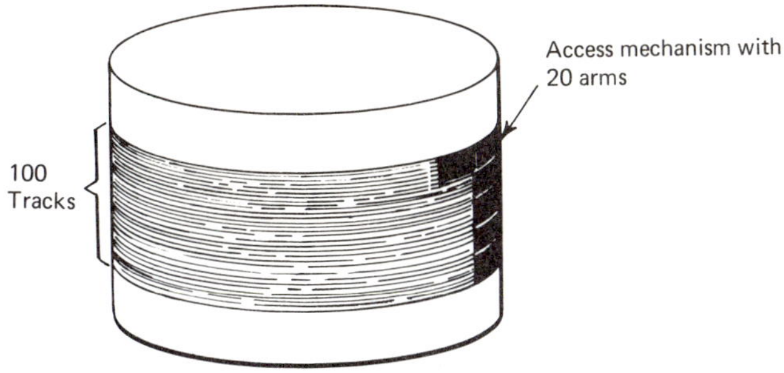

Fig. 45 Data cell access mechanism. Each position of the access mechanism can read 20 tracks of a strip.

contains the required record, the strip is placed around a drum. Each strip has five cylinders and each cylinder has 20 tracks. As in the case of all direct-access devices, there is one access arm for each track of a cylinder. Hence the 2321 access mechanism consists of 20 arms. These 20 arms are moved as a unit when going from one cylinder to another (Fig. 45).

Control Units for Data Cell and Drums

As in the case of all tape and direct-access devices, a control unit is required to check the validity of data to or from the devices and to control the operations of the device. The control unit for the 2321 Data Cell Drive is the same as the control unit for the 2311 and 2302 Disk Storage—the 2841 Storage Control Unit. In the capacity and transmission-speed chart for drum we said that the transmission speed of the 2301 is 1.2 million bps. This high speed is achieved by transmitting four bits at a time (rather than one bit at a time as the 2841 Storage Control Unit permits). Therefore, a special control unit had to be designed.

DISK I/O OPERATIONS

Retrieving or recording a record from a Direct Access Storage Device (DASD) involves a fairly complex combination of I/O operations. Some of the commands used with DASD I/O operations are SEARCH, SEEK, READ and WRITE. The functions of READ and WRITE are the same for DASD as for the other I/O devices. The seek operation is used primarily to position the access mechanism at the cylinder where the record in question is to be retrieved from or recorded to. The search operation is used to find the exact location of a record on a track; it locates the record by successfully comparing the identification of the desired key (determined directly or indirectly by the problem program) with the key recorded on the track. What happens if the search is unsuccessful? Then the SEARCH command must be executed again. So that another SIO instruction doesn't have to be issued by the CPU to get another search initiated, the SEARCH command is followed by a branch operation called *Transfer In Channel* (TIC). As soon as an unsuccessful SEARCH command has concluded, the channel obtains the next Channel Command Word (CCW) in sequence. If the next CCW is a TIC command, and the branch-to address in the TIC is the location of the SEARCH command, then the same SEARCH command is executed again. What if the comparison of the search operation is successful? When the search operation is successful, the channel does *not* obtain the next CCW in sequence; that is, it skips the CCW just after the SEARCH command and obtains the following one. This "following one" is usually a READ command. Thus the channel can execute the same SEARCH command repeatedly with only one SIO instruction.

The programs required to perform the various DASD I/O operations and the DASD interrupt handling programs are supplied by IBM (these programs reflect several years of programming effort).

PROBLEM PROGRAM— I/O PROGRAM RELATIONSHIP

The SIO instruction is privileged; the I/O programs supplied by IBM are in core storage locations with a protection key not available to the problem program. Hence a problem program cannot branch to the I/O program. If it tried to do this, an unmaskable interrupt would occur and the interrupt handling routine would end the problem program. How then does the IBM-supplied I/O programs get called upon? To obtain the services of the I/O program, a problem program must issue a *Supervisor Call* instruction. The execution of an SVC instruction causes one of the five major types of interruption; it is appropriately called an SVC interrupt. A new *SVC* PSW gains control of the CPU. The SVC PSW will contain the proper key to unlock the storage in which the I/O programs are residing. The address in the SVC PSW is not, however, the location of the I/O program's first instruction. This is because the interrupt handling program doesn't yet know the specific identity of the SVC instruction (there is a possibility of 256 different identities for an SVC). Not until the Interrupt Handling program determines that the SVC's identity reflects a request for an I/O operation, does the I/O program get the use of the CPU.

INSTALLATION LAYOUT

For an idea of how many of the I/O devices, control units, channels, and the CPU appear to an observer, see Fig. 46.

(a)

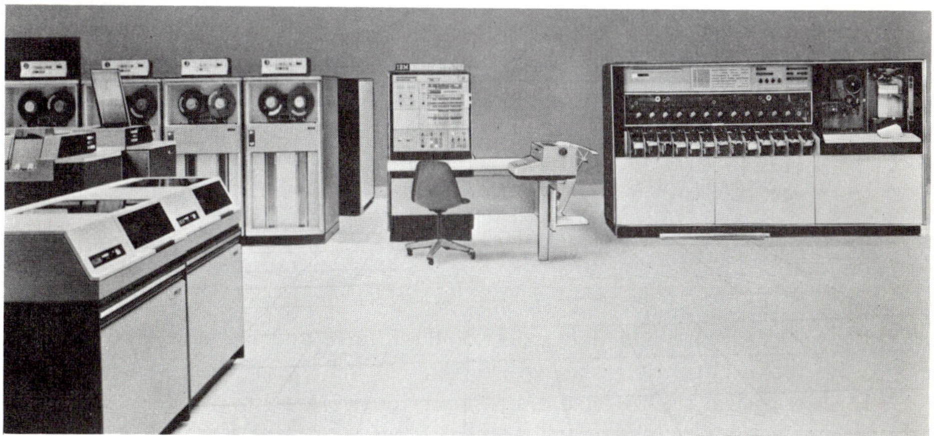

(b)

Fig. 46 (a) An installation using the Model 85 as its CPU; (b) an installation using the Model 40 as its CPU.

SUMMARY

1. Data sets to which inquiries, requiring rapid response (under 7 to 8 seconds), are made should be on direct access and not on tape.
2. A data-processing disk has concentric tracks in which data is recorded.
3. When the disk receives a write command, any previously recorded data is erased immediately before the writing of the new data.
4. The mechanism that reads and writes data on disk is called an access arm.

5. The positioning of the access arms is controlled by an access mechanism.
6. The tracks of a pack that are vertically aligned comprise a cylinder.
7. All the data recorded in a cylinder can be read or written without moving the access mechanism.
8. A series of disks mounted on a common shaft is called a disk pack.
9. Three disk drives are the IBM 2311, 2314, and 2302. These drives use packs whose numbers are 1316, 2316, and 2302. The 1316 and 2316 are removable; the 2302 is not.
10. Each 2311 Disk Drive can accommodate one 1316 pack. Each 2314 Disk facility can accommodate eight 2316 packs. A 2302 Model 3 Disk Drive accommodates one 2302 pack. A 2302 Model 4 Disk facility accommodates two 2302 packs.
11. The byte capacity, transmission speed, average rotational delay, and minimum, average, and maximum access time for one of each of the three disks, the data cell, and drums are as follows:

	Byte Capacity	Transmission Speed, bps	Av. Rotational Delay, msec	Access Time, msec Min.	Access Time, msec Av.	Access Time, msec Max.
2311	7,250,000	156K	12.5	25	75	135
2314	29,176,000	312K	12.5	25	75	135
2302	112,790,000	156K	17.0	50	165	180
2321	400,000,000	55K	25.0	100	500	650
2301	4,100,000	1,200K	8.6	0	0	0
2303	3,900,000	312.5	8.6	0	0	0

12. Disks, drums, and data cells should receive and transmit their data via selector channels.
13. A physical record on a direct-access device consists of
    a. an address marker followed by a gap.
    b. an identification (called a count area) followed by a gap. The area contains
        (1) the cylinder number.
        (2) the track number.
        (3) the record number.
        (4) the length of the key (a zero if there is no key).
        (5) the length of the physical record.
    c. the key [if item b(4) is not zero] followed by a gap.
    d. the data of the physical record.
14. An indexed sequential data set contains records that are in sequence. One track of each cylinder contains a copy of the highest key in each of the other tracks; this is called a track index. Higher indexes can be created such as taking the highest key of each cylinder and recording that on a separate track; this is called a cylinder index.

15. Indexed sequential organization is used for a data set when inquiries requiring rapid responses are made.
16. A data set is organized directly when the key of a record is identical to, or can be transformed into, an address on disk, drum, or data cell.
17. The process of computing a direct-access address from a record's identification number is called key transformation.
18. The advantage of direct organization is that it allows very rapid response to inquiries. Its main disadvantage is that *sequential* processing of transactions against the directly organized data set is not possible; hence transaction processing is quite slow.
19. The main DASD I/O operations are SEARCH, SEEK, READ and WRITE.
20. An unsuccessful search operation causes the channel to execute the next CCW in sequence. A successful search operation causes the channel to skip the next CCW in sequence.
21. A branch operation in a channel program is effected by a Transfer In Channel (TIC) command.
22. The SIO instruction is privileged and cannot be executed while the CPU is in the problem state.
23. IBM-supplied I/O programs are kept in protected main storage. A problem program cannot branch to an I/O program.
24. A specifically identified SVC instruction must be used by a problem program to obtain the services of the I/O program.

SUGGESTED READING ASSIGNMENT

IBM System/360 Component Descriptions
2314; 2844 (A26-3599)

Listed below are the section names, major topics and minor topics to read if you want more in-depth knowledge of the IBM 2314. This reading assignment is also appropriate if you wish to know more about the IBM 2311.

IBM 2314 Direct Access Storage Facility

- Introduction
  - IBM 2314
  - IBM 2844
- Functional Description
  - IBM 2316 Disk Pack
  - Access Mechanism and Disk Organization

- Data Format
  - Information Transfer
- Track Format
  - Index Marker
  - Gaps
  - Home Address Area
  - Track Descriptor Record
  - Data Records
  - Data Checking
- Record Capacities
- Timing Considerations
  - Access Times
  - Rotational Delays
- 2314 Channel Attachment

Input/Output Operations

- Chaining
  - Disk I/O operations
- Termination of I/O Operations
- I/O Instructions
  - Addressing
  - Channel Status Word

Channel Commands

- Branching in 2314 Channel Programs
- Search Commands (general description)
- Record Overflow

Two Channel Switch Special Feature

- Channel Selection Switch
- Device Reservation

4 VARIETIES OF DATA PROCESSING

REVIEW OF BATCH PROCESSING

Many of the data-processing applications we've described so far deal with data sets whose records are read or written once a day or more seldom. That is, not more than once a day, all the transactions concerning records in a given data set are sorted into sequence and then, in one batch, processed against the master data set. When transactions are collected over a relatively long period of time and then processed in a relatively short period of time, we say that *batch processing* is taking place. Here are some examples of batch-processing applications:

1. Preparation of the employee payroll—During the course of the week the payroll department collects from each employee such data as
   a. number of hours in attendance.
   b. amount of time worked on different jobs.
   c. changes in number of dependents, marital status, and so on.

   From the employee's manager or from the personnel department, the payroll department may receive such data as
   d. new rate for a job.
   e. cost-of-living adjustment factor.
   f. flat raise in pay.

   At the end of the work week, the payroll department prepares all the above transactions for processing by the computer. This preparation phase may include punching cards, sorting them into employee-number sequence, and transcribing the cards onto tape. At the conclusion of the preparation phase, the master employee payroll data set (on tape or disk) and the transaction records are brought to the computer for processing. The various payroll programs now prepare such documents as checks and earning statements for the employee, employee attendance summaries for departmental managers, and the amount of time and money spent on various jobs for the project leaders. In addition, the master employee payroll data set is made current to reflect such data as year-to-date gross, year-to-date withholding taxes and FICA, and amount deducted from gross for purchases of savings bonds and company stock.

2. Report card preparation—During the course of the marking period, each instructor records in his grade book the marks his students receive for quizzes, examinations, laboratory projects, term papers, class participation, and so on. At the end of the marking period, the data recorded in all of the grade books is punched into cards (including such items as instructor's and student's names, student number, and absence frequency). These cards are then sorted by student number in preparation for processing. At the conclusion of the preparation phase, the transaction records (student's intraterm marks) and the student master data set are brought to the computer for processing. The various student processing programs prepare such documents as report cards for students, performance summaries of students for the instructor, and attendance summaries of students for the school administrators. In addition, the master student data set is updated (made current) to reflect the notations made in each instructor's grade book.
3. Here are three other applications where the processing of batched transaction data and the master data set is done on a periodic basis:
   a. scheduling of classrooms, teachers, courses, and students
   b. life insurance premium preparation
   c. gas and electric bill preparation

INQUIRY PROCESSING

In the section on direct-access devices we said that people frequently need to know the contents of a record in just a few seconds. When this is the case, batch processing is certainly inappropriate. That is, even when direct-access devices are used, and data sets are organized indexed sequentially or directly, batch processing will not produce rapid responses to inquiries. What the inquirer needs is

1. a typewriter-like device where he can sit, type out a coded inquiry, and transmit it to the computer.
2. to have a program in the computer that can decode the inquiry, find the

record that contains the data for the response, and extract and process or edit the data.

3. to have the program in the computer transmit the response back to the typewriter-like device where the inquirer can see it (see Fig. 47).

A typewriter-like device, when used in a data-processing application such as making inquiries of a master data set, is called a *terminal.* (A terminal is an I/O device where a data-processing answer ends up or where data to be processed originates.) Certain employees of many commercial, industrial, governmental, and educational institutions require rapid responses to inquiries. Other examples of using terminals for inquiring into magnetically recorded data sets include the following:

1. What is the balance in the savings account that has the number 785-321?
2. How many of the part number PB8-732-9K are supposed to be in the warehouse in Cleveland?
3. Who is the owner of a 1968 Dodge with the New York registration DU-0015?
4. What are the names of the students who are enrolled in Electrical Engineering 234 taught by Dr. Yadaraf?

Terminal for Inquiry/Response

IBM has a large selection of terminals that can be used for making inquiries and receiving responses. One of these terminals that looks very much like a typewriter is the IBM 2740 (twenty-seven forty) Communications Terminal (see Fig. 48). The maximum transmission speed of this terminal is about 15 characters per second (about as fast as the fastest typist could type). One of the main advantages of using the 2740 is that the inquirer has a printed copy of both his inquiry and the response. The facility of a printed copy can, however, be a disadvantage if it isn't needed (visual output cannot be produced any slower than with a typewriter).

When a visual but nonprinted copy of a response is required, the data-processing organization can use a *display station.* One of the display stations offered by IBM has a typewriter-like keyboard for entering the inquiry and a cathode-ray tube (such as a television screen) for displaying the response (see Fig. 49). The display station shown in Fig. 49 can display a response 10 to 20 times faster than the 2741.

Connecting Terminals to S/360

From the standpoint of control units, terminals are no different than the I/O devices we've described to date. That is, between the terminal and the channel there must be a control unit. Three main control units can be used. These are the

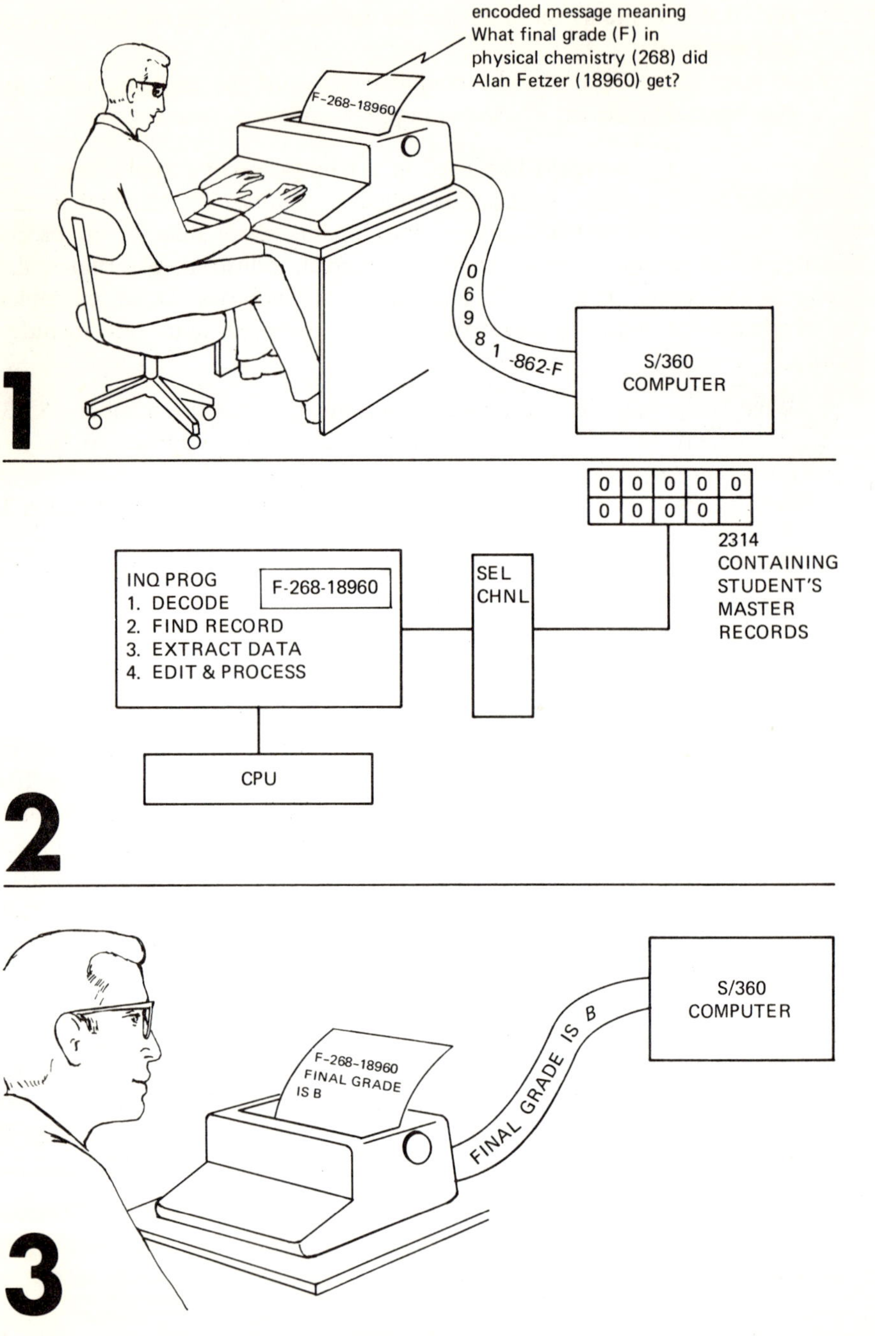

Fig. 47 Inquiry/response sequence.

(a)

(b)

Fig. 48 (a) The IBM 2740; (b) the 2741 communications terminal.

IBM 2701 Data Adapter Unit, the IBM 2702 Transmission Control Unit, and the IBM 2703 Transmission Control Unit. Although the capabilities and capacities of these three control units varies somewhat, their basic function is to condition the transmitted data and to control the terminals.

Fig. 49 IBM 2265 display station with alphameric keyboard.

Transmitting Data to and from Terminals

The S/360 with its I/O devices are frequently in the same room and almost always in the same building. The close proximity of the I/O devices, control units, channels, storage, and CPU makes it economically feasible to use very high quality cables for transmitting data at very high rates (hundreds of thousands of bytes per second).

When someone is going to use a terminal, he wants to use it at his work station (e.g., a desk on the production floor, a place to stand behind a counter in a bank, a large carpeted office, a laboratory, shipping and receiving platform, or a ticketing counter at an airport). That is, he doesn't want to go to the computer room, or to the building that contains the computer, or even to the city or state where the building with the computer is located. Quite obviously the computer manufacturer cannot supply cables (at a low-enough cost) to connect terminals and computers that are several thousands of feet and more distant (thousands of miles) from each other.

The dilemma is solved by using the lines that are provided by the telephone and telegraph companies (which have been designed primarily for telephone conversations and the sending of telegrams). Although the quality of these lines does not permit the ultrahigh transmission speeds of local cables, the quality of these lines is adequate to handle the capacity of most terminals. Hence most institutions use telephone and telegraph lines to transmit data between the place where the computer is located and the remote terminals (see Fig. 50). Depending upon how much data-transmission activity there can be, the user of the data-processing equipment can either lease a line or lines for private use or he can use the public telephone lines. If he chooses the latter, both the terminal and CPU need a phone number that can be dialed. The dialing at the data-processing center may be done by a person or by a program in the S/360. If the terminal user wants to connect the terminal and the computer, he must dial manually.

A single leased line can connect a computer with several terminals. This is particularly useful when a lot of data is transmitted between the computer and any one of several terminals but where none of the terminals alone has much to send to the S/360. When one leased line has more than one terminal attached to it, it is called a multidrop line (see Fig. 51). When several terminals are attached to a single leased line, a program in the S/360 must be used to select the appropriate terminal. This selection must be done either when the terminal is to send data or when it is to receive data.

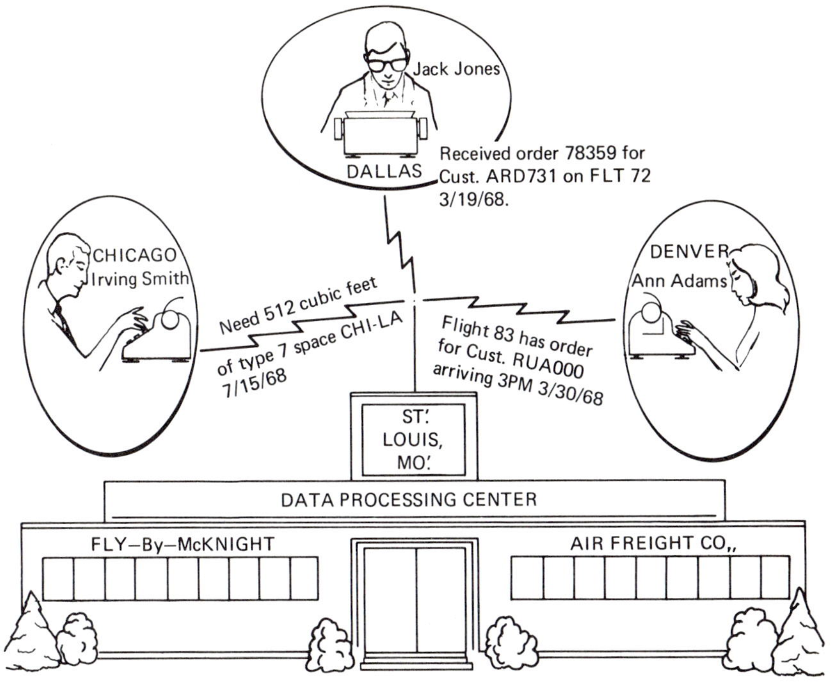

Both IRV and JACK are entering service requests into a typewriter-like Terminal. The data they type is sent in a split second by some combination of telephone, telegraph, and microwave transmission facility to the IBM System/360 in St. Louis. There the System/360 processes the service request to make sure it can be carried out when the time comes.

Each employee who operates a terminal receives an acknowledgement from the computer whenever it receives an employee's message. Just to make sure . . .

Whenever an article is in flight to a particular city, the computer sends a message to the operator there. As it is doing to ANN ADAMS in Denver.

Fig. 50 Using telephone and telegraph facilities to send data.

USING TERMINALS TO TRANSMIT BATCHES OF DATA

Although the main type of terminal used in data-processing applications looks like the keyboard of a typewriter, no law was ever passed forbidding the use of nonkeyboard devices. Thus data-processing equipment designers have developed terminals that can read cards, punch cards, read tape, write tape, and in one operation print an entire line (see Fig. 52).

Most of these terminals were developed so that branch locations could locally prepare their data-processing input and transmit it by telephone or telegraph lines

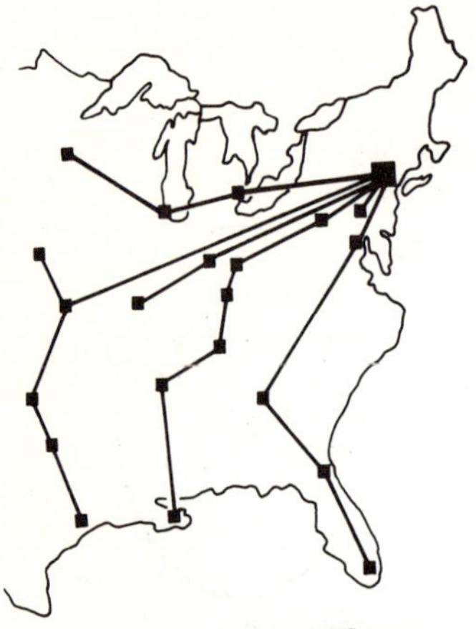

Fig. 51 Multidrop lines. Five of the above 6 lines have more than one terminal connected.

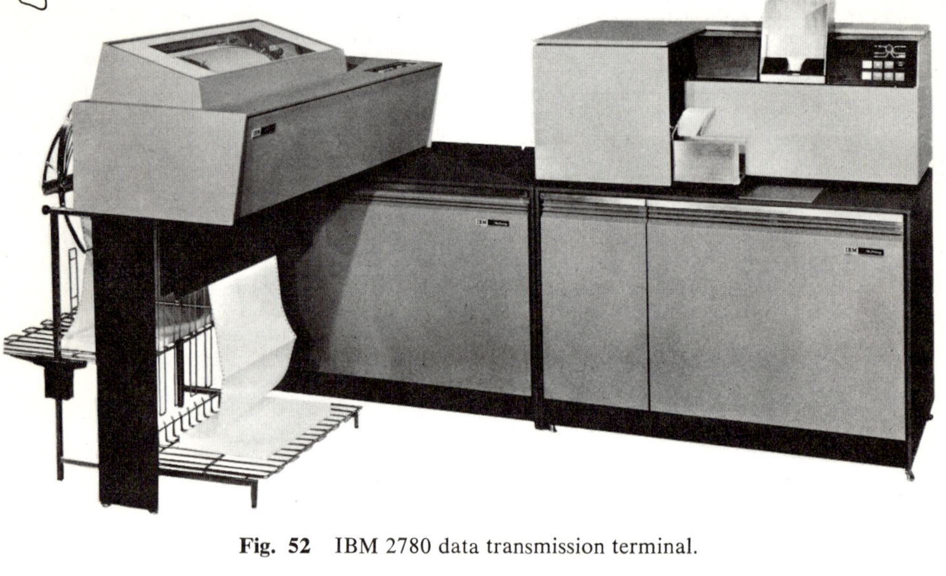

Fig. 52 IBM 2780 data transmission terminal.

to the data-processing center; there it would be stored as one batch on cards or on tape or a direct-access device. Later, when the schedule allowed, the computer would process the batch of transmitted data and then either send the results directly back to the branch's terminal or store the results on tape or a direct-access device. (If the latter alternative is selected, then at an even later time, the computer would send to the terminal the results it had stored during processing.) In recent years a CPU itself has qualified to be a terminal, especially when it exchanges data over telephone and telegraph lines with another CPU. Such an arrangement is particularly useful when one computer's capacity is exceeded at the same time that the other computer is relatively idle (see Fig. 53).

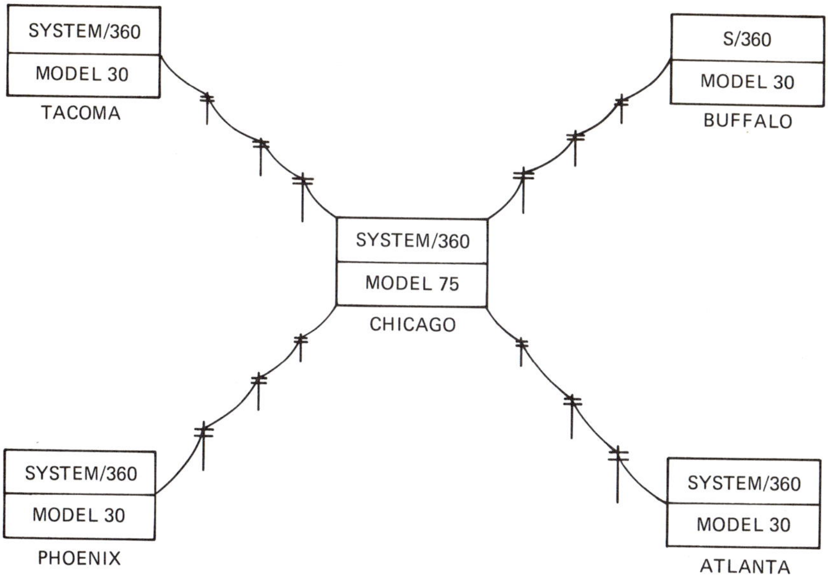

Fig. 53 S/360 Model 75, using Model 30's as terminals.

SENDING MESSAGES BETWEEN TERMINALS VIA THE COMPUTER

Another common application of terminals and computer is the sending of messages from one place to another via the computer (where a message is distinguished from a data-processing record; i.e., the body of the message is more of a short note or letter for someone else to read—it is not usually data to be processed).

The originator of the message prefixes his text with such information as his identification and the terminal (or terminals) to which he wants the message sent. When the computer receives the message a program records the message, including the prefix on disk. Later (within seconds if necessary) a program examines the prefix and, based upon the information in it, sends the message to the destination terminals. This activity is generally referred to as *message switching.*

REAL-TIME PROCESSING

A very popular term in data-processing circles is *real time.* It means that a computer system with terminals is used to process data sets whose records are kept current within seconds of any transactions. Real-time processing is required in applications where the computer is keeping track of a limited, rapidly changing and popular inventory item (such as available seats on passenger planes).

Let's say, for example, that a passenger/airline company has recorded on direct-access devices such data as

1. its schedules between all the cities it services.
2. the schedules of other airlines that land at the same airports.
3. the capacity of each plane (seat inventory) that would fly the scheduled flights.
4. the number of seats on each plane for which reservations have not been made (i.e., seats are still available).

Let's assume that the data set for Flight 591 of January 18 shows that there are three empty seats. Now within seconds of each other, four people (one each in New York, Chicago, Denver, and San Francisco) ask ticket agents in their respective cities for space on Flight 591 of January 18. Which of the four people should get seats? The first three who ask should get them. The only way that such a priority can be guaranteed is to process each request the instant it is made. As soon as the request is received by the computer, the data sets that might be affected are "frozen," the appropriate records processed and updated, the frozen data sets released, and the confirmation of reservation transmitted to the terminal. All of this must take place in a short-enough period of time (2 or 3 seconds) that the customer thinks he's getting immediate results (i.e., results in real time).

ELECTRONIC SKETCH PAD

Many people who are involved in designing new products invariably make dozens and perhaps even hundreds of sketches on paper before they construct a model. This is true of automobiles, kitchens, clothes, bridges, schools, roads, apartment houses, airplanes, radio and television circuits, rockets, and spaceships. Why so many sketches? Often the designer wants to know what his creation will look like when viewed from many different angles (from above, below, the left or right, the front or rear, and the many variations in between).

Even the most talented and speediest designers require many, many hours to prepare their sketches, especially when they make changes. Now the computer age has come to the designer's rescue; engineers have designed an electronic sketch pad called the IBM 2250 (twenty-two fifty) Display Unit (Fig. 54). Using the 2250, designers can create drawings, work on them for awhile, and when it's time to go home, store the drawing on tape or direct access and let someone else use the 2250. When it is his turn again to use the 2250, he calls for his drawing and immediately it appears before him on the 21-inch screen (cathode-ray tube). While the designer is sketching on the tube with his electronic "light pen" he can

Fig. 54 IBM 2250 display unit, Model 1.

rotate his drawing so it can be viewed from a different angle, magnify the image he's creating, or, if it's too big, miniaturize it.

You may well ask how this is all possible with a television-like screen. To answer this question, let's look at the screen (display area) first and then the pen. The screen is like a piece of graph paper with just over 1,000 vertical lines (x lines) and just over 1,000 horizontal lines (y lines). The intersections of these invisible x and y lines provide over 1 million points, each of which has an address (made up of one x value and one y value). Together with a special pen, a person can "write" upon the screen; what he's really doing is drawing lines between points, very much like kids do when they "connect the dots." The *address* of each point that the sketcher connects with a line is stored in a special core storage buffer. This is necessary so that the image on the screen can be regenerated continuously (the material of which a screen is made cannot keep an image visible for more than a few milliseconds).

The pen is really not a pen at all; that is, it does not draw the lines. Instead, it tells the 2250 to draw the lines (the lines are written on the back surface of the screen). The sketcher places the pen at a point of the image where he wants to start. When the pen is at this point, he depresses a foot pedal. The light sensor of the pen detects the light at this point, the address of which is determined by the 2250. Then he moves the pen to another point, where he wants the line to terminate. As soon as the address of this point is determined by the 2250, a line is drawn on the screen connecting the two points. See Fig. 55, which shows various images on a 2250 screen.

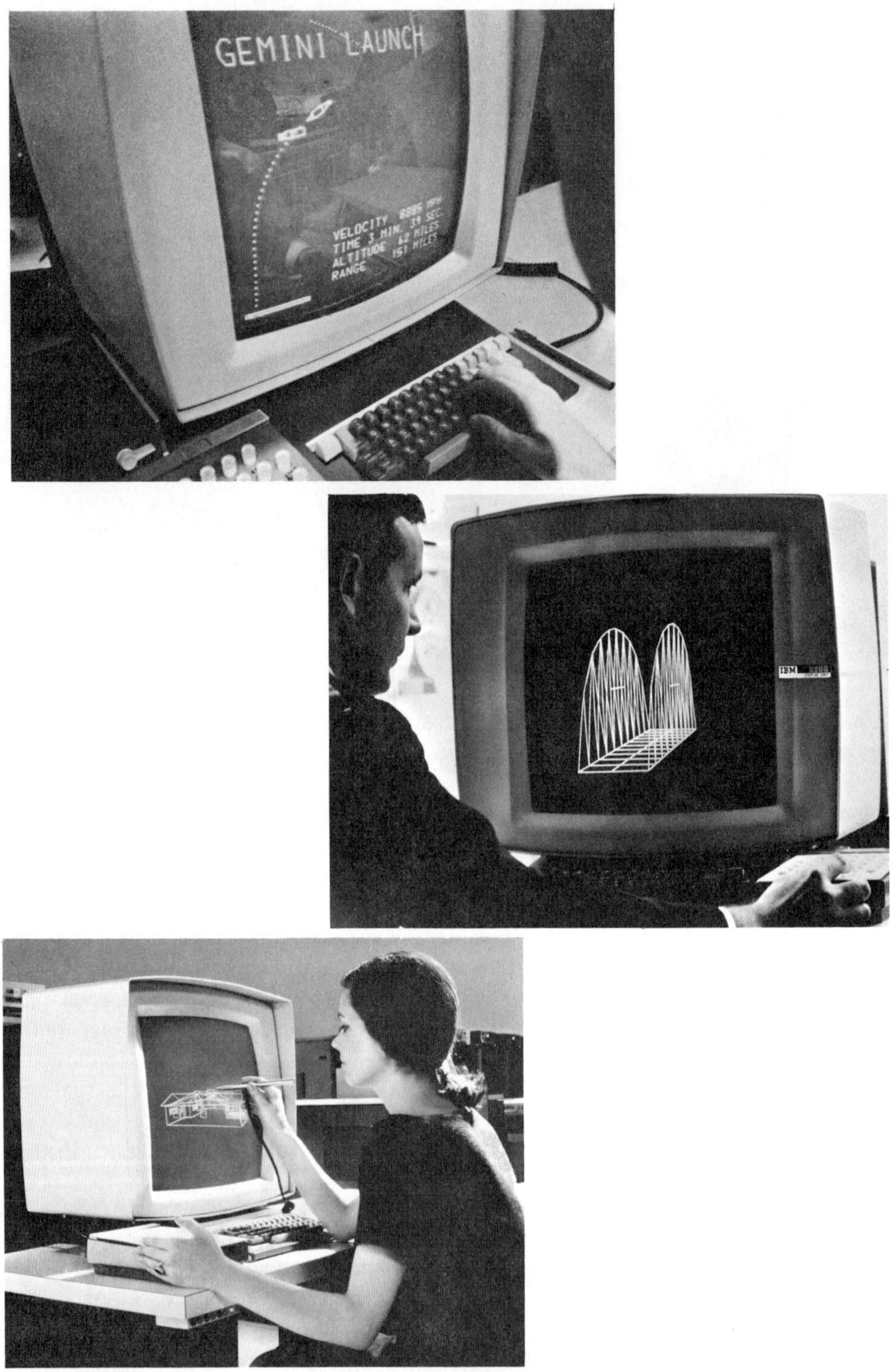

Fig. 55 Images from a 2250 screen.

Other Uses of the 2250 Display Unit

Some data-processing departments provide a 2250 for their computer operator to use. During the execution of programs, messages from the program can be displayed on the 2250, instructing the operator to perform some function. It can also be used to tell the operator which I/O devices are being used.

Another use of the 2250 is for computer-assisted instruction. Students sit at the 2250 and choose one answer from multiple choices, construct answers in narrative or pictorial form, and match problems with answers as they learn new subjects. A program in the computer evaluates the student's responses and directs his progress.

Control Unit and Channel

The control unit for the 2250 Display Unit is the IBM 2840 (twenty-eight forty) Display Control Unit. The 2840 contains the buffer storage for regenerating the picture on the screen of the 2250. The 2840 Display Control Unit is attached to the S/360 main storage by way of the selector channel.

MISCELLANEOUS INPUT DEVICES

Ever since electronic data processing has become accepted, engineers have been designing ways to reduce the amount of data that has to be key punched into cards before it can be processed. One of the earliest inventions was *mark sensing,* meaning that a device could *sense* the presence of a *mark* if it were made by a special pencil, were about $\frac{1}{3}$ inch long, and were made within a certain area on a card or piece of paper. Some of the more popular uses of mark sensing were for multiple-choice and true-or-false exams and for recording the readings on electricity-usage meters. In most cases, data in mark-sense form does not enter the computer directly. Generally speaking, it is first processed by an independent card punch.

Devices for Reading Magnetic and Optical Characters

In recent years the banking industry has been responsible for the development of a device that can read numeric and a few special characters when these characters are written with special magnetic ink. Magnetic-ink character recognition is used primarily for checking accounts. When a subscriber gets a supply of checks, each check bears the subscriber's checking account number and the bank's

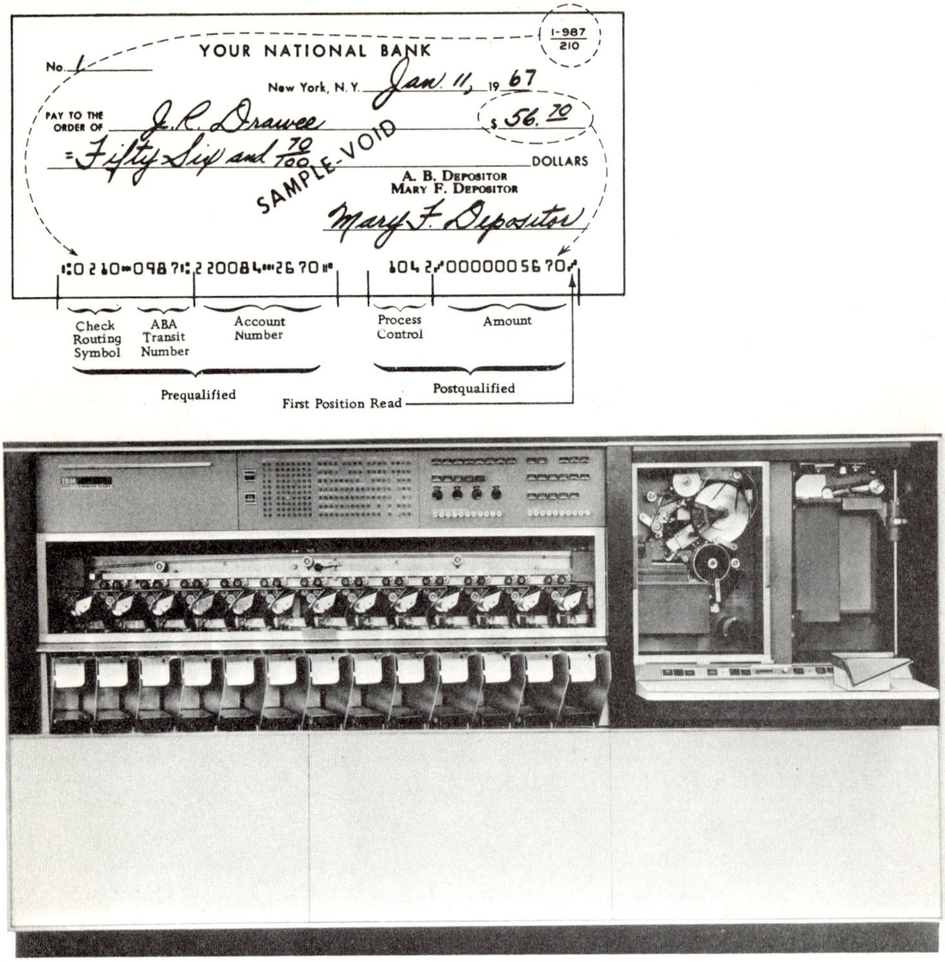

Fig. 56(a) An IBM 1412 Magnetic Ink Character Reader and a magnetically inscribed bank check.

identification. The first bank that gets the check after it is cashed records on the check the amount for which the check was cashed. As the check goes from bank to bank in its journey to eventual redemption, the check gets processed by S/360 computers having devices that can read the magnetically inscribed characters. Optical readers come in several varieties. One of them can read marks made by an ordinary lead pencil. These marks are very similar to the ones made in the mark-sensing applications mentioned earlier. Other optical readers can read documents with a limited number of different characters. Still others can read all the numeric and alphabetic characters as well as certain symbols. The primary virtue of these input devices and the documents they read is to eliminate key punching. When this equipment can be economically justified, it provides the ability to process transactions shortly after they have taken place. Figure 56 shows magnetic and optical character readers and a document read by each.

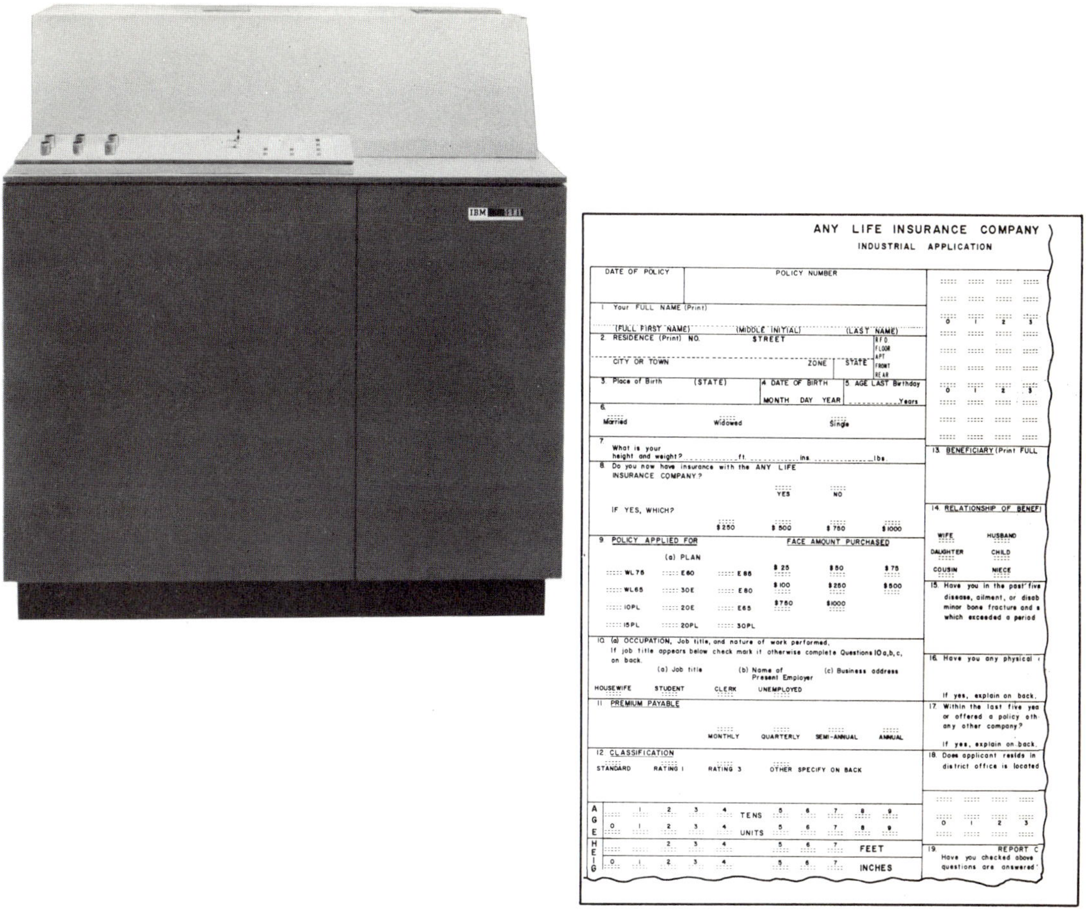

Fig. 56(b) An IBM 1231 Optical Mark Page Reader and a sample data sheet.

ADDRESSES OF I/O DEVICES

Let's consider a data-processing installation that has 12 tape drives; four 2311's; eight 2314's; a drum, several printers, card readers and punches, 100 terminals (of several varieties) in remote cities, magnetic and optical character readers (one each), and several 2250 Display Units. How does the computing system distinguish any one device from all the others? Each of the devices is given an address. The address of any device is made up of three hex digits. The digit in the leftmost position identifies the channel (or channels) through which the data may travel. The standard digits for each of the channels on the S/360 are as follows:

0 multiplexor
1 selector channel 1
2 selector channel 2
•
•
•
6 selector channel 6

Therefore, if a tape unit is to use channel 1, the tape unit's leftmost address position is a 1. If a 2311 is also going to use channel 1, it's leftmost address position would also be 1. The second digit identifies the control unit to which the I/O device is attached. The standard digit for the first 2841 control unit is 9. (Among other devices, the 2841 controls the 2311 drive.) The rightmost digit identifies the device itself. For example, when there is only one 2481 Control Unit attached to selector channel 1 and there are five 2311's attached to the control unit, the addresses are 190, 191, 192, 193, and 194.

The standard digit for the first tape control unit is 8. If this control unit is attached to selector channel 2 and there are six tape drives attached to the control unit, their addresses are 280, 281, 282, 283, 284, and 285.

When there is just one 2821 Control Unit for a printer, card reader, and card punch, the digit identifying the control is 0 (zero). Since the 2821 Control Unit is attached to the multiplexor channel, the first two digits identifying the address of a printer or reader punch will be zero, zero. The standard address for the 1403 Printer is 00E, for the card reader it is 00C, and for the card punch it is 00D. A visible, metallic sticker of the device's three-digit address is usually glued to the I/O device (see Fig. 57).

The same three-digit address is used in the Start I/O (SIO) instruction, which the CPU must execute if the channel is to execute its commands. That is, a command is conditioned by the device address in the SIO instruction. For example, if the command code is 02 and the SIO instruction contains the address 00C, a card will be read. With the same command code (02) and an SIO operand of 180, a tape record will be read.

SUMMARY

1. Batch processing implies the collection of transaction records over a relatively long period of time and then processing the transactions over a relatively short period of time.
2. Batch processing usually pertains to a master data set whose records are in sequential order and a transaction data set that has been sorted into the same order as the master data set.

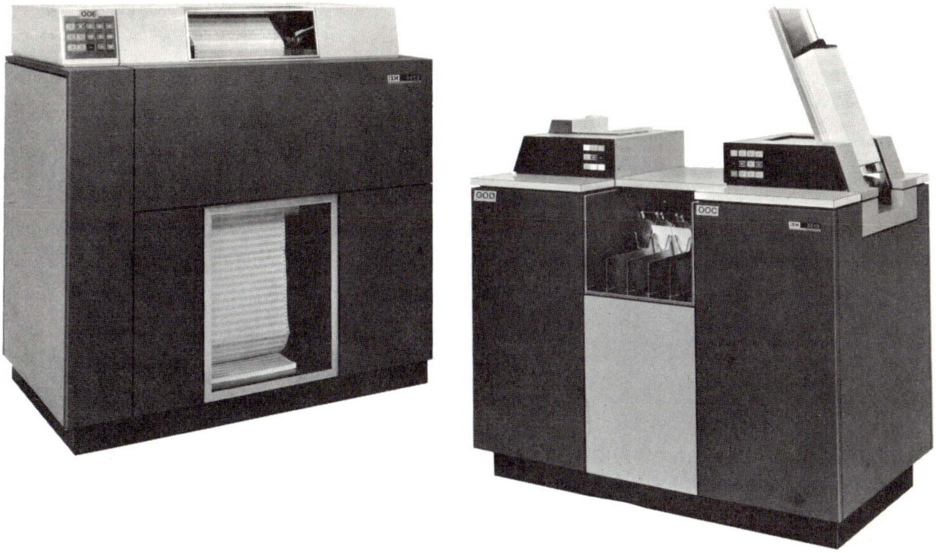

Fig. 57 Physical address stickers on IBM 1403 Printer and IBM 2540 Card Read Punch.

3. Some examples of batch-processing applications are report card preparations; payroll checks and attendance records; scheduling of classrooms, teachers, courses, and students; life insurance premium-notice preparation; and, gas and electric bill preparation.
4. There are many occasions when an institution must inquire into the contents of a data record and have the contents of the record displayed within seconds.
5. Two terminals for making inquiries and receiving responses are the 2741 Communications Terminal (Fig. 47) and the 2265 Display Station (Fig. 48).
6. When telephone and telegraph company facilities are used to transmit data between terminals and a centralized CPU, the process is called teleprocessing.
7. Most teleprocessing terminals send and receive their data through a multiplexer channel via a special transmission control unit.
8. Either leased lines or the public telephone and telegraph lines can be used for transmitting data between a computer and terminals.
9. When public lines are to be used, the connection between computer and terminals is made by dialing. Dialing may be manual or automatic (i.e., programmed).
10. Several terminals on a single leased line is described as a multidrop line. The selection of which terminal is to use the line is made by a program in the computer.

11. Terminals can also be used for transmitting batches of data from distant places. After the batch has been collected, the computer can process the data just as though it had originated locally.
12. Using terminals and the computer to send messages from one remote location to other remote locations is called message switching.
13. Processing transactions and changing the status of the master file within seconds of the transaction's occurrence is called real-time processing.
14. The 2250 Display Unit can be used as an electronic sketch pad. To create and change on the screen of the 2250, one uses a light pen.
15. The 2250 Display Unit can be used as a computer operator's console when it is not being used as an electronic sketch pad.
16. Input devices that can read characters magnetically and optically can be attached to an S/360.
17. The address of an I/O device is made up of three hex characters. The leftmost character identifies the channel, the next character identifies the control unit, and the rightmost character identifies the device.

SUGGESTED READING ASSIGNMENT

Data Communications Primer (C20-1668)

The above IBM publication consists of a number of data communications topics. The major topics are listed below.

Communications Concepts

Communications Channels

Communications Service Offerings

Communication Systems

Common Carriers

Network Design

5 USING THE COMPUTER INSTALLATION

In the section on addresses of I/O devices we spoke of a somewhat large data-processing installation, which has the following I/O configuration:

12 tape drives
4 2311's
8 2314's
1 drum
several printers
several card readers and punches
100 terminals
1 magnetic character reader
1 optical character reader
several 2250's

Although it wasn't mentioned previously, the existence of the proper control units, the proper number of channels, a fairly powerful CPU (e.g., a Model 65), and an adequate amount of main storage (e.g., 1 million bytes, often referred to as a megabyte) should be inferred.

Who would use such an array of data-processing equipment? What do they do with all these devices? Who decides when the equipment can be used, by whom, and for how long?

A DESCRIPTION OF A "TYPICAL" INSTITUTION

To help answer these questions, let us say that there exists in the city of Alkaka Rapids, state of New York, the manufacturing division of the Jemeke Company, which makes and markets scientific toys, games of strategy, and gym equipment; at the manufacturing plant are 30,000 employees. To support the manufacturing requirements, the plant management has created departments with diverse functions. The function of some of these departments and how the employees use the computing facility are described below.

Design Department

In this department are employees who design new toys, games, and gym equipment. Many of these people are artists and/or engineers. They use 2250 Display Units to design new products. After the product is designed, feasibility engineers use the computer to determine how much it will cost to manufacture. If the computer program determines that the cost is so high as to jeopardize a profit, the product will not be built.

Personnel Department

This department sets the standards for job performance and does the hiring and firing. It also controls a data set in which is recorded the job, education, skills, ambitions, and special accomplishments of each employee. When a new job is defined or a vacancy exists, a program searches the data set for the records of persons who match the required qualifications. This data set must be continually updated to reflect newly hired people; employees who have changed their job, skills, education level, and so on; and employees who have left the company.

Production Scheduling Department

These people must schedule the variously skilled production employees, the manufacturing equipment, the arrival of raw materials, and the departure of finished goods in such a way to get maximum production at minimum expense and to keep the production employees happy (i.e., they must not be overworked or allowed to be idle over long periods of time).

Scheduling for optimum performance can be very complex. Although there are literally millions of alternative schedules that would be profitable, there is only one that can be most profitable. (Although there are many other important considerations for optimum scheduling, profitability receives the greatest consideration.) To determine the most profitable alternative in a reasonable amount of time requires a computer and various data sets. The data sets must describe the capabilities and location of each piece of equipment, the required skills and the people who have them, the machining steps required to make a product or part of a product, the location and quantity of special tools, the rate at which materials can be brought to the work stations, the speed with which finished products can be removed from work stations, a description of the items to be made, and so on.

Accounting and Bookkeeping

These employees make sure that the bills get paid (accounts payable), that invoices are prepared for shipped goods, and that payments received are credited to proper accounts (accounts receivable). They also write the orders for all raw materials and send acknowledgements to customers who've ordered some products directly from the plant. This department keeps its accounts payable, accounts receivables, and its orders on magnetically recorded data sets. This department uses the S/360 to prepare its payment checks, to prepare invoices, to write orders, and to write acknowledgements.

Plant Engineering

The people in this department use the S/360 to design the production environment.

Property Control

This department's employees keep an inventory of all the manufacturing equipment, tools, typewriters, and furniture in the plant. The inventory data set contains such data as location of equipment, age, purchase or rental price, name of person or department to whom charged, and the date when the equipment is to be replaced.

Payroll

The personnel in payroll use the S/360 to prepare checks and earnings statements for each employee, provide attendance reports to personnel, employee performance reports to departmental managers, and project costs to project managers. These people also prepare all the reports required by the federal government on various withholding programs.

Others

Let's assume that for this company there are 17 other departments, each with its own computing requirements. In addition to the manufacturing people, there are the marketing people scattered throughout the world. Each major city in the United States and each foreign country has a branch office from which the marketing people direct their efforts. The marketing division's headquarters are in New York City. Not only do the marketing people sell the company's products, they are also responsible for promotional campaigns; for determining the satisfaction level of the buyer; for recognizing desires for new toys, new games, and new gym equipment; for appraising the profit potential of new products; and for holding demonstrations.

The marketing division of the company has its own S/360, primarily for personnel and payroll purposes. It is located in New York City.

Each branch office has at least one terminal; that is, they all have one typewriter-like terminal for sending and receiving messages and for making inquiries into data sets maintained by the production department. The larger branch offices have terminals for sending large batches of data that have to be processed by the manufacturing or marketing division's S/360.

PROGRAMMING THE COMPANY'S COMPUTERS

As the competition in the marketplace becomes more and more active, the company must be sure to implement as quickly as possible new management science techniques; new ways of organizing, storing, and retrieving data; and new ways of keeping its marketing force informed. The computers of the company will be relied upon to a great extent in realizing the implementation. This means that the company must have a great many systems analysts and programmers, especially if the implementation is to be realized in a reasonable amount of time.

For the most part, each department has its own programming talent. For many of these employees, programming is a full-time job (particularly true in those departments that require the traditional data-processing reports); for other employees, programming is an extension of their regular job; this is the general case for engineers, technicians, and designers. The language used by the programmer depends to some extent on the type of data-processing problem he has to solve: Engineering and design departments make heavy use of FORTRAN; the commercial departments' programmers write many of their programs in COBOL. Programmers implementing management science techniques may choose PL/1; some data-processing problems may require very special programming that can best be solved using the Assembly language.

COMPILER PROGRAMS

Whatever programming language is used, every program written in one of these languages must be translated into a machine language program. As you already know, the translation is accomplished by using a compiler program; here the *computer itself* is used to compile a machine language program from a program written in COBOL, PL/1, or other language. (If you don't know this, either you haven't met the prerequisite for this course or you haven't read Appendix I.) These compilations take a fair percentage of the computer's time. (Many of the professional programmers have two, three, or more programs in development at a time. Such an arrangement allows the programmer to debug one or more of his programs while the computer is compiling one of his "corrected" programs. In the course of the day it is not unusual for a programmer to have each of his programs that are in early stages of development compiled three or four times—with intervening periods for corrections, of course.)

Almost without exception, each programming language has two or more compilers. Why so many? After a program is compiled and debugged, it may be used only once for a period of a minute or two (maybe less, such as a few seconds). Then again, after being compiled and debugged, it may be used frequently and for long periods of time (payroll calculation).

As you know, the main objective of a compiler program is to translate. However, the translation and its resultant product must be economically justified. For example, if the machine language program produced by the compiler is going to be used frequently and for long periods of time, then the machine language program should be efficient in its use of the CPU. In contrast, if the machine language program is used once or twice for 10 or 15 seconds each, it doesn't matter so much if it's efficient.

A compiler that has as its main objective the production of a very efficient machine language program (usually referred to as object code) is more complex and takes more computer time than a compiler whose main objective is to translate in the shortest amount of time—hence the choice of several compilers for each programming language.

A COMPILER PROGRAM'S I/O REQUIREMENTS

What are some of the I/O requirements for compiling? The I/O requirements of a compiler depend to a great extent upon its size and the language used in writing the program.

The two most common I/O devices used are the card reader and the printer. The card reader is the usual input device for entering into storage the statements of the symbolic program. The printer is the usual output device on which appears each *statement* and the machine language instructions compiled from it (see Fig. 58).

In addition to these devices, the compiler may need some tape or disk devices on which to record the intermediate results of compilation. In general, either tape or disk can be used whenever the compiler has not been designed to accommodate its intermediate results in main storage.

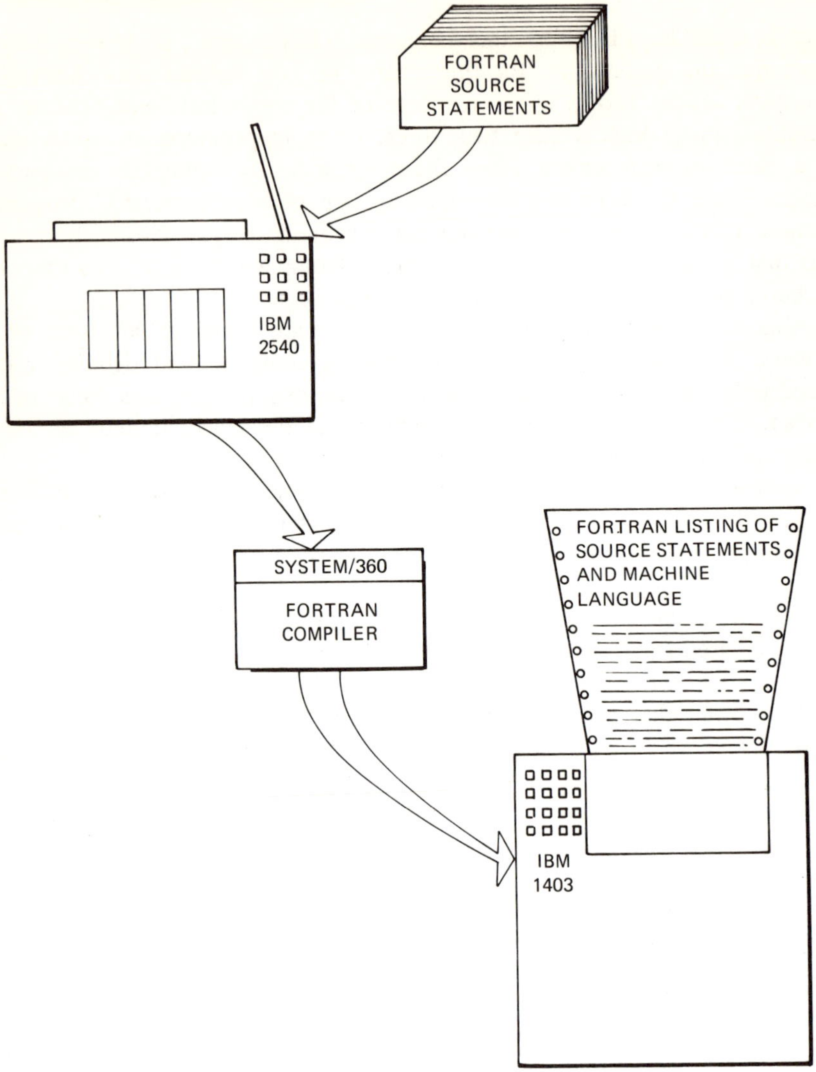

Fig. 58 Program preparation sequence.

If disks are chosen for recording the intermediate results, the amount of space required depends upon the specific compiler and the number of symbolic statements that have to be compiled.

SUBMITTING PROGRAMS TO BE COMPILED FROM TERMINALS

The last three topics (on compiling) allude to the *batch processing* of symbolic programs. That is, each programmer writes his entire program (or an integral section of a program), has the statements punched into cards, and submits them to the computer, where his batch of source statements is compiled (see Fig. 59).

As Fig. 59 implies, not too much effort is required to bring the punched card statements to the computer room or to get the compiler listing back to the programmer when the programmer and computer are in the same building or at least not more than a mile or two away. What about programmers who are many miles from the computing center? Can they write their programs, punch the statements into cards, and then, in one batch, send them to computer? (Since this textbook doesn't ask too many questions to which the answer is no, the answer must be "Yes, they can.")

By having a 2780 or 1050 (a typewriter-like device) Terminal System at a branch office, a remote programmer can submit a batch of source statements, have

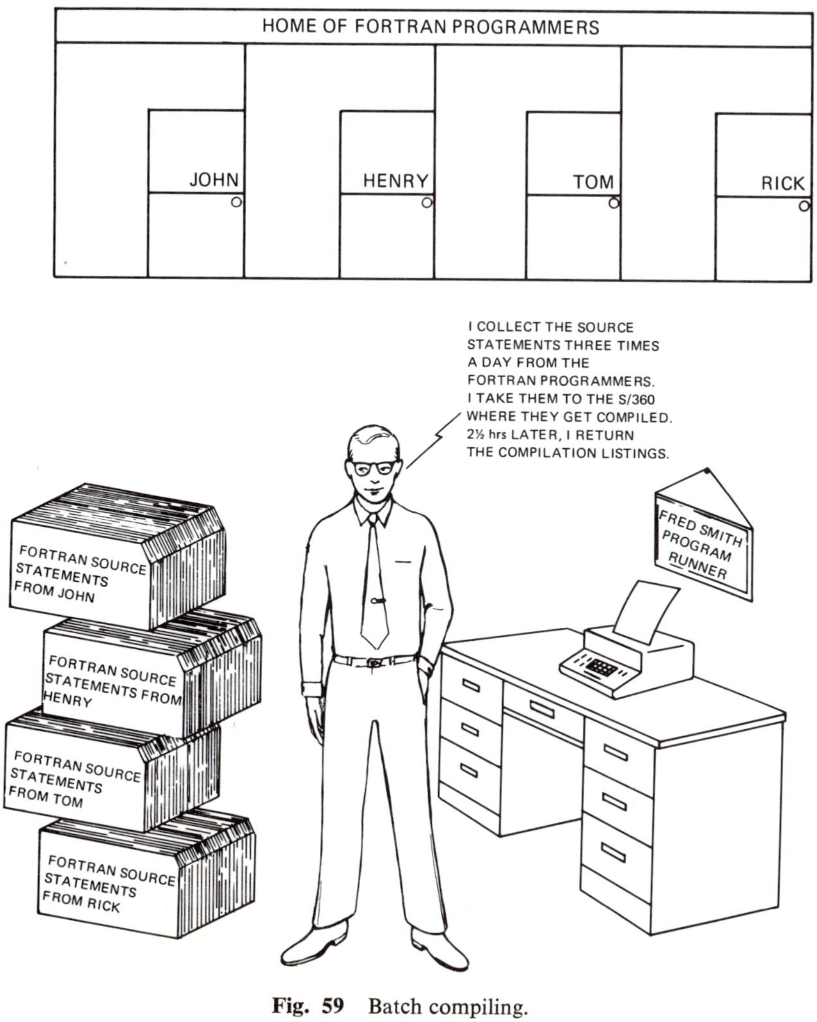

Fig. 59 Batch compiling.

them compiled, and receive by return transmission a listing of his compiled program (see Fig. 60).

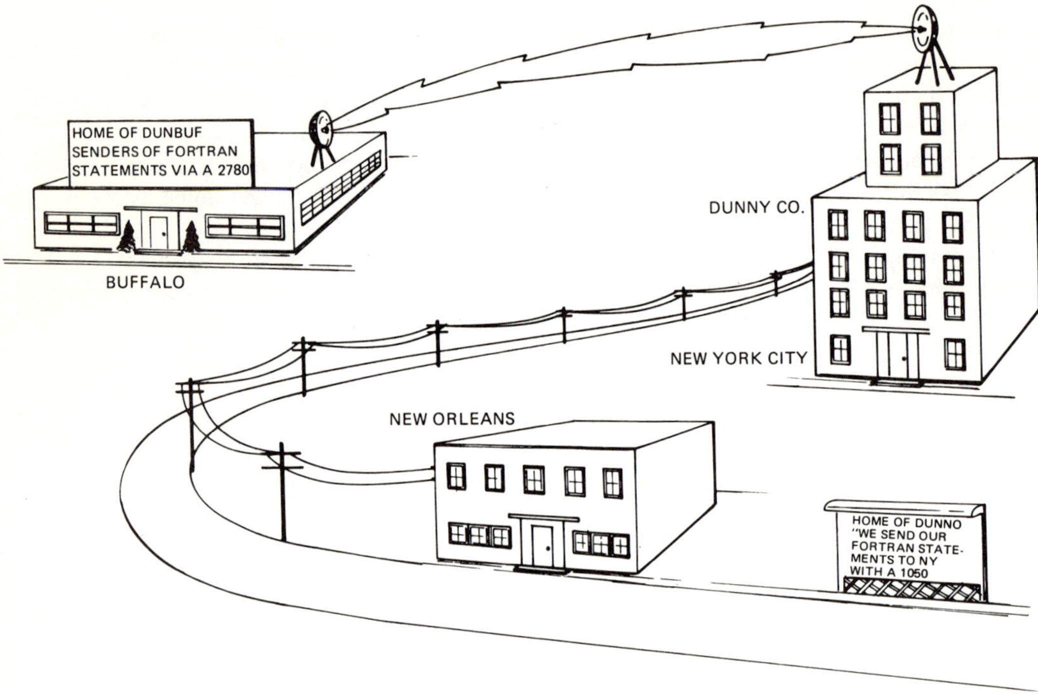

Fig. 60 Telecompiling.

CONVERSATIONAL PROGRAMMING

One of the most aggravating acts committed by the "beginning" or once-in-a-while programmer is the violation of some simple rule concerning the construction of a program statement. It is particularly aggravating when it takes several hours for the compiler listing (which points out the error) to be returned to the programmer. [Most programming languages have some very strict rules. If these rules are violated in the writing of a program, either the program will be compiled incorrectly or not compiled at all. For example, the omission of a comma where one was expected, the leaving of a space where one should not have been, or the misspelling of a key word in the statement are all violations that could produce an improperly compiled program. (Even if the compiler program can be *"fooled"* into accepting improperly constructed statements and produces a "properly compiled program," the execution of the machine language program would probably produce faulty results.) Although the compiler program does detect many grammatical and syntactical errors and highlights on the listing where the error was committed, it does not make the correction (although sometimes it tries). Only the programmer or someone else closely connected with the program can ascertain what the correction should be.]

The ideal situation would allow the programmer to create his program, *one statement at a time,* and transmit it to the computer by way of a typewriter-like terminal. In the computer would be a program that edits each statement. If the statement is in error, the program sends an error message back to the terminal, identifying the nature of the error as accurately as possible. If the statement is correct, the editing program places it on disk. The editing program must also keep track of where on disk it stores successive statements from each terminal. (The last sentence means to imply that one program in the computer can handle statements from several programmers, each using a different terminal.) When a programmer has completed the writing of his source statements, he can type a special command instructing the computing system that his program is ready for compilation (see Fig. 61).

When a programmer constructs his statements at a terminal, sends them to a computer program for evaluation, and receives diagnostic messages when a statement is incorrect, the process is called *conversational programming.*

MANAGING THE COMPUTER INSTALLATION

It must have occurred to you by now that the installation we've been describing is quite complex—scores of programmers (both local and remote) writing in different languages, each wanting to get his program compiled in the least amount of time; designers and engineers, who want the computer and its display units when they are creatively inspired; the "bread-and-butter" data-processing departments, which need their periodic reports on time and require the data sets under their control to be kept current; marketing and manufacturing executives, who want an answer within a few seconds after making an inquiry into a confidential data set.

Who are the people that manage the computer room and schedule the data-processing jobs? What are some of the aids at their disposal? Are there any special attributes of the S/360 and the operating system that can assist in the managing of the computer complex? These questions shall be discussed in Chapter 6.

SUMMARY

1. The programmers of a data-processing installation may use one or more of several programming languages. The most popular programming languages are FORTRAN, COBOL, PL/1, and Assembler.

Fig. 61 Terminal programmer.

2. Most programming languages have two or more compilers for producing machine language statements from the programming language statements.
3. The two most common I/O devices required for compilations are the card reader and the printer.

4. Certain compilers need tape or disk drives on which to record the intermediate results of compilation.
5. The output of a compiler must be processed by the Linkage Editor before the machine language statements are executable.
6. The symbolic statements of a program may be submitted from a remote location to the central computing facility in one batch over telephone and telegraph lines.
7. Conversational programming means that the programmer constructs his statements at a terminal, sends them one at a time to the computer for evaluation, and receives from the computer diagnostic messages when a statement is incorrect.

SUGGESTED READING ASSIGNMENT

Organizing the Data Processing Installation (C20-1622)

This IBM publication is a guide for organizing the data processing department. It describes the functions that must be performed to ensure a successful data processing operation.

6 THE SYSTEM/360 OPERATING SYSTEM

In the beginning of this book, a computer is likened to a data factory where processing headquarters (CPU) retrieves one instruction at a time from the main warehouse. Once an instruction is deciphered, data is obtained from or sent to the main warehouse. One of the inefficiencies of the data-factory operations, you may recall, results from a speed discrepancy. That is, the speed with which processing headquarters and the main warehouse can communicate with each other is much higher than the speed with which the main warehouse can receive or dispense information from or to shipping/receiving or the auxiliary warehouses. Such an imbalance in speeds causes the processing headquarters to have many costly coffee breaks. To reduce the number of coffee breaks to something reasonable, the factory can concern itself with several concurrent tasks (e.g., task X can be worked on while tasks A, B, C, and so on are waiting for fresh data or for their distribution area to be emptied).

FACTORY MANAGERS

Who in the data factory determines which task the employees should be processing? Why a manager, of course! Because he is responsible (according to certain rules) for the proper execution of tasks, he is called the *task manager.* Since the task manager has all he can do to keep track of each tasks status, the responsibility of deciding when to start a new job, or what to do with a completed job, is given to another boss—he is called the *job manager*. Another boss is responsible for all the data traffic between the main warehouse and shipping/receiving or the auxiliary warehouses—this boss is called the *data manager*.

Whenever there are three bosses of relatively equal rank, there had better be a person who can coordinate them—he is referred to as the *master*. In computer terminology, the master and his three immediate managers and their books of rules, procedures, and duties are called an *operating system*.

OPERATING SYSTEM: DEFINITION

In the past several years the operating system has been defined in many ways. The objective of these definitions is to describe in several well-chosen sentences the purpose of the operating system. The definition is usually unsatisfactory to the person who is trying to find out what an operating system is. This is because the operating system is a complex collection of many programs, some large, some small, whose objectives are to automate the data-processing installation. As a single topic, the operating system is about equivalent to organic chemistry. It is just as difficult to find out what organic chemistry is all about by reading a two- or three-sentence definition as it is to "know" the operating system by reading a similar definition. However, in keeping with tradition, here is a general definition of the operating system (the specific definition is given in the remaining pages): The operating system is a collection of programs written and supplied by IBM for a data-processing installation to use in meeting its data-processing responsibilities.

COLLECTION OF PROGRAMS IN AN OPERATING SYSTEM

Now for a look at *some* of the programs in the collection:

1. All the compiler programs (FORTRAN, COBOL, PL/1, etc.).
2. Programs for sorting data sets into different sequences.
3. Programs for managing the input and output operations for all types of IBM devices and all types of data set organization.
4. Programs for keeping track of how much available space is left on various direct-access devices.
5. Programs for diagnosing and analyzing I/O devices suspected of faulty operation.
6. A "master" program, which, when in main storage, controls all the other programs in main storage. The master program is called the *Supervisor*.

7. Programs that keep track of the location on disk of all the application programs and the programs listed in 1 through 6.
8. Programs that write messages to the computer operations staff when something is needed or when something is wrong.
9. Programs that keep a catalog of data sets, noting the serial number of the volume on which the data set is recorded.

Each of these nine types of operating system programs performs a service for the data-processing installation. There are many more in addition to these nine.

EACH INSTALLATION GENERATES ITS OWN OPERATING SYSTEM

The data-processing requirements of today's installations are so diverse that it would be impossible to expect every installation to use the same operating system. Hence IBM provides a *kit* with which each installation generates its own system. The kit consists of every conceivable type of program, including the nine categories above. Each installation must choose the parts it requires and then it must put those parts together. This process is referred to as *system generation.*

THE SUPERVISOR

One of the major capabilities of the operating system (OS, pronounced oz, as in "the wizard of") is to allow several programs to share the CPU. Figure 62 shows three different layouts of main storage, each with more than one program placed into main storage.

It probably occurred to you as you were looking at Fig. 62 that if several programs are in main storage sharing the CPU, there had better be a Supervisor program in main storage also (to referee the sharing). We shall now describe the way the Supervisor works.

The Supervisor is given control of the CPU at the beginning of the data-processing day (see Fig. 63). As soon as the Supervisor program has completed its initial functions, some of the programs it will be controlling can enter main storage. Figure 64 shows main storage with the Supervisor informing the program STATISTIX that it can use the CPU. Now that the program STATISTIX has control of the CPU, when is the Supervisor going to regain control of the CPU? The Supervisor can obtain control of the CPU when one of the following events takes place:

1. The amount of time that the Supervisor gave to STATISTIX for using the CPU has expired (Fig. 65a).

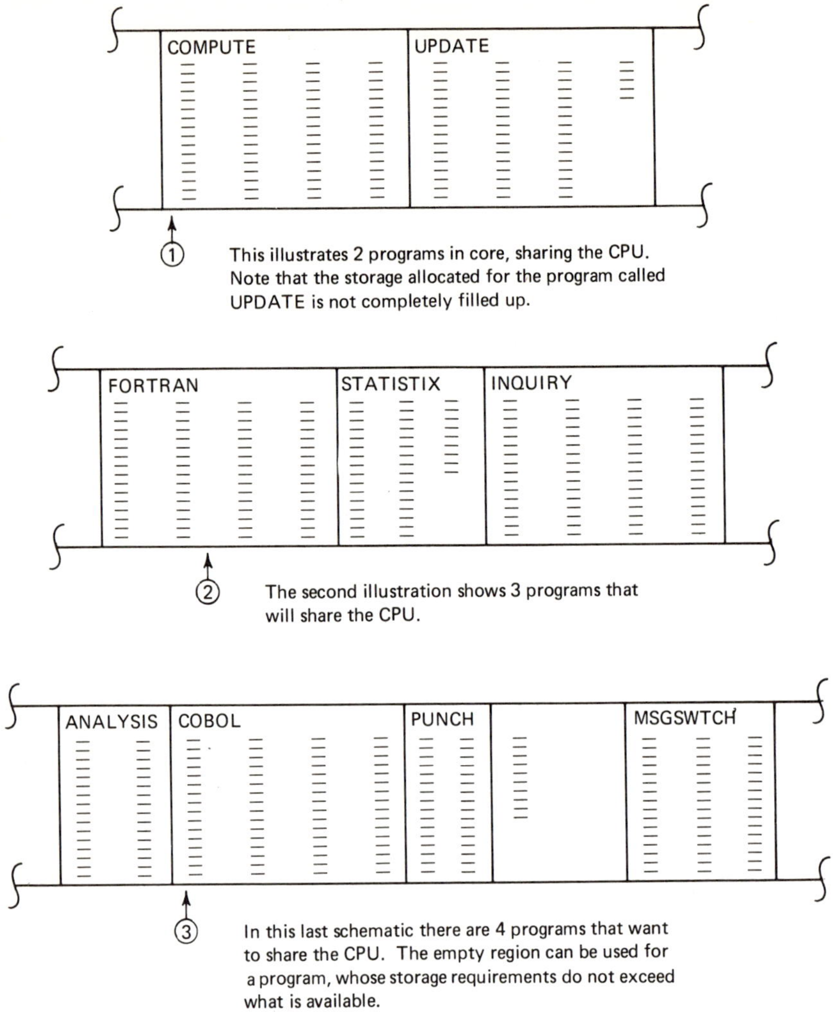

Fig. 62 Multiple programs in storage.

2. One of the instructions in STATISTIX (the program using the CPU) was not properly set up (the CPU can detect many mistakes in programming) (Fig. 65b).
3. An input or output operation has completed (Fig. 65c).
4. A special instruction requesting that CPU control be returned to the Supervisor is executed by STATISTIX (Fig. 65d). The instruction may have been issued because STATISTIX needs an input record and has to wait until it's available.
5. There has been a malfunction of a component in the CPU (Fig. 65e).

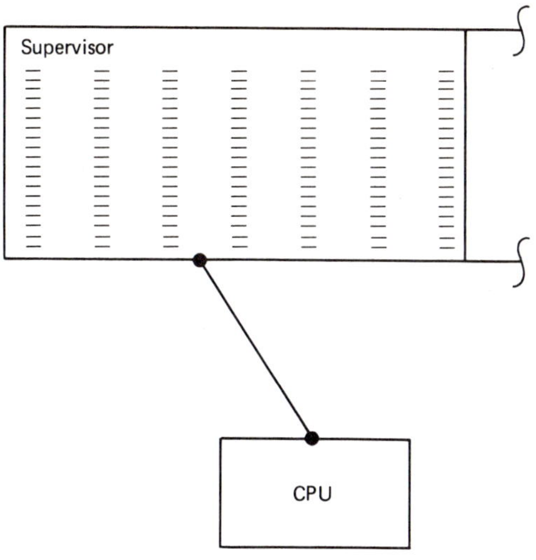

Fig. 63 Supervisor/CPU relationship.

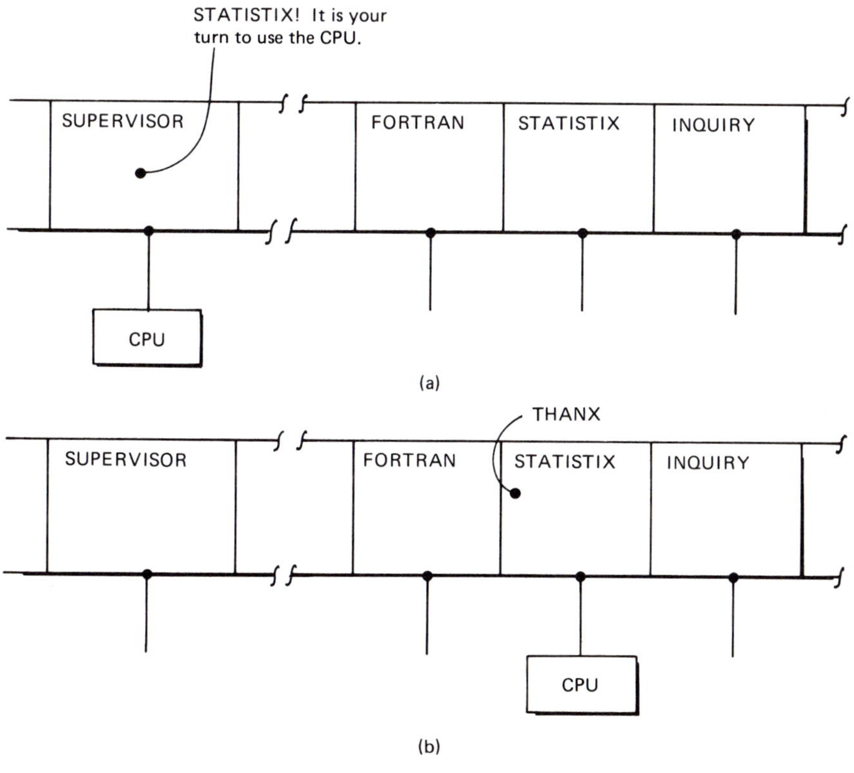

Fig. 64 Supervisor/application program talk-back.

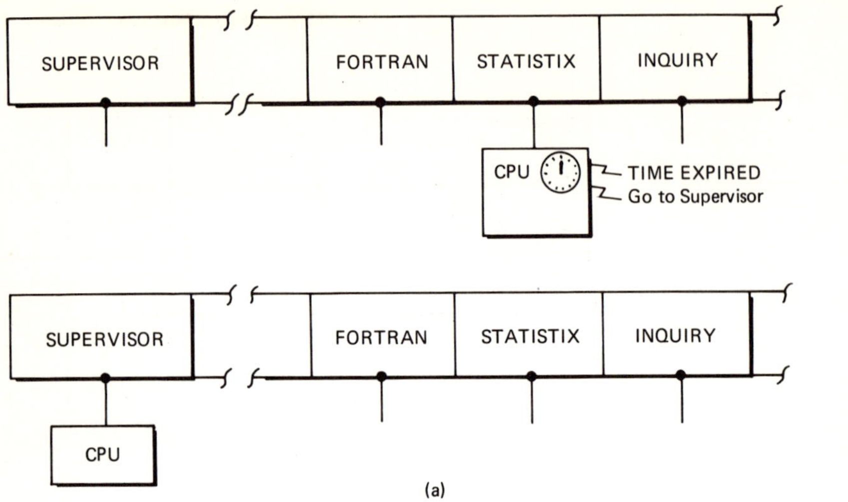
SUPERVISOR
FORTRAN
STATISTIX
INQUIRY
CPU
TIME EXPIRED
Go to Supervisor
SUPERVISOR
FORTRAN
STATISTIX
INQUIRY
CPU

(a)

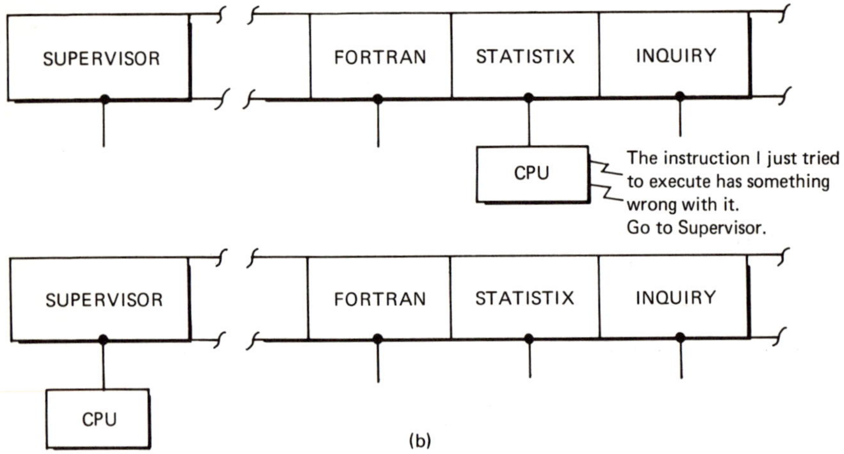
SUPERVISOR
FORTRAN
STATISTIX
INQUIRY
CPU
The instruction I just tried
to execute has something
wrong with it.
Go to Supervisor.
SUPERVISOR
FORTRAN
STATISTIX
INQUIRY
CPU

(b)

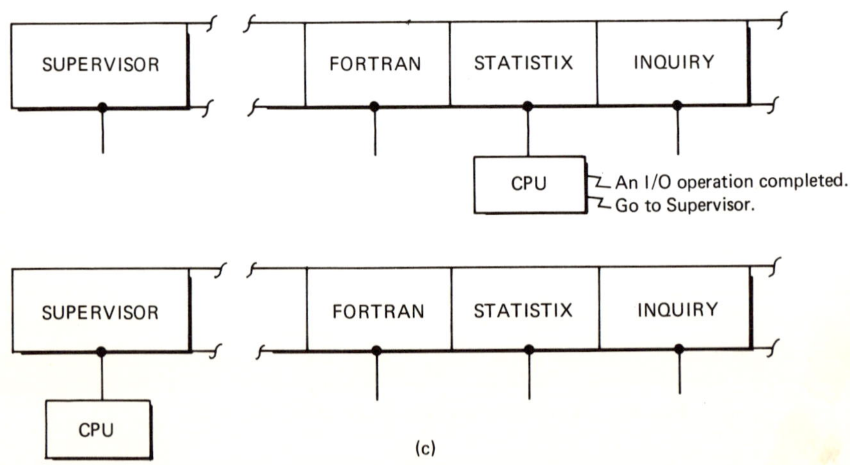
SUPERVISOR
FORTRAN
STATISTIX
INQUIRY
CPU
An I/O operation completed.
Go to Supervisor.
SUPERVISOR
FORTRAN
STATISTIX
INQUIRY
CPU

(c)

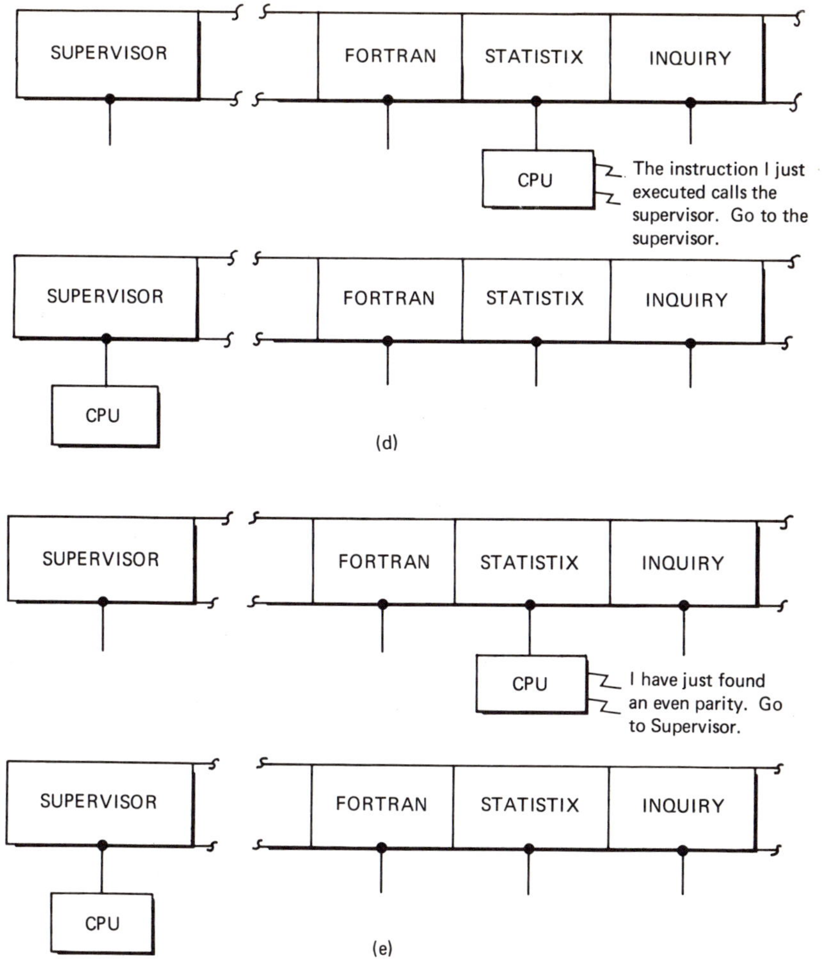

Fig. 65 Take-over of CPU control by supervisor.

THE S/360 INTERRUPT SYSTEM

Each of the illustrations in Fig. 65 shows the Supervisor receiving control as a result of an *interruption* during the execution of a program. That is, whenever one of five *types* of events (as exemplified above) occurs, the program that has control of the CPU is interrupted and control is turned over to the Supervisor. Each of the five types of interrupts is named as follows:

1. Figure a—External Interrupt
2. Figure b—Program Interrupt
3. Figure c—I/O Interrupt
4. Figure d—Supervisor Call (SVC) Interrupt
5. Figure e—Machine Check Interrupt

The Supervisor Processes the Interruption

When the Supervisor gets control after an interruption, it is aware only of the *type* of event that caused the interruption. The Supervisor must now determine the specific event. The Supervisor program is made up of many parts, called *routines.* The determination of which specific event caused an interruption is made by an Interrupt Handling Routine. For example, the I/O Interrupt Handling Routine determines

1. the channel and device when an I/O operation has completed.
2. the channel and device when an error occurs during an input operation. The I/O operation Handling Routine (IHR) also determines the exact nature of the error.
3. If the interrupt is caused by an error, the I/O IHR may try to reperform the I/O operation a certain number of times. If a retry of the I/O operation is successful, processing continues as though nothing had happened; if unsuccessful, the program for which the I/O operation was started is terminated, and a message will so inform the operator.

When an interrupt occurs, the PSW that had been controlling the CPU is replaced by a PSW related to the type of interrupt. For example, if there is an I/O interrupt, the current PSW is replaced by an I/O PSW. In the I/O PSW is the address of the routine that processes the interrupt (Fig. 66). Depending upon the action taken by the IHR, the Supervisor will either return CPU control to the interrupted program or give CPU control to a different program. Generally speaking, after the interrupt has been processed, the Supervisor reloads the replaced PSW so that the interrupted program can continue (see Fig. 67).

SYS1.LOGREC

Whenever a mechanical or electronic malfunction takes place, its occurrence is recorded. The recorded data is used to assist the IBM Customer Engineer in diagnosing and correcting the errant equipment. The data set in which the information is recorded is called SYS1.LOGREC.

The I/O Supervisor

The part of the operating system that sets up the channels to execute the input and output operations is called the *Input/Output Supervisor.* The I/O Supervisor

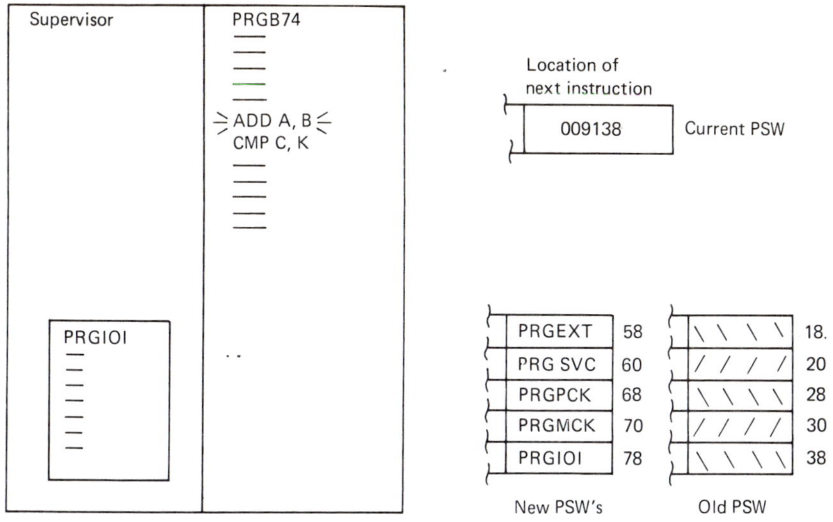

This figure illustrates that an I/O interruption is about to take place. The machine instruction equivalent to ADD A, B has just been executed and the address of the next instruction has just been calculated.

The current PSW contains the address of the next instruction, 009138.

Each of the new PSW's is in a particular storage location. Here the storage locations of the PSW are given in hexadecimal. (Of course, the addresses in the new PSW must be in machine language to be executed. We show them here with symbolic addresses for ease of reference.)

When a PSW is to be substituted, it will be moved out and saved in a storage location that is reserved for the type of interruption occurring. After a PSW is moved and saved it is referred to as the old PSW.

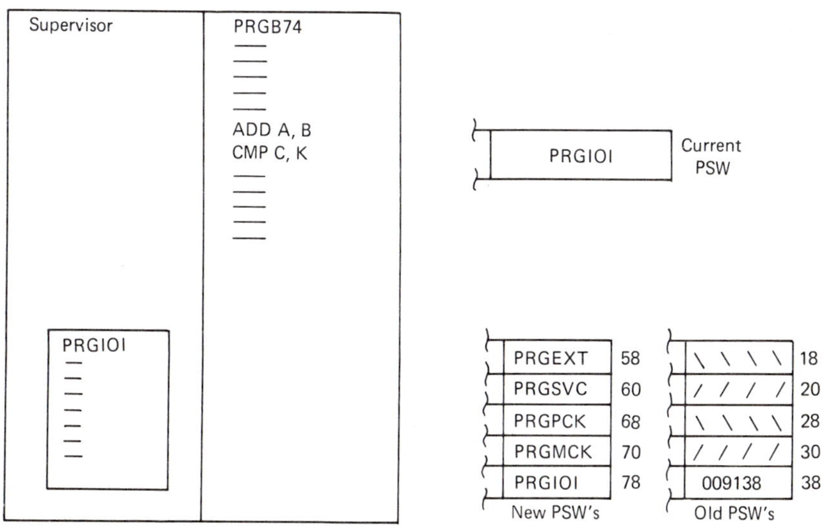

Here we see that two major events have occurred.

1. The PSW which was in control when the interrupt occurred has become what is called "The Old I/O PSW."

2. The new PSW from hex location 78 (i.e., the "new I/O PSW") has become the current PSW. The address now in the current PSW is where the next instruction to be executed comes from.

Fig. 66 New, current, old PSW's.

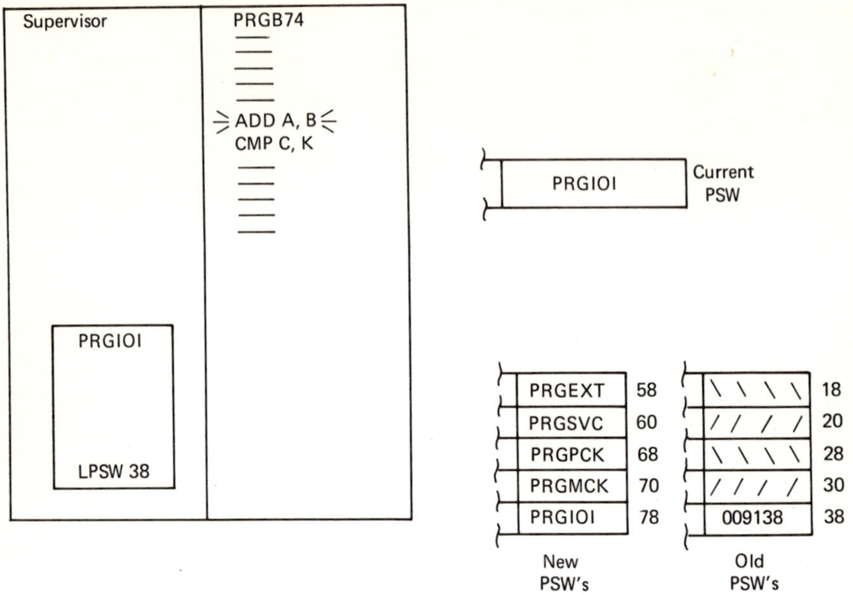

The last instruction of an interrupt handling routine should restore the old PSW to a current status. This is accomplished by issuing the instruction called "Load Program Status Word" (LPSW). The operand for LPSW is the location of the old PSW to be restored.

(a)

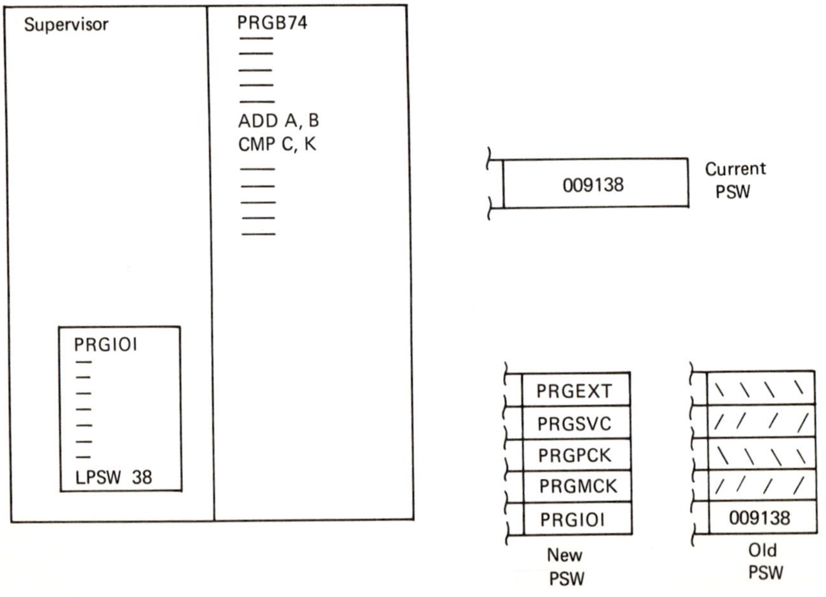

This figure shows that the current PSW now contains the address of the next instruction of the problem program which previously had been interrupted.

(b)

Fig. 67 (a) Restoring old PSW: (b) old PSW restored.

selects the proper series of channel command words (for the device to be started) and issues the Start I/O command. The I/O Supervisor is the most complex program of the operating system. (For an installation such as the one we've been describing, the I/O Supervisor might easily require 5,000 bytes. A program of this size and complexity would require a talented, experienced programmer about 1 year to write.)

Access Method Programs

The I/O Supervisor does not, however, communicate directly with the application program. When an application program requires an input record or wants to dispose of an output record, it informs a program called an *Access Method.* The Access Method program keeps a supply of input records in main storage. It also receives the output from the application program. When all the records in an input area have been processed, the Access Method informs the I/O Supervisor to start an input operation. When an output area has been filled up, the Access Method asks the I/O Supervisor to start an output operation.

The main purpose of the Access Method is to tell the application program where in main storage to get the next input record from or where to put the next output record. Figure 68 shows the relationship among the application program STATISTIX, the Access Method program, and the I/O Supervisor.

Some of the major Access Methods are the Sequential Access Method (SAM), Direct Access Method (DAM), Teleprocessing Access Method (TAM), and Indexed Sequential Access Method (ISAM, pronounced eye sam).

PROGRAM LIBRARY

The installation we've been describing could reasonably be expected to have many hundreds of application programs, a dozen or so compiler programs, the Linkage Editor program, sorting programs, and several other varieties. Where are these programs kept? In general, all the programs are kept in one data set on either drum or disk storage. This data set is called SYS1.LINKLIB (pronounced sis one point link libe; one usually refers to it by its nickname, however, which is pronounced link *libe*). When a program in LINKLIB is to enter main storage, it is brought in by a Supervisor routine called Program Fetch.

Placing and Finding the Program in LINKLIB

When a program is placed into LINKLIB, it follows the one previously entered into the data set. In other words, the position of a program in LINKLIB depends upon its entry sequence; the first program entered into LINKLIB is near

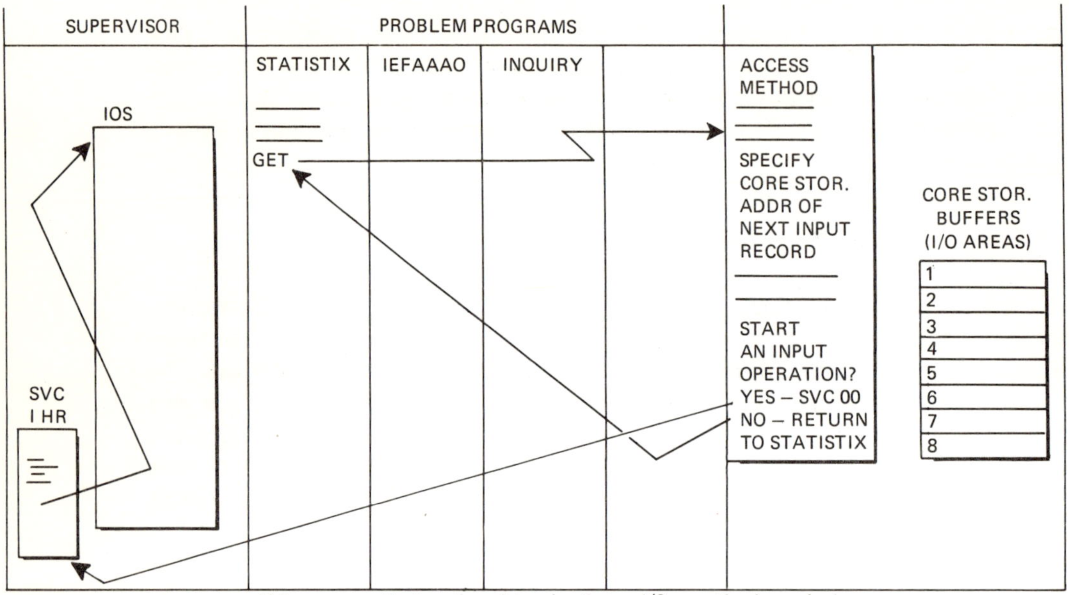

If the access method routines determine that an I/O operation is required, an "SVC 00" instruction is issued. This causes an SVC Interrupt. The SVC Interrupt Handling Routine (IHR) determines that the number associated with the SVC is "00". Upon determing this fact, control of the CPU is given to the I/O supervisor.

The I/O supervisor fills the core storage buffers, which are used to stockpile I/O records. It is not uncommon to have three, four, five or more input buffers filled with records waiting to be processed. Keeping core storage buffers filled minimizes the amount of time a problem program has to wait for input.

Fig. 68 I/O supervisor, access method, problem programs relationship.

the front of the data set. Thus we see that the member programs of a program library are not in alphabetical sequence (see Fig. 69). How, then, is the required program found in a reasonable amount of computer time? Just in front of the first program in LINKLIB is an area called the *directory*. In this directory is recorded the program's name, the track and record number of where the program begins, and how long it is. The *directory* of LINKLIB is kept in alphabetical sequence (see Fig. 70). When a new program is added to LINKLIB, all the entries in the directory higher in sequence are shifted to make room for the program's name, location, and length.

A program library, consisting of programs and a directory, is an example of a partitioned data set. The data set is called *partitioned* because each program, recorded in its own partition, is insulated from its neighbor. The only way to determine where in the data set a program is located is to look it up in the directory. The content of each partition is often referred to as a member. Hence a compiler program (such as the FORTRAN compiler) is a member in the partitioned data set called LINKLIB.

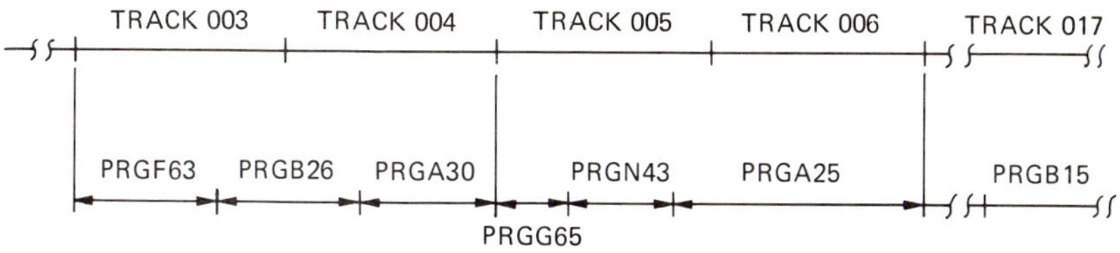

This is a schematic of how several consecutive tracks projected in a straight line would keep a few of its programs. Note the alphameric value of each program name: they are not in ascending order of alphameric values- - -they don't have to be. As a matter of fact, these values are all mixed up- - -i.e., F63 is higher in alphameric value than B26, which in turn is higher than A30, which in turn is lower than G65, and so on.

The order in which these programs reside on consecutive tracks is the same as the order in which they were initially written onto the tracks. Those programs that are used most are intentionally written first so that they will be closest to the beginning of the set.

Fig. 69 Organization of programs in a DASD library.

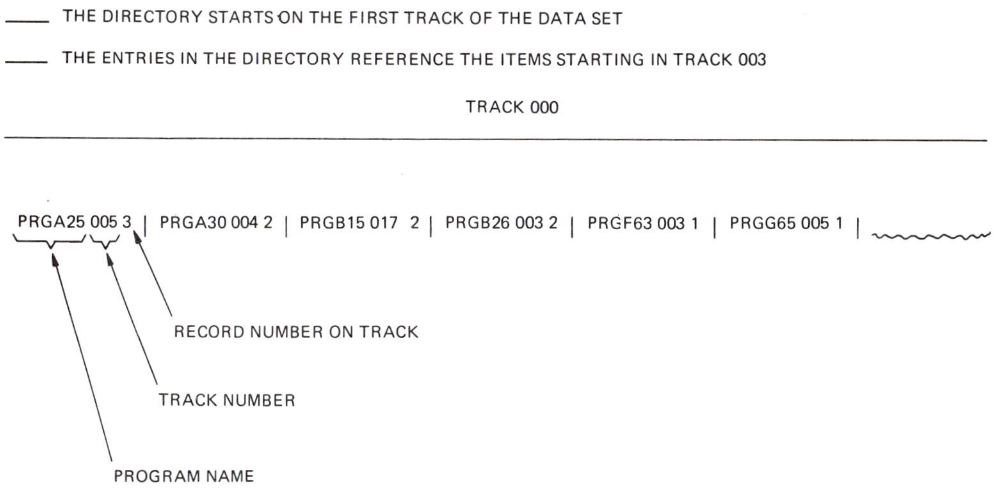

Fig. 70 Directory schematic.

SUBROUTINE LIBRARIES

In the course of time, the programmers who used the various programming languages discovered that many of their problems have common parts. For example, all FORTRAN programmers at some time or another need to find the square root of a number or find the value of a trigonometric function. Rather than require each FORTRAN programmer to write his own series of ADD's, COMPARE's, and so on, to find the square root or whatever, the operating system comes with a basic collection of subroutines for the FORTRAN programmer to use. The collection of FORTRAN subroutines is kept in a library called SYS1.FORTLIB (called FORTLIB). FORTLIB comes only with some basic subroutines, and each installation may add its own routines. Also, if some of the basic subroutines are inappropriate for the installation's FORTRAN programmers, the subroutines can be removed.

Companions to FORTLIB are SYS1.COBLIB for the COBOL programmers and SYS1.PLILIB for the PL/1 programmers. Another library is SYS1.SORTLIB. In this library are the subroutines for constructing a program that will sort the records of a data set from one sequence to another. The organization (not the content) of all the subroutine libraries is the same as the organization of LINKLIB. That is, each subroutine's name, beginning track and record number, and length are kept in the directory of the library.

The omission of any comments concerning a library for the Assembly language programmer was intentional. The main reason is that the Assembly programmer does not use previously written subroutines, as such. He does, however, have a library containing collections of Assembly language instructions. Each collection is like a superinstruction and is referred to as a *macro*. The name of the library containing the macros is called SYS1.MACLIB.

Use of Subroutine Libraries and MACLIB

When a compiler program is processing source statements, it evaluates each statement to see if it refers to a subroutine (for COBOL, FORTRAN, etc.) or macro (for the Assembly language). For some of these, the compiler requests the Supervisor to go to the corresponding library and retrieve the requested subroutine or macro. After the subroutine or macro is retrieved, it is compiled just as though it had been included in the source statements. In other cases, the subroutines are not incorporated until the Linkage Editor programs are executed.

MULTIPLE DATA SETS PER VOLUME: THE VTOC

Although each operating system data-processing installation will have different library requirements (regarding their size and intraorganization), most of these installations will have several libraries on a drum or disk pack. (Each disk pack and drum is called a data-processing *volume*. Each reel of tape is also called a volume.) Since a volume consists of several libraries (each library is a data set), each volume has a table of contents (as do textbooks and encyclopedias). In data-processing terminology, this is usually referred to as the volume table of contents (VTOC). There is one slight difference, however; in a conventional booklike volume the table of contents is traditionally at the beginning. In a data-processing volume (drum, disk pack, etc.) the table of contents may be anywhere in the volume (wherever the installation wants to keep it). Since the table of contents can be anywhere, an additional facility is provided to make it easy to find. At the beginning of the volume is the volume's *label*. One of the items of information in the table is the track address of the beginning of the VTOC. Figure 71 shows the relationship between a volume's label and its VTOC.

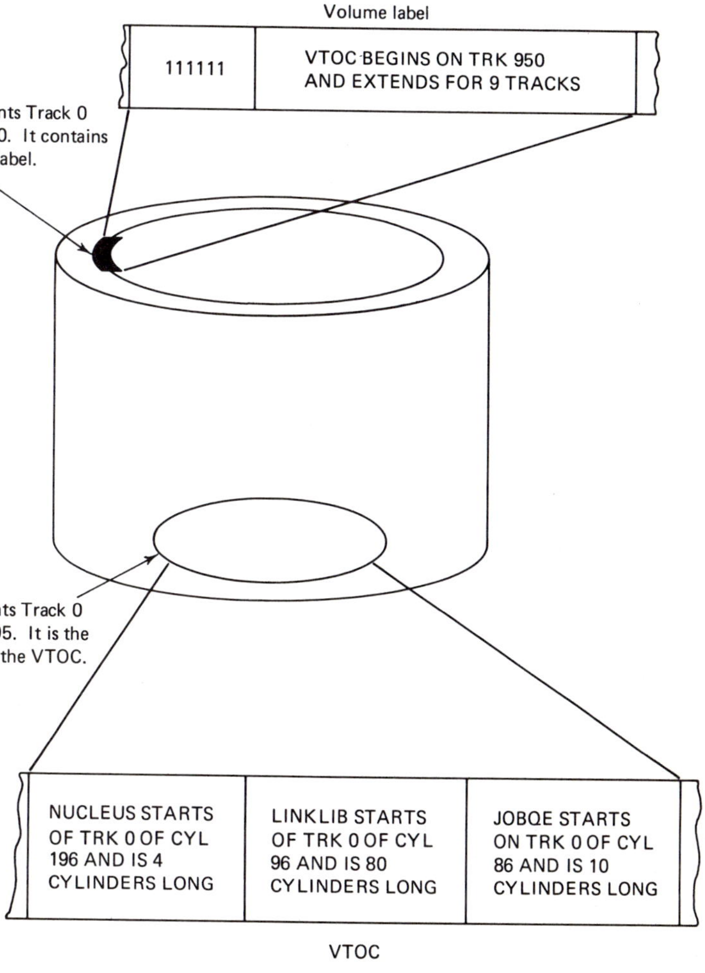

Fig. 71 Volume label/VTOC relationship.

HOW THE OPERATING SYSTEM GETS PROGRAMS (TASKS) STARTED (INITIATED)

Up to this point we have avoided talking about how the operating system (OS) gets programs started. We can avoid it no longer. Getting a program into main storage is a relatively simple operation. Once a program has been brought into storage it is usually referred to as a *task*. (The distinction between the words *program* and *task* is not sharp. Generally speaking, the word "task" is used after the program has been brought into main storage for execution.) The major concerns of getting a task initiated are:

1. Is there enough main storage for the program?
2. Are the input and output devices needed by the task available for use?
3. Are the data sets and the volumes on which they reside (or, if output, are to reside) available for the task?

Answering these questions is the responsibility of an OS program called the *Initiator*. (Since the Initiator is a program, it must be in main storage before the application program or compiler program or whatever it is going to initiate.)

For the Initiator to perform its responsibilities, it must be provided with information. There are two major categories of information the Initiator requires. These are

1. the name of the program
2. the I/O requirements of the program

Once the Initiator has determined that the requested program exists, that there is enough main storage, and that all the I/O requirements can be met, the program is brought into main storage and becomes a task. As soon as it is in main storage, it must share the CPU along with the other tasks, as was shown in Fig. 62.

DESCRIBING THE I/O REQUIREMENTS AND NAMING THE PROGRAM

Before the Initiator can perform its responsibilities, the name of the program and the I/O requirements must have been recorded in a data set called SYS1.SYSJOBQE (pronounced sis one point sis job cue but usually referred to as job cue). The most popular way of getting this information recorded into JOBQE is to punch it into cards. Then have a special task read the cards (from a card reader such as the 2540) into main storage followed by recording the information into JOBQE. The name of the task used to read these cards is generally referred to as the "Reader." (Another name for this task is *Reader/Interpreter.* The word Interpreter is used because there are many items of information in the card; how the Initiator is to use this information is interpreted by the reader.) Figure 72 shows how the responsibilities of the Reader and Initiator are related. (In case you're wondering how the Reader program got initiated, let us say for now that the Reader receives special consideration.)

SYSTEM TASKS

Because the Reader and the Initiator are not tasks started by an Initiator as are applications programs, but rather are parts of the operating system's control program, the Reader and the Initiator are called *system tasks.*

THE READER AND SOURCE STATEMENT CARDS

One of the common procedures for compiling source statements (FORTRAN, COBOL, etc.) is to place the source statement cards directly in back of those naming the program to be executed (in this case, a compiler) and the ones describing the I/O requirements (see Fig. 73). Figure 73 shows that the information for the Initiator is placed in the data set named SYS1.SYSJOBQE and that the FORTRAN source statements are recorded in a data set named *TEMPORARY.-DS.#1.* The space and the name for this data set is automatically provided by OS. The space and the name are kept by OS until the FORTRAN compiler has compiled the source statements. After the compilation is over, the space is automatically reclaimed by OS. (The name *TEMPORARY.DS#1* is fictitious; we chose it to illustrate the concept of a *temporary* data set. The names composed by OS for temporary data sets are coded and rather lengthy—more about this later).

To make it easier for the Reader task to distinguish the cards describing the program and I/O requirements from the data cards (such as source statements), the former require slashes in columns 1 and 2 (see Fig. 74). The card describing the required program is distinguished from the cards describing the I/O requirements. The former requires the term *EXEC* and the latter the term *DD.* EXEC stands for *execute* and DD stands for *device description* or *data definition* (see Fig. 75).

In addition to the slashes and the terms (EXEC and DD), each card should have a name so that it can be distinguished and referred to. When the card does have a name, it must start in column 3 and consist of no more than eight characters;

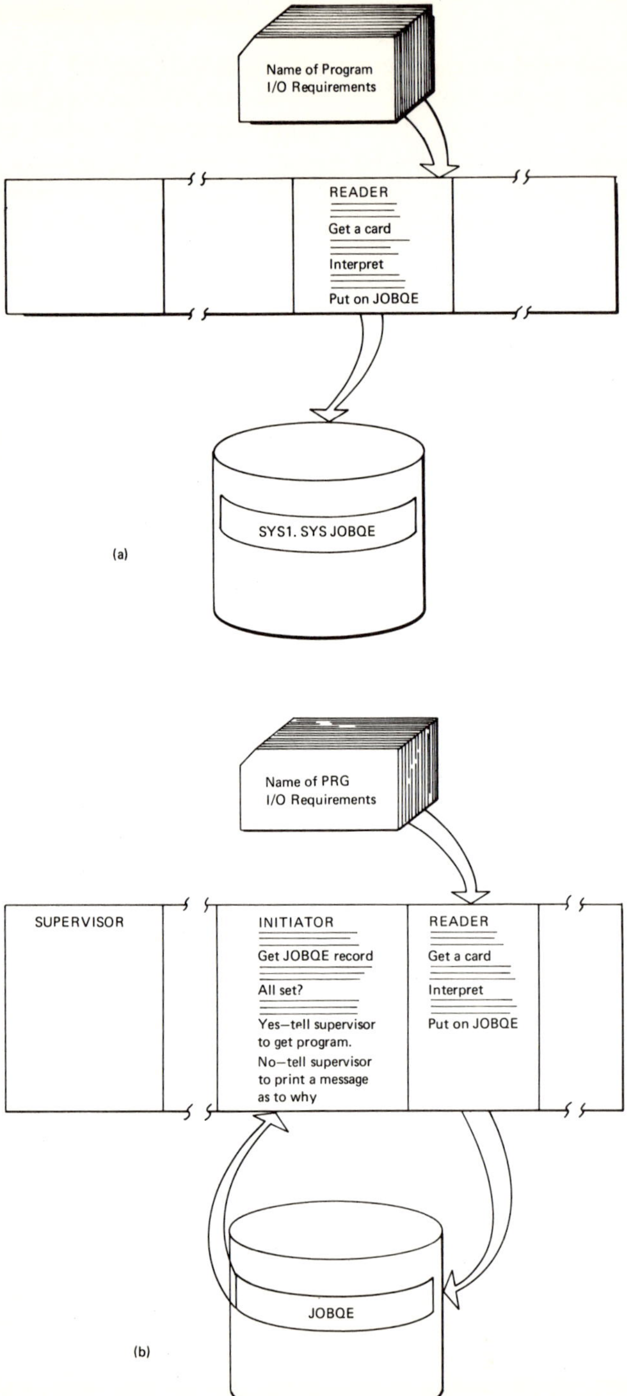

Fig. 72 Reader/JOBQE/Initiator relationship.

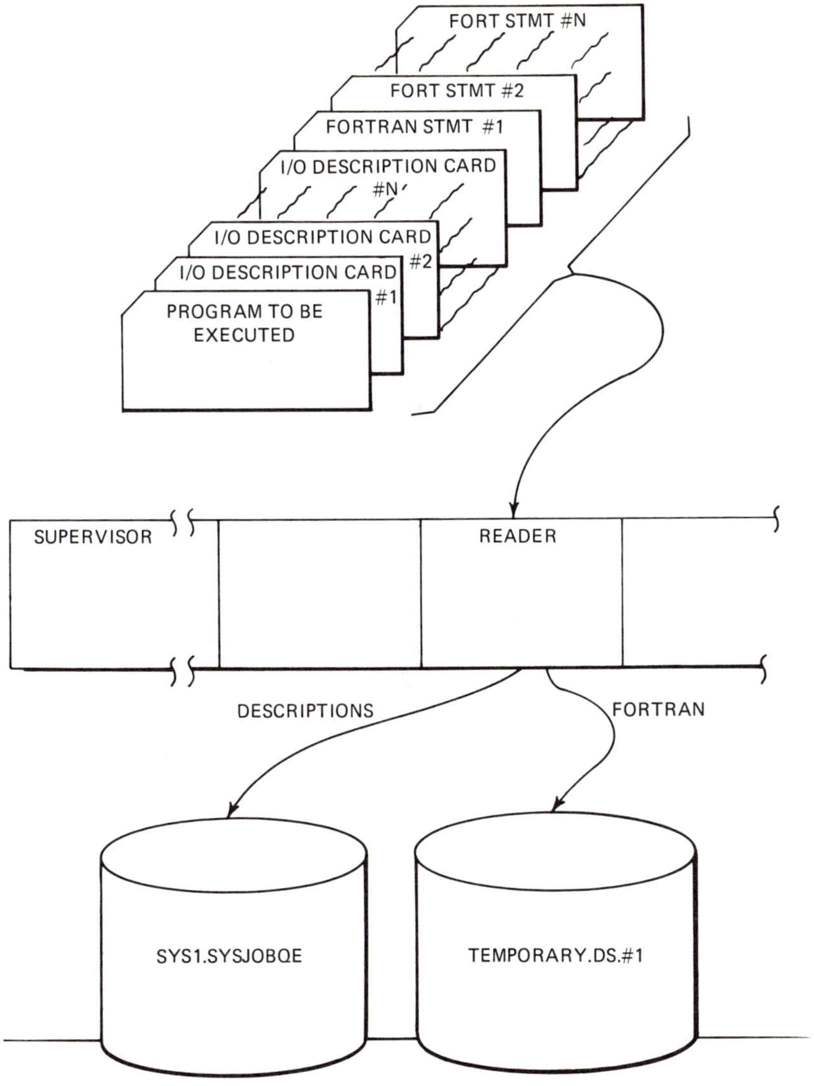

Fig. 73 Recording contents of job stream.

the name must always be followed by a space of at least one column. Figure 76 shows the left end of the cards necessary to compile the FORTRAN source statements (using the compiler known as FORTRAN F). The names used in the DD cards and the EXEC card are pretty much the standard names used when a compiler's I/O requirements are described. (Remember, IBM has written the compiler programs to be used with OS/360. The IBM programmers who wrote the compiler programs are responsible for composing the names of the DD cards. When *you* become a programmer and want to process data sets, one of *your* responsibilities

Fig. 74 Marks of distinction.

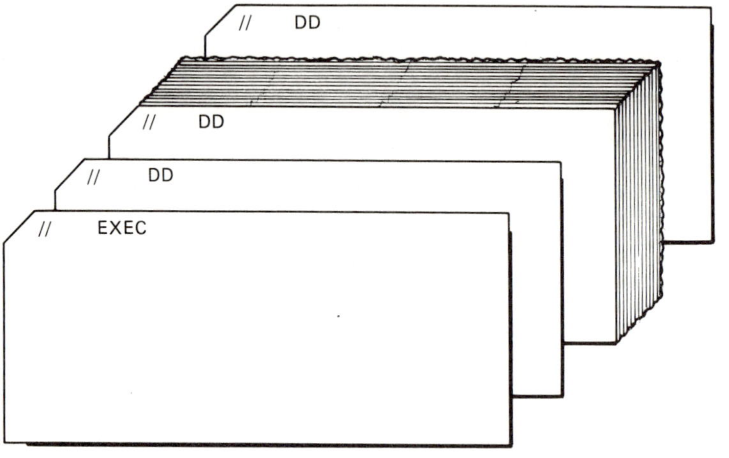

Fig. 75 EXEC and DD terms.

will be to specify the names to be used in the DD cards describing your I/O requirements.)

DEFINITION OF A JOB STEP

The program that is to be executed and its I/O requirements comprise a job step. The EXEC card and its associated DD cards are referred to as *job step cards.*

DEFINITION OF A JOB

It would seem that if there is an entity called a job *step*, there certainly should be something called a *job*. What then is a job? A job is a series of related job steps. (Of course, if none of the job steps is related, there will be only one job step per job.)

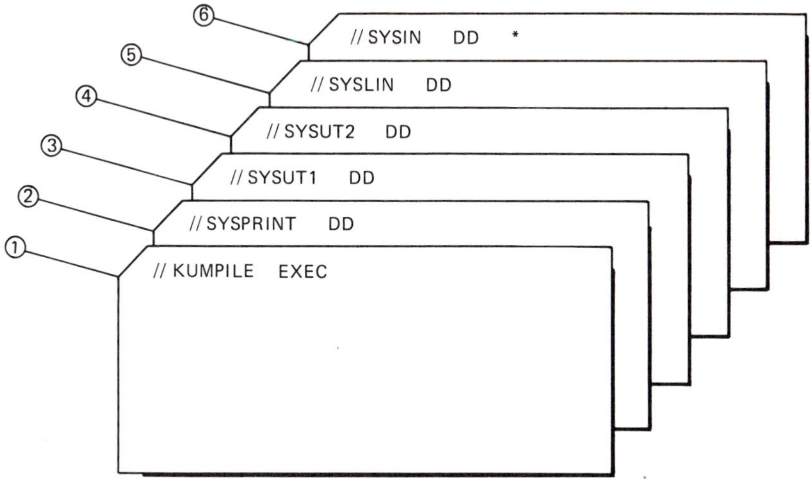

① The EXEC card has been named KUMPILE
② This DD card, named SYSPRINT, will be used to request eventual printed output
③&④ These DD cards, named SYSUT1 and SYSUT2, will request space on a DASD for intermediate results
⑤ This DD card, named SYSLIN, will request space on DASD for recording the results of compilation
⑥ This card, named SYSIN, and containing an asterisk, informs the Reader program that source statements are about to follow

Fig. 76 Sample EXEC and DD Cards.

RELATED JOB STEPS COMPRISE A JOB

The output of a compiler, although consisting of machine language instructions, is not executable. To make it executable, a compiler's output must be processed by a program called the *Linkage Editor.* The output of a compiler is certainly closely related to the Linkage Editor's input (they are the same). Here, then, is an example of related job steps. Figure 77 shows parts of the EXEC and DD cards required for a job consisting of two steps. (The EXEC cards also show how the FORTRAN compiler and the Linkage Editor program are named: The FORTRAN G compiler's *official* name is *IDYFORT* and the Linkage Editor's official name is *IEWL.*) Note also that intermediate results do not have to be recorded on direct-access space.

THE JOB CARD

To distinguish one job from another (i.e., one series of related job steps from another series of related job steps) requires a job card. This card, like the EXEC

1. A DD card requesting a punch (the output of the compiler is going to be punched into cards).
2. The EXEC card for specifying the Linkage Editor (IEWL)
3. A DD card requesting SYS1.FORTLIB, a library of FORTRAN subroutines.
4. A DD card requesting space for the output of the Linkage Editor. This card is usually named SYSLMOD, meaning load module.
5. A DD card for requesting space for intermediate Linkage Editor results.
6. A DD card for requesting the data set on which had been recorded the output of the Compiler.

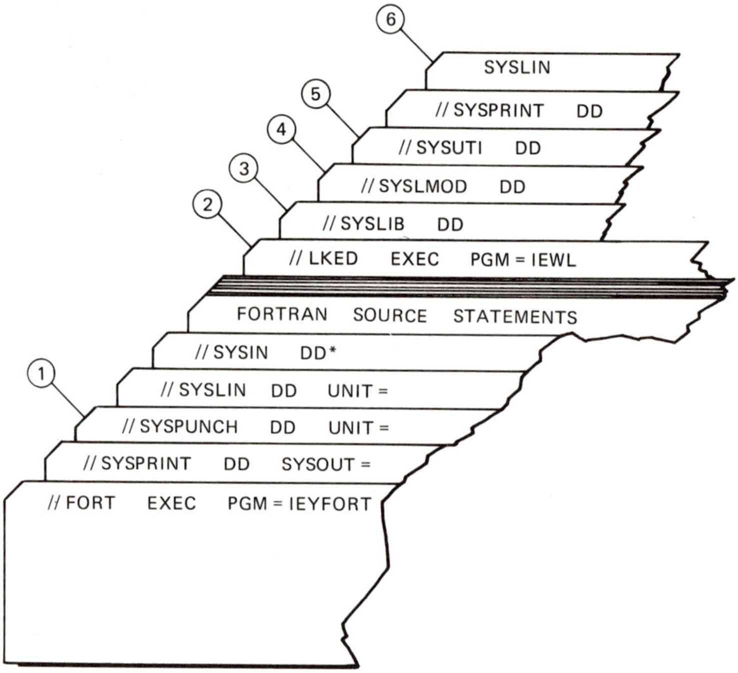

Fig. 77 Sample job step statements.

and DD cards, requires slashes in columns 1 and 2 and a name beginning in column 3; it also requires the term JOB, which comes after the name (see Fig. 78).

THE JOB STREAM

During the course of a data-processing day, jobs are assembled and prepared for the Reader task. The collection of assembled jobs is called a *job stream.*

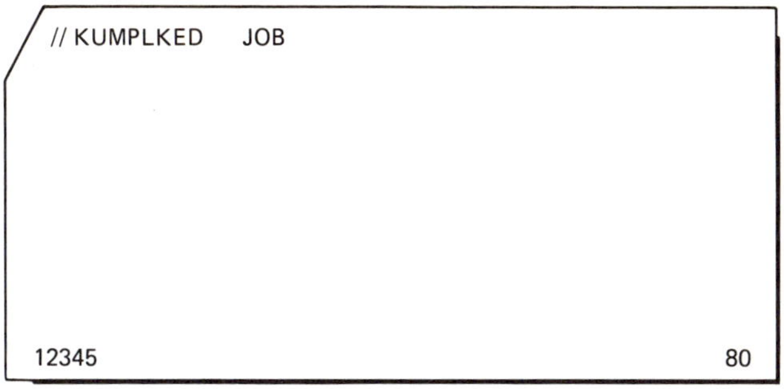

Fig. 78 Job statement.

MULTIPLE JOB STREAMS

An installation such as the one we described previously may have more than one job stream. In addition to the conventional job stream (which is prepared and assembled locally), another job stream might be prepared and assembled in another part of town, transcribed into magnetic tape, and brought in person to the data-processing center or transmitted by terminals (see Fig. 79). In any event, if the jobs originating at the two different locations are to be entered into the JOBQE simultaneously, there will have to be two Reader tasks, each reading its own job stream. The alternative is to hand-carry or mail the remotely prepared job stream to the computer installation and then combine the two job streams as one.

CLASSIFICATIONS OF JOBS

One of the most important decisions the operations staff of the data-processing center must make is: Which jobs should be in main storage at the same time? Think of what would happen if one wanted to execute three jobs each requiring six tape drives but with only 10 tape drives on the system; only one of the jobs would get initiated. The Initiators for the other two jobs would be in storage waiting for the devices they need; they'll have to wait until the first job terminates. The main storage occupied by the two waiting Initiators would be unavailable for any other programs. To prevent such a hangup from occurring, jobs should be classified according to some scheme. For example, an installation could classify jobs as follows:

Class D jobs requiring three to four tape drives and 10 to 15 minutes of computer time.

Class E jobs requiring three to four tape drives and 15 to 30 minutes of computer time.

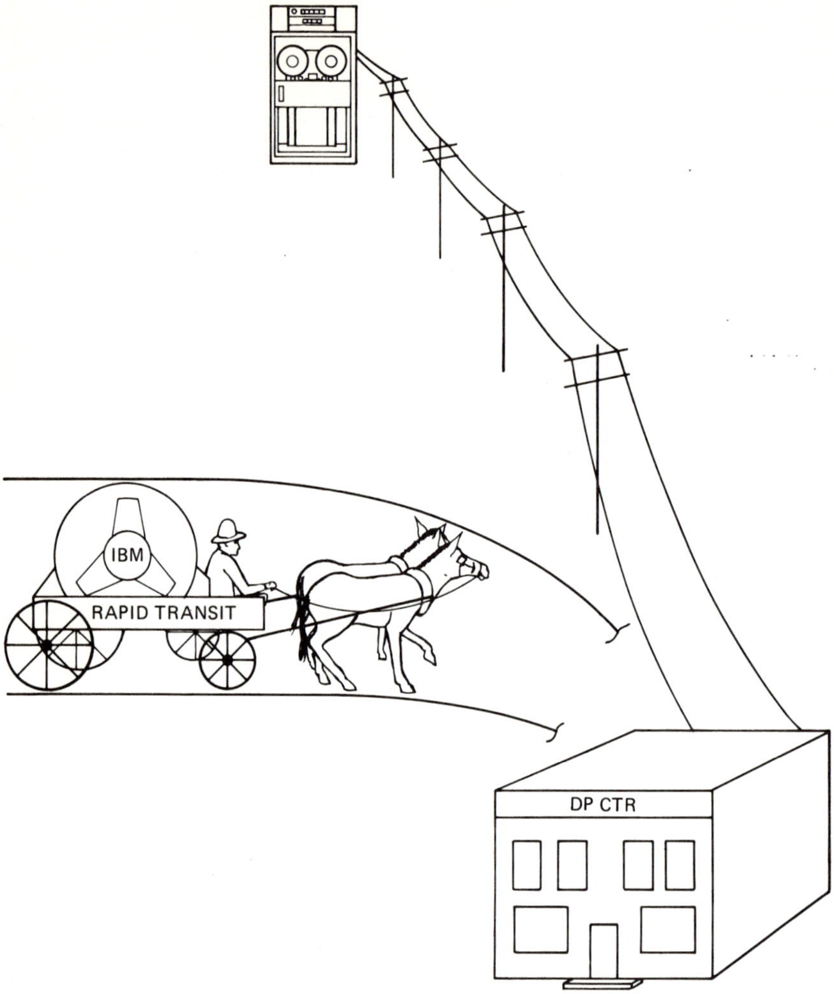

Fig. 79 Data transmission techniques.

Class F jobs requiring three to four tape drives and $\frac{1}{2}$ to 2 hours of computer time.

Class G jobs requiring five to eight tape drives and 10 to 30 minutes of computer time.

Class H jobs requiring five to eight tape drives and $\frac{1}{2}$ to 2 hours of computer time.

Class I jobs requiring no tape drives, little or no I/O operations, and 10 to 20 minutes of computer time. (These are called high compute jobs —once they get the CPU, they rarely give it up, because they don't have to wait for I/O operations.)

The operating system has been designed with the capability of recognizing the class of a job. Here is the way it works. The class code of each job is placed into the JOB card. When the Reader task reads the job stream, the class code is used to place the control information about the job into a unique area in the JOBQE for each possible job class. The unique area is often referred to as the *class queue* (see Fig. 80).

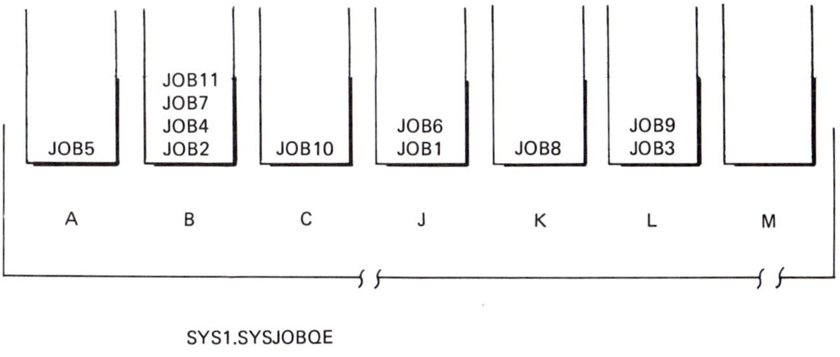

This illustrates the job queue subdivided into class queues. The numerical part of each job's name represents its order in the input stream.

Fig. 80 SYS1.SYSJOBQE compartments.

When each Initiator is started by the computer operator, he assigns to the Initiator the job class codes which the Initiator is permitted to start. When the Initiator is looking in the JOBQE for job steps to initiate, it looks only in those class queues authorized by the operator. An Initiator may have a primary class, a secondary class, and a tertiary class. (The number of levels of classes which an Initiator may be associated with depends upon the authors of the operating system. One version of the operating system may have up to eight classes.) When the operator starts an Initiator he does so with a command—START INIT, CDE, where C, D, and E are the respective primary, secondary, and tertiary class codes. As long as there are jobs in the class C queue of JOBQE, the Initiator will start only class C jobs. When there are no more class C jobs, the Initiator will start class D jobs. (Of course, if the reader places another class C job in the queue, then the next time the Initiator is looking for work, it will choose the class C job.) If there are no class D jobs, the Initiator will start class E jobs. When all three of its class queues are exhausted, the Initiator will just wait. It will start up again if the Reader places a job in either of its class queues. If there is no possibility of any more class C, D and E jobs, the operator can stop the Initiator by issuing the command STOP INIT, CDE. The main storage space occupied by the Initiator will then be made available for other tasks. Perhaps one of these will be another Initiator specifying different classes.

PRODUCTION OF OUTPUT—OUTPUT WRITER

In a multiprogramming operating system it is very possible that several application tasks may require a printer or a punch. Does this mean that the installation should have several printers and punches? Fortunately, the answer is usually no (although many installations do have two or more printers and two or more punches). To accommodate printed and punched output for a large number of tasks, the operating system employs a scheme of recording output data (to be printed or punched) on a direct-access device. The to-be-printed or to-be-punched output data set remains on the direct-access device until a printer or punch is available. As soon as it is available, a system program called an output writer transfers the output data set from the direct-access device to the printer or punch (Fig. 81).

Output Classes

An output writer must have some way of knowing which of the many possible output data sets it is to print or punch first. To apply the concept of priorities to output data sets, each output data set to be produced is assigned an output class code. The class code of an output data set is placed into a DD statement. (For each output data set there must be a separate DD card.) For example, if the output class is K one would place SYSOUT=K onto the DD card. For each output data set that is temporarily recorded on a direct-access device, the operating system makes an entry into a list called the *output data set queue*. The output data set queue is, in many respects, structured in the same way as the input job queue (which consists of job class queues). An output writer task is started by an operator (he types a command). When he issues the command to start a writer, he also specifies the class of output data sets it is to transcribe from disk to printer or punch.

Choosing Output Classes

What qualifies an output data set to belong to a given class? Output classes are assigned by an installation's systems personnel or operations personnel according to printing or punching requirements. For example, let's say that there are five report forms used for printing operations, three punch card forms for punching operations, one 1403 Printer, one 1443 Printer, a 2540 Card Punch, and one 2501 Card Punch. This means that there are 10 printing combinations and 6 punching combinations. For each of these combinations (16 in all), the installation may assign an output class code. Then when the operator starts an output writer task, he includes the proper class code with his start writer command.

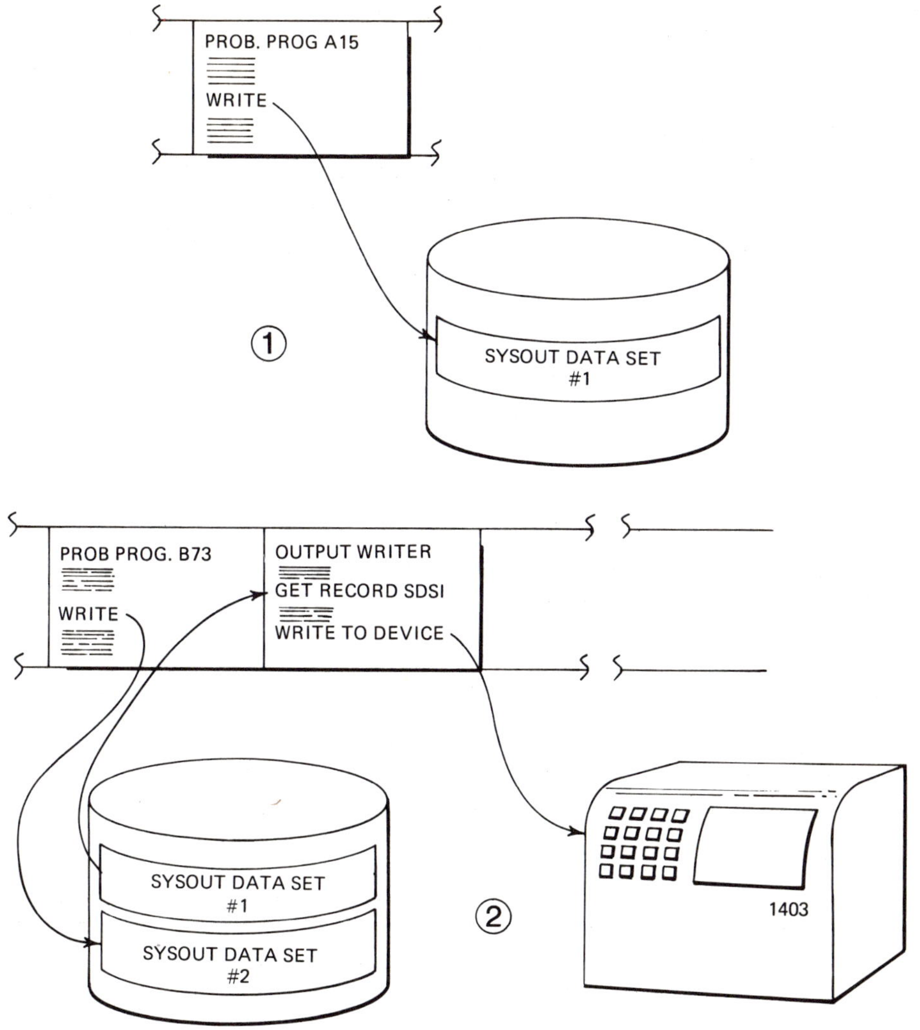

Fig. 81 Output data set preparation.

PROGRAM PRODUCTION IN AN OS/360 INSTALLATION

In an OS/360 installation the responsibility of writing a problem program is often done by a team of programmers (sometimes called the *modular* approach). Each member of the team is given the responsibility of writing a module of the program. This responsibility includes not only writing it, but also debugging and testing it as though it were a complete program. When all of the modules are "error free," they must be combined and tested as an integral unit. Producing programs in modular form has several advantages, the most important being early completion of a programming project.

The relationships of these modules is sometimes fairly simple. That is, Module A is completely executed before it branches to Module B; then Module B is completely executed before it branches to Module C, and so on. Often the relationships are much more complex. For example, the module that programmer B is writing is required in the middle of the program written by programmer A.

(a)

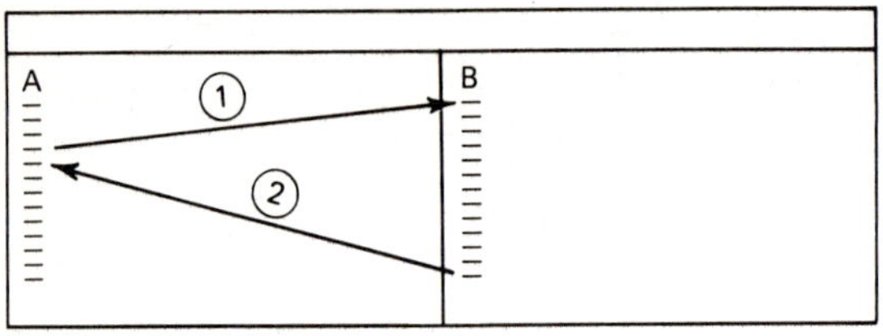

Likewise, the module that programmer C is writing is required in the middle of Module B (example b), and that toward the end of its execution, Module A needs Module C (example c).

(b)

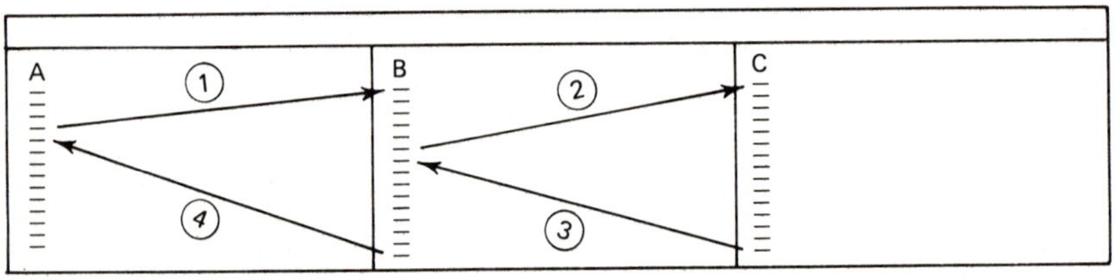

(c)

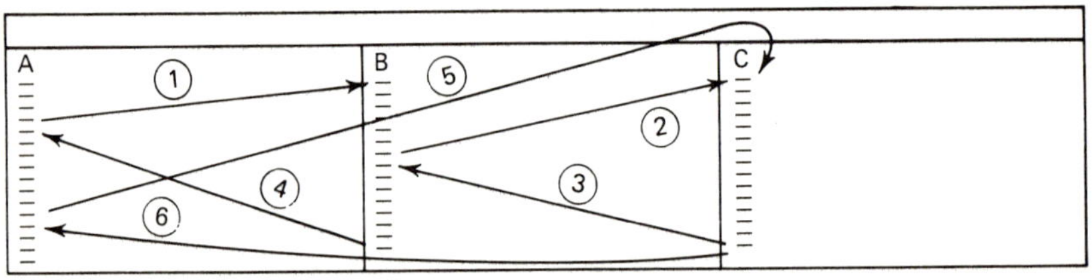

In examples b and c, are modules that are referred to as *calling* modules and *called* modules; A is a calling module (it calls on both B and C); Module B is both a calling module (it calls Module C) and a called module (it is called upon by Module A); and Module C is a called module (it is called upon by both Module A and Module B). A programmer can accomplish the transfer of CPU control to another module by issuing a special branch instruction. This branch instruction, as its first order of business, automatically places the address of the next instruction into a register (usually register 14). [In example d, the next instruction is a move characters (MVC) operation.]

(d) 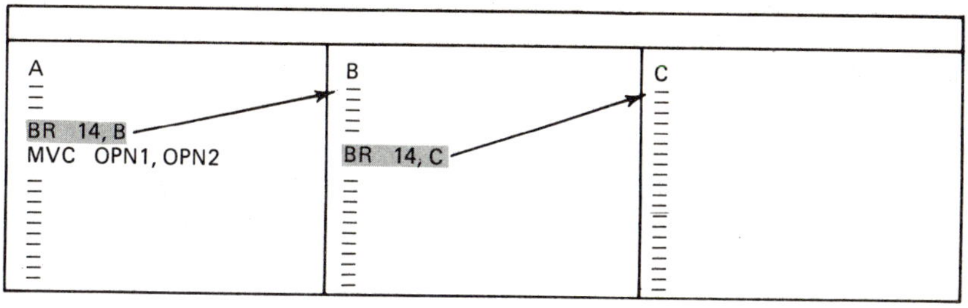

Although modular programming has the major advantage of early completion, it carries with it a major responsibility; that of assuring the preservation of the contents of the registers (so that when a module eventually regains control of the CPU and the 16 registers, it can continue as though it had never lost control).

Each *calling* programmer (who gives up control of the CPU and registers) must provide in his own module, an area of storage where the contents of the registers can be stored by the called module. To tell the called programmer where his save area is, the calling programmer loads his save area's address into register 13 (Load 13, SAVE) as shown in example e.

(e) 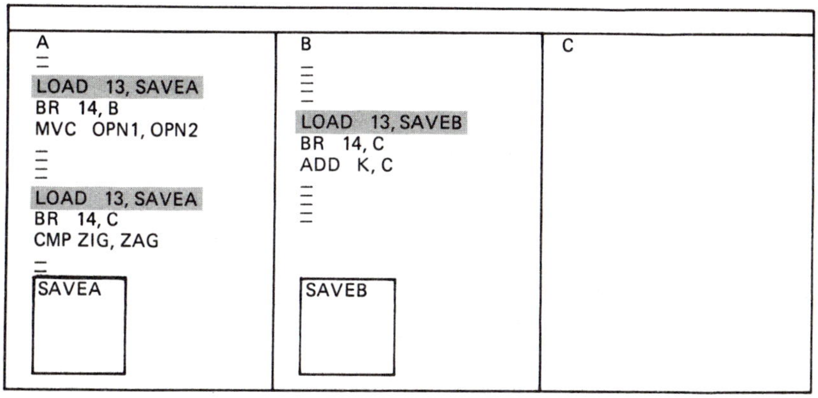

The first thing the called programmer writes in his module is an instruction to store the contents of the registers in a storage area provided by the calling programmer. The instruction (example f) in effect says, "store the contents of the registers in a storage area the address of which is specified by the contents of register 13" (Save 13). After *saving* the contents of the registers, the called programmer can do anything that he wants to with most of the 16 registers.

(f) 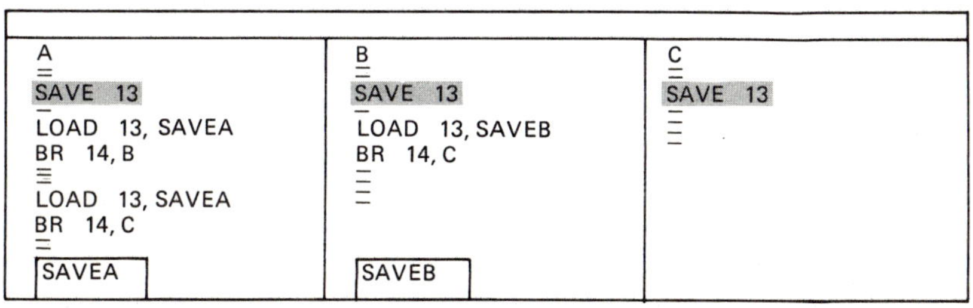

When the called programmer has finished his work, he gives an instruction (it is a macro instruction) called *Return,* as shown in example g. The Return instruction will restore the contents of the registers to the way they were before the called module got control of the CPU; the return instruction then causes a branch operation. The place branched to as a result of the Return instruction is determined by the contents of register 14.

(g)

A	B	C
SAVE 13	SAVE 13	SAVE 13
LOAD 13, SAVEA BR 14, B	LOAD 13, SAVEB BR 14, C	
LOAD 13, SAVEA BR 14, C		
RETURN	RETURN	RETURN
SAVEA	SAVEB	

Save and Return have been included in Module A with the anticipation that some day it will be "just the module someone needs" (of course he'll also have to need modules B and C). That is, even though Module A is now a calling module only, it may someday be a called module.

UNIPROGRAMMING

Before the days of multiprogramming, one merely distinguished between the Supervisor and the *one* problem program. There was no prefix to the term *programming.* As soon as the concept of multiprogramming was proposed, data processing people constructed the term *uniprogramming* where *uni* means one.

The version of OS/360 that supports the uniprogramming concept is called the Primary Control Program (PCP). In a PCP operating system, the Reader, Initiator, and Problem Program sequentially occupy the *same* area of main storage. That is, the first program in main storage is the Reader, the next program is the Initiator, and then follows the Problem Program, each occupying the space vacated by its predecessor.

ORGANIZATION OF MAIN STORAGE FOR MULTIPROGRAMMING

Main storage can be thought of as consisting of two distinct divisions. One division is referred to as the *fixed area.* This is where the various Supervisors reside. The other division is called the *dynamic* (changing) *area.* It is in the dynamic area where the application programs, the Initiators, the Readers, and the Output Writers come and go (see Fig. 82). There are two basic multiprogramming variations of the

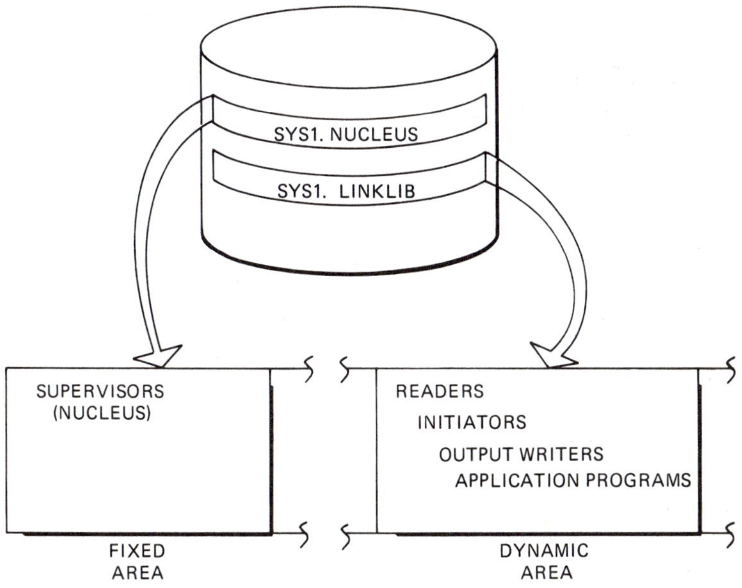

The Supervisors that reside in the fixed area make up the nucleus. The nucleus is the first part of the Operating System that enters storage at the beginning of a data processing cycle. The nucleus is recorded in a special data set called SYS1. NUCLEUS. The reader, initiators, output writers, and most application programs are kept in SYS1. LINKLIB.

Fig. 82 Fixed and dynamic areas.

operating system. These are called MFT-II (meaning multiprogramming with a fixed number of tasks, version two) and MVT (meaning multiprogramming with a variable number of tasks). Let's briefly examine each of these.

MFT-II—Partitions for Tasks

One type of multiprogramming system requires that the installation specify the maximum number of tasks that can be in the dynamic area of main storage. This specification must be done at the time that the installation is generating its operating system. The size (number of bytes) of each of these tasks' areas must also be specified at system generation time. The main storage area in which the tasks are to reside are called *partitions*. Can the number and size of partitions be changed? After the operating system has been "fired up" for the day's activities, the number and size of the partitions can be changed. The change is effected by having the operator issue a special command. There are a number of conditions the operator must be aware of; hence it is not a good practice to continually change the number and size of partitions in an MFT-II system.

The F in MFT-II means that the number of tasks is fixed, one task per partition. Installations with requirements consisting mostly of batch-processing applications and with jobs that can be scheduled with reasonable accuracy usually select the MFT-II system.

MVT—Regions for Tasks

There are many installations with requirements that are relatively unpredictable, particularly when the applications require teleprocessing. Why should this be so? Most teleprocessing applications imply the presence of many human beings sitting at typewriter-like terminals. Each of the terminal operators may require a different program to retrieve and process information from a large variety of data sets. It is not at all predictable when a given terminal operator will require a given program. Hence programs (tasks) of various sizes will continually be swapped in and out of main storage.

If an operator continually had to adjust partition sizes to accommodate the various-sized tasks, a fair percentage of the data-processing day would be taken up by making the adjustments. Therefore, an operating system option is the capability of the Initiator to have partitions adjusted as it selects each job (or job step). However, instead of calling these divisions of main storage *partitions*, they are called regions.

The V in MVT stands for variable. Not only can the number of regions vary according to the job's requirements, but the number of application program tasks *per* region can vary also. What is the significance of this? As was just said, the task requirements of teleprocessing applications are rather unpredictable. It is not uncommon for one terminal operator to enter such combinations of data that to process it might require either

1. hundreds of thousands of main storage bytes for a single program (task), or
2. several successive programs (tasks) proportionately smaller.

The first alternative (hundreds of thousands of bytes) is not economically feasible, especially if these are to be dozens of terminals all contending for main storage bytes. What about the second alternative? If done right it could be the solution. The implementation of the second alternative is called *subtasking*.

Subtasking in MVT

Here is the way subtasking is accomplished. Along with several batch-processing tasks, one teleprocessing task is initiated. Each time a terminal operator provides some *data* (either in the form of a query or conventional data), the teleprocessing task first determines its nature. Based upon this determination, the teleprocessing task brings into its region the appropriate program to process the data. (Hence the teleprocessing task acts like a small-scale Initiator.) The programs brought in by the teleprocessing task are called *subtasks*. When one of these subtasks is waiting for something to happen (so it can continue), another subtask can use the CPU. In other words, CPU control can be switched back and forth between the subtasks rather than give CPU control to an altogether different task. (This does happen but only if *all* of the subtasks are waiting.) The number of subtasks per region can be anything reasonable. Since the number of tasks (regular and sub) can vary, this option of the operating system is called multiprogramming with a variable number of tasks (MVT).

SEQUENTIAL SCHEDULER

When PCP is the type of operating system used, the reading of the job stream is interleaved with the initiation and execution of jobs. For example, if there are several jobs in the job stream, the Reader stops reading the input stream when one of the following happens:

1. A SYSIN DD * card has been read. This card implies that data cards to be read by the problem program are next in the input stream.
2. Another job card has been read. Certain data processing jobs, which might consist of several steps, do not have any data cards. When this is the case, the Reader reads the cards from all of the job's steps before the Initiator is brought in to Initiate the first step.

In PCP, jobs are executed in the same sequence as the job's control cards are read by the Reader. That is, the third job in the input stream is the third job executed; the eighth job in the input stream is the eighth job executed, and so on. Hence, the Job Scheduler (the collective name given to the Reader/Interpreter and Initiator) in a PCP environment is often referred to as the *Sequential Scheduler*.

SCHEDULING JOBS FOR A MULTIPROGRAMMING OPERATING SYSTEM

If a data processing installation is to implement an operating system capable of multiprogramming, it obviously cannot use the Sequential Scheduler.

One of the major requirements of multiprogramming is to have a Reader that can read an entire job stream without once stopping. That is, the information in the job control cards is recorded in SYS1.SYSJOBQE and each set of data cards is recorded on disk as a separate data set.

After enough information about a job has been recorded in the JOBQE, one or more Initiators can be started. In general, one Initiator must be started for each problem program task.

Any input stream data cards that had been recorded as a data set on a direct access device are read from the direct access device once the problem program has been initiated.

PRIORITY SCHEDULER AND JOB PRIORITIES

Unless some priority scheme is implemented, the Initiator selects jobs for Initiation in the same sequence as they entered the class compartments of the JOBQE. To *automate* preferential ordering of jobs, each job can be given a relative priority with which it will be identified when it is in its JOBQE class compartment awaiting selection. The scheme used for MVT and MFT is to assign high numeric values to high priority jobs and low numeric values to low priority jobs.

Since MFT and MVT use the priority scheduling concept, the Job Scheduler in multiprogramming operating systems is referred to as the *Priority Scheduler.*

HOW THE SUPERVISORS REMEMBER WHAT'S GOING ON

So far we have talked about or implied the existence of certain supervisor programs; these are the *I/O Supervisor* (responsible for all operations related to input and output), the *Interrupt Handlers* (responsible for determining the nature of the interrupt and what to do about it), the *Task Supervisor* (the one that remembers the status and condition of each task in core storage), and the *Task Dispatcher* (it chooses the next task that is ready to use the CPU). Another supervisor keeps track of the amount of core storage that isn't being used and, therefore, available. It is called the *Main Storage Supervisor* (MSS). When the Initiator wants to start a new task, it is the MSS that must get the required main storage and then inform the Initiator of its availability and location. When the Terminator wraps up a task's operation, it is the MSS that marks as available the main storage that had been used by the terminating task.

One supervisor manages the electronic clock in the S/360 and keeps track of time. It is responsible for maintaining the time of day and calculating the amount of time used by each task. It is known as the *Time Supervisor.*

Still another supervisor keeps a list of names of programs (modules, routines) that are in core storage at any given time. A name list of each module that is in core is kept up to date by the *Contents Supervisor.* When one of the tasks in core requires the service of another program module or routine (written either by IBM or a problem programmer) the list of programs in core is examined by the Contents Supervisor to see if it is already in core. If it is not in core, a *request* is made of yet another program to obtain it.

RESOURCES

The objects managed by each of the Supervisors are called *resources.* That is, the electronic clock is a resource, modules and routines required by other tasks are resources, available main storage is a resource. When a problem program task or a system task needs one of these resources it is very probable that another task is already using the resource. Not only is it possible that another task is using the resource, there may be several other tasks waiting ahead of it. The operating system must not forget about a task's request for a resource. These requests must be remembered in some kind of order; one could almost say that the requests of each task are recorded and placed into a pile. Some of these requests get put on top of the pile (given preferential treatment), some are placed on the bottom of the pile, and some are placed in between. (However, the word *pile* is not used; the preferred term is *queue*; the word queue means a *waiting line.*) Wherc the record of request in the queue is placed is not done on a random basis; rather a fairly strict rule is followed.

A *record* of each task that is in storage is kept by the task supervisor. This record contains the identity of the task and an up-to-date account of its status. [When the task is initiated, the MSS gets a block of main storage for creating the record. This block of main storage is called the Task Control Block (TCB).]

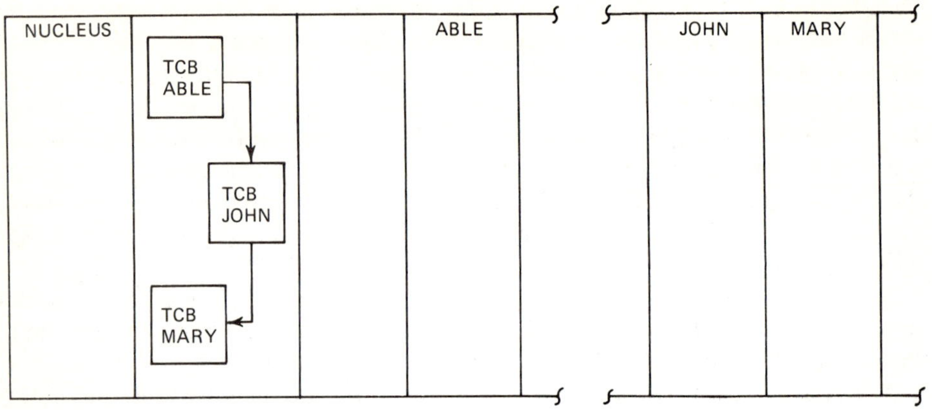

The programming technique used for request queueing is to create a record in main storage of the task's *request* for a resource. The place in main storage where each request for a resource is recorded is called a request block (RB). (There are several types of RB's; each type is related to the kind of resource being requested.) Each time a request for a resource is made, OS creates an RB and places it into the proper queue. How is the order of the RB's in the queue maintained? Each time a new RB is created in storage, its address is stored in the previous RB. The address of the task's first RB is kept in the task control block (TCB). The most recently created RB contains the address of the TCB. (The address in a control block is often referred to as a pointer; on a diagram a pointer is indicated with an arrowed line.)

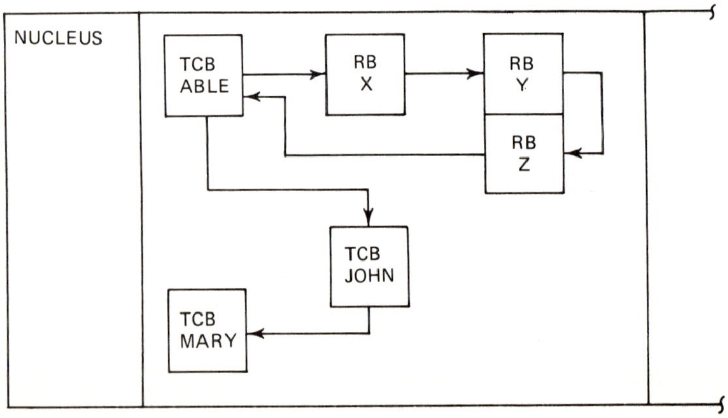

The linking of a TCB with its chain of RB's is appropriately called the *RB Chain.* Whenever a resource becomes available for use, its RB is disconnected from the chain and the remaining RB's are rechained.

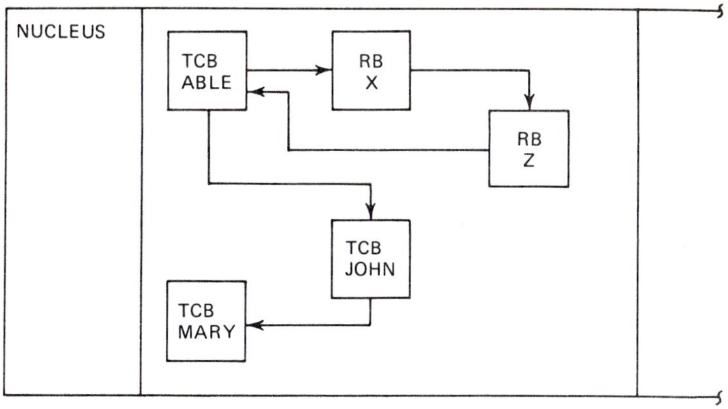

THE ATTACH MACRO

In order to permit the creation of subtasks, the writer of the "parent" task writes a special macro instruction together with the name of the problem which he determined is to become the subtask. The name of this macro instruction is ATTACH. When the ATTACH macro is expanded into machine language, one of the instructions is an SVC identified with the number 42. When the program with the SVC 42 is executed, the SVC 42 causes an interrupt; the SVC Interrupt Handling Routine recognizes the 42, has a TCB created for the program named in the ATTACH macro, and then requests the program to be brought into main storage. Two main relationships between the parent task and the ATTACH'ed subtask are that both will have the same storage protection key and that the parent task, if it so desires, can cause the subtask to end prematurely (also referred to as *end abnormally* or ABEND) for any reason whatsoever.

HIERARCHY RELATIONSHIPS BETWEEN SYSTEM AND PROBLEM PROGRAM TASKS

The Initiator is regarded as a System task. It is the Initiator's responsibility to initiate a Problem Program Task. When the Problem Program task has finished its responsibilities, the Terminator (the opposite of the Initiator) is responsible for terminating the Problem Program task.

How is the relationship between the Initiator/Terminator (I/T) and the Problem Program tasks maintained? In the same way that a parent Problem Program task maintains its relationship with one of its descendant tasks—via the ATTACH macro. That is, the Initiator/Terminator attaches a Problem Program task to it. (Even a parent problem program task is a subtask of the Initiator.)

In the hierarchy of tasks, even the Initiator is a subtask. Each Initiator is a subtask of the Master Scheduler [the Master Scheduler (MS) is the system task that oversees the entire administration of the operating system]. That is, when the console operator issues the command (Start Init) to start an Initiator, the Master Scheduler attaches the Initiator to it. In both MFT and MVT, the Master Scheduler can attach up to fifteen Initiators, and each of these Initiators is a subtask of the Master Scheduler.

REENTRANT, REUSABLE AND NON-REUSABLE PROGRAMS

There are many different binary categories into which routines (programs) can be placed—here are a few "either ors": commercial or scientific; application or system problem state or supervisor state; and there are several others. With the advent of multiprogramming it became necessary to develop a tertiary categorization of routines; that is, a routine is either *nonreusable,* or *serially reusable,* or *reentrant.*

A routine that is *nonreusable* is one that is brought into core storage, executed just once, and then becomes useless. Why useless? Because the programmer constructed it in such a way that during execution some of its instructions or constants are changed and then never restored. For each execution a new copy of a nonreusable routine must be brought into main storage.

The nonreusable routine can be made *serially reusable* by having some extra instructions at either its beginning or end; these extra instructions would insure the restoration of the main instructions and constants to their initial state. This is the way most problem or application programmers write their routines. Serially reusable routines work on one unit of I/O data at a time. That is, there is only one set of records being processed at a time; record set $(n + 1)$ does not begin getting processed until record set (n) is finished. Let's say that two or more programmers discover that they can use this routine and that their programs might all be in main storage at the same time. If one copy of the serially reusable routine is in core storage, then each programmer must write an instruction that enqueues upon (gets into the waiting list) the routine when it becomes available. If the routine is popular (that is, it is needed often), then each program will have to do a lot of waiting to use the routine. An alternative which greatly reduces the waiting time, but requires more core storage, is to bring into main storage a copy of the routine for each of the programs. If the routine consists of 250 bytes, this solution may be tolerable; but if each copy of the routine requires several thousand bytes, one may be reluctant to use the multiple-copy alternative.

A *reentrant* routine can be used by any number of programmers, *as soon as they need it.*

To illustrate the concepts of nonreusable, serially reusable and reentrant programs (routines), we will show the coding necessary to calculate a trivial sum:

$$SUM = A + B + C$$

Symbolic Location	Operation	Operands	Comments
BEGIN	CSECT		(CSECT informs the Assembler that a complete section of a symbolic program follows.)
	ADD	SUM1,FACTORA	(Add factor A to SUM1.)
	ADD	SUM1,FACTORB	(Add factor B to SUM1.)
	SUB	SUM1,FACTORC	(Subtract factor C from SUM1.)
	BR	SKIPOVER	(Unconditional branch to instruction named SKIPOVER.)
SUM1	DS	8 BYTES OF SPACE	(Allocate 8 bytes of space and associate with SUM1.)
SUM2	DS	10 BYTES OF SPACE	(Allocate 10 bytes of space and associate with SUM2.)
SKIPOVER	LOAD	SUM2,FACTORD	(Load Factor D into SUM2.)

The above program is an example of a nonreusable code (that is, a nonreusable program). Let's see why.

When the program is translated into machine language by the Assembly Compiler, the symbolic address SUM1 is transformed into a *displacement* from the beginning of the program. SUM1 will be assigned and associated with a storage area of 8 bytes. When the machine language program is brought into core storage for execution, the 8 byte storage area where SUM1 is to accumulate will contain any data that had been stored there from a previous program. The only exception to this is at the beginning of the data processing day, right after the IPL program. (The IPL program sets all core storage positions to blank.) Unless the programmer writes some instructions to assure the presence of zeros in the core storage locations assigned to SUM1, his program will not be usable (to say nothing of it being *reusable*). The programmer could assure first-time usability by changing the *define storage* (DS) operation to a *define constant* (DC) operation; together with the DC operation he would state the value of the constant which in this case would probably be zero.

```
          ADD   SUM1,FACTORA
          ADD   SUM1,FACTORB
          SUB   SUM1,FACTORC
          BR    SKIPOVER
SUM1      DC    8 BYTES OF ZEROS  (allocate 8 bytes of stor-
                                   age and fill with zeros)
SUM2      DC    10 BYTES OF ZEROS (allocate 10 bytes of
                                   storage and fill with
                                   zeros)
SKIPOVER  LOAD  SUM2,FACTORD
```

The above program will work the first time it is executed; during assembly, the Assembler compiler not only allocates 8 bytes of Main Storage space but also provides for eight bytes of zeros. When the program is brought into storage for execution, the *area* assigned to SUM1 will be loaded with zeros.

Although the program will work properly with the first set of factors, it won't for subsequent ones (unless one wants to develop a running total of SUM1's). That is, when the program is processing the second set of factors, SUM1 will already contain a total leftover from processing the first set of factors. Hence the program is not reusable. To make the program reusable for a second set of factors, the program must contain some instructions near its beginning to reduce the contents of SUM1 to zero.

One of the programming techniques used is to subtract the value from itself.

```
          SUB   SUM1,SUM1  Subtract the contents of SUM1
                           from itself
          ADD   SUM1,FACTORA
          ADD   SUM1,FACTORB
          SUB   SUM1,FACTORC
          BR    SKIPOVER
SUM1      DC    8 BYTES OF ZEROS
SUM2      DC    10 BYTES OF ZEROS
SKIPOVER  LOAD  SUM2,FACTORD
```

Now the program is reusable.

Most problem programs are of the serially reusable type. The program generally is used by only one task. If another task needs to use the program, either a second copy is brought in or the program is enqueued upon (put into a wait list). This is not the case, however, for systems programs—that is, the same copy of a system program may be concurrently required by a number of tasks. An example of such a system program is the I/O Supervisor; there is only one I/O supervisor in core storage to service the requirements of all the problem program tasks. The same copy of the I/O Supervisor could very well be concerned with the Input/Output requirements of three, or five, or ten or twenty and more tasks *at the same time:* (If the IOS were serially reusable, each task requiring its use would have to wait until IOS had completely finished servicing the request of the previous task.) How can this be possible? Let's say that the I/O Supervisor, as a result of a request from TASK1 proceeded to the 17th instruction when it discovered it must wait for some event to finish (like the required channel is busy). Since IOS has to wait, its contents of the registers are saved; then the task dispatcher gives CPU control to TASK2.

Now suppose that TASK2 requires the services of IOS right from its beginning. If the first 17 instructions include operations on areas of storage within the program (like SUM1 and SUM2), these areas cannot be *"cleared out."* If they were cleared out, they wouldn't contain the proper information when IOS once again works on TASK1's request. One of the solutions to the problem is to develop the sums outside of the program's storage area. How is this area of main storage obtained? The problem program must make a request to the MSS (Main Storage Supervisor) to get main storage area; he makes the request with a macro instruction called *GETMAIN*. In the program example we've been describing, the programmer would request 18 bytes. When MSS has obtained the 18 bytes, it places the address of the first byte into register 0. Now the programmer writes:

```
GETMAIN    18 bytes
LR         5, 0 (transfer contents of Reg zero to Reg five)
SUB        0(5), 0(5)  [0 (5) means: R5 contains base address and
                        displacement is 0]
ADD        0 (5), FACTORA
ADD        0 (5), FACTORB
SUB        0 (5), FACTORC
  ⋮               ⋮
LOAD       8 (5), FACTORD  [8 (5) means: R5 contains base ad-
  ⋮               ⋮         dress and displacement is 8]
FREEMAIN   18 bytes
```

The last instruction above shows how the programmer releases to MSS the main storage he previously requested but no longer needs.

The program is now *reentrant;* that is, no matter when the program's execution is interrupted (in servicing the request of a task), another task can use the program. Each time a task uses the program, the MSS gets a different block or core storage. Each block's identity is maintained so there is no possibility of an erroneous interchange.

Examples of Reentrant Code; Link Pack Area

Most of the routines in the nucleus are reentrant programs. So are the Access Methods; certain parts of the Initiator/Terminator are also reentrant.

In certain versions of OS, reentrant programs and routines that are not part of the nucleus are placed into a section of main storage called the Link Pack Area.

RESIDENT SVC'S

Previously we talked about several macro instructions that the programmer may use. GET and PUT are used to request the input/output supervisor (IOS) to obtain or dispose of records; GETMAIN and FREEMAIN are used to request the Main Storage Supervisor (MSS) to obtain or release Main Storage; ATTACH is used to request the Task Supervisor to create a subtask (DETACH is used to request the Task Supervisor to no longer recognize a subtask). There are many other macro instructions which the programmer may use; to create input/output buffers, (rather than have it done automatically by the Access Methods), he uses BUILD; to obtain the time of day from Time Supervisor he issues the macro instruction TIME.

Each of the above macro instructions is expanded into a series of machine language instructions the last of which is a specifically numbered SVC (Supervisor Call Instructions). When the SVC instruction is executed it causes an interrupt. The SVC interrupt handling routine identifies the type of SVC after which the appropriate Supervisor program is branched to. The instructions in the supervisor that are executed as the result of a SVC are referred to as *SVC routines.* Many of the SVC routines are permanent parts of the nucleus and are referred to as *resident SVC*'s.

SVCLIB

Resident SVC's come into the nucleus during the IPL procedure. Other SVC routines are required so seldom that to require permanent residence in the nucleus would be an example of poor storage utilization. These SVC routines are kept in a system data set called SYS1.SVCLIB; these SVC routines are referred to as being non-resident. When a non-resident SVC routine is required, it enters into a storage area within the nucleus appropriately called the *transient area.*

JOB CONTROL STATEMENTS

Now that you have become acquainted with some of the concepts and techniques of multiprogramming and the operating system, let us return to the topic of how an installation describes its requirements to the operating system.

Because job control statements are usually punched into cards, they are referred to as *job control cards.* The following are job control cards:

1. The JOB card—identifies the beginning of a job (which consists of one or more job steps).
2. The EXEC card—identifies the program to be executed.
3. The DD cards—describe the data sets and I/O devices required by the program named in the EXEC card.

Why the word *control* in job control cards? The word *control* implies that the initiation and execution of the program in each of the job's steps is going to be controlled by the operating system as to

1. the maximum amount of time the job can remain in main storage after its initiation.
2. the maximum amount of time a task can have the CPU before another program has a turn.
3. whether the Initiator can evict a task of lesser priority to start a program of higher priority.
4. which kind of I/O devices can be used or which specific I/O devices are required.
5. whether a data set either
   a. already exists and is not going to be changed,
   b. already exists but may be modified, or
   c. doesn't exist yet.
6. whether OS is to keep track of the data set for future reference or is to be forgotten.
7. if the data set doesn't exist yet, how much direct-access space is required, or the number of reels of tape.
8. whether a disk pack or tape reel is to be removed after the task has terminated.
9. whether a data set can be used by more than one task at a time.
10. the number of records to be read into storage each time the Access Method determines that input is required.
11. the relative priority of a job (with respect to other jobs).
12. the type or class of job.

Encoded information of each of the sample items above must be part of a JOB statement, EXEC statement, or DD statement.

REDUCING THE NUMBER OF JOB CONTROL CARDS TO BE HANDLED

It is quite likely that the dozens of jobs an installation has to run each day may require several thousand job control cards, which might be in several different file drawers. This necessitates a manual operation of retrieving the control cards in the morning and replacing them in the evening. Many of these jobs are run quite frequently: some every other day, some once a day, and some several times a day. It would certainly be advantageous to have on disk the job control information of frequently used jobs. Hence a scheme was implemented whereby job control information for any job could be kept on disk. Then the question arose of how to refer to specific job control information. The answer was to call each specific group of job control cards a *procedure* and give each procedure a name. Then, instead of punching the name of the program into an EXEC card, you would punch the name of the procedure. When the Reader/Interpreter identifies the contents of the EXEC card as a request for a procedure, the Reader/Interpreter tells the control program to read the procedure. Each of the entries in the procedure is then treated just as though the information had come from the card reader.

Procedures Are Kept in SYS1.PROCLIB

The procedures are kept in a special partitioned data set on disk. This partitioned data set is called SYS1.PROCLIB. Each of the procedures in the library has a name. This name and the beginning track address of the procedure are kept in the directory of the procedure library (i.e., in the directory of SYS1.PROCLIB).

SUMMARY

1. The operating system is a collection of programs written by IBM for a data-processing installation to use in meeting its data-processing responsibilities.
2. The main areas of responsibility of the operating system are the master scheduler, data management, task management, and job management.
3. IBM provides a "kit" with which each installation generates its own operating system. Choosing the parts and putting them together is called system generation.
4. The Supervisor program controls the applications programs' use of the CPU.

5. The Supervisor regains CPU control whenever an application program is interrupted.
6. The five types of interrupt are External, Program, I/O, Supervisor Call, and Machine Check.
7. The I/O Supervisor selects the proper series of channel commands and it issues the Start Input/Output instruction.
8. The Access Method programs inform the I/O Supervisor program that an I/O operation is required.
9. The Application programs request input records from the Access Method programs.
10. The Application programs request the Access Method programs to dispose of output records.
11. The main purpose of the Access Method programs is to tell the application programs where in main storage to get the next input record from or where to put the next output record.
12. Most of the programs (Application and System Tasks) of an installation are kept in a data set library called SYS1.LINKLIB. Conversationally this data set is referred to as LINKLIB.
13. LINKLIB is a partitioned data set.
14. Each program in a library is called a member.
15. The location of each member in a partitioned data set is recorded in the directory of the partitioned data set.
16. A collection of programming language statements is called a subroutine.
17. Popular and commonly used subroutines are recorded in subroutine libraries. Some of these libraries are SYS1.FORTLIB, SYS1.COBLIB, SYS1.PLILIB, and SYS1.SORTLIB.
18. Macro instructions are recorded in SYS1.MACLIB.
19. A volume is a reel of tape, a disk pack, or a drum.
20. The contents of each volume is recorded on the volume. The place where the contents is recorded is called the volume table of contents (VTOC).
21. Once a program has been brought in storage for execution, the program is referred to as a task.
22. The Initiator program is responsible for determining the availability of resources required for data-processing programs. The major resources are main storage, I/O devices, and data sets and volumes.
23. To perform its function the Initiator needs to know the name and the I/O requirements of the program.
24. The name of the program and its requirements must be recorded in SYS1.SYSJOBQE before the Initiator can perform its task.
25. A program called the Reader/Interpreter records the program name and its I/O requirements on SYS1.SYSJOBQE (JOBQE).
26. The Initiator and the Reader/Interpreter are called System Tasks.
27. The program name is provided to the Reader/Interpreter in an EXEC statement.

28. The program's I/O requirements are provided to the Reader/Interpreter in a DD statement.
29. The program to be executed and its I/O requirements make up a job step.
30. A job is a series of related job steps.
31. One job is separated from another job with a job statement (job card).
32. A collection of assembled jobs is called a job stream.
33. Jobs should be classified according to the resources they require. Examples of resources are amount of CPU time, number of I/O devices, types of data sets, and amount of main storage.
34. Jobs are recorded in JOBQE according to their class code.
35. Initiators are permitted to select jobs according to the job's class code.
36. Output data sets are recorded on direct-access storage devices. When the eventual output device is available, an Output Writer transcribes the data set from direct-access storage to the device.
37. Output data sets are categorized according to classes.
38. Main storage is divided into a fixed area and a dynamic area. The Supervisor resides in the fixed area. Application programs, Initiators, Readers, and Writers reside in the dynamic area.
39. The dynamic area of an MFT-II system is subdivided into sections called partitions. The dynamic area of an MVT system is divided into sections called regions.
40. In an MVT system, an application task can "initiate" a subtask. Application tasks cannot "initiate" subtasks in an MFT-II system.
41. The EXEC and DD cards of a job step may be recorded as a procedure in a partitioned data set called SYS1.PROCLIB.
42. The Supervisors that reside in the fixed area of main storage make up the Nucleus. The Nucleus is the first part of the operating system that enters storage at the beginning of the data-processing cycle. The Nucleus is recorded in a special data set called SYS1.NUCLEUS.
43. Each module of a program may call upon, and be called upon by, another module. In the first case the module is referred to as the *calling;* in the latter case as the *called.*
44. Modular programming requires each programmer to provide an area of storage in his own module where the contents of the sixteen registers can be saved (when he gives up control of the CPU). The preservation of the calling programmer's registers is the responsibility of the called programmer. The called programmer fulfills his responsibility by issuing the SAVE macro. He restores the registers for the calling programmer by issuing the RETURN macro.
45. Uniprogramming means that there is only one problem program in core under the control of the supervisor.
46. The version of OS/360 that supports uniprogramming is called PCP (Primary Control Program).

47. The collection of the Reader/Interpreter, Initiator/Terminator and the Output Writer are referred to as the Job Scheduler.
48. The Job Scheduler used in a PCP environment is called the Sequential Scheduler. The one used in either an MFT or MVT environment is called the Priority Scheduler.
49. The objects managed by each of the Supervisors are called resources. Examples of resources are: input/output devices, data sets, direct access storage space, programs that are part of the operating system, and main storage and the CPU.
50. When a task requests the use of a resource, a record of the request is made; the record is referred to as a block.
51. The blocks (records) of successive requests for a resource are chained together according to some rule of priority.
52. The TCB (Task Control Block) of each task is used to keep track of the task's status.
53. Requests for a resource are recorded in an RB (Request Block).
54. To create a subtask, the parent task must issue the ATTACH macro, along with the name of the program that is to become the subtask.
55. The hierarchy of tasks is: Master Scheduler, Initiator/Terminator, Problem Program task, Problem Program subtask, Problem Program sub-subtask, and so on. (In PCP and MFT there is only one level of Problem Program task.)
56. Before a module can use a serially reusable program which it has called, the module must wait until the program has finished processing the data for which it is currently responsible.
57. Each time a reentrant program is executed, it obtains a fresh supply of storage in which the reentrant program stores its results.
58. A module that calls for the use of a reentrant program does not have to wait for the reentrant program to finish its current processing responsibility. A reentrant program can be entered at any time.
59. The Access Methods, parts of the Initiator/Terminator, and most of the routines in the Nucleus (such as the supervisors) are reentrant programs.
60. Reentrant programs that are not part of the Nucleus are kept in a section of main storage called the LPA (Link Pack Area).
61. Many macro instructions expand into a series of machine language instructions the last of which is an SVC. Each uniquely identified SVC calls upon a program referred to as an SVC routine.
62. Resident SVC's are a prominent part of the Nucleus.
63. Nonresident SVC routines are recorded in SVCLIB.
64. When a nonresident SVC routine is required, it enters into a storage area of the Nucleus named the transient area.
65. Mechanical and electronic malfunctions of the S/360 are recorded on a data set named SYS1.LOGREC.

SUGGESTED READING ASSIGNMENT

IBM System/360 Operating System MFT GUIDE (C27-6939)

IBM System/360 Operating System MVT Control Program Logic Summary (Y28-6658)

7 DATA MANAGEMENT

You will recall that there are three main management areas in the operating system—task, job, and data. The management area that programmers are mostly concerned with is data management, for if the operating system doesn't have all the information it needs to obtain or create a data set, the program to process the data won't get started. Before the operating system can begin a task it must have answers to many questions. Here are *some* of the questions:

1. Does the data set already exist or is it going to be created? (New or old?)
2. If a new data set is to be created, how much direct-access storage space, or how many reels of tape, will be required?
3. What is the name of the data set?
4. What is the identification (serial number) of the volume on which the data set resides?
5. What kind of input or output device should be used?
6. Are the records blocked or unblocked?
7. If the data set already exists on a direct-access storage device, will it be needed again? (If not, the space it used can be reclaimed for a new data set.) (Keep or delete?)

There are many other questions which have to be answered. However, before the above questions are answered and before any more questions are asked, it will be helpful to review and expand upon the topics related to data and its management.

REVIEW OF DATA

1. Data is information that is to be processed.
2. The information about a particular object is called a logical record.
3. Each item of a logical record is called a field.
4. The length of a logical record may be fixed, variable, or undefined.
5. All the logical records of a collection of similar objects are called a data set.
6. Data sets to be processed by tasks under the control of the operating system must have names.
7. Rapid retrieval of data set records is possible when the data set is recorded on magnetic tape, magnetic disks, or magnetic drums.
8. Digits, letters, and symbols that make up the data are encoded. The main codes are BCD, EBCDIC, and card.
9. Data sets may be organized
   a. sequentially.
   b. randomly (direct).
   c. sequentially with indexes (indexed sequentially).
   d. in order by arrival and with a directory (partitioned).
10. Data must be in main storage to be processed by the CPU.

REVIEW OF MEDIA ON WHICH DATA IS RECORDED

1. Most recorded data exists in punched cards, on reels of magnetic tape, on magnetic disk packs, and on magnetic drums.
2. Each magnetic tape reel contains one continuous ribbon of tape.
3. A physical record consists of all the data that is recorded between two inter-record gaps.
4. Any number of logical records between gaps is called a physical record.
5. Data can be magnetically recorded on seven- or nine-track tape.
6. Data on disk and drum is recorded in EBCDIC.
7. The recording surface of disks and drums is divided into tracks.
8. A disk track may contain more than one physical record.
9. The number of tracks that can be read without moving the Access mechanism is called a cylinder.
10. Punched cards can accommodate up to 80 characters of data (digits, letters, and symbols). Stub cards that can accommodate up to 51 characters also exist.

REVIEW OF I/O DEVICES

1. Input data is read by an input device; output data is recorded on output devices.
2. Some I/O devices share control units; other I/O devices have their own, private control unit.
3. The numerical name of the most popular IBM tape unit is 2400.
4. The numerical names of the various disk units are 2311, 2314, and 2302.
5. The numerical name of the most popular card reader punch is 2540.
6. The numerical name of the most popular printer is 1403.
7. All data to and from I/O devices passes through a channel.
8. A multiplexor channel is used with slow-speed devices; selector channels are used with high-speed devices.
9. Each I/O device has a physical address consisting of three hexadecimal characters. The leftmost character identifies the channel, the center character identifies the control unit, and the rightmost character identifies the specific device.

REVIEW OF ACCESS METHODS

1. The instructions and commands needed to control the access of input and output data are supplied by IBM. A collection of these instructions and commands is called an Access Method.
2. The Access Methods and the data set organization with which they are used are:
   a. Sequential Access Method—the sequential reading or writing of records no matter how they may be stored.
   b. Indexed Sequential Access Method—the reading and writing of records that have their storage addresses located in an index.
   c. Direct Access Method—the reading and writing of records that have been stored according to some relationship between their identification field and a physical location on a direct-access device.
   d. Partitioned Access Method—for accessing records (i.e., reading and writing records) for small collections of records that have been stored in the sequence in which they arrived. The location of where the record has been stored is placed in the *directory* of the data set. The identification fields in the directory are in sequence.
   e. Teleprocessing Access Method—for accessing records that are transmitted over facilities provided by common carriers (telephone and telegraph companies).

f. Graphics Access Method—for accessing records that are displaced on devices with television-like screens.

HOW THE PROGRAMMER COMMUNICATES WITH THE ACCESS METHODS

1. Programmers inform the Access Method that they want an input record by using a GET or READ instruction. The Programmers use PUT or WRITE to inform the Access Method that they have produced an output record.
2. Programmers use GET and PUT when they want to use multiple input/output areas, (buffers) and have the Access Method control the filling and emptying of these buffers. Because this Access Method may have many records *waiting* in main storage (to be processed or written), we say that it is the *queued* version of the Access Method.
3. When programmers want to control the filling and emptying of buffers without assistance of an Access Method, they use the READ and WRITE instructions. This is the *basic* version of the Access Method.
4. The Access Methods that have a queued version are Sequential, Indexed Sequential, and Teleprocessing (QSAM, QISAM, and QTAM).
5. The Access Methods that have a basic version are Sequential, Indexed Sequential, Teleprocessing, Direct, Partitioned, and Graphics [BSAM, BISAM, BTAM, BPAM, and GAM (no B)].
6. When an Access Method determines that an input or output operation is required, the Access Method calls on the Input/Output Supervisor for assistance.

OS DATA-RETRIEVAL SCHEMES

The data set requirements for the company we described earlier might be as follows:

1. 39 data sets on direct-access disk packs and drums
   a. 20 system data sets (e.g., LINKLIB, COBLIB, SORTLIB, PROCLIB, JOBQE)
   b. 4 large-application data sets (e.g., Product Inventory, Engineering Drawings)
   c. 14 small-application data sets, consisting mostly of mathematical tables.
   d. Space for temporary data sets. The number and size of these data sets depends upon different programs' requirements for intermediate results.
2. About 220 data sets on magnetic tape. In some instances it takes many tape volumes to record one data set. In other cases, up to five or six data sets may be recorded on one tape volume.

Recording a Data Set's Location in a Catalog

Many of the 258 data sets on which the data is recorded are referred to on a periodic basis. (For some, the period is daily, weekly, or monthly; for others, especially system data sets, the reference can be as frequent as several times per job step.) As you know, before a task begins it must have been informed of a data set's residence. That is, the answers to the following questions must be provided.

1. What is the name of the data set?
2. What is the serial number of the volume on which the data set resides?
3. What type of device does the volume require?

The answers must be provided so that the Initiator can find the data set for the processing task. The information, reflected by the answers to these three questions, must be made available to the Initiator in a DD card.

When an installation has data sets that will be referenced over and over, it seems that a great deal of keypunching time could be saved if one didn't have to punch the volume serial number and device type into a DD card every time the data set was to be used in a job step. The technique for providing the required information of device type and volume serial number without punching it into a DD card is called *cataloging.* The activity of cataloging (a verb) is associated with a data set called a *catalog.* The official name of the catalog is SYSCTLG (the only known pronounciation for this collection of letters is sis catalog). The catalog of the operating system contains the data set name, the volume serial number, and the device type on which the volume is to reside. When a data set has been cataloged, it is not necessary to place the device type or volume serial number into the DD card (only the data set name is required). When only the data set name is provided, the Initiator assumes the rest of the required information is in the catalog (Fig. 83).

DATA SET NAME	VOL IDENTIFICATION (i.e. serial number)	DEVICE TYPE
SYS1.COBLIB	KLC001	2311
SYS1.FORTLIB	KLC001	2311
SYS1.LINKLIB	KAC002	2311
SYS1.MACLIB	KLC001	2311
SYS1.NUCLEUS	KLC001	2311

Fig. 83 OS catalog schematic.

Qualifying Data Set Names

A classification system for data sets has been developed so that reference to them can be simplified. As an example, it is convenient to distinguish those data sets that are part of the operating system (program libraries, procedure library) from those containing application records (employee master data set, insurance policy master data set). Operating system data sets are usually referred to as *system* data sets, and application data sets are usually called *user* data sets. It might happen that a system data set has the same name as a user data set. To avoid the possibility of confusion, the operating system allows names to be qualified. For example, most of the system data sets talked about in this book have been qualified to one level with the characters *SYS1.* (SYS1.PROCLIB, SYS1.LINKLIB). Although most system data sets are qualified to only one level, as many levels of qualification as necessary may be used. Several levels of qualification are common with user data sets. For example, Fig. 84 shows two data sets named XPENS. To refer to a specific XPENS, one would write

USER.ADVTZNG.XPENS

or

USER.SALES.XPENS

whichever is appropriate.

As another example, USER.ADVTZNG.XPENS refers to the data set of expense records for the advertising department; USER.ADVTZING.CARRIERS refers to the data set containing the names of newspapers, magazines, radio stations, and television stations that advertise the company's products; USER.SALES.XPENS refers to the data set of expense records for the sales department. The categorization of the data sets we have mentioned so far can be shown by index level, as illustrated in Fig. 84.

Relationship of Catalog to VTOC

Let's get back to the Initiator's function of locating a data set requested in a DD card. Let's say that the catalog (or DD card) has revealed to the Initiator the device type and serial number of the volume on which the data set resides. Since it is quite possible that the volume's contents consists of many data sets, it will be necessary for the operating system to look at the VTOC. To find out where the VTOC is, the operating system looks at the volume label (see Fig. 85). After determining from the label where the VTOC can be found, the location of the data set on the volume can be determined. In some instances, a data set may be so large that only part of it is on one volume—in that case the volume contains less than one data set. In general, however, a volume contains several data sets; it is not uncommon for a disk volume to contain 20 or more data sets. For each of the data sets on the volume, there will be *at least* one entry in the VTOC. Each entry describes, in coded form, information about the data set that is required by the operating system. For example, if there are 3 data sets on the volume there will be *at least* three entries in the VTOC; if there are 20 data sets, there will be at least 20 entries in the VTOC. Each individual entry in the VTOC is called a *data set*

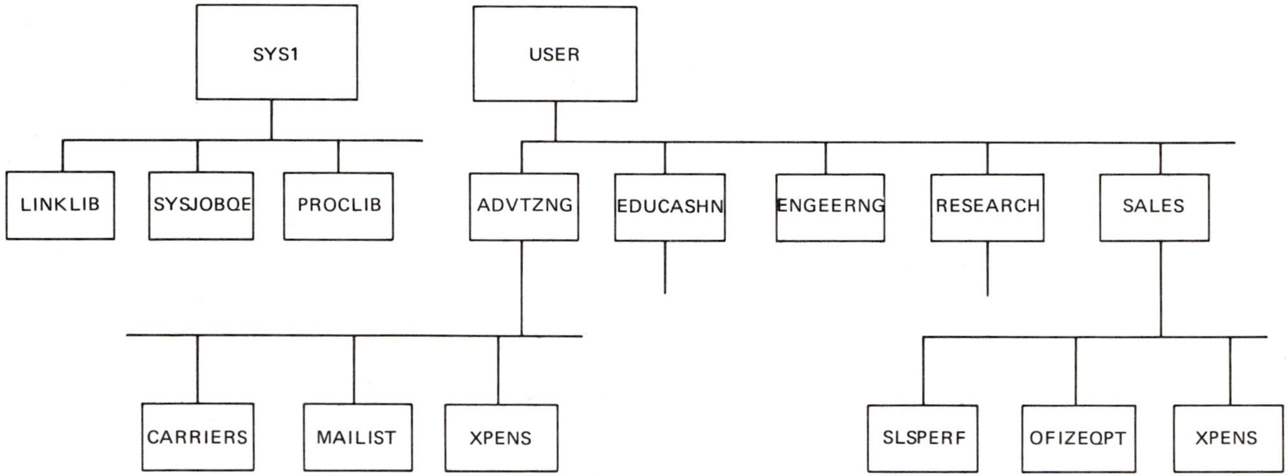

This figure schematically illustrates the levels of index for qualified names. Note that all of the indexes of the second level USER have a lower level except ENGEERNG. Thus USER. ENGERRNG refers to a data set whereas USER.SALES refers to nothing (another level of qualification is needed to specify the required data set).

Fig. 84 Levels of index for qualified names.

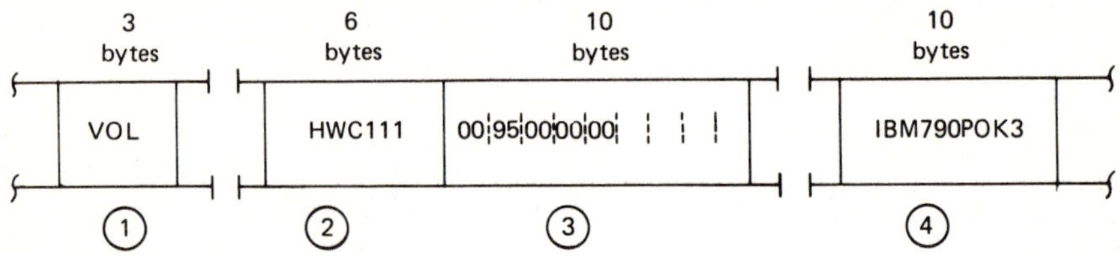

1. This is the first field of the volume label. It consists of the three letters VOL.
2. This is the volume serial number. It consists of six alphameric characters.
3. 0095 is the cylinder address,
   0000 is the track address,
   00 is the record number within the track of the beginning of the VTOC
   These ten hexadecimal characters (5 bytes) are followed by 5 blank bytes.
4. This is the name and address code of the installation that owns the disk pack.

Fig. 85 Volume label contents.

control block (DSCB). In this DSCB will be such information as the name of the data set, the date when the space for the data set was first allocated, the date after which the data set may be destroyed, and the track address of where on the volume the data set begins (see Fig. 86).

Some additional information may be

1. how the data set is organized (sequentially, direct, etc.).
2. type of record length (fixed, variable, etc.)
3. size (length) of physical records.
4. size of logical record.

TYPES OF ENTRIES IN VTOC

DSCB's—Formats 1 and 3

In the last paragraph we stated that there will be *at least* one DSCB in the VTOC for a data set. It would seem then that there may be conditions in which it is possible to have more than one DSCB for a data set. From Fig. 86 we can calculate that the amount of space for the data set TEST.DATA is 15 *contiguous* cylinders (or 150 tracks). Suppose, however, that the amount of space requested for TEST.DATA had been *70 cylinders* and that although this amount of space was available on the disk pack, not more than 16 cylinders are available in one contiguous batch or extent. Now we certainly would not want the Initiator to say it could not allocate 70 cylinders for the data set just because the available spaces weren't contiguous. Therefore, the Initiator *does* allocate 70 cylinders. And if,

VTOC entry for the Data Set TEST.DATA Stored on a 2311 Disk Pack

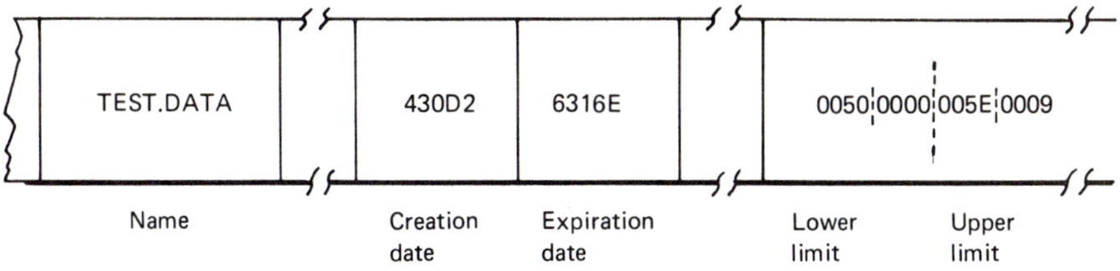

Name - There are 44 positions available for the name of a data set. Nine positions are used for TEST.DATA.

Creation date - The date on which the data was created. The first two digits (hexadecimal) represent the year (43 in hex is equivalent to 67 in decimal). The last three digits (also hexadecimal) represent the day of the year (0D2 in hex is equivalent to 210 in decimal and the 210th day of 1967 is July 29).

Expiration date - The date after which the data set may be "scratched" or deleted so that the disk space the data set occupies may be used for other, new data sets.

Lower limit - The cylinder (0050) and track (0000) in hexadecimal of where the data set begins.

Upper limit - The cylinder (005E) and track (0009) in hexadecimal of where the data set may end.

NOTE:

The amount of space calculated by taking the difference between the upper and lower limits, *is contiguous*. That is, each track of the data set is *adjacent to* the next track of the same data set.

Fig. 86 VTOC entry schematic.

for example, the extents or batches of available space consist of 15, 12, 14, 10, 12, and 16 cylinders, respectively, the Initiator will allocate all of the first five extents (for 63 cylinders) and seven cylinders of the last extent to round out the request for 70 cylinders. Since there now are six different extents there will have to be six lower and upper limits shown for the data set. Figure 86 illustrates part of a DSCB in which are recorded the data set name, some dates, and *one* lower and upper limit. If more parts of this DSCB were illustrated, you would see that it contained the lower and upper limits of two or more extents for a total of three (Fig. 87). Since this DSCB can record only three extents, we'll need another DSCB in the VTOC for recording the remaining extents. Now the operating system will have to know where in the VTOC this next DSCB is located. Therefore, the *first* DSCB for the data set will state where the next DSCB is. This is illustrated in Fig.

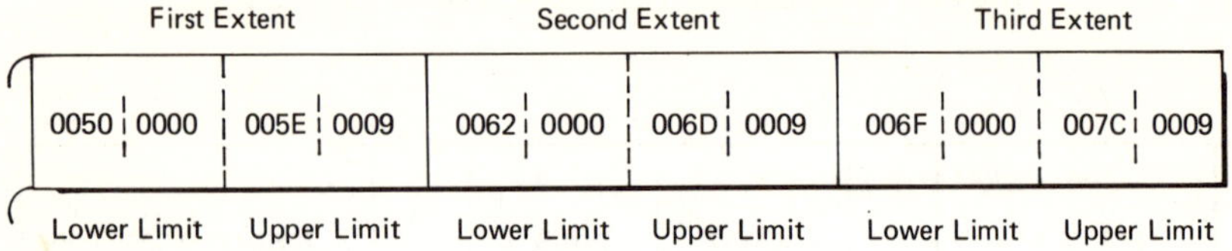

This figure is an extension of the right-hand end of Figure 86. It shows the lower and upper limits of the extents for 15, 12 and 14 cylinders respectively for the data set named TEST.DATA.

Fig. 87 Three extents.

88. What does the remaining-extents DSCB look like? First, let's say what it does not contain. It does not contain the data set name or the creation and expiration date. Its main purpose is to contain the upper and lower limits of the extents that don't fit into the main DSCB. The maximum number of extents that this DSCB can describe is 13 (see Fig. 89).

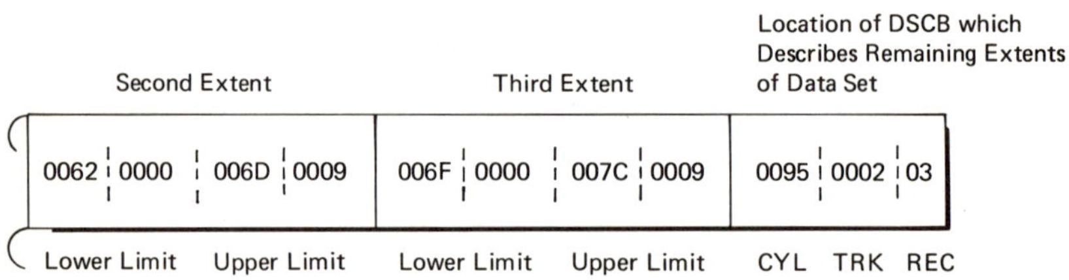

This figure is an extension of the right-hand end of Figure 86. It shows that the location of the DSCB which describes the remaining extents of the data set called "TEST.DATA" is the third record of the second track of the 95th cylinder.

Fig. 88 Recording location of next DSCB.

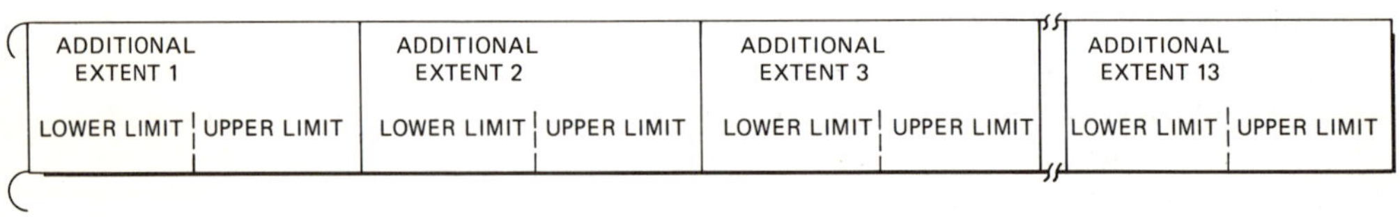

This type of DSCB describes up to 13 additional extents that cannot be described in the main DSCB.

Fig. 89 Format 3 DSCB.

We have just described two types of DSCB's. The main DSCB, which contains such information as the data set's name, the creation date, and expiration date is called a *Format 1* DSCB. The DSCB that contains the upper and lower limits of up to 13 overflow extents is called a *Format 3* DSCB.

DSCB for Available Space—Format 5

When a data set is deleted, the space that had been allocated to it is returned to the free-space inventory. In general, this *free space* is referred to as available space (i.e., available for allocation to NEW data sets). During the course of a period of data-processing time (where a period of time may be a few minutes to several days) there may be many requests by the Initiator for disk space interspersed with many "givings up" by the terminator of disk space no longer needed. To keep an accounting of the extents of available space, there is a special format of DSCB. It is referred to as a *Format 5* DSCB (see Fig. 90). So far we have talked

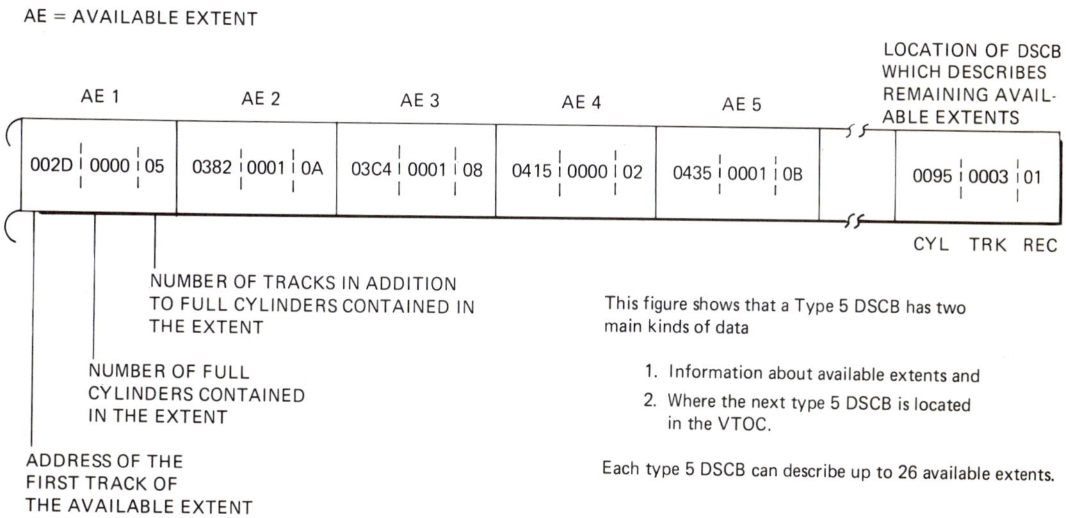

Fig. 90 Format 5 DSCB.

about three DSCB's—Formats 1, 3, and 5. Figure 91 illustrates how this variety of DSCB's might appear in a VTOC.

DSCB for the VTOC—Format 4

Since the VTOC consists of *data* which describes data sets, the VTOC is *itself* referred to as a data set. Hence the VTOC must also have a DSCB to describe its extent (notice that we said extent and not extents; all the records of the VTOC *must* be contiguous). The DSCB that describes the VTOC is referred to as *Format 4* DSCB (see Fig. 92). Figure 93 shows that the first DSCB in a VTOC is a type 4 and that the second DSCB is a type 5—the third and subsequent will be some order

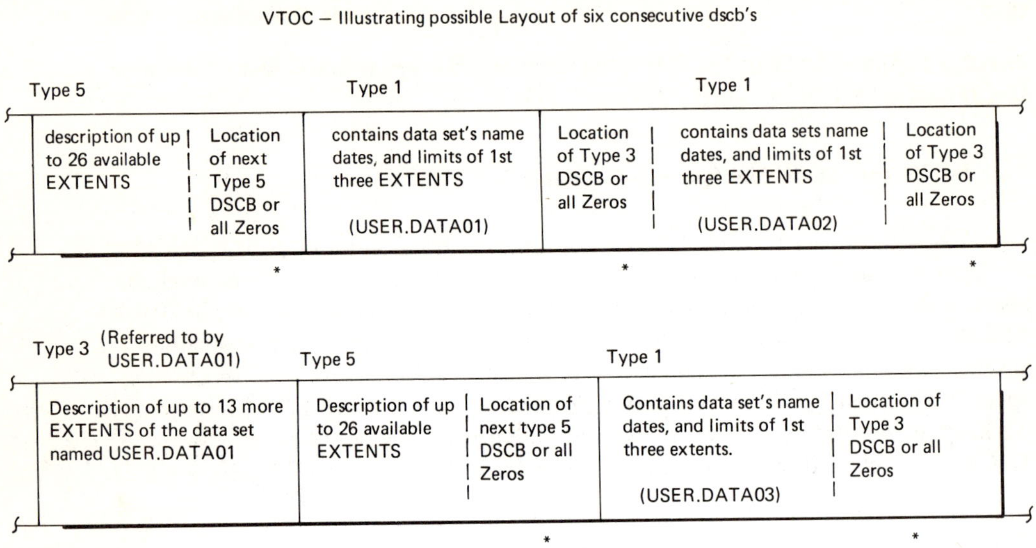

* This figure illustrates that if a continuation of a Type 5 or Type 1 DSCB is <u>not</u> needed, the <u>area</u> reserved for location of next DSCB contains zeros.

Fig. 91 VTOC schematic with various DSCB's.

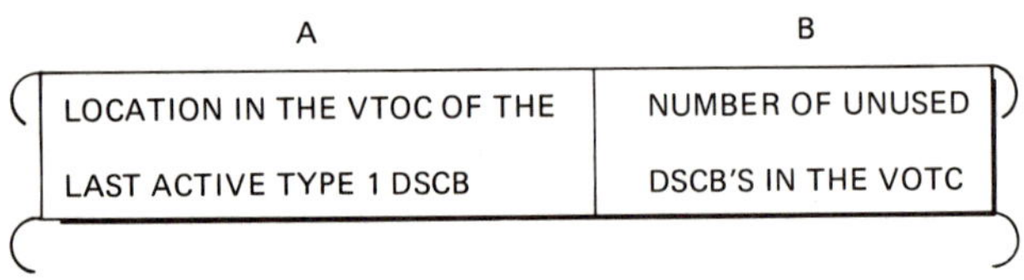

This figure shows two of the main information fields in a Type 4 DSCB. Whenever a DSCB for a NEW data set is created, the value in B is decreased by one. Whenever a data set is deleted, its data set control block is also deleted and the value in B is increased by one.

Fig. 92 Format 4 DSCB.

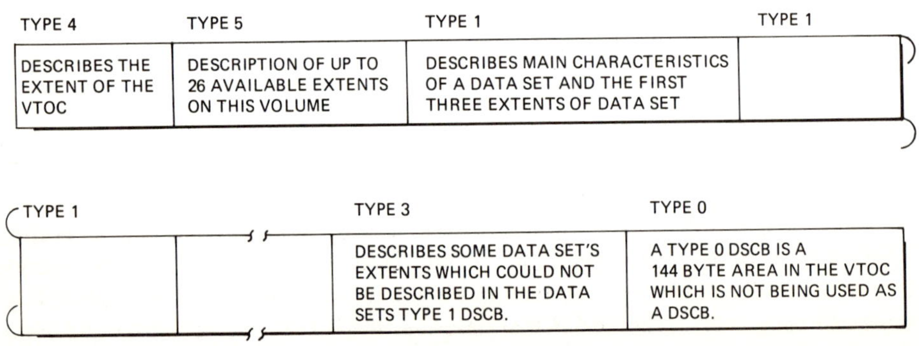

Fig. 93 Various format DSCB's in VTOC.

of types 1, 3, and 5. Also note that *available* DSCB's are referred to as *Format 0* DSCB's.

Number of DSCB's in a VTOC

The amount of space allocated for a disk pack's VTOC is accomplished with a program called DASDI (direct-access storage device initialization). Let us say that an installation requires one cylinder (10 tracks) for the VTOC of a particular disk pack. How many DSCB's can a VTOC of 10 tracks accommodate? The answer is 150. (Each DSCB is 144 bytes long and is considered to be one record. Since DSCB records are unblocked, 15 of them can be accommodated on one 2311 track.)

DESCRIBING A DATA SET AND SPECIFYING ACCESS METHOD INFORMATION

Certain characteristics of a data set (especially new ones about to be created) are often described by the programmer within his program. (If he doesn't supply them in his program they will have to be supplied before the program is executed.) In addition, the programmer also specifies certain information required by the Access Methods whose service he will use. Some of the information the programmer might specify are

1. data set organization (e.g., sequential)
2. type of I/O device (magnetic tape, printer, disk, etc.)
3. Access Method (GET, i.e., queued)
4. record form (e.g., fixed length and blocked)
5. number of bytes required per block (e.g., 400)
6. length of each record (e.g., 100 bytes)
7. number of buffers required (e.g., 3)
8. length of each buffer (e.g., 400 bytes)

DATA CONTROL BLOCK

The place in his program where the Assembly language programmer lists such information as the eight preceding items is called a *data control block*. [High-level language programmers (FORTRAN, COBOL, etc.) don't use a data control block as such. Rather, they state the data management requirements in some other way. Then, during the compilation process this information is brought together into a list similar to the one prepared by the Assembly language programmer.] It is called a data control block because the information about the *data* is kept together (making up a *block of information*), and because the information is going to *control* the I/O functions.

Naming the DCB

The programmer, in addition to *listing* certain items of information about the data in his program's data control block, must also *name* the data control block. Figure 94 shows how a programmer using the Assembly language would name and code the eight items of information.

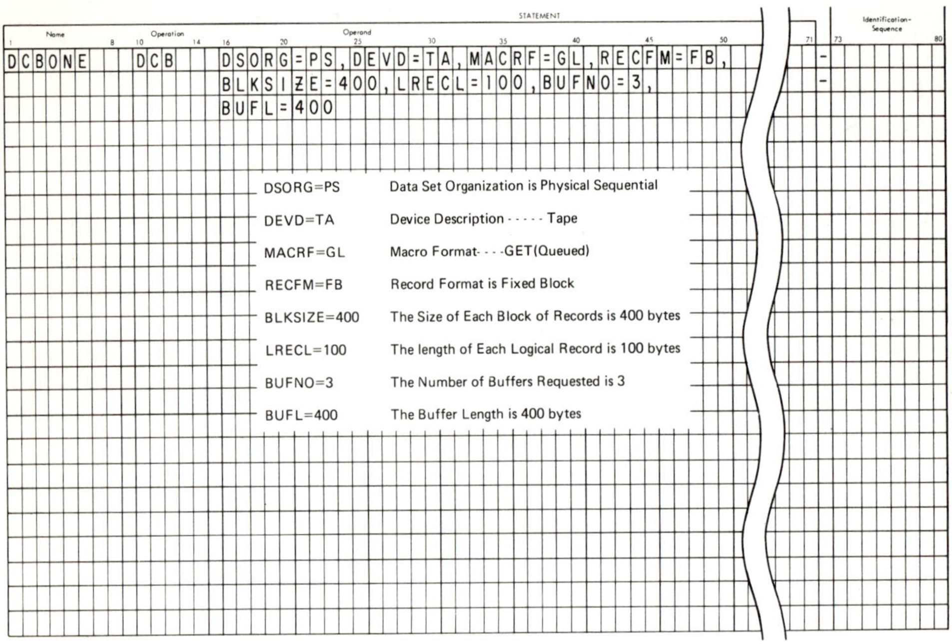

Fig. 94 Programmer's recording of DCB.

CHANGING ACCESS METHOD REQUIREMENTS

On several previous occasions we've mentioned that a company may have several S/360's, each with a different amount of core storage. When such a situation exists and the company wants to process a data set on a S/360 with a different core size, it may be advisable to change the number of input and output buffers in core storage. Assume that the S/360 on which a particular job is normally run has 512K of core storage—hence core storage is relatively abundant and a request for 4 to 5 input buffers of 500 bytes each might not be considered extravagant. The alternate S/360, however, may have only 256K of core, where one could afford, at most, two input buffers.

One of the ways that the installation could respond to such a situation is to compile two separate programs—one in which the number of buffers (BUFNO) in the DCB requested in *5*, and one in which the number requested is *2*. This solution unfortunately, has several drawbacks. The major drawbacks are:

1. Each of the otherwise identical programs needs to be stored separately.
2. Each program needs a separate name.

When the operating system was being designed it was realized that an installation might want to change, among other things, the number of buffers requested. It was therefore decided that this and certain other information shouldn't have to be stated until the job (of which the program is a part) was ready to be put into the job stream. In other words, it was decided that a lot of information doesn't have to be determined and written by the problem programmer.

Placing DCB Information into the DD Card

The information (such as number of buffers) that can be supplied just prior to job execution time should be punched into a DD card. Figure 95 shows the information required for requesting three buffers.

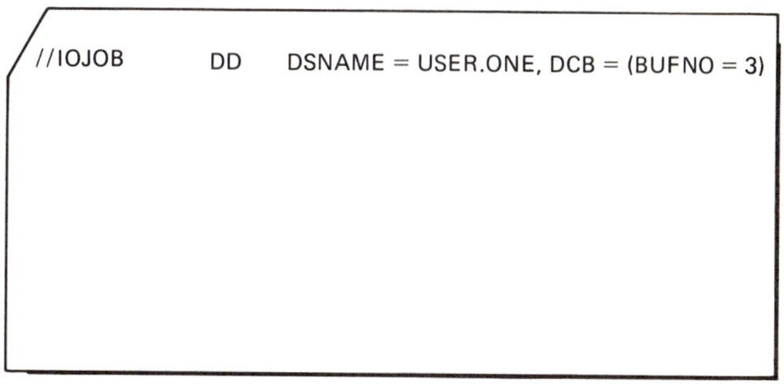

Fig. 95 Sample information in a DD card.

Some of the other changes an installation might wish to make are

1. writing on a seven-track tape instead of a nine-track tape.
2. writing output with three records per block instead of five records per block.
3. writing on a tape whose recording density is 800 bpi instead of 556 bpi.

All these changes can be effected through the use of the DD card only if the programmer has fulfilled his responsibility. That is, only if the programmer leaves the appropriate DCB field blank in his program will the information supplied in the DD card become effective.

Linking DCB's and DD Cards Together

With certain data-processing applications it is quite possible that a programmer may process three differently organized data sets. When this is the case, he'll probably require three different Access Methods. For each of these Access Methods, he'll have to write a DCB. For each of the data sets, the installation needs a DD card. Now the question is: If some of the DCB information for an Access Method has to be given in a DD card, how does the operating system *know* which DD card and DCB are related? This problem is solved by informing the problem programmer of the name of the DD card. The programmer then must write this DD name in the DCB of his program (see Fig. 96). Then, at some time prior to the problem

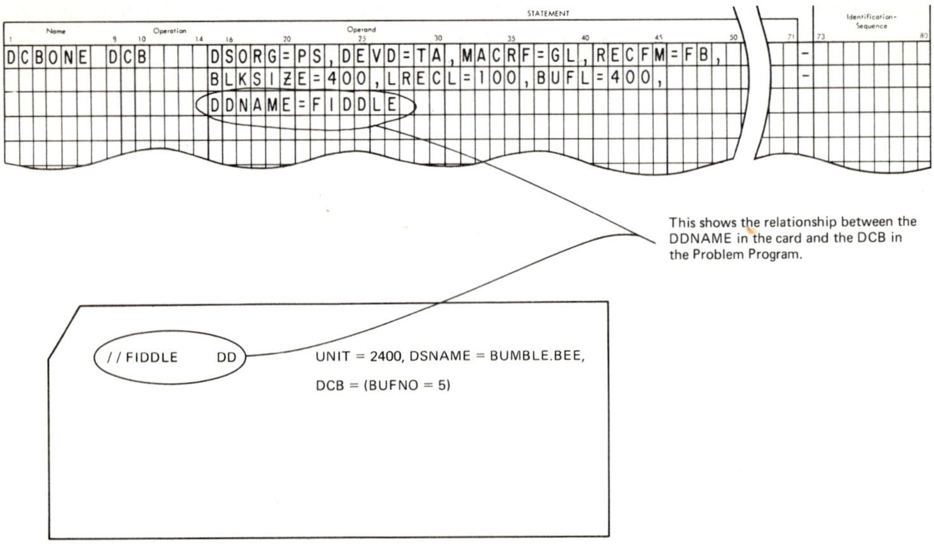

Fig. 96 Providing the relationship between DD statement name and DCB.

program's execution, the related DCB information is automatically merged together by the operating system.

Device Independence

One of the more impressive features of the S/360 operating system is that most programmers don't have to be concerned about the I/O devices their programs are to use. For example, it may be the responsibility of a programmer to update records of a data set that has been recorded on a reel of tape. In his program he would process and arrange all the data according to the format that has been specified. Suppose, though, that the tape drive for receiving the updated data set is in the process of being maintained but that a disk pack and disk drive are available. All that the installation has to do is prepare a DD card to reflect the device changes and to request the required amount of disk space (see Fig. 97). Of course, the installation also has to have an appropriate DD card when this data set will be used as input.

```
// DDCARD1      DD      UNIT=2400,DSNAME=USER.OUTPUT,
                        DISP = (NEW,KEEP),LABEL = (,SL),
                        VOLUME = SER = TAPE01
```

1. Shown above is the DD Card normally used for allocating a tape volume. The term "LABEL = (, SL)" means that the Label of this data set has a standard format.

```
// DD CARD1     DD      UNIT = 2311,DSNAME = USER.OUTPUT,
                        SPACE = (TRK,(50,5)),DISP = (NEW,KEEP)
```

2. Shown above are some changes required to have the data set written on disk. The unit must be different and a request for space must be added.

Fig. 97 Sample changes for DD statement.

RETRIEVING A SPECIFIC GENERATION OF A DATA SET

Many companies have master files which are updated on a periodic basis. This is particularly true of their payroll data set, which is usually updated on a periodic basis (weekly, biweekly, or semimonthly). The main input for the update process is the previous period's output data set. Figure 98 illustrates the original creation of the master file and the update process over a three-week basis. Each week at the end of the processing run, the master file data set that was the input is placed into a

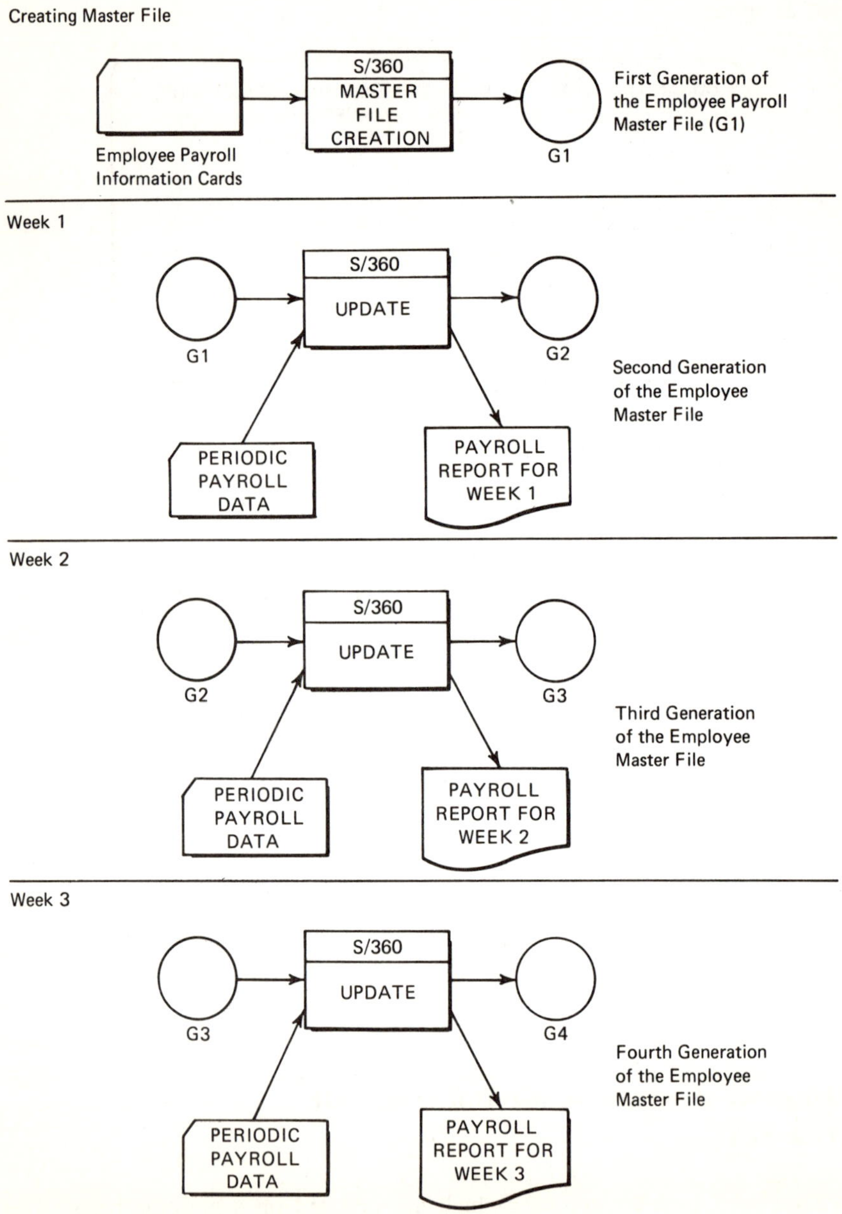

Fig. 98 Three-week processing cycle.

tape vault for safekeeping. Depending upon such factors as state and local laws and company policy, the data-processing department will have many generations of the master file data set in the tape vault.

Naming Related Data Sets

Let us assume that the company which pays its employees on a weekly basis keeps 52 generations (one year's worth) of the employee master file in the tape vault. Suppose that a question arises about several employees' pay records for a particular period during the past year. It will be necessary to retrieve the proper tape volume and then print out the required records (under control of the operating system, of course). The DD card required for allocating the data set would have to have punched in it, the data set name, device type, and volume serial number. Of course, if the data set were cataloged, the DD card would require only the DS name. Of course (from what you've learned so far) when 52 data sets are cataloged, there will be 52 entries in the catalog.

As you can see, cataloging each new generation with a unique data set name would be quite inconvenient—you would have to be sure that duplicate names weren't used. There would also be the problem of uncataloging the fifty-third generation each week. To eliminate these little nuisances, there has been designed into the operating system a special cataloging facility that allows a collection of chronologically related data sets to be called by a single name. To distinguish one generation from another, the operating system assigns a generation number. For example, the collection of payroll data sets could be given the group name of YRTODATE.PAYROLL. As soon as a new updated master file has been prepared, it will be regarded by data management as the current generation and will be assigned the number of its generation, e.g., G007 (pronounced gee zero zero seven). In addition to the generation number, it was decided to provide a *version* number also. That is, if a particular generation of a data set has to have some of its records replaced (corrections may have to be made) it would be a good idea to keep a record of this. Hence, a version number is suffixed onto the generation number. For example, the first version of the fifth generation of the master payroll data set would be referred to as YRTODATE.PAYROLL (G0004V00) and the second version of the fifth generation would be YRTODATE.PAYROLL (G0004V01). The third generation would be referenced as YRTODATE.PAYROLL (G0002-V00). Figure 99 illustrates the special cataloging facility for a group of generation data sets.

Relative Generation Number

It may have already occurred to you that punching up a DD card with something like *G0001V00* is cumbersome and awkward. To make it easier to refer to a particular generation in a DD card, the operating system recognizes YRTODATE.-

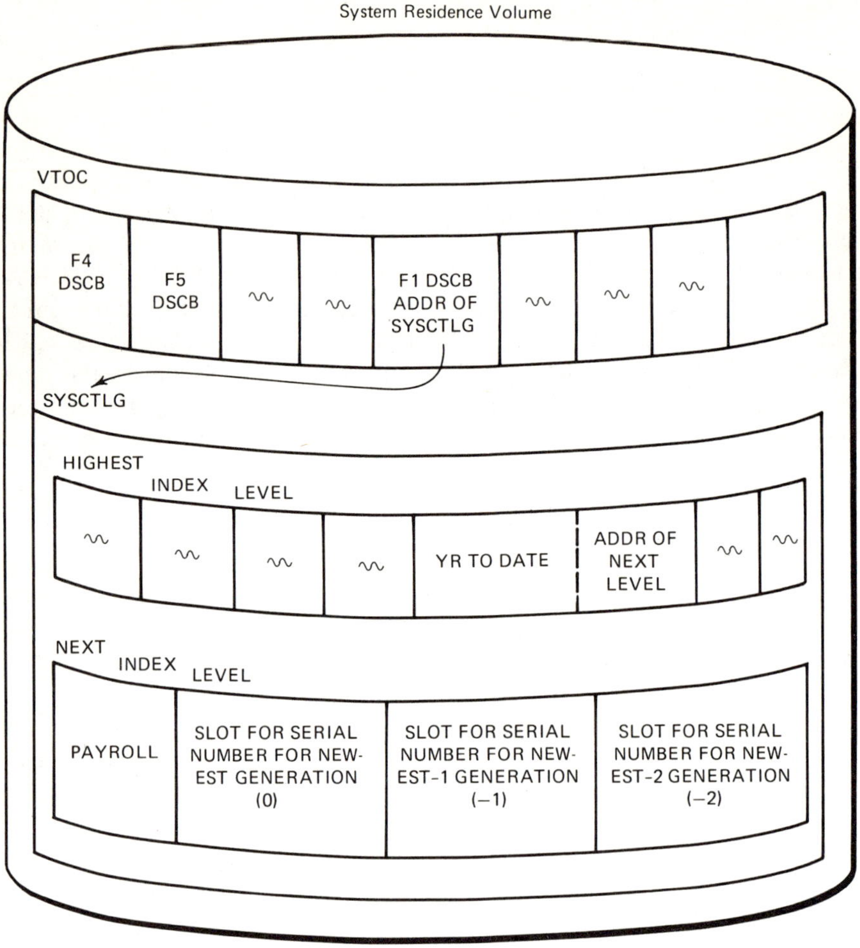

This figure illustrates how the "VTOC" is used to find the catalog. Once the catalog is found, the index levels are searched until the lowest level is found. The generation index is searched until the required generation's volume serial number (and device type) is found.

Fig. 99 VTOC catalog relationship.

PAYROLL (0) as the current generation, YRTODATE.PAYROLL (−1) as the generation created last week, and YRTODATE.PAYROLL (+1) as the generation about to be created. The values (0), (−1), and (+1) are referred to as the relative generation number, whereas such values as *G0012V00* and *G0015V02* are called the *absolute* generation number.

Maintaining the Catalog

Each week (or any other desired time period) as a new generation is being created, the other generations become one week older. That is, those that had been regarded as —1, —2, —3, and so on, before the update run will be regarded as —2, —3, —4, and so on, after the update run. The aging process and keeping record of it in the catalog is accomplished by the Terminator. Figures 100 and 101 show how a generation is *aged*.

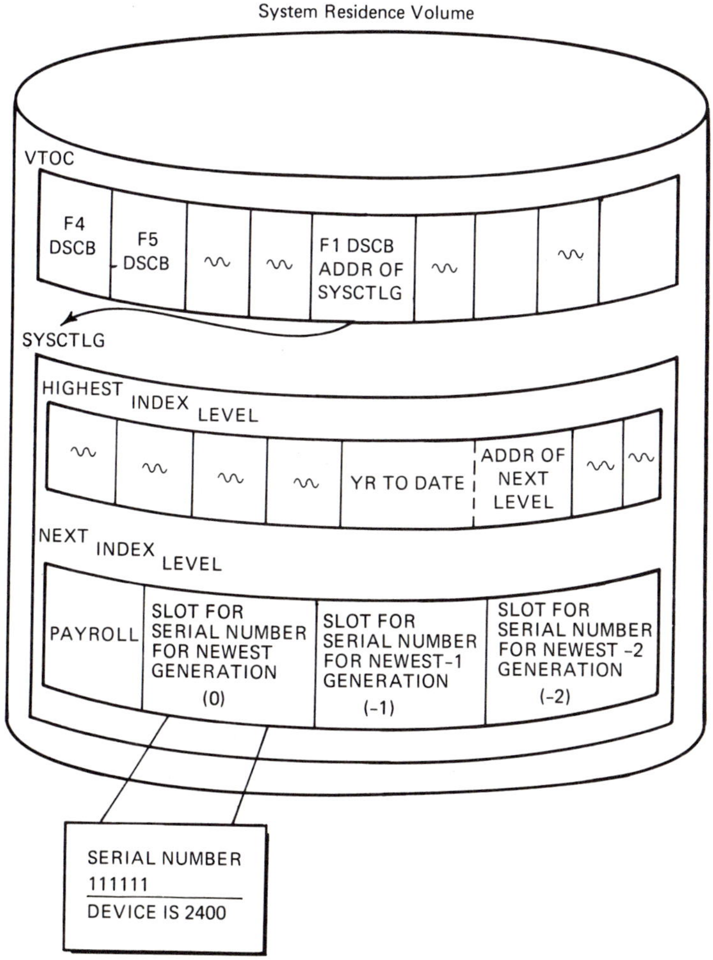

The first generation occupies the slot for the newest generation.

Fig. 100 Slot for newest generation.

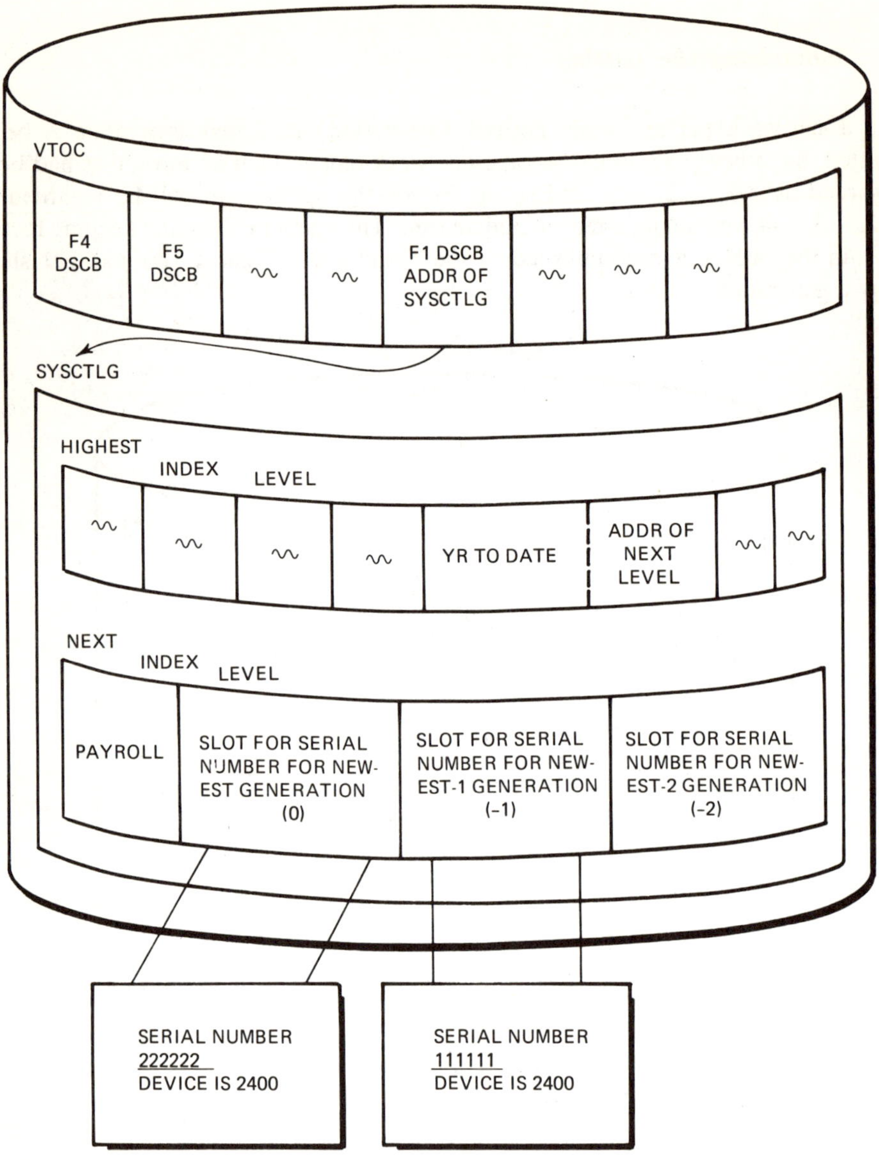

When a new generation is created, the reference data for the old ones is moved up a slot in the generation index.

Fig. 101 "Moving" reference data for new generation.

Also, what had been cataloged as the next-to-the-oldest generation before the update run becomes the oldest after the job is run. The generation that had been the oldest has its entry in the catalog removed by the Terminator (i.e., uncataloged). As an alternative to just uncataloging the oldest generation during an update run, it is possible to uncatalog *all* generations after the desired maximum number of generations has been accumulated. For example, an installation may wish to clear out the catalog at the beginning of each year. When this is the case, the attempt by the Terminator to catalog the fifty-third generation will cause the entire *index* to be emptied.

Creating the Index for a Generation Data Group

Before a generation of a data set can be cataloged, a special index in the catalog (SYSCTLG) must be built. To build this index requires the execution of a special program. The name of this program is IEHPROGM—it is a program categorized as a utility program and is supplied by IBM as part of a standard operating system kit.

OPERATIONAL FACTORS CONCERNING DATA MANAGEMENT

Passwords

One of the great concerns of the data-processing industry as well as the general public is the matter of protecting information in confidential data sets from unauthorized use. This is particularly true of installations employing multiprogramming and having many, many data sets on line at the same time. Let's just take a simple case where the executive payroll data set is on a disk pack along with the apprentice-training-status data set and several others. Suppose it is known that the apprentice-training-status data set is to be processed on next Wednesday between 10 A.M. and 12 noon. What is to keep someone from "faking" a job request to execute a "program in development" during which the contents of the confidential data set is printed? In the traditional sense, the answer is "very little."

The designers of the operating system realized this problem area and therefore devised the password principle. The essentials of the password principle are illustrated in Fig. 102. In item 4 of Fig. 102 we said that a special or *master* password for the PASSWORD data set is invented. Only when this master password is given could anyone make changes, add to, or read from PASSWORD.

Why would anyone want to change or add passwords? New passwords would be added when new confidential data sets are created. Passwords would be changed if it is suspected that some unauthorized person has "discovered" it. How does one discover a password? The password is printed on the console typewriter sheet (when the operator makes his reply), where all may see.

1. The installation makes a list of the names of the data sets which are considered as containing confidential information.

1.	USER.TOPCKRET
2.	USER.RUFMADLN
3.	USER.PROPOSLS
4.	USER.ADVTG.XPNSES
5.	USER.ADVTG.GROTR
6.	USER.XEKPAYRL
7.	USER.TESTPRGS.AUTOMSHN
8.	USER.TESTPRGS.NEWPRODS
9.	USER.TESTPRGS.KEMRSRCH

2. To be associated with each of the data set names, the installation concocts a password and writes it on the list.

	DATA SET NAME	PASSWORD NAME
1.	USER.TOPCKRET	SSSSSSSH
2.	USER.RUFMADEL	FAGUTIME
3.	USER.PROPOSLS	GNUBIZZZ
4.	USER.ADVTG.XPNSES	VSPENDOE
5.	USER.ADVTG.GROTR	MEANSNIL
6.	USER.XEKPAYRL	RICOHOMB
7.	USER.TESTPRGS.AUTOMSHN	MEKNEYES
8.	USER.TESTPRGS.NEWPRODS	MAKESAKK
9.	USER.TESTPRGS.KEMRSRCH	HOKUSPOK

3. After preparing the list, it should be punched into cards. The data in these cards should be recorded on disk as a data set. The data set should be named PASSWORD.

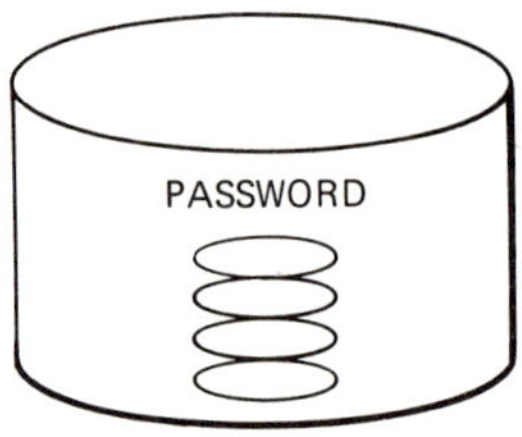

4. All of the confidential data sets (except PASSWORD itself) now have a password. Therefore, to prevent unauthorized access to PASSWORD several very responsible and trustworthy data processing people now invent a super password to be associated with it. This super password (e.g., NO1NOZIT) becomes part of the PASSWORD data set.

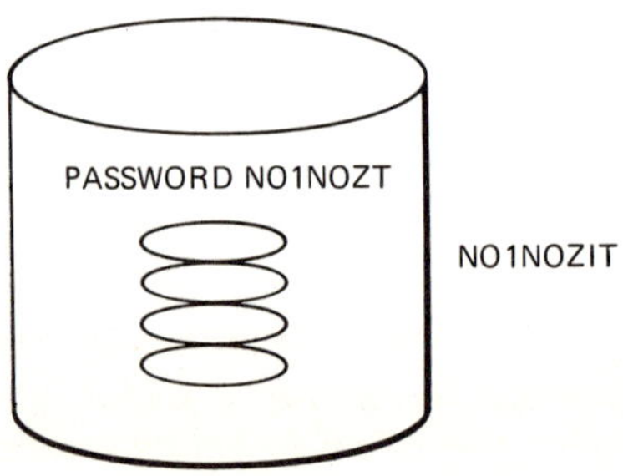

Fig. 102 Password list preparation and use.

5. So that the appropriate data management routines know whether or not a data set requires a PASSWORD, the installation must make a notation in the DSCB of the data set.

DSNAME	PASSWORD NEEDED?	IF YES PASSWORD IS NEEDED TO
USER. PROPOSLS	YES	READ DATA SET
USER. COMNNOLJ	NO	———
USER. XEKPAYRL	YES	READ OR WRITE DATA SET
USER. CONFONE	YES	WRITE DATA SET
PASSWORD	YES	READ OR WRITE DATA SET

6. Before a problem program can access the records of a data set its dscb is checked to see if the data set requires a PASSWORD.

If it does require one, the following sample message may appear.

```
IEC301A   S   DSNAME   USER.XEKPAYRL
```

The message text essentially means, "The data set whose name (DSNAME) is USER.XEKPAYRL requires a password (S).

The operator must then issue a formal reply which contains the password, i.e., REPLY 00, 'RICOHOMB'.

7. The effect of a password is nullified after a CLOSE instruction has been executed.

Fig. 102—*Cont.*

Deferred Mounting of Volumes

Installations are sometimes faced with data-processing problems wherein certain data sets may not be required by a program until sometime after the program has begun execution. For example, an engineering program may be run which requires several data sets containing special mathematical values (recorded on tapes) only after the program has been executing for several minutes. It would be an advantage to the installation if the mounting of these tapes could be deferred until after the program begins, rather than have to mount them before the Initiator gets executed. This consideration is implemented in S/360 and the method of implementation is shown in Fig. 103.

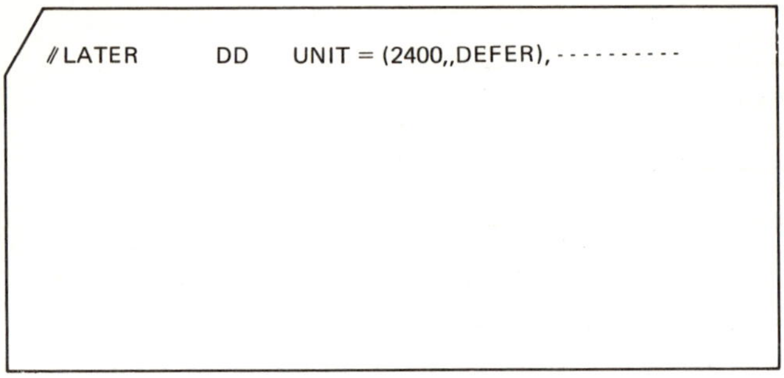

When one asks to DEFER the mounting of a data set, it eventually will be mounted when the program requiring it is under execution.

To defer the mounting of a data set's volumes until the execution of the program, one uses the word DEFER following the number of units: for example, UNIT = (2400, 3, DEFER). If the data set requires only one unit, it is permissable to write UNIT = (2400, , DEFER) rather than UNIT = (2400, 1, DEFER). It is not permissable to leave out the "extra" comma eg. UNIT = (2400, DEFER); if this is done, the reader interpreter will reguard it as an error.

Fig. 103 Request to defer mounting.

Volume Allocation

The following discussion will again make evident to you the interrelationship between the Initiator and data management. One of the most difficult decisions that the Initiator makes for you concerns the interrelated requirements of data sets, volumes, and I/O devices. Of course, you must tell the Initiator what you want. (What you want and what you *say* you want are often two different entities.) The way you normally tell the Initiator what you want is through the use of DD cards. Of course, before you can say what you want the Initiator to do concerning data sets, volumes, and I/O devices, you'll have to be familiar with the characteristics of data sets, volumes, and I/O devices.

DATA SET CHARACTERISTICS

The primary characteristic that the Initiator looks for in a data set is its probable longevity—that is, will it still be in existence or will it be deleted after the job in which it was created is terminated? If it is to be deleted during the termination of the job in which it was created, we call the data set *temporary*. If it is not deleted during the termination of the creating job, we call the data set *nontemporary*. (Notice that we are not using the word permanent, which implies eternal existence.)

What are temporary data sets used for? You should recall that compilers need work space for the intermediate results of compilation. The space is usually requested in the DD cards named SYSUT1 and SYSUT2, as shown in Fig. 104.

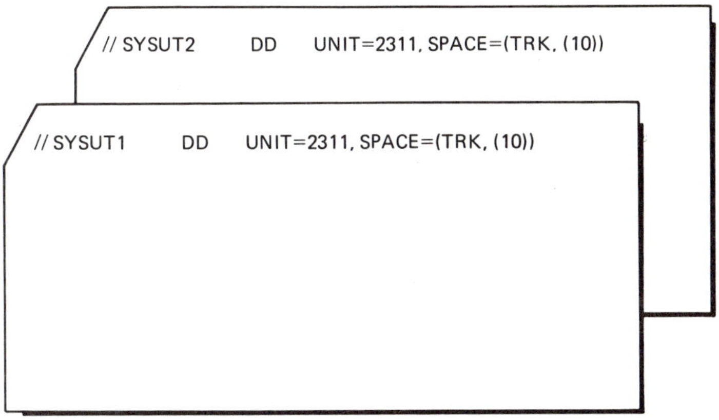

Notice that there is no data set name in either of the DD cards. Whenever a request for a data set space is made in a DD card, but no DSNAME = is given, the Initiator automatically assigns a name.

Also notice that no disposition information is given, Whenever the DISP= information is missing, the Job Scheduler automatically assumes the dispositions of NEW, DELETE.

Fig. 104 Space request for unnamed data set.

Another example of a data set that is often considered temporary is the machine language output of a compiler. We usually want this data set to last only long enough for the Linkage Editor to use it. Now the output data set of a compiler is very important to the programmer even though it's only temporary. To give the programmer a feeling of security, the operating system allows him to participate in naming temporary data sets. This is illustrated in Fig. 105.

REQUESTING THE VOLUME ON WHICH A DATA SET IS LOCATED

In the topic of cataloging we said that the job scheduler finds old data sets by referring to either of two sources: the DD card alone or the DD card and catalog. In either case, when an old data set is requested, the serial number of the volume must be specified; otherwise the operating system won't be able to find the data set.

However, as we saw in the previous section, it is not necessary to specify volume serial number when requesting space for a new data set. Notice that we said *not necessary*—we didn't say you cannot. As a matter of fact, if you are creating a new data set and you want it to be recorded on a specific volume, you had better make your request with a volume serial number. Therefore, when you

```
// SYSPUNCH   DD   DSNAME=&NOFFVGO, UNIT=2311,
                   SPACE=(CYL,(1)), DISP=(NEW,PASS)
```

In this DD card, the data set has been given the name NOFFVGO. The Job Scheduler knows that it is temporary because the name has been preceded by an ampersand (&).

Fig. 105 Temporary data set name.

ask the operating system to decide where a new data set is to be recorded, we say you are making a *nonspecific* request. On the other hand, when you specify the serial number of a volume, we say you are making a *specific* request.

DISMOUNTABILITY OF VOLUMES

If you have worked in a data-processing installation you have probably noticed the *occasional* message from the operating system telling you to dismount a disk pack and wondered why this happened. The reason for such a message is quite simple; the operating system has determined that someone wants very much to keep a data set just created (the data set being on the volume mentioned in the message).

Now why does the operating system print this message only occassionally? Is the operating system arbitrary, printing the message only when it feels like it? On the contrary, it really knows what it is doing. How then does it decide whether or not to issue a dismount message?

First, volumes are either absolutely dismountable, dismountable by operator command, or just plain dismountable with no strings attached. For example, an absolutely undismountable volume is one that contains such data sets as SYS1.-LINKLIB, SYS1.SYSJOBQE, SYS1.NUCLEUS, or the PROCLIB. It certainly is a good idea to have the volumes on which these data sets reside absolutely undismountable. (Think of what would happen if the operating system suddenly wrote a message to the operator to remove the pack with LINKLIB on it. Since LINKLIB is the main program library, no more new programs would be started with LINKLIB removed.) The volumes that fall in the category of being absolutely undismountable are called *permanently resident*.

Another category of volumes is almost identical to those called permanently resident with one exception: The operator, by issuing a certain command, can make them dismountable. For example, volumes that contain such data sets as SYS1.-COBLIB or SYS1.FORTLIB should be regarded as being resident only when either

COBOL or FORTRAN compilations are being run. There is no need, however, to force them to stay mountable after the compilations have been run. Therefore, the operator, by issuing the command UNLOAD, qualifies the volume for dismounting. Note that we did not say that the UNLOAD command actually dismounts the volume—it only *qualifies* it for dismounting if the need should arise. The *volumes* that can be made dismountable by an operator command belong to the category called *reserved*.

The next category concerns those volumes which are just plain dismountable. They are called *removable*. Why would the operating system want to remove a volume? Let's suppose that a four-drive S/360 has volumes KMC001, JCC002, APC003, and MLC004 mounted, when along comes a job's DD card requesting the volume KAC005—where is KAC005 going to go? The operating system first has to determine which of the four mounted volumes is dismountable. After determining this, it will print two messages—one to dismount the removable volume and another to mount the requested volume. However, if none of the four volumes is dismountable, there will be a problem. To minimize the probability of such a problem requires careful planning.

Now suppose that a volume usually considered as being removable received a data set that must be available for subsequent jobs. It would not be in the best interests of the installation if the operating system considered this volume as being removable. Therefore, something had better be done about it. Again, it is the operator who does the something; he issues the command called MOUNT. When the operating system gets this command, it changes the status of the volume from *removable* to *reserved*.

The topic "dismountability of volumes," which we have just been describing, is referred to as the *mount characteristics* of a volume.

VOLUME AVAILABILITY

So far we have talked about

1. temporary and nontemporary data sets.
2. specific and nonspecific requests for volumes.
3. permanently resident, reserved, and removable volumes.

Another aspect of volumes that the Initiator is concerned with is closely related to the topic of specific and nonspecific requests. That is, if your request is specific, the system must determine if the allocation is possible: If the request is nonspecific, the system must determine which volume is best for providing the requested space. Therefore, to determine the availability of a volume for allocation, direct-access volumes are classified as being either private, public, or storage.

Private of course, means restricted use—like private property. The space on a volume that is regarded as private will never be allocated for a nonspecific request—even when the entire volume is empty. Space on a public volume can be granted for a nonspecific request. It is also possible by way of certain information in a DD card to make a public volume into a private volume. Then the next time the volume is used, it will be regarded as private.

A storage volume is like a public volume except that a storage volume cannot be made private.

These three classifications, private, public, and storage, are regarded as the *allocation characteristics* of a volume.

Volume Sharing in a Multiprogramming Environment

As you know, there may be more than one task in storage when the operating system is set up for multiprogramming. You also know that each task will need one or more data sets. Suppose that in a multiprogramming environment are two tasks, each using a different data set but with both residing on the same private volume. As soon as one of the tasks finishes, the Terminator (realizing that the volume is private) will issue a dismount message. The second task could no longer access its data set. To prevent such a catastrophe from occurring, the operating system must be informed that the volume is sharable by several tasks. The information concerning the sharability of a volume is usually placed into a DD card.

Informing OS about the Characteristics of Volumes

There are two major ways of informing the operating system's Initiator about the allocation characteristics (public, private, storage) and the mount characteristics (permanently resident, reserved, removable) of a volume. One way is to specify it in a DD card. The second way is to put a coded description of these characteristics into a system data set called SYS1.PARMLIB. (Entries made into PARMLIB are called members and these members must be named.)

In the case of the volume's characteristics, the member name is PRESRES. (The term PRESRES is made up of the words *p*ermanently *res*ident and *res*erved.) Each entry in PRESRES indicates the volume serial number, the *mount* characteristics, and the *allocation* characteristics for direct-access volumes. At IPL time, the volume serial numbers of all mounted direct-access volumes are checked with the entries in PRESRES. If these volumes are mounted, the operating system assigns to the volume, the characteristics listed in PRESRES. Figure 106 is a copy of a console print out while IPLing an MVT SYSTEM. (IPL means initial program load. The IPL procedure is performed to "start up" the operating system. The IPL procedure is usually performed at the beginning of the day or after the computing system has had a "nervous breakdown." The IPL procedure brings the Nucleus into the fixed area of main storage.)

```
    IEA101A    SPECIFY SYSTEM PARAMETERS
    r 00,'U'
    IEA1061    IEFSD105  NOT FOUND IN SYS1.LINKLIB
    IEE101A    READY
    S WTR,00E  *
    S RDR,00C  *
    S INIT  *
    set date 166.222
    IEE3091  SET       KEYWORD MISSPELLED
    SET DATE=67.222
    IEF4201  RDR=SYSRDR
    IEF4211  INIT=PRINT2.PRTPROC  (1)
(1) IEF2491  FOLLOWING P/R & RSV VOLUMES ARE MOUNTED
    111111  ON 190       (P/R-PUB)
(2) 222222  ON 191       (P/R-STR)
    SPLIT2  ON 192       (P/R-PUB)
    IEF2501 FOLLOWING MAY BE MOUNTED
(3) 333333  ON A 2311
    00 REPLY DEVICE ADDRESSES OR GO
    r 00,'GO'
    IEF4291 INPUT QUEUE EMPTY
    d jobnames
    IEA000A   INT REQ,00C,**,0200,4000
```

Refer to Shaded Printing Only

(1) During system IPL, this message describes the volumes mounted for PRESRES (meaning permanently resident and reserved), which is a member of PARMLIB

(2) The serial number of each MOUNTED volume is written followed by the device address.

Next comes the characteristics that have been recorded in PRESRES. These may be:

P/R-PUB - Permanently Resident - Public
P/R-PRV - Permanently Resident - Private
P/R-STR - Permanently Resident - Storage
RSV - PUB - Reserved - Public
RSV - PRV - Reserved - Private
RSV - STR - Reserved - Storage

(3) If a volume described in PRESRES has not been mounted, this message is written. The operator can either reply with a device address (if the volume is to be mounted), or the word GO, if the volumes are not to be mounted.

Fig. 106 Informing operator of status of mounted volumes.

Volume Request Summary

The combinations of (1) temporary and nontemporary data sets, (2) specific and nonspecific requests, (3) allocation characteristics of private, public, and storage, and (4) mount characteristics of permanently resident, reserved, and removable are so great that it is not possible to memorize them. Therefore, each installation should have a chart summarizing the combinations. Such a chart is shown in Fig. 107.

VOLUME REQUEST SUMMARY

If you		and your request is:		and your data set is:		IT CAN BE SATISFIED WITH A VOLUME WHICH IS:						
						FIXED (Permanently resident or reserved)			REMOVABLE			
									Not Mounted	MOUNTED		
Do Not Specify PRIVATE	Specify VOLUME=PRIVATE	SPECIFIC	NONSPECIFIC	TEMPORARY	NONTEMPORARY (PERMANENT)	PUBLIC	PRIVATE	STORAGE		Not Allocated Public	Allocated Public	Allocated Private
X		X				X	X	X	PU	PU	PU	PR
X			X	X		X	No	X	PU	PU	PU	No
X			X		X	No	No	X	PR	No	No	No
	X	X				X	X	X	PR	PR	PR	PR
	X		X			No	No	No	PR	No	No	No

SYMBOLS
PU = PUBLIC
PR = PRIVATE
X = CAN SATISFY REQUEST
No = CANNOT SATISFY REQUEST

Fig. 107 Volume request summary.

Data Set Integrity

Closely related to the topic of *sharable volumes* in a multiprogramming environment is the area of *sharable data sets.* You may wonder why the sharing of data sets should be of concern. Let's suppose that the Reader/Interpreter program has just read an EXEC card in which is punched a request for a procedure from the data set PROCLIB. Also in main storage at the same time as the Interpreter is a utility program—it is going to change some of the procedures in PROCLIB. As you have already guessed, this could produce, at least, a minor conflict. To considerably reduce the probability of such a conflict, data sets in multiprogramming can be classified as being available on a *shared* basis or on an *exclusive* basis.

Any time that a data set is to be effected by a writing operation, the data set should be considered as the exclusive property of the program doing the writing. On the other hand, if many programs are only *reading* records from the data set, the data set can be shared—even if a dozen or more programs are reading from it. Figure 108 illustrates how to tell the Initiator that a data set is regarded as being sharable.

SUMMARY

1. Before the Initiator can begin a task it must have answers to the following questions:

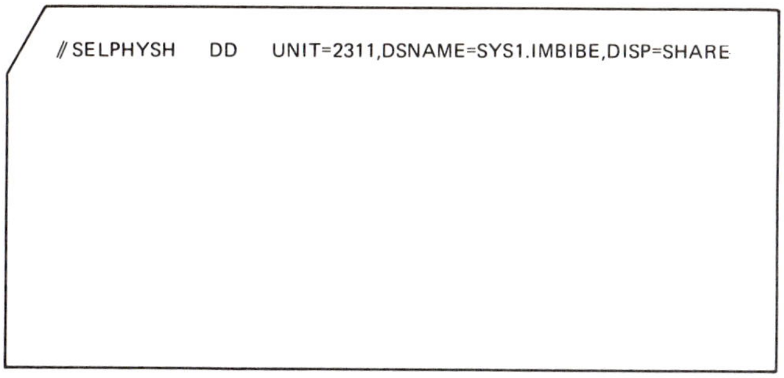

Sharing of a data set is indicated in DISP=SHARE. When SHARE is used with DISP, it implies OLD and KEEP.

If a data set is to be exclusive property of a task, its exclusiveness is indicated merely by not using the word SHARE. In other words, exclusive control is indicated by using DISP with anything valid other than SHARE.

Fig. 108 Request to share a data set.

a. Is the data set new (to be created) or is it old (already exist)?
b. If it is a new data set, how many cylinders or tracks of disk space are required or how many reels of tape are required?
c. What is the name of the data set?
d. What is the serial number of the volume on which the data set resides?
e. What kind of output device should be used?
f. Are the records blocked or unblocked? Fixed-length or variable-length records?
g. Shall reference to the data set be kept or deleted after the job has been processed?

2. Programmers inform the Access Method they want an input record by using a GET or READ macro instruction. Programmers use PUT or WRITE to inform the Access Method that they have produced an output record.
3. When an Access Method determines that an I/O operation is needed, the Access Method calls on the I/O Supervisor for assistance.
4. The queued Access Methods keep I/O buffers filled automatically. The filling and emptying of I/O buffers when using the basic access methods is the responsibility of the programmer.
5. The OS data set catalog contains the name of a data set, the type of device on which the data set is recorded, and the serial number of the volume.
6. Qualified data set names are used to distinguish among classes of data sets.
7. The contents of each volume is recorded in a data set called the volume table of contents (VTOC).
8. For each of the data sets on a volume there will be at least one entry. The entry is called a data set control block (DSCB).

9. A DSCB that defines the first three extents of a data set is referred to as a Format 1 DSCB.
10. A DSCB that defines extents of data sets beyond the third is called a Format 3 DSCB.
11. A DSCB that defines available storage is called a Format 5 DSCB.
12. A DSCB that describes the VTOC data set is called a Format 4 DSCB.
13. The place in his program where the Assembly language programmer describes data sets and specifies Access Method information is called a data control block (DCB).
14. Certain information about a data set's characteristics and about the Access Method does not have to be included in the programmer's DCB, it can be placed into the DD statement just before submitting the job for execution.
15. DCBs and DD cards are linked together by writing the name of the DD card in the DCB.
16. A collection of data sets related by time is called a generation data group.
17. Members of a generation data group are distinguished from one another by a generation number. The generation number is assigned by the operating system.
18. The OS data set catalog is automatically updated each time a new generation of a data set is created.
19. To make a password-protected data set available for allocation by the Initiator, the computer operator must provide the proper password.
20. The passwords for protected data sets are kept in a data set named PASSWORD. To make changes or additions to the PASSWORD data set requires the issuance of a master password.
21. The request to the operating system for the mounting of a volume to be deferred can be made in a DD statement.
22. Data sets deleted during the termination of the job in which they were created are called *temporary.*
23. Data sets whose life spans two or more jobs are called nontemporary.
24. Leaving the responsibility of selecting a volume for a new data set to the operating system is regarded as a nonspecific request.
25. Stating the serial number of a volume (to the operating system) is called a specific request.
26. The mount characteristics of a volume are permanently resident, reserved, and removable.
    a. The operating system will never ask the operator to unload (remove) a permanently resident volume.
    b. A reserved volume will not be asked to be dismounted.
    c. A removable volume will be asked to be dismounted if another volume is required by a job or job step.
    d. By issuing certain commands, the computer operator can change the status of volumes from reserved to removable and vice versa. He cannot change the status of a volume from (or to) permanently resident.

27. A volume's eligibility for allocation depends on its allocation characteristics: private, public, and storage.
    a. Private volumes will not be used for granting space to nonspecific requests.
    b. Public volumes can be used for granting space to nonspecific requests. A public volume's allocation characteristics can be changed to private.
    c. Storage volumes can be used for granting space to nonspecific requests. A storage volume's allocation characteristics can not be changed to private.
28. The premature dismounting of a private volume being used by two or more concurrent tasks can be prevented by informing the operating system that the volume is sharable.
29. The allocation characteristics of a volume can be recorded in a member of SYS1.PARMLIB named PRESRES.
30. The initial program load (IPL) procedure is performed to "start up" the operating system.
31. As soon as a data set is allocated to a task, the data set is regarded as exclusive property of the task. To inform the operating system that other tasks can use the data set concurrently, the data set must be described as sharable.

SUGGESTED READING ASSIGNMENTS

IBM System/360 Supervisor and Data Management Services (C28-6646)

Section II: Data Management Services

- Part 1: Introduction to Data Management
  - Data Set Characteristics (all—a good review)
  - Direct Access Device Characteristics (all)
  - Interface With The Operating System
    - Data Set Description
    - Processing Program Description (first two paragraphs)
    - Sharing a Data Set
- Part 2: Data Management Processing Procedures
  - Data Processing Techniques
    - Queued Access Technique (all)
    - Basic Access Technique
      - Read
      - Write
      - Check

- Wait
- Data Event Control Block
- Error Handling (first paragraph only)
- Selecting An Access Method
- Opening and Closing a Data Set (first 6 paragraphs)
- Buffer Acquisition and Control
  - Buffer Pool Construction (first 4 paragraphs)
  - Buffer Control (first 5 paragraphs)
- Processing a Partitioned Data Set (first 4 paragraphs)
- Processing an Indexed Sequential Data Set
  - Indexed Sequential Data Set Organization
  - Additional Records in an Indexed Sequential Data Set
  - Indexed Sequential Data Set Maintenance
- Processing a Direct Data Set
  - Organizing a Direct Data Set
  - Referring to a Record in a Direct Data Set (first paragraph only)

8 THE JOB STATEMENT

REVIEW

In Chapter 6 you were introduced to the three main components of job control: the Job statement, the Execute statement, and the DD statement. You should recall that the major purpose of the Job statement is to identify a collection of job steps as being related. Information for controlling the selection, execution, and disposition of a job by the operating system can be placed into the Job statement. Figure 109 lists 12 items of information that can be provided to the operating system in a Job statement.

THE JOB STATEMENT FORMAT

Perhaps the most difficult things to remember about the Job statement are the rules for construction and punctuation. Many a Job statement containing well-planned information has been misunderstood or rejected by the Reader/Interpreter because the preparer of the statement forgot to provide a comma where one was required or left a blank space where he shouldn't have. Therefore, before exploring the items of Fig. 109 further, let's look at some of the mechanical rules for constructing Job statements.

RULES ABOUT JOB STATEMENTS

1. A Job statement can consist of several horizontal lines. (One usually writes a Job statement on paper before punching it into cards.)

Description of Information to be Placed into the job statement	Name of Description
1. Name of the job	Jobname
2. Number of department or number of project and other accounting information which is to be used for charging of computer's use.	Job accounting information
3. Name of person responsible for this job	Programmer's name
4. Which job control statements and which messages are to be displayed (i.e., printed)	MSGLEVEL
5. Conditions under which the job is to be terminated (other than normal end)	COND
6. Classification code of job	CLASS
7. Priority of the job (for selection by initiator)	PRTY
8. Output device on which messages are to be displayed	MSGCLASS
9. Amount of Main Storage Required (MVT)	REGION
10. Preventing a job from being initiated	HOLD
11. If job is evictable from main storage and if it can evict other jobs from main storage	ROLL
12. If the job fails and is to be restarted at other than the beginning	RD RESTART

Fig. 109 Job statement components.

2. Each line of a statement consists of 80 consecutive columns.
3. Columns 1 and 2 must contain slashes (//).
4. Columns 73 through 80 must not be used for JOB information. The information in these columns is not used by the Reader/Interpreter. These columns usually contain sequencing or identification data.
5. If all the information required to describe a job cannot be accommodated on a line, column 72 should contain a character to signify that another line follows. These subsequent lines are referred to as *continuations*. If there are no subsequent lines, column 72 must be blank.
6. The first line of the statement must contain the name of the job. The first character of the name must start in column 3 and be a letter. It must consist of eight characters or less. The characters used in the name can be alphabetic, numeric, or those referred to as "national" characters. These are the dollar sign ($), the number sign (#), and the commercial "at" sign (@).
7. One space (or more) must follow the name of the job; following this space must be the term JOB. One space (or more) must follow this term.

8. Any information (parameters) about the job must come after the term JOB. Some parameters must be provided first and in a certain order. Such parameters are referred to as *positional*. Parameters that are *not* positional must be provided together with an identifying term and an equal sign (=). This identifying term is called a *keyword*. Sometimes a keyword is used to provide several subitems of information (called *subparameters*) each of which must be in a certain order. When this is the case one could say that positional subparameters are supplied within a keyword.
9. When a collection of more than one item of information comprises a parameter, the collection must be enclosed in parentheses.
10. Parameters and all levels of subparameters must be separated from each other by commas. Positional parameters, on occasion, may be deliberately omitted. To signify that one has been omitted requires two consecutive commas. If two consecutive positional parameters are omitted, one must provide three consecutive commas, and so on. For example, assume that you usually have to supply in order, the name of the project, the project number, the name of the project leader, and the number of the department responsible for the project, with the keyword *PROJECT=*. Now suppose the only information that exists is the first and last parameter. Here is the way you'd specify these parameters: PROJECT=(POKER , , ,79D). When a keyword parameter is deliberately left out, no special indication of any kind is required.
11. The person preparing the Job statement may wish to annotate (comment on) his choice of parameters. He may do so in several ways:
    a. Write comments after supplying all parameters. Leave one space (or more) after the last parameter and then begin writing comments.
    b. Intersperse comments between keywords. Leave one or more spaces after the separation comma and then write the comment. (When this option is used, the person must be sure to supply a subsequent keyword on the next line and indicate in column 72 that a continuation follows.)

The above list of 11 rules may look somewhat formidable now. After you have had some practice, however, the formidability will diminish; not go away, mind you, but it will diminish.

Let us now return to the subject of supplying the information described in Fig. 109. The first parameter (positional) to be considered is job accounting information.

JOB ACCOUNTING PARAMETERS

The basic item of job accounting data is called the *account number*. This is the number to which the use of the computer is charged. In addition to the account number one may wish to provide other accounting information, provided the total amount does not exceed 142 characters. This may consist of such subparameters as the date on which the job was submitted, the number or name of the project for which this job is to process the data, the name of the project director, and a telephone number to call if certain characteristics of the job are abnormal. Accounting parameters must be the first information provided after the term JOB in the Job statement. If the accounting information consists of only the account number, parentheses are not needed. If the accounting information consists of subparameters, the account number must be listed first and the subparameters list must be enclosed in parentheses.

Let us assume that an installation has an accounting routine that can expect up to four subparameters: the account number, date of submission, a project number, and a project director. Figure 110 shows several variations on the submission of accounting data. Just to show you some of the kinds of errors a person can make, examine Fig. 111.

```
1.  //GOODONE  JOB  790
2.  //GOODTWO  JOB  (790,02-18-69,3661A,HARVEY-MAX)
3.  //GOODTHRE   JOB  (790,,3661A,HARVEY-MAX)
4.  //GUD4WOT  JOB  (790,,,HARVEY-MAX)
5.  //GUDFIFTH    JOB    (790,                               C
                          02-18-68,                          C
                          3661A,                             C
                          HARVEY-MAX)
```

Notes:
1. Only the account number is given, hence parentheses are not required.
2. This shows that the installation expects 4 accounting sub-parameters and all of these are provided. Because the accounting information consists *of a sub-parameter list*, it is enclosed in parentheses.
3. This is just like item 2 except the submitter of the job did not want to specify the date (i.e., the second positional sub-parameter). To indicate that the second positional sub-parameter was *deliberately* left out, he places the second comma immediately after the first comma.
4. Again, just like item 2 except that this time the submitter of the job did not specify either date or project number. To indicate that the second and third positional sub-parameters were deliberately left out, he places the second and third commas immediately after the first comma.
5. This is the same as item 2 except that each sub-parameter is placed into a separate card. Installations use this technique to facilitate visual reading. The price to pay is extra cards to be punched. Then too, the Reader program has to read more cards.

Fig. 110 Sample job accounting data.

1.
```
//BADONE   JOB790
```
2.
```
//BADTWO     JOB   (790, 02-18-68,3661A,HARVEY-MAX)
```
3.
```
//BADTREY  JOB   (790,3661A,HARVEY-MAX)
```
4.
```
//BAD4OS   JOB   (790,HARVEY-MAX)
```
5.
```
//BADFIFTH   JOB   (790,                                            C
//                  02-18-69,                                       C
//                  3661A,                                          C
//                  HARVEY-MAX
```

Notes:
1. The account number has been concatenated with the term JOB. The Reader program can not distinguish between terms and operands when they are concatenated.
2. There is a blank between the first comma and the beginning of the second sub-parameter.
3. Here we are assuming that the operating system is expecting 4 sub-parameters. In this case, it is getting only 3 with no indication of which one is to be left out. Hence, OS will assume that the fourth one has been deliberately left out, and the ones given will be treated as sub-parameters 1, 2 and 3.
4. Again assuming that OS is expecting 4 sub-parameters. In this case it is getting 2 which will be treated as the first and second sub-parameters (instead of being treated as the first and fourth).
5. The sub-parameter list does not conclude with a right parenthesis.

Fig. 111 Incorrect specification of job accounting data.

PROGRAMMER NAME

The second positional parameter in the Job statement must be the programmer's name (which cannot exceed 20 characters). If the name contains special characters (slashes, spaces, etc.) the name must be enclosed in apostrophes (not parentheses). For example, if T. O'Neill were the name, it would have to be recorded in the Job statement as 'T.O"NEILL'. (Note that when the name includes a legitimate apostrophe, it must be followed by a second apostrophe. Figure 112 shows examples of correct and incorrect recording of accounting information and programmer name in a Job statement.

MESSAGE DISPLAY

As part of the output for every job, the operating system automatically displays (this usually means printing) on its output device the Job statement, improperly

```
//OK1 JOB ,JONES

//OK2 JOB 790,JONES

//OK3 JOB (790,02-18-69,3661A,H-M),JONES

//OK4 JOB (790,,3661A,H-M),JONES

//OK5 JOB (790,,,H-M),JONES

//K01 JOB  JONES

//K02 JOB  790JONES

//K03 JOB  (790,02-18-69,3661A,H-M)JONES

//K04 JOB  (790,,3661A,H-M),    JONES

//K05 JOB  (790,,,H-M),J O N E S
```

1b The comma required for signifying deliberate omission of the accounting information was left out. Hence Jones will be regarded as accounting information

2b Because account number and the name are concatenated, the eight characters are considered as the first positional parameter, i.e., as the account number

3b The accounting information sub-parameter list is not separated from the name by a comma.

4b There is a blank space between the comma which follows the accounting subparameter list and the first character of the name.

5b There is a blank after the first character of the name. This signals the end of the name. O N E S will be regarded as comments.

Fig. 112 Correct and incorrect job statement samples.

constructed EXEC and DD statements (i.e., ones with errors in them), and associated diagnostic messages. In many cases the computing installation wants the operating system to display (print) *all* the job control statements. (Printing all the job control cards produces irrefutable evidence of what had been punched in the cards. It is a good argument settler.) To receive this additional system's output it is necessary to use the keyword MSGLEVEL and equate it to the digit 1 as follows:

MSGLEVEL=1

If the keyword is omitted or equated to 0 (zero), only the Job statement, incorrect control statements, and diagnostic messages will print.

TERMINATION CONDITIONS

In multistep jobs, the successful execution of an early step usually dictates whether subsequent steps are to be initiated. For example, in a compile and Link Edit job, it is of little value to Link Edit if the compilation is unsuccessful.

To request OS to terminate a job upon the detection of an unsuccessful job step requires the two following related items:

1. The writer of the program (either IBM or the installation personnel) in which the failure occurs must place a value into register 15 before he issues an instruction telling the operating system that he is finished processing. The value he places into register 15 is called the *return code*.
2. In the Job statement must be stated the value or range of values of the return codes which the Initiator will consult on each step of the job for causing early termination. The keyword required to state these values is COND (which stands for condition).

The condition parameter provides the installation with the means to compare each return code with up to eight different values. (There can be only one return code in register 15 from the job step task, but there may be different return codes for each step of the job.) If any one of the comparisons is satisfied, subsequent steps are bypassed and the job is terminated.

To specify the conditions one must provide OS (via the job card) with a *code* and an *operator* as follows: COND=((code,operator)...,(code,operator)). The term *code* refers to a decimal value from 0 to 4095 which is to be compared with the return code provided by the job step task. The term *operator* refers to the type of comparison to be made with the return code. The operators are as follows:

GT (greater than)
GE (greater than or equal to)
EQ (equal to)

LT (less than)
LE (less than or equal to)
NE (not equal to)

Let's look at an example. If you wrote

COND=((50,GE),(60,LT))

it would mean: If 50 is greater than or equal to the return code of the job step task, or if 60 is less than the return code of the job step task, the rest of the job steps are to be bypassed. In other words, the job continues as long as the return codes range from 51 through 60. (*Note:* If the keyword COND and its parameters do not appear in the job card, no return code tests are made.)

CLASSIFICATION CODE OF THE JOB

As you may recall, the Reader task places onto SYS1.SYSJOBQE the encoded *description* of a data-processing job as it appears in the JOB, EXEC, and DD cards. This encoded description is used by the Initiator for the selection of a job.

To minimize conflicts regarding the concurrent or overlapping selection of jobs of similar type, all jobs should be classified with a one-letter code (in the range of A through O). To specify a job's class one must use the keyword *CLASS.* For example, if a job has been assigned the class code F, the JOB card would be punched with

CLASS=F

All the information concerning this job will be recorded in the *F* class queue (a compartment of SYS1.SYSJOBQE). When an Initiator which has been authorized to select class F jobs is ready to initiate its next job, it will select the job from the F class queue.

PRIORITY OF THE JOB

Many installations have classified their data-processing jobs into three or four categories. Hence there will be at most three or four class queues in the JOBQE. These same installations may have many jobs in each of the class queues. Obviously some of the jobs are more important than others; the more important a job is, the sooner it should be considered for selection by an Initiator. An installation can code the relative importance of a job by giving it a selection priority. High-priority jobs have a high number and low-priority jobs have a low number. The range of priority numbers that should be used with application programs is a high of 12 to a low of 0.

The keyword is PRTY (meaning priority). If a job is to be given a priority of 10, *PRTY=10* would be placed into the JOB card.

OUTPUT DEVICE ON WHICH MESSAGES ARE DISPLAYED

From the time that the Reader task records a job's description on JOBQE until the job is terminated, the operating system is "taking notes." These notes consist of information about all aspects of the job. Some of the "notes" consist of the following information:

1. What, if anything, was wrong with the coding in the job control cards? (misspelled words, missing commas, etc.)
2. Which I/O devices were allocated by the Initiator?

These notes (referred to as *system messages*) will be written by an Output Writer task; hence the messages must have been recorded on a direct-access device as an output data set. The system message output data set is generally associated with the output class code A.

Whenever the operating system is started up, an Output Writer task assigned to output class A is also started up. The I/O device generally associated with output class A is the main printer.

Many of the jobs that are processed in the course of a day require simple printed output. The paper used for this output is usually nothing more than ordinary fanfold paper. It bothers no one to print the system messages between the output of a job's steps. Some jobs require special forms, however, such as payroll checks, savings bonds, and prenumbered invoices. One would not want to print system messages on any of these documents. One way to ensure that it doesn't happen is to assign an output class other than A for system message. This can be accomplished by using the keyword MSGCLASS. For example, if the output class were to be X, one would place the following information into the job card:

MSGCLASS=X

As long as no Output Writer task with class X has been started, the messages will not be printed.

AMOUNT OF MAIN STORAGE REQUIRED FOR A REGION (MVT)

To inform the Initiator how many bytes are required for an MVT region, one can use the keyword REGION. The *amount* of storage has to be specified in blocks of

1,024 bytes each. For example, if one requires 10,000 bytes he would punch

REGION=10K

in the job card. The amount of storage that would actually be allocated is 10,240 bytes, 240 bytes more than was actually required. ($10 \times 1{,}024 = 10{,}240$). If storage of different hierarchies is required, it can be requested by specifying two amounts. The first amount is for storage of hierarchy 0 and the second for hierarchy 1; for example, if one requires 20,000 bytes of hierarchy 0 storage and 70,000 bytes of hierarchy 1 storage, he would punch the job card with

REGION=(20K,70K)

What happens if the keyword REGION and its parameter are not applied? At the time that the installation is generating its operating system, it is possible to specify how large the *standard* region is. Thus, if the region amount is not supplied in the job card, the standard one will be assumed by the Initiator.

PREVENTING A JOB FROM BEING INITIATED

Although data-processing installations make every effort to place in the job stream only those jobs for which the probability of initiation is high, there are occasions when at the time of job submission it is impossible to assure the presence of all resources required by the job (I/O devices, data sets). Should this job be placed on the shelf (where it might be forgotten)? To get this job recorded in the JOBQE and yet make it ineligible for selection by the Initiator (unless some special action is taken by the operator) can be accomplished by punching

TYPRUN=HOLD

in the job card. This keyword and its parameter will cause the job to be classified as *uninitiatable.* (Systems programmers say the job has entered the hold queue.) To make it eligible for initiation, the operator can issue a command to release the job. The actual command he gives is RELEASE, together with the name of the job.

ROLLOUT/ROLLIN (MVT)

Although the majority of the applications programs written by the "typical" installation require 30,000 bytes (or less) of main storage, there are many occasions when a program may require as many as several hundred thousand bytes. The greater the number of main storage bytes required for a region, the less likely it is that the Initiator will get those bytes, even if the job has been assigned the highest possible priority. Several techniques can overcome the dilemma. One technique is to make several smaller programs out of the big program and then execute the smaller programs as a series of job steps. The disadvantage of this technique is that the Initiator and Terminator task must be used between job steps, and, as efficiently written as the I/T is, its entry into main storage and its execution does take time. Another technique is to have the operator *cancel* enough jobs to make the required amount of main storage available. The disadvantage of this technique is obvious.

One of the accepted techniques is to sectionalize the program into two parts—one small and one large. The small part would be regarded as an *entire* program. Its region requirements are relatively small, so its chances of getting initiated are pretty good. When the first part recognizes the need for the second part, the first part would request the operating system to make available enough main storage for the remaining section. If the operating system cannot find enough vacant main storage for the second section, a task of lower priority (or several tasks of lower priorities) can be temporarily evicted from main storage. (These tasks are recorded on disk.) This activity is referred to as *rollout.* The main storage that has been vacated by the rolled-out tasks is then assigned to the second part of the program. When the oversize task is terminated, the rolled-out tasks are rolled back in. The entire activity is usually called *rollout/rollin.* Tasks cannot be rolled out indiscriminately, however. That is, a task must be categorized as being "rolloutable" before it is evicted. Neither can a task request that other tasks be rolled out unless it has received permission to do so. That is, a task must be given permission to *request* rollout of another task. Both permission to request rollout of other tasks and being regarded as rolloutable is specified by the keyword ROLL. There are two positional parameters associated with the keyword. The first one states whether or not it is rolloutable. The second one states that all steps of a job can be rolled out. To state that (1) the steps of a job are rolloutable and (2) all steps of the job can request other tasks to be rolled out requires

ROLL=(YES,YES)

To specify that all tasks (or job steps of a job) can be rolled out but cannot request rollout of other tasks requires

ROLL=(YES,NO)

CHECKPOINT/RESTART

One of the most annoying events in an installation is the abnormal termination of a time-consuming job that has been under execution for some time. Some of the jobs in this category are multitape volume sorts and the updating of multivolume master data sets. The usual action taken after a job has abnormally terminated is to restart the job from the *beginning.*

If the job has been running for 5 minutes, the effect is somewhat annoying to the operations staff but not too disruptive to the processing schedule. But, if a job has been running for an hour or two or even 20 minutes, the effect of having to restart the job at the very beginning would be very annoying and it would certainly disrupt the rest of the schedule. To minimize the amount of time lost because of abnormal terminations, the operating system permits restarting at points other than the very beginning of the job. There are two main places within a job where a restart may be requested. These are

1. at the beginning of a job step.
2. at selected points within a program of a job step.

Which of the two categories is appropriate for a given job is the responsibility of the system's programming staff.

Taking a Checkpoint within a Program

To restart a job within a program of a job step requires that the programmer include in his program a special instruction called CHKPT (meaning take a checkpoint). When this instruction is executed, the program (in which CHKPT occurs) is recorded, as a series of records on a special data set appropriately called the *checkpoint data set.* In addition to recording an exact copy of the program (as it exists at that instant), there will also be recorded a copy of all the information that the Supervisor needs about the program and an indication of the progress of processing input and output records. The series of records which reflect the above information is called a *checkpoint entry.* Each time a checkpoint entry is made it is given an identifying number. This identification is used when and if the job has to be restarted. When a restart is to be made from a checkpoint, one usually chooses the most recently assigned identification number.

Defining a Step Restart

We have seen that a job can be restarted at the beginning of a job step or at a checkpoint. The next question to answer is: Should the restart be automatic or should it be deferred until someone has looked over the situation? The choice of automatic or deferred restart at the beginning of a job step may be defined in a job control card. The term signifying the *restart definition* is RD. If an automatic restart at a job step is desired, the RD is equated with an R (RD=R). If a deferred restart (not automatic) at a job step is the choice one equates RD to NR (RD=NR). The choice of an automatic or deferred restart at a checkpoint entry is specified by the programmer as part of the CHKPT instruction.

Requesting the Deferred Restart

If a restart is to be deferred (for a relatively long time after the job terminated abnormally), the job card for the restarted job must contain the keyword RESTART. If the deferred restart is to begin at a job stop, the term RESTART is equated to the name of that job step. If the RESTART is to begin at a checkpoint entry, the term RESTART must be equated to a concatenated name, consisting of the name of the job step and the checkpoint identification number.

Further Definition of a Restart

So far two alternatives for defining a step restart have been defined: RD=R gives us an automatic restart and RD=NR prohibits an automatic restart. RD=NR also prohibits an automatic checkpoint restart even though it has been requested in the CHKPT instruction; however, checkpoint entries are recorded. The coding to prevent a checkpoint from being taken even though the programmer requested it is

RD=NC (NC means "no checkpoint to be taken")

To request an automatic step restart but prohibit the execution of the CHKPT instruction if one happens to be in the program of this step is accomplished by coding

RD=RNC (RNC means "perform a job step restart but don't take any checkpoints")

SUMMARY

1. Accounting data must be the first positional parameter in a job card.
2. The programmer's name must be the second positional parameter of a job card.
3. The keyword MSGLEVEL is used to specify whether all job control statements and diagnostics are to print or just diagnostics.
4. The keyword COND can be used with return codes from tasks to request OS to terminate a job.
5. The keyword CLASS is used to place jobs into specific compartments of the JOBQE.
6. The keyword PRTY can be used to assign a priority to a job.
7. The keyword MSGCLASS is used to inform the operating system that OS messages are to be written by an Output Writer assigned to an output class other than standard.
8. The keyword REGION is used to inform the Initiator how many bytes of storage are required for each of the steps in the job.
9. The keyword TYPRUN is used with the parameter HOLD to keep the job from being initiated.
10. The keyword ROLL is used to specify whether the tasks created from the steps in this job can request roll out of other tasks and whether the tasks can be rolled out.
11. The keyword RD is used to tell OS what kind of restart is allowed for a job's tasks and when the restart may be taken.
12. A Job statement *must* be named.

9 *THE EXECUTE STATEMENT*

REVIEW

In Chapter 6 you were told about the main function of the Execute statement, that of informing the operating system of either the name of a program or the name of a procedure recorded in PROCLIB. Information to control the execution of the program can also be specified in the Execute statement. Figure 113 lists nine items of information that can be provided to the operating system by the EXEC statement.

THE EXECUTE STATEMENT FORMAT

The grammar and syntax rules for composing an Execute statement are just as numerous as for the Job statement. Therefore, before the items in Fig. 113 are explored further, let us review the mechanical rules for constructing EXEC statements (many are similar to the rules for constructing Job statements).

RULES ABOUT THE EXEC STATEMENT

1. An Execute statement can consist of several horizontal lines. (One usually writes an EXEC statement on paper before punching it into cards.)

	Description of Information to be Placed into the EXEC statement	Name of Description
1.	Name of the step	step name
2.	a. Name of the Program b. Name of the Procedure	PGM PROC
3.	Passing Parameters to the Program	PARM
4.	Job step Accounting Information	ACCT
5.	Job Step Time Limit	TIME
6.	Amount of Main Storage Required (MVT)	REGION
7.	Conditions under which the job step is to be bypassed or executed	COND
8.	If a job step is evictable from main storage and if it can evict others from main storage	ROLL
9.	Defining a Restart	RD

Fig. 113 Execute statement components.

2. Each line of a statement consists of 80 consecutive columns.
3. Columns 1 and 2 must contain slashes (//).
4. Columns 73 through 80 must not be used for EXEC statement information. The information in these columns is not used by the Reader/Interpreter. These columns usually contain sequencing or identification data.
5. If all the information required to describe the job step cannot be accommodated on a line, column 72 must contain a character to signify that continuation lines follow. If there are no subsequent lines, column 72 must be left blank.
6. The first line of the statement should contain the name of the job step. (Although the JOB statement must have a job name, the EXEC statement doesn't have to have a step name. However, it is a good idea to provide a step name. Later you will see how cross-references between job control cards can be made. To make cross-references, the EXEC statement must be named.) The first character of the name must be a letter and it must start in column 3. The characters used in the name must be alphabetic, numeric, or those referred to as "national" characters. These are the dollar sign ($), the number sign (#), and the commercial "at" sign (@).
7. One space (or more) must follow the name of the job step. Following the space must be the term EXEC. One space (or more) must follow this term.
8. Any information (parameters) about the job step must come after the term EXEC. Some parameters must be provided first and in a certain order. These are referred to as "positional parameters." Parameters that are not positional must be provided with a keyword and an equal sign

(=). When a keyword is used to supply several subitems of information (called subparameters) the subparameters must be in a certain order. When this is the case, one could say that positional subparameters are supplied with a keyword.

9. When a collection of subparameters is provided, the collection must be enclosed in parentheses.
10. Parameters, and all levels of subparameters, must be separated from each other by commas. Positional parameters, on occasion, may be omitted. To signify that one has been deliberately omitted requires two consecutive commas. If two consecutive positional parameters are omitted, one must record three consecutive commas, and so on.
11. The person preparing the EXEC statement may wish to annotate his choice of parameters. He may do so in several ways.
    a. Write his comments after supplying *all* parameters. He can do so by leaving one space (or more) after the last parameter and then begin writing comments.
    b. Intersperse comments between keywords (not positional parameters). He must leave one or more spaces after the separation comma and then write the comment. (When this option is used, the person must make sure to supply a subsequent keyword on the next line and indicate in column 72 that a continuation line follows.)

We shall now return to the subject of supplying the information referred to in Fig. 113. The first parameter to be considered is the name of the program to be executed.

NAME OF THE PROGRAM

The name of the program that is to be executed must be made available to the Initiator so that the program can be fetched into main storage for execution. The program that is to be requested must be in a partitioned data set and the program's name must be in the directory of the partitioned data set. A program is named by using the keyword PGM and an equal sign. For example, if the name of the program is KALQL8, the EXEC statement would contain

PGM=KALQL8

NAME OF THE PROCEDURE

If the job step (or a series of job steps) is performed very often, it is quite probable that its EXEC and related DD cards are recorded as a procedure on PROCLIB (remember, the procedure was given a name). If this is the case, the procedure can be requested by using the keyword PROC, an equal sign, and the name of the procedure. For example, if the name of the procedure is FORTLEGO, the EXEC statement would contain

PROC=FORTLEGO

It is also possible to request a procedure merely by placing it as the first positional parameter after the term EXEC.

Installations that prefer to identify procedure requests with a keyword rather than by its position feel that *positive identification* of a procedure request (as opposed to a program request) is more of an advantage than saving five columns of a statement. That is, specifying PROC=FORTLEGO eliminates any doubt that a procedure, and not just a program, is being called; stating *FORTLEGO* alone does not have the same element of assurance.

PASSING PARAMETERS TO THE PROGRAM

Two or more departments (or people) often have very similar data-processing requirements, but not similar enough to agree on all points. The differences of opinion might concern such problems as whether to single space, double space, or triple space an output listing; whether results are to be printed only, or printed and punched, or punched only; the name of the department that is to be printed at the top of each page; the value of an adjustment factor to be used in a crucial calculation; and so on. When such diverse requirements exist, the programmers can select one of two alternatives:

1. Write a separate program for each of the departments. (Each slightly different program would have to be kept in a partitioned data set. This greatly increases the disk storage required for storing programs.)
2. Write one general-purpose program for all the departments. Write it in such a way that by providing specific information (parameters) in the execute card the general-purpose program becomes tailored for a specific department's use. (A general-purpose program is usually larger than specific-purpose programs, but one general-purpose program requires a lot less space for storage than several specific-purpose ones.)

The second alternative is obviously (?) the one selected. The main part of the program could be written by leaving the "variable" constants out (i.e., use blanks in place of variable constants). Preceding the main part of the program would be a tailoring routine for taking the parameters supplied in the EXEC card and placing them into the blank areas. If expected parameters are not present, the tailoring routine could either supply some standard ones or cause the job step to be abnormally terminated. For example, a general-purpose program may have been written for printing the results of a company's United Fund drive. The program permits either a listing of each employee's donations (LIST), or a summary listing of donations by department (SUMRY), or a combination of the two (BOTH). Also the listing may be either single spaced (1), or double spaced (2).

Built into the general-purpose program would be the instructions to test for special instructions from the requestor. The test could be to see if the requestor specified either LIST, or SUMRY, or BOTH and 1 or 2; whatever the requestor specifies in the EXEC card will be honored by the program. For example, if he wants a double-spaced combination report he would specify *BOTH,2*. If he specifies neither, the general-purpose program would have been written to supply, for example, SUMRY,1 that is, a single-spaced summary.

The keyword for supplying the parameters is PARM. Up to 100 characters of data can be supplied with this keyword. Of course, separate subparameters have to be separated by commas and enclosed in either parentheses or apostrophes. Many of the IBM-written compliers have been written with possible alternatives. For example, the FORTRAN complier was written with the capability of preparing several optional outputs. Two of these outputs are

1. a listing of the results of compilation (called a map).
2. a *deck* of cards containing the compilation results. If both options were chosen, one would place in the EXEC card the following:

PARM='MAP,DECK'

JOB STEP ACCOUNTING INFORMATION

In addition to charging computer usage to a job account number, it is possible to allocate charges on a job step basis. However, job step accounting information is provided with a keyword in contrast to its being provided by *position* in job accounting.

The keyword is ACCT. If the job step accounting information consists of subparameters, they must be enclosed in parentheses. For example, if the job step accounting routine were expecting four subparameters (let's say account number or name, project name or number, date submitted and project location) one might specify

ACCT=(WE241,FPC,091695,SPFLA)

If the second and third subparameters were to be deliberately left out, one would specify instead,

ACCT=(WE241,,,SPFLA)

JOB STEP TIME LIMIT

Earlier we said that installation managers get very annoyed at abnormally ended jobs that have been under execution for some time. Just as annoying are those jobs that never seem to end but should have. How can this happen? Even though a newly written program has been successfully compiled and link edited, it is quite possible that the program has a logical flaw in it. One of these logical flaws is the *endless loop*. An endless loop can occur when the programmer uses the wrong condition for a branch instruction. (He wanted to branch to the beginning of a routine on a zero condition but he actually wrote an instruction to branch on a nonzero condition.) To prevent such a condition from wasting computer time (or any other undesirable condition) it is possible to limit the amount of computer time that a job step may have. This is accomplished by placing a maximum time limit (expressed in minutes and seconds) in the EXEC card with the keyword TIME. For example, if a job step is expected to complete in 2½ minutes or less, one would specify

TIME=(2,30)

A time limit of ½ minute would be expressed as

TIME=(,30) [Note the parameter-missing-indicator comma. It would have been equally correct to state TIME=(0,30).]

A time limit of 1½ hours would be expressed as

TIME=(90)

If the job step doesn't terminate normally in the amount of time specified, the job (starting with this step) will be terminated abnormally by the operating system.

AMOUNT OF MAIN STORAGE REQUIRED (MVT ONLY)

When all the steps of a job require about the same amount of main storage, one usually makes the request for main storage in the job card. However, when the main storage requirements of each step vary widely, it doesn't make much sense to request the same amount of main storage for all the steps of the job. For example, suppose in a Compile and Link Edit job, the compiler needs 200K bytes and the linkage editor 45K bytes. It would benefit the installation if the difference between the number of bytes in the Compiler and Linkage Editor could be made available to start another job. To implement this benefit one can request main storage in an EXEC card. Each of the job step's EXEC cards (mentioned above as Compiler and Linkage Editor) would then have, respectively,

REGION=200K and REGION=46K

(Even though the estimated linkage editor size was given as 45K, requests for main storage should be made in 2K-byte increments.) If a program has been written so that part of it may reside in main storage of hierarchy 0 and another part in hierarchy 1, the request for region size can be made in the same way as it is in a job card. For example, if 80K bytes are required for hierarchy 0 and 150K bytes for hierarchy 1, one would specify the request as

REGION=(80,150)

BYPASSING JOB STEPS

In certain applications where jobs consist of many steps, it is not uncommon for some of the steps to be unnecessary on occasion. For example, the third step of an accounts receivable job might be to sort tape records of delinquent accounts by age. Suppose, however, that during step 1, when all the active records in the master data set were extracted, no delinquent accounts were detected. It certainly would be a waste of time to initiate the third step, especially when there is no data. Depending upon the conditions detected in previous steps, the *bypassing* of a job step can be carried out as follows:

1. Have the writer of the program where the condition is detected place a return code in register 15.
2. Place into the EXEC card of the step that may be bypassed the code representing the condition under which bypassing is to occur.

For example, let's say that the programmer of step 1 will place a return code of 8 into register 15 if there are no delinquent account records. To bypass step 3, one would place into the EXEC card of step 3 the operator EQ (for equal), the value 8 (to be compared with the return code to see if an equal condition exists), and the step name of the EXEC card in step 1 (assume the name is PARTONE) as follows:

COND=(8,EQ,PARTONE)

Executing

There are times when one wants to execute a job step *even* though a previous step has failed. Alternatively, one may want to execute a job step *only* if a previous step has failed. (Remember, the normal sequence of events is that all subsequent steps are bypassed when an abnormal termination occurs.) For whatever reason the installation may have for executing the job step under these conditions, the execution may be requested by stating

COND=EVEN

(i.e., the step is to be executed *even* though a previous step has failed) or by stating

COND=ONLY

(i.e., the step is to be executed *only if* a previous step of the job has failed). The ONLY and EVEN conditions can be further qualified by using them in conjunction with the code and operator (GT, GE, EQ, etc.) For example, the narrative of what is desired might be, "Execute this step *only if* a previous step failed *except* when the return code of some previous step (named ZWEITE) was equal to 20." This narrative would be coded as

COND=(ONLY,(20,E,ZWEITE))

In the case of EVEN, the narrative might be, "Execute this step *even though* a previous step failed *except* when 20 is greater than the return code of step 3 (named DRITTE), or when 40 is equal to the return code of step 2 (named DEUXIEME)." This statement would be coded as

COND=(EVEN,(20,GT,DRITTE),(40,E,DEUXIEME))

ROLLOUT/ROLLIN

When permission for rollout is granted or denied in a job card, each step of the job must abide by the permit or denial. There are many cases where it is appropriate to just consider rollout for one of the job's steps. Job step rollout can be implemented by using the keyword ROLL in the EXEC card, with exactly the same terms (yes or no) as ROLL is used in the job card.

DEFINING A RESTART

When all the steps of a job are to receive the same consideration for restart, the definition of the restart type is placed in the job card by using the RD (restart definition) keyword. As in the case of the inappropriateness of always having to specify the parameters for *region size* and *rollout* permission in a job card, so, too, it may be inappropriate to define restart in a job card—hence the capability to define restart in an execute card.

To review, if one wants an automatic step restart, he would code

RD=R

If he doesn't want an automatic step restart, he would code

RD=NR

If he wants neither an automatic step restart nor checkpoint entries to be made, he would code

RD=NC

And last, if he does want an automatic step restart but wants the CHKPT instruction nullified (should it be in the program), he codes

RD=RNC

When the restart options are specified in an execute card, they apply to the respective job step; when the restart options are specified on the job card, they apply to all the steps in the job.

SUMMARY

1. The EXEC statement names a program or a procedure.
2. The keyword for specifying a program is PGM.
3. The keyword for requesting a procedure is PROC.
4. A procedure may be requested by placing its name in the place for the first positional parameter.
5. The keyword PARM is used to supply a general-purpose program with information to make it a specific-purpose program.
6. The keyword ACCT is used to supply the operating system with job step accounting data.
7. The keyword TIME is used to specify the maximum amount of time that a job step's task may use the computing system.
8. The keyword REGION is used to inform an Initiator how many bytes of storage are required by the job step's program.
9. The keyword COND is used to tell the operating system the conditions under which a task is to be bypassed or executed.
10. The keyword ROLL is used to grant permission for the job step's task to request rollout and to specify that it (the job step's task) may itself be rolled out.
11. The keyword RD is used to state what kind of restarts are permissible and whether the restart is automatic or deferred.
12. An EXEC statement does not have to be named except when other EXEC or DD statements in the job will refer to it, or when one wants the name to print on the console typewriter.

10 THE DD STATEMENT

REVIEW

The primary purpose of the DD statement is to provide the operating system with information. The information will be used for the allocation of data sets, direct-access space, I/O devices, and volumes for the program that is specified in the EXEC statement.

STATUS AND DISPOSITION OF DATA SETS (DISP)

One of the characteristics of a data set that the Initiator must be informed of is its relative age. If the data set was previously created and named, it is OLD. If the data set is to be created by the problem program about to be run, it obviously doesn't exist yet and hence it is NEW. Also, a NEW data set may have to have space allocated to it.

After the problem program is through processing, the Terminator must be told what to do with the data set: whether to KEEP its name in the active file or DELETE its name from the active file. (You know if a data set is recorded on disk, the name file is actually the VTOC.) When the name of a data set (that has been on disk) is deleted from the VTOC, the space that had been allocated to the data set is returned to the free-space inventory.

Sometimes in a multistep job, a data set created by one of the first steps is required by one of the later steps. For example, the data set produced by the compiler is the input to the Linkage Editor. To tell the Terminator of such an intrajob desire it is necessary to PASS the data set from the earlier step to the later step.

The Initiator and the Terminator are informed of a data set's age and what is to be done with it by means of an entry in the DD card. This entry is called DISP (for disposition).

Parameters for Initiator

The first parameter after the equal sign is information for the Initiator. The first parameter may be one of the four following terms:

1. NEW—This means that the data set didn't exist before this step (i.e., the data set is to be created on this step). In other words, it represents an output data set.
2. OLD—The data set did exist before this step was started. All input data sets are regarded as being *old.*
3. MOD—This is somewhat similar to being OLD. It means that records are to be added to the data set. The parameter MOD is unique. That is, if the data set is not found by the Initiator, the data set will be regarded as NEW. (Of course, if the data set is in reality NEW, one had better request space. How to request space is explained a little later.)
4. SHR—Again similar to OLD. In addition, it means that the data set can be used simultaneously by more than one program. [When it is not explicitly stated to the Initiator that a data set is sharable, it is assumed by OS that the problem program (for which the Initiator is allocating the data set) will have exclusive use of the data set.]

Parameters for Normal Termination

The second parameter for *DISP=* is used to instruct the Terminator what is to be done with a data set when the job step terminates normally (i.e., successfully). The second parameter may be one of the following:

1. KEEP—This means that the data set's DSCB is to be retained in the VTOC after the Terminator deallocates the data set.
2. PASS—The Terminator is not to deallocate the data set at the end of the step. The volume containing the data set automatically remains mounted between job steps.
3. DELETE—The data set's DSCB is deleted from the VTOC and the space that had been allocated to the data set is made reallocatable. If the catalog was used to locate the data, the disposition of delete causes the data set name to be uncataloged. However, if the DD card contained the volume serial number and unit type (i.e., the catalog was not used), the data set name will remain cataloged even though its DSCB is deleted from the VTOC.

4. CATLG—The Terminator causes an entry to be made into the catalog. The entry will contain the volume serial number and device type of the data set named in the DD card. When the disposition is CATLG, the data set's DSCB is retained in the VTOC.
5. UNCATLG—The Terminator removes from the catalog the reference to the volume serial number and device type of the data set. The data set is not deleted, however. (This is an important point to remember.)

Parameters for Abnormal Termination

The parameters that can be used for normal termination can also be used when a job step terminates abnormally. Whatever parameter is placed in the third position of the DISP= keyword will be considered by the Terminator if the step ends abnormally. If the third parameter is not included in the DISP= keyword, then whatever is placed in the second position applies to both normal and abnormal termination. Figure 114 shows several examples of the keyword DISP=.

1. A new data set is being created. Upon normal termination it should be catalogued (which assumes keeping). If the step ABENDS the data set should be deleted.

```
DISP = (NEW, CATLG, DELETE)
```

2. An old data set is to be deleted if the step terminates under normal conditions but is to be kept if the step ABENDS.

```
DISP = (OLD, DELETE, KEEP)
```

3. A new data set is to be kept upon successful completion of the step otherwise it is to be deleted.

```
DISP = (NEW, KEEP, DELETE)
```

4. An old data set is to be kept whether the step terminates either normally or abnormally. (Note that the absence of the third parameter has the same affect as though it were included).

```
DISP = (OLD, KEEP)
```

Fig. 114 DISP coding examples.

Defaults

In the previous paragraph we said that if the third parameter is absent the Terminator assumes one (i.e., whatever is in the second parameter applies to both normal and abnormal termination). Does the Terminator or Initiator make any other assumptions? There are several instances where the omission of a parameter, whether accidental or planned, causes the Terminator or Initiator to make some assumptions. For example, the complete omission of DISP= and its parameters causes the Initiator to assume NEW and the Terminator to assume DELETE,-DELETE. Many installations take advantage of these "automatic" parameters (which are generally referred to as *default* parameters). That is, the preparor of the DD card intentionally leaves out DISP=(NEW,DELETE,DELETE) because he knows the Initiator/Terminator assumes this disposition when it is absent from the DD card.

Some other examples of assumed defaults are

1. DISP=OLD
2. DISP=(,KEEP)
3. DISP=(,PASS)

In the first example the information provided is for the Initiator—the Terminator assumes KEEP whenever the first parameter is OLD (or implies that it is old). In the second and third example, the first parameter is absent. When the first parameter is not supplied, the Initiator assumes NEW.

Disposition of System Output Data Sets

You should recall that in a multiprogramming environment one does not usually request allocation of printers or punches directly. That is, instead of having the operating system record a data set directly on an output device, it is possible to have the data set recorded temporarily on disk and then later, using a program known as the Output Writer, prepare the final data set with the printer or punch.

You should also recally that each output data set should be classified with a letter or digit (its output class). (Also, Output Writers select data sets for printing or punching according to a list consisting of these letters and digits. When a data set has been assigned the same class letter or digit that the Output Writer can recognize, the output is produced.)

The device on which the data set is ultimately recorded (printer, punch, etc.) is specified in a Writer procedure (which is in PROCLIB). The Initiator refers to the requested procedure for allocating the output device. To request this allocation requires a DD card in the job step. In this DD card, one places the keyword SYSOUT and the class associated with the desired device. For example, if the class is F, the DD card might appear as

```
//RESULTS DD SYSOUT=F
```

DATA SET NAMES

Review of Temporary and Nontemporary

Earlier in the text you were told that data sets can be regarded as being either temporary or nontemporary. Temporary data sets are ones whose longevity is limited to the life of a step or a job. Generally speaking, one does not provide names to temporary data sets, because the operating system itself is the only entity making reference to them. Examples of temporary data sets are the *work areas* required by the Compilers and the Linkage Editor. Nontemporary data sets are ones that can best be described as having a disposition of KEEP or CATLG. Data sets to which *future* reference has to be made are regarded as nontemporary.

Naming the Data Set

The operating system allows a data set to be named almost anything according to the following rules:

1. A data set name can consist of up to 44 characters (including periods).
2. For each eight alphameric characters or less, there must be a period.

Figure 115 illustrates the two rules.

SHORTEST POSSIBLE

DSNAME = A

LONGEST POSSIBLE

DSNAME = ABCDEFGH.IJKLMNOP.QRSTUVWX.
YZ012345.67899876

DSNAME = A.B.C.D.E.F.G.H.I.J.K.L.M.N.O.P.Q.
R.S.T.U.VW

Fig. 115 Data set name extremes.

Referring to Part of a Data Set

When someone wants to refer to a member of a PDS or to a generation of a generation data group, it is necessary to qualify the data set name with a member name or a generation number. For example, to refer to the generation about to be created (for the data set JENRASHN) requires the keyword and parameter

DSNAME=JENRASHN(+1)

On the other hand, if one wants to refer to the generation produced three weeks ago one would specify

DSNAME=JENRASHN(−3)

When a member of a PDS is referred to, the member name can be given as a suffix to the data set name. For example, to refer to the program called IEHLIST in LINKLIB one could state

DSNAME=SYS1.LINKLIB(IEHLIST)

When a partitioned data set is specified without a member name, the entire PDS will be referred to.

Assigning Names to Temporary Data Sets

In the developmental stages of a program, many installations use the technique known as COMPILE-LINK EDIT and GO. In the first step of a job, the source program is compiled and the results are placed into a *temporary* sequential data set. This temporary data set is *passed* to step 2. Then in the second step the results of compilation are link edited and these results are placed into a temporary partitioned data set. In the third step, the link-edited program is executed.

To facilitate reference to a temporary data set created in a previous step of the job, one can assist the operating system by providing a "temporary" name. (This is particularly helpful if there are several temporary data sets produced in earlier steps. Temporary data sets must be named if one is to distinguish among them.) This can be accomplished by placing two ampersands in front of the name. The "temporary" name often used for the data set receiving the results of compilation is

&&LOADSET

Also, the temporary partitioned data set that receives the Linkage Editor output is generally named &&GOSET. Figure 116 schematically summarizes the use and naming of temporary data sets. In Fig. 116 we say that the temporary data set is *partially* defined. This means that the operating system takes part in the naming ceremony. That is, the operating system, upon detecting the two ampersands, takes the "temporary" name and concatenates (do you remember the meaning of this word? It means to place adjacent to) it with the job name. For example, if the data set name is &&TEMPRARY and the job name is JOBONE, the complete temporary data set name would become

JOBONE.TEMPRARY

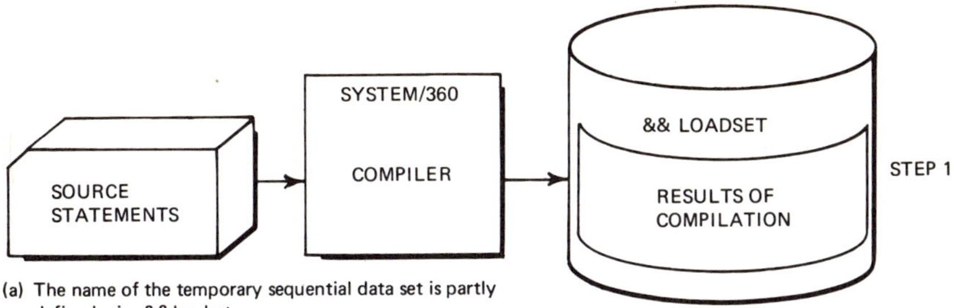

(a) The name of the temporary sequential data set is partly defined, viz., &&loadset.
(b) The sequential data set &&loadset is passed to step 2.

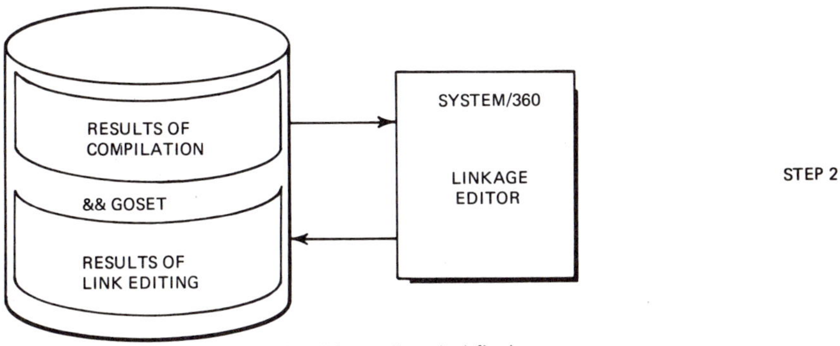

(a) The name of the temporary partitioned data set is partly defined, vis., &&goset.
(b) the PDS is passed to step 3.
(c) The temporary data set &&loadset is deleted at the end of step 2.

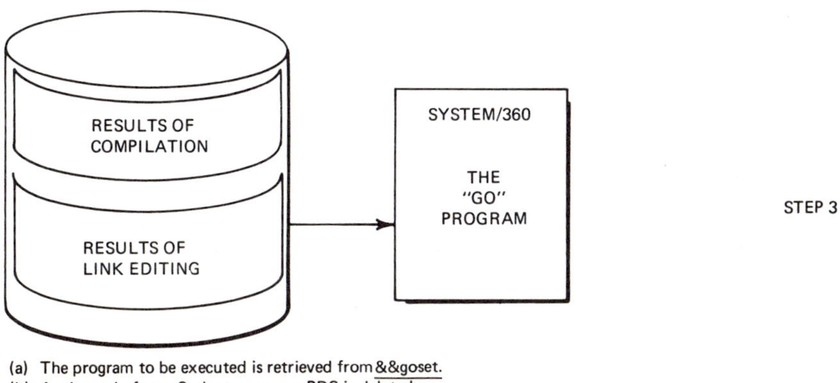

(a) The program to be executed is retrieved from &&goset.
(b) At the end of step 3, the temporary PDS is deleted.

Fig. 116 Temporary data set naming and use.

SPECIFYING AND REQUESTING I/O UNITS (UNIT=)

In one way or another, the operating system must be made aware of the type of unit that the data set resides on or is going to reside on. That is, if a device is to be allocated by the Initiator, some indication of the device type or unit must be specified.

Requesting a Specific Unit

A specific I/O unit can be requested by giving the physical address of the device. For example, if one wanted to allocate the disk drive whose address is 193, one would state

UNIT=193 (one ninety-three)

Requesting a specific unit can have serious consequences in getting the job step executed. For example, suppose that in multiprogramming environment, unit 193 had already been allocated for a job and that now a new job is started—this new job has a DD card specifically requesting unit 193. What will happen? For one thing, the new job might not get started until the other job terminates. In some cases this would be allright. However, if one were requesting work space for a temporary data set from the volume on unit 193 and the volume on unit 193 had no space and was permanently resident, the job requesting the work space would NEVER get started.

There are, of course, occasions when there is no alternative but to request a specific device. For example, if the immediate output has to be in the form of a card deck, and there is only one card punch with a physical address of 00D, there is little else to state except

UNIT=00D (i.e., ZERO, ZERO, DEE)

Requesting a Type of Unit

One can usually have a higher degree of assurance of getting a request satisfied if he asks the operating system to find an available unit. For example, if one wants space on a 2311 for a temporary data set and he doesn't care which volume or unit is to be used, he can specify the type of unit:

UNIT=2311

Of course, if the type of unit is to be a tape drive, then one must use

UNIT=2400

Requesting a Class of Unit

From the discussion of the previous paragraph one might assume that he could make only exclusive requests—for example, a request for a 2311 *or* a 2314. If this assumption were true, the allocation of I/O devices by the operating system would be restricted to one type of device for each DD card. As you may have guessed, it is possible to make a request in a DD card so that *any* appropriate device can be allocated. What is an "appropriate" device? For sequential data sets it could be a 2400 Tape unit, or a 2311 Disk Drive, or a 2314 Disk Drive, or part of a 2321 Data Cell; for partitioned data sets it could be any of the above except the tape units. (Remember, PDS's consist of members whose locations are specified in a directory.)

To make it possible for OS to allocate *any* appropriate device requires some preparation on the part of the installation at the time it is generating its system. First, it would make lists of devices to be used for meeting various allocation requirements. Then each of the lists would be given a name that reflects what the devices in the list represent. Figure 117 illustrates three lists. Once the list has been constructed, it is coded and placed into cards as input to the system generation process. During the system generation process the coded list becomes part of the

DEVICES IN THE LIST TO BE USED FOR	SEQUENTIAL DATA SETS	TAPE RESIDENT SEQUENTIAL DATA SETS	PARTITIONED OR DIRECT DATA SETS
NAME OF LIST	SYSSQ	TAPE	SYSDA
PHYSICAL ADDRESSES OF DEVICES IN THIS LIST (IN ORDER OF CONSIDERATION FOR ALLOCATION)	180 181 182 183 192 193 230 231	182 183 184 185 186	190 191 192 193 230 231 232 233

Note: The above addresses represent the following device types:

180, 181, 182, 183, 184, 185, 186 – 2400'S
190, 191, 192, 193 – 2311'S
230, 231, 232, 233 – 2314'S

Fig. 117 List of allocatable units.

installation's operating system. Once the list is part of the operating system one can give the list's name as a parameter to the UNIT keyword. For example, if one needed a volume for a sequential data set and didn't care on which device the volume would be mounted, he would specify

UNIT=SYSSQ

From this request the Initiator searches the list for the device that first satisfies the request.

Requesting Devices for Multivolume Data Sets

On many occasions, particularly with data sets on tape, one may require several devices because the data set is on several volumes. To minimize waiting time for mounting and dismounting it is possible to state the number of volumes required. For example, if three tape drives are needed, one merely has to state

UNIT=(2400,3) or UNIT=(TAPE,3)

This keyword and its parameters will get three tape drives allocated (if they are available).

Deferring the Mounting of a Volume

If it isn't necessary to get a volume mounted by the Initiator, one can specify a request for a deferred mount. For example, if a reel of tape with a particular serial number won't be needed until many seconds or several minutes after the step has started, one can ask for deferrment as follows:

UNIT=(2400,,DEFER)

(The unit type, the number of volumes, and the term DEFER are positional parameters, so the absence of the number of volumes in this example had to be denoted by two consecutive commas. When the number-of-volumes amount is absent, the Initiator *assumes* that it is 1.)

Requesting Separate DASD's for Different Data Sets

Of primary importance to the operations management in a data-processing center is the optimization of I/O flow. By seeing to it that highly active data sets are recorded on different volumes (rather than on the same volume), one can assure a relatively higher performance. For example, in the case of using the Assembler F Compiler there are three separate work areas required (the DD names for these work areas are SYSUT1, SYSUT2, and SYSUT3). Assuring that the SYSUT3 work area is *not* allocated space on the same volume as SYSUT1 and SYSUT2 greatly reduces the time in waiting for the access arms to be positioned (see Fig. 118).

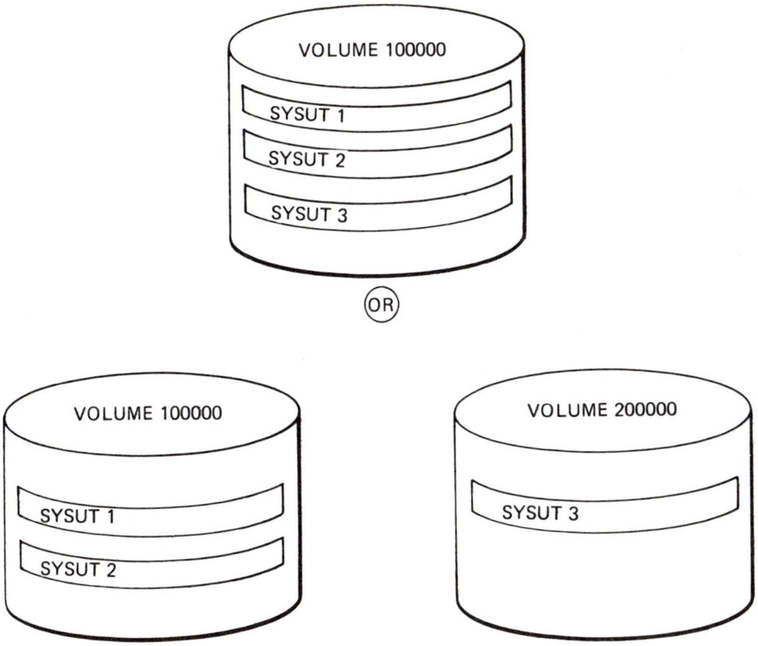

Fig. 118 Two alternatives for data set space allocation.

To request separate access mechanisms for direct-access data sets requires the subkeyword SEP= as the last operand of the UNIT= keyword. The subparameters of the SEP= subkeyword refer to the DD cards (i.e., to the name of the DD card) which describe the data sets to be kept separated. For example, to keep SYSUT3 from getting space on the same volume as SYSUT1 and SYSUT2, one would prepare the following DD cards:

```
//SYSUT1 DD UNIT=2311
//SYSUT2 DD UNIT=2311
//SYSUT3 DD UNIT=(2311,SEP=(SYSUT1,SYSUT2))
```

Requesting the Same Device for Different Data Sets

Another concern of operation's management is assuring that several data sets get recorded on the same volume. Although it appears that this concern is in contradiction to the previous one, it is not. For example, if the data sets OBJMODS and LOADMODS are to be on the same pack (see Fig. 119), one would prepare the following DD cards:

```
//OBJECT DD DSNAME=OBJMODS,DISP=(NEW,KEEP),UNIT=2311
//LOAD DD DSNAME=LOADMODS,DISP=(NEW,KEEP),
            UNIT=AFF=OBJECT
```

In the above DD card excerpts you see that there is a double keyword, UNIT=AFF= (AFF means affinity), and that the parameter is the name of the DD card that describes the other data set with which this one is to coreside.

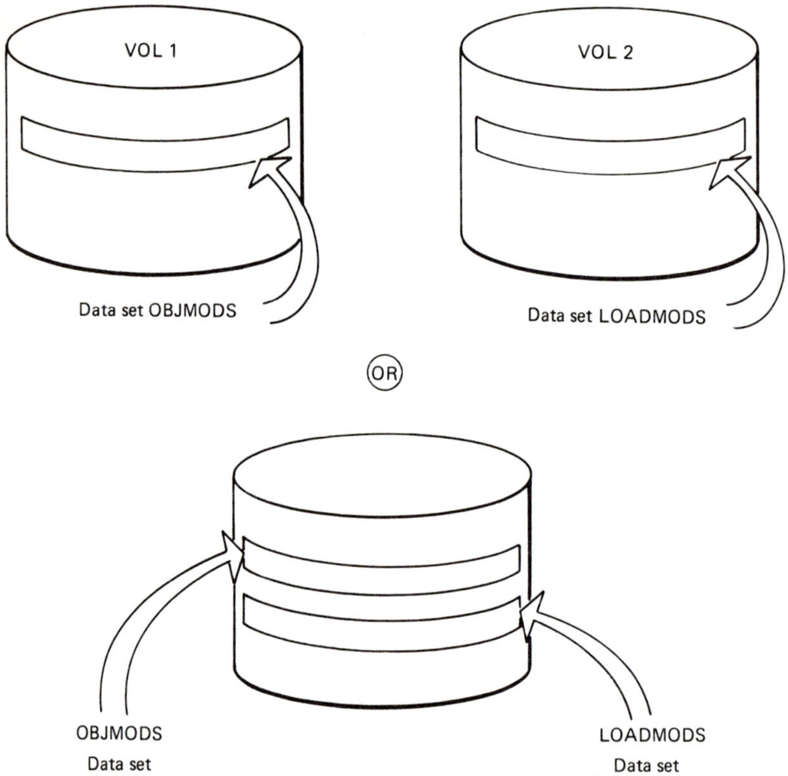

Fig. 119 Two more alternatives for data set space allocation.

Allocating the System's Input Device for Reading Data

There are two main techniques for allocating the system's input device for reading data in the input stream (see Fig. 120). The first technique, as shown in Fig. 120, uses the asterisk. When this character is in a DD card, it is a signal to the

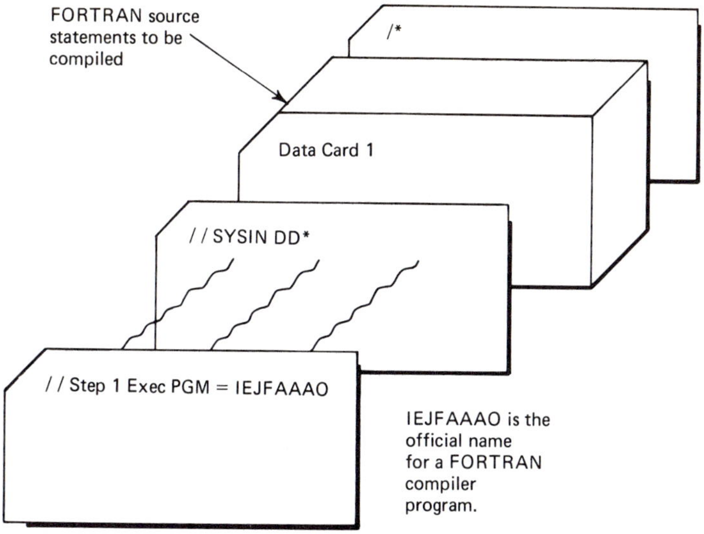

Fig. 120 SYSIN DD * statement.

Initiator that the card reader is to be allocated for the purpose of reading data cards (i.e., cards that are to be processed by the program named in the execute card of the step). The asterisk loses its effect as soon as a slash-asterisk card (i.e., a card with a /* in columns 1 and 2) or another job control card is encountered in the job stream.

The second technique, similar to the first, uses the term DATA instead of the asterisk. The term DATA has the same effect as the asterisk except that it retains its effect when a JCL card is encountered. Therefore, the term DATA is used instead of an asterisk for such functions as reading JCL statements for placement into PROCLIB as a procedure.

IDENTIFICATION OF THE VOLUME

Private Volume Requests

Programmers working on special projects often require that the volume on which they are recording data or from which they are reading data be *dismounted* after the job step is finished. They want the dismounting to take place because they don't want the operating system to grant space requests from this volume for new data sets of someone else's data-processing jobs. To ensure that dismounting takes place, one can state that the volume is private property

VOLUME=PRIVATE

Suppose, however, that the programmer has a two-step job in which he wants to use the private volume in both steps. He certainly wouldn't want to delay the computing center operations by causing a dismount followed by a remount of the same pack. Therefore, he can request with the VOLUME keyword that the volume be *retained* (i.e., not dismounted until the end of the subsequent step):

VOLUME=(PRIVATE,RETAIN)

Requesting the Nth Volume of a Multivolume Data Set

Quite often a data-processing installation finds that it has to process only a small collection of records of a rather large data set. For example, an insurance company may want to examine the policy records written between two dates, such as February 1958 and June 1959. It knows what the policy numbers issued during these dates are and that these records are on the third volume of the eight-volume master policy file data set. Now, when the job is run to examine these records one doesn't want to have all eight volumes allocated, just the third one. Requesting the third volume of the multivolume data set can be done by placing the volume's order number in the third positional operand. To obtain the third volume one merely states

VOLUME=(,,3)

Requesting More than One Volume

As has been already alluded to several times, there are many data-processing applications where a data set requires more than one volume. To specify that more than one volume is required, one can state the number of volumes as the fourth positional parameter of the VOLUME keyword. For example, to allocate four volumes one could state

VOLUME=(,,,4)

In each of the four positional parameters for VOLUME discussed so far, no mention has been made of serial numbers (i.e., the values that identify specific volumes). Therefore, if the keyword and its parameters were

VOLUME=(PRIVATE,RETAIN,,4)

there would be allocated four private volumes to be kept mounted at the end of this job step. Suppose, however, that one wishes to *read* some data set records—can the operating system predict what the volume serial numbers are? The answer is obviously no! Somehow the serial numbers must be stated if the request is for specific volumes.

Requesting a Specific Volume or Volumes

If a data set is not cataloged, the volume serial number (or numbers) has to be provided in a DD card. There are two techniques for indicating the volume serial numbers. We shall call one the direct method and the other the indirect method.

DIRECT REFERENCE

When a direct reference is made it means that the volume serial numbers are in the same DD card that refers to the data set. For example, if one wants the three volumes whose serial numbers are HWC111, KAC008, and CCC039, one states as follows:

VOLUME=SER=(HWC111,KAC008,CCC039)

If only one volume is required, for example, HWC111, it can be specified as

VOLUME=SER=HWC111

(Note that when there is a list of serial numbers, they are enclosed in parentheses, but when only one serial number is given, parentheses aren't needed.)

Now let's look at an instance where two specific private volumes are to remain mounted after the step in which they are first used. If the serial numbers are APC010 and JCC006, one would state

VOLUME=(PRIVATE,RETAIN,SER=(APC010,JCC006))

Note that when the *last* two positional parameters are not required it is not necessary to indicate their absence with commas. (Reminder: These last two positional parameters are related to the number of volumes and the *N*th volume.)

INDIRECT REFERENCE

What does a person do when a data set that he needs for his program is on a volume whose serial number he doesn't know? One obvious answer is that he can ask enough people until he finds out. An alternative that requires less extensive research is to find out what catalogued data sets are on that volume. Once the name of the catalogued data set is known, it can be used as an indirect reference to the serial number. For example, if the catalogued data set is COBLIB, one merely has to state

VOLUME=REF=SYS1.COBLIB

(REF stands for *reference*).

Now let's assume another situation. In step 1 of a job a nonspecific request is made for a volume. Because it is nonspecific, almost any volume will be used: in step 4 a data set is to be recorded on the same volume that was assigned in step 1. How does one ensure that the same volume is used in both steps? A technique known as the refer-back can be used. What one refers back to is a DD card of a previous step. The referring back to the desired activity is indicated by an asterisk,

VOLUME=REF=*

Two more items of information are required. One is the name of the step (i.e., the name of the execute card) and the other is the name of the DD card. For example, if the volume information for the DD card in step 4 is to be obtained by referring back to a DD card named URLYER in a step named STEPONE, one would state

```
//STEP4 DD  ~~  ,VOLUME=REF=*.STEPONE.URLYER,  ~~
```

When two data sets are to be created in the same job step and they are both to reside on the same volume obtained with a nonspecific request, it is not necessary to include the name of the step; only the name of the DD card is required. For example, if the nonspecific request is first made in the DD card named PREESEED and the refer-back is being made in the DD card named KURRENT, one would specify

```
//KURRENT DD  ~~  ,VOLUME=REF=*.PREESEED,  ~~
```

(When this technique is used one must make certain that the DD cards are in the correct order in the input stream.)

REQUESTING SPACE ON DIRECT-ACCESS STORAGE DEVICES

Before a new data set can be recorded on DASD's the space required by the data set must have been allocated by the Initiator. There are two major items to specify when a space request is made. One is the unit of space measure—these are a track, cylinder, and block length. The other item is the quantity or number of space units.

If tracks are to be allocated one uses the keyword SPACE, the term TRK, and the quantity or number of tracks. The following examples show how different requests could be made.

Whole No. of Tracks Required	Keyword and Parameters
35 tracks	SPACE=(TRK,35)
190 tracks	SPACE=(TRK,190)
4 tracks	SPACE=(TRK,4)

If cylinders are to be allocated the term CYL is used instead of TRK:

SPACE=(CYL,5)

SPACE=(CYL,70)

Sometimes it is not too appropriate to make requests for space using the TRK or CYL as units of measure. This is because the type of unit used may change. For example, a track on a 2311 can accommodate a maximum of 3,625 bytes, whereas a track on a certain model of a 2314 can hold up to 7,294 bytes. Hence a request for the same number of tracks on a 2314 allocates twice the amount of space as would be allocated on a 2311. Another example of track or cylinder being inappropriate is that the numbers of bytes they represent is not appropriate for the length of the records to be written. Therefore, one can request space in terms of block length. The two following examples show how this is done:

Block Length and No. of Blocks	Keyword and Parameters
100 blocks, each 1,024 bytes long	SPACE=(1024,100)
1,000 blocks, each 80 bytes long	SPACE=(80,1000)
80 blocks each 1,000 bytes long	SPACE=(1000,80)

Although the second and third examples would get the same amount of space allocated, they differ greatly in the length of the block to be written (80 bytes versus 1,000 bytes) and the *number* of blocks to be written (1,000 blocks versus 80 blocks).

Future Space Requirements

Sometimes it is difficult to predict how much larger a data set may become in the future. Faced with such a predicament, a programmer might request two or three times as much as he needs, "just to make sure." It is not a good idea to tie up large chunks of storage just to make sure that enough space will always be available. One solution is to request "conditional" space (i.e., space to be granted at some future time if the need should arise). The future-requirements space is specified as the second parameter (immediately following the original quantity). The conditional value is placed into the DSCB of the data set. Each time the data set runs out of space, the extra space is allocated (on the same volume) until no more space exists.

Examples

1. 35 tracks now with 5 conditional,
   SPACE=(TRK,(35,5))

2. 70 cylinders now with 7 conditional,
   SPACE=(CYL,(70,7))

3. 1,000 eighty-byte blocks with 50 conditional,
   SPACE=(80,(1000,50))

Allocating Space for Partitioned Data Sets

Some of the space allocated to a partitioned data set must be used for a directory. The directory space for a PDS is divided into units called records, which are 256 bytes each. The number of directory records to be set up is specified as the third positional subparameter for space amount.

Examples

1. 5 cylinders with 1 conditional and 15 directory records,
   SPACE=(CYL,(5,1,15))

2. 10 cylinders with no conditional cylinders and 25 directory records,
   SPACE=(CYL,(10,,25))

When the Initiator detects the existence of the third positional parameter, it assumes that the space request is for a partitioned data set. This is the only way to distinguish the request for creating a PDS from creating a non-PDS.

Releasing Unneeded Space

When there is no possibility of future growth for a data set being created on the current step, it is a good idea to have the Terminator return any space left over at the end of the step for reallocation. Since the Terminator can release unused space, it makes the planning of space requirements a little easier. That is, a person can make a rough estimate of his space requirements, add a 10 or 20 percent safety factor (so that the step won't terminate abnormally), and then have the Terminator release unused space. To specify the *release* function requires the positional operand RLSE.

Examples

1. 20 cylinders for a partitioned data set with 40 directory records,
   SPACE=(CYL,(20,,40),RLSE)

2. 75 tracks for a sequential data set,
   SPACE=(TRK,(75),RLSE)

Requesting Contiguous Space

The operating system, after determining that enough total space for a request exists on a volume, will attempt to allocate continguous tracks or cylinders. If the tracks or cylinders are not contiguous, OS allocates smaller blocks to satisfy the request. There are occasions when under no circumstances does the installation want requests to be fulfilled by allocating small blocks. That is, contiguous space is to be allocated or none at all. Contiguous allocation can be specified by using the positional parameter CONTIG. (If there is no contiguous space when it is requested, the job will not get run and will have to be rescheduled after the problem has been analyzed and eliminated.)

Examples

1. 20 contiguous cylinders for a sequential data set; release the excess space:
   SPACE=(CYL,(20),RLSE,CONTIG)

2. 30 contiguous tracks for a sequential data set; do not release the excess space:
   SPACE=(TRK,(30),,CONTIG)

SPLITTING DATA SETS INTO SMALLER SETS

Occasionally an installation has to determine whether to put all the data concerning certain items into one data set or into two or more data sets. For example, employee data may consist of such diverse information as that which is personal (home address, make of automobile, and automobile registration number) and that which is business (payroll data, skill and education, seniority, and relocatability). The total amount of data for each employee could realistically consist of 400 to 500 characters. Suppose that for a particular and frequent data-processing application (e.g., payroll) only one half of the data is required. It would be wasteful of time to read in a 400-character record when only 200 characters are needed most of the time.

To make the I/O operations more efficient, one can split the data into two (or more if desired) data sets (see Fig. 121). On occasions when all 400 characters are required, corresponding records from both data sets can be read in such a way that it isn't necessary for the access arms to move when getting records from alternate data sets. That is, a collection of cylinders can be allocated in such a way so that each cylinder is split between corresponding records of the two data sets. As you know, a cylinder is comprised of tracks which are "stacked" one above the other. Such an arrangement makes it possible for the access mechanism to remain stationary when the reading or writing operation transfers from one track to the next. As long as the access mechanism remains motionless, many milliseconds of

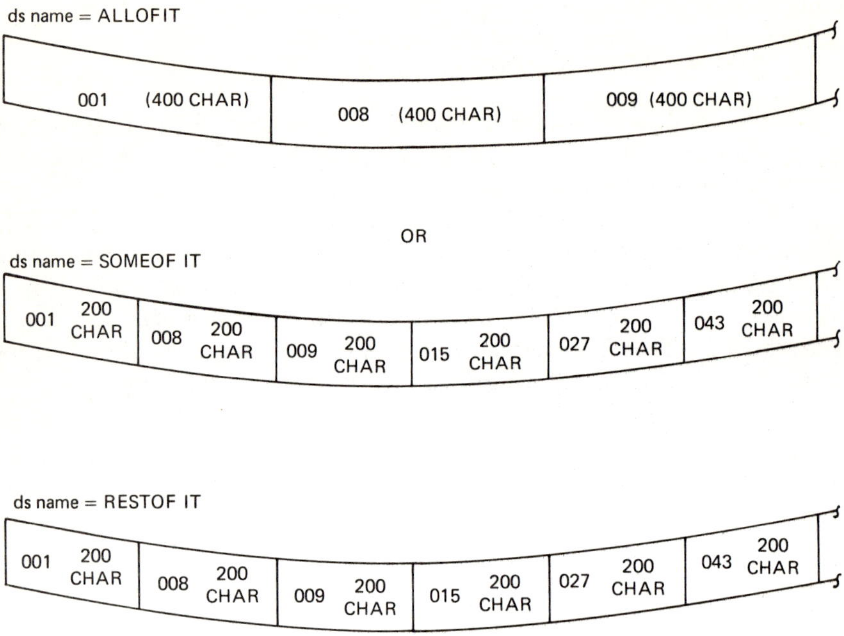

Fig. 121 Alternative of integral or split data sets.

time can be saved. Getting a collection of cylinders allocated in such a way that each cylinder is split between corresponding records is accomplished by the keyword SPLIT= instead of the keyword SPACE=. Two units of measure can be used to request split allocation: cylinder and block size.

Cylinder—Split Allocation

To request split allocation for cylinders, the DD cards must be in a certain sequence. That is, the first DD card must specify the amount of space required by the "upper" data set and the total amount of space required for all data sets sharing the split cylinders. For example, if the upper data set is to have 6 tracks per cylinder and 30 cylinders are required for all the split data sets, one would write

SPLIT=(6,CYL,30)

Each "lower" data set needs to state only how many tracks per cylinder it is to use. If it is four tracks, one writes

SPLIT=4

Conditional space for future requirements can be requested in the same way as when using the SPACE= keyword. For example, suppose there are to be three data sets requiring a total of 50 cylinders now and 5 conditionally for future use, with 3 tracks per cylinder for the upper data set, 4 tracks per cylinder for the middle data set, and 3 tracks per cylinder for the lower data set. The three DD cards would contain the following:

SPLIT=(3,CYL,50,5)

SPLIT=4

SPLIT=3

Block Size—Split Allocation

Just as space can be requested by block size with the SPACE= keyword, so can space be requested by blocksize with the SPLIT= keyword. The major difference is that one asks for the percentage of the blocks rather than a specific amount. (The operating system figures out the number of blocks from the percentage and the total space request. When blocks are requested the operating system rounds off the request to whole cylinders.) For example, suppose one wants three data sets requiring a total of two thousand 200-character records now, and 400 conditionally for future use, to be split as follows: Upper data set, 40 percent; middle data set, 35 percent; lower data set, 25 percent. The request would be written

SPLIT=(40,200,(2000,400))

SPLIT=35

SPLIT=25

Figure 122 shows three more examples of requesting split allocation.

Split Requests

1) CYLINDER, NO CONDITIONAL SPACE

```
//DDONE     DD ~~~, SPLIT = (6, CYL, 30),
//DDTWO     DD ~~~, SPLIT = 4
```

2) CYLINDER, CONDITIONAL SPACE

```
//DDEIN     DD ~~~, SPLIT = (3, CYL, 50, 5)
//DDZWEI    DD ~~~, SPLIT = 4
//DDDREI    DD ~~~, SPLIT = 3
```

3) BLOCKSIZE, CONDITIONAL SPACE

```
//DDUNO     DD ~~~, SPLIT = (40, 200, (2000, 400))
//DDDUE     DD ~~~, SPLIT = 35
//DDTROIS   DD ~~~, SPLIT = 25
```

Fig. 122 Examples of split requests.

ARRANGING DATA SETS INTO A SERIES

Another requirement of some data-processing installations is the assurance that a series of data sets gets recorded on one volume and that they appear in a certain sequence. One of the main techniques used to meet this requirement is to request the Initiator to allocate *in the first step of a job* enough space for all the related data sets. (You know that to grant such a request, the Initiator looks at the Format 5 DSCB for locating available space.) Then in subsequent steps of the same job, requests for "subspace" are made (i.e., space is to be granted from the supply given to the first data set rather than from the free space described by a Format 5 DSCB). Naturally, you must distinguish the request for subspace from a request for free space. This is accomplished by using the keyword SUBALLOC= instead of SPACE=.

To use the SUBALLOC keyword, one must identify the data set from which the suballocation is to be granted. The data set is identified indirectly. That is, one must include in the suballocation request the name of the step and the name of the DD card in which the data set was first created. For example, suppose that in the step named PREVSTEP a data set named MASTER was allocated 50 cylinders of space. Then to get 10 cylinders of this data set suballocated one would have to write

```
SUBALLOC=(CYL,(10),PREVSTEP.MASTER)
```

OPTIMIZING CHANNEL USAGE

When a S/360 has two or more selector channels the installation can get optimum use from them by requesting separate channels for transmitting data from highly active data sets on *different devices.* For example, if there are many simultaneous requests to both LINKLIB and SVCLIB (old data sets) and each has been placed on a separate volume, then having the data from these two libraries come over separate channels would be an improvement over having the data come over one channel. To request channel separation requires the keyword SEP=. (This keyword is spelled the same as the subkeyword for requesting the separation of *new* data sets onto different devices in the UNIT= keyword.) To specify the other data set(s), which are to use a different channel, requires the names of the DD cards that describe the other data sets. For example, if the respective data sets DSONE, DSTWO, and DSTHREE are described with the DD cards named ENGLISH, N05, and HUDSON, then to use a different channel for the data set name NEWDS requires the following:

//CHNLSEP DD DSNAME=NEWDS,SEP=(ENGLISH,N05,HUDSON)

If several DD cards are to express the desire for channel separation (for data sets on *different devices*), there is a technique that can minimize the duplication of the SEP=DDNAMES keyword. For example (assuming the same job step as above), if still another data set NEWERDS is to have its records transmitted over a different channel than DSONE, DSTWO, and DSTHREE, one could either state (this illustrates duplication)

//MORESEP DD DSNAME=NEWERDS,SEP=(ENGLISH,N05,HUDSON)

or use the shortcut technique in which reference is made to the DD card already specifying separation, via

//MORESEP DD DSNAME=NEWERDS,AFF=CHNLSEP

The above example shows the keyword AFF=, which means *affinity*. It literally means that this data set (NEWERDS) is to have channel affinity with the data set named in the DD card called CHNLSEP. (That is, it is to have the same channel separation from the other data sets as does the data set mentioned in CHNLSEP.) Figure 123 shows the relationship between several DD cards and the keywords SEP and AFF.

Optimizing Channel Usage

```
// ENGLISH   DD  DSNAME = DSONE, ~~~
// NO5       DD  DSNAME = DSTWO, ~~~
//HUDSON     DD  DSNAME = DSTHREE ~~~
// CHNLSEP   DD  DSNAME = NEWDS,
                   SEP = (ENGLISH, NO5, HUDSON), ~~~
__ __ __ __ __ __ __ __ __ __ __ __

// MORESEP   DD  DSNAME = NEWERDS,
                 SEP = (ENGLISH, NO5, HUDSON),~~~

                      – OR –

// MORESEP   DD  DSNAME = NEWERDS, AFF = CHNLSEP
```

Fig. 123 Equivalent use of SEP and AFF.

IDENTIFICATION OF DATA SETS ON TAPE

In addition to supplying volume label information, it may be necessary to supply data set label information. On direct-access devices, data set labels are referred to as *data set control blocks* (DSCB's). You will recall that the DSCB's are in the

VTOC, which the operating system finds by consulting the direct-access volume label. (A direct-access volume must *always* have a standard label if it is to be used by the operating system.) In contrast, volume labels are not mandatory on tape. And when there is no volume label on tape there will be no data set label. There can also be data set labels on tape that are not standard.

Whereas a data set on DASD can be found by getting the cylinder, track, and record number address from the data set's DSCB it is not so automatic a procedure for finding other than the first data set on tape (magnetic tapes don't contain address markers). The operating system must be told the data set's order on tape when the data set is not first. (To do this, the tape data set must have labels—if there are no labels there is just "one" data set.) For example, if the fourth data set were required it would be necessary to state

LABEL=4

To specify the type of label on tape (both volume and data set), or that one doesn't exist or that one exists but is to be ignored, requires one of the following positional parameters:

SL—The volume and data set labels are *standard.* (Standard refers to a format required by IBM-supplied data-management routines.)

NSL—The labels are *not standard.*

NL—There are *no labels.*

SUL—There are both *standard* volume and data set labels and *user* data set *labels.*

BLP—There are some kinds of *labels* but they are to be *bypassed* (i.e., ignored).

Examples

1. The data set in question is the third one and there are standard labels,
   LABEL=(3,SL)
2. The volume has no labels,
   LABEL=(,NL)

PROTECTING THE DATA SET

If this is a data set being created on this step and future retrieval is to be password protected, the operating system will place a code in the data set's label if it is stated that

LABEL=(,SL,PASSWORD)

Then, at retrieval time, the proper password will have to be given by the console operator.

Note. If you have any questions about password protection, it might be a good idea to review Fig. 102. A somewhat weaker method of protecting a data set is by using the retention-period or expiration-date technique. That is, at the time of creating the data set one can specify either the number of days from today or the date *before* which it will be necessary to issue a formal operator reply if the data set is to be used.

Examples

1. The data set is to have a protected retention period of 156 days:
   LABEL=RETPD=156
2. The data set is to have an expiration date of no earlier than Sept. 22, 1971:
   LABEL=EXPDT=71265

SPECIFYING DATA SET ATTRIBUTES AND ACCESS METHOD REQUIREMENTS

The Access Methods get the information they need from three major sources. These are:

1. The DCB in the problem program.
2. The label of the data set.
3. The DCB keyword in the DD card.

If the information required is in the DCB of the problem program, the Access Method uses it. If the information is not in the DCB of the problem program, the Access Method looks for it in the DCB keyword of the DD card. If the information is neither in the problem program DCB nor the DD card, the Access Method looks for it in the data set label. Figure 124 shows the decisions made for each parameter that is required.

When Should DCB Information Be Placed in a DD Card?

When a data set's disposition is OLD, its attributes are pretty well established and they have probably been already recorded in the data set label (DSCB or header record). If the old data set is on an unlabeled tape, however, the data set attributes are not automatically available (unless they were all included in the DCB of the program that is to process the data). When such an old data set is to be processed, its attributes may have to be supplied by the DCB keyword in the DD card. (Of course, it can't be supplied unless someone knows what the information is or where to find it. The answer is "good documentation and retrieval system" or, better yet, use standard labels.)

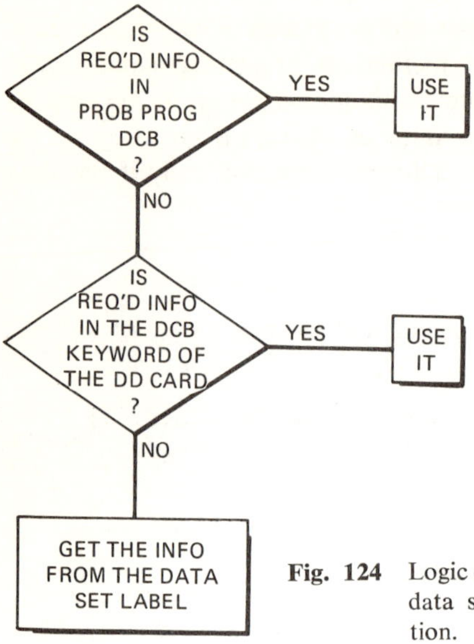

Fig. 124 Logic of obtaining data set information.

The most important DCB information that has to be supplied are logical record length (LRECL), tape recording density (DEN), record format (RECFM), and block size (BLKSIZE). When seven-track tape is used it may be necessary to specify the tape recording technique (TRTCH).

When the data set's disposition is new, it means that it is about to be created as a result of executing a program. One of the items in the program is the list of DCB information in which the programmer stated as many permanent attributes of the data set as he could (e.g., LRECL). It may be, however, that RECFM couldn't be decided upon at the time the program was written (i.e., should it be fixed and blocked or fixed and unblocked). Therefore, RECFM will have to be supplied in a DD card.

Examples

1. Fixed records, 240 characters each, with a blocking factor of 4, a density of 556 characters per inch on seven-track tape with the data conversion feature. [The data conversion feature allows the writing of 4 BCD tape characters (24 bits) from 3 EBCDIC characters in storage; it allows the reading of a group of 4 BCD characters and converting them into 3 EBCDIC characters.]

```
~~,DCB=(RECFM=FB,LRECL=240,BLKSIZE=960,DEN=1,TRTCH=C),~~
```

(Block size is the product of LRECL and the blocking factor; the 1 in DEN=1 is the code for 556 characters per inch; TRTCH=C means the tape recording technique is conversion; the B in RECFM=FB means that there is more than one record per block.)

2. Fixed and unblocked records, 80 characters per record, nine-track tape:
∿,DCB=(RECFM=F,LRECL=80,BLKSIZE=80),∿

In addition to supplying data set attributes, the DCB keyword can state to the Access Method the number of I/O buffers required. (If no buffer requirements are stated, the operating system automatically creates two.) This is accomplished by specifying BUFNO=.

Example

A high I/O job is to be run on a S/360 with more core storage than the job really needs. This may allow for an increase in the number of buffers to make the I/O operation more efficient. Let's say someone has determined that five buffers represents the best balance between cost of storage and speed of processing. Hence the keyword and parameter

BUFNO=5

Using DCB Information Previously Specified

When DCB information about a data set has to be supplied in a DD card, it may be that there already exists another data set with DCB information identical to what is required. When this is the case, it is possible to equate the DCB keyword to the data set name. There are two prerequisites to using this technique:

1. The data set's name must be in the catalog.
2. The volume upon which the data set resides must be in a mount condition. (The DCB information is obtained from the DSCB of the mounted data set.)

Example

If LINKLIB is the data set whose attributes can be used for PRIVLIB, one would state

DCB=SYS1.LINKLIB

Sometimes the same DCB information must be used for several new data sets being created in the same job. When this is the case, the DCB information has to be provided *directly* only once. Thereafter (as long as it is in the same job), one can refer to the DD card in which the DCB information was first recorded. For example, suppose the step named URLYSTEP had a DD card named ORIGDCB in which *several* DCB parameters were given; then one would refer back as follows:

1. DCB=*.URLYSTEP.ORIGCDB (when the steps are different) or
2. DCB=*.ORIGDCB (when this is the same step).

DEFINING THE CHARACTER SET FOR THE PRINTER

The printer most often used with a S/360 installation is the 1403. A special feature of the 1403 is the interchangeability of type chains or type trains (chains and trains contain the type slugs for printing the graphic symbols), each of which corresponds to a certain character set (there are about a dozen different character sets). Each of these chains and trains is controlled by the print buffer in the 1403. This buffer must be conditioned each time a new character set is used and it should be reconditioned when power has been turned off. (If the buffer receives the EBCDIC representation of a character for which it isn't conditioned, the printer regards this as an I/O error and stops.)

The conditioning (or reconditioning) must be done with the keyword *UCS*. The parameter supplied with the keyword should be equivalent to the identification code of the character set. The following is a partial list of the character set names and their identification code.

alphameric	AN
FORTRAN/COBOL	RN
text printing	TN
high-speed alphameric	XN

If one were to use the FORTRAN/COBOL set, he would specify

UCS=RN

INFORMING THE INITIATOR TO LOOK FOR A PROGRAM IN A PRIVATE LIBRARY

As you know, the Initiator starts its search for the program (named in the execute card) in SYS1.LINKLIB. In LINKLIB may reside hundreds of modules; these are the ones most frequently used by the installation. There are several considerations for not putting a program into LINKLIB. For example, a program may be under development—one should not clutter up LINKLIB with programs in the development stage. Another reason for not placing a program into LINKLIB is that very few people use the program or that it is seldom used by anyone. To accommodate the people whose programs don't meet the LINKLIB entrance requirements, the OS architects made it possible to put these programs into "private" libraries. Then, when one of these programs is required, the Initiator can be instructed to start looking for the requested program in the private library. To instruct the Initiator to look in a private library requires a DD card named JOBLIB. This card must appear immediately after the JOB card.

Although there can be only one DD card per job named JOBLIB, there can be several unnamed DD cards immediately following the JOBLIB card (and preceding the execute card of the first step). Into each of these unnamed DD cards one places the name of the data set in which the Initiator should look for programs that are named in the execute cards of the job. (When unnamed DD cards follow named DD cards, one refers to the collection as concatenated DD cards.)

The disposition information is of great importance also. The first parameter is usually either OLD or SHR (share) unless the JOBLIB is going to be created during the first step of the job, in which case it would be NEW. Regardless of what the first parameter is, the second one must not be either KEEP or DELETE. (Why it must not be delete is obvious.) When a data set is given the disposition of KEEP, the Terminator will at the end of the job step make the data set unavailable for further steps of the job. Since there can be only one JOBLIB DD card per job regardless of the number of steps, the disposition of KEEP would make the JOBLIB data set available *only to the first step* of the job. (Why? The Terminator at the end of the step would deallocate it.) The designers of the operating system consider the KEEP disposition in the JOBLIB card an error. Therefore, to assure the availability of the JOBLIB data set to all steps of a job requires the parameter PASS [e.g., DISP=(OLD,PASS) or DISP=(SHR,PASS)]. When PASS is used in conjunction with OLD, the data set is KEPT at job termination time.

To make a private program library available for only the life of a job step, one can prepare a STEPLIB DD card instead of a JOBLIB DD card. Of course, the STEPLIB DD card must precede the EXEC card of the job step.

SUMMARY

1. The information in a DD statement is used for the allocation of data sets, direct-access space, I/O devices, and volumes for the program requested in the EXEC statement.
2. The keyword DISP is used to tell the Initiator/Terminator of the status and disposition of data sets. The status of data may be NEW, OLD, MOD, or SHR. The disposition of data sets may be KEEP, PASS, DELETE, CATLG, and UNCATLG.
3. The disposition of output data sets is requested with the keyword SYSOUT.
4. A member or part of a data set may be referred to by providing the member name or relative generation number.
5. Programmers may assist the operating system in naming temporary data sets. A temporary data set is defined by placing two ampersands in front of the name.

6. Requests for I/O units can be specific by type, and by class. The keyword to request a unit or units is UNIT.
7. Two or more units may be specified with one request.
8. The parameter DEFER used with the keyword UNIT makes it unnecessary to have the volume mounted on the unit until after the job step has started executing.
9. One can request different data sets to be mounted on the same unit or on different units.
10. The system input device can be allocated for data in the input stream by placing an asterisk or the term DATA immediately following the DD.
11. Volumes can be defined with the keyword VOLUME.
12. A volume may be designated as private.
13. To keep a private volume mounted between job steps, one must specify RETAIN.
14. The *N*th volume of a multivolume data set may be requested.
15. If a specific volume is required, one may refer to it directly by providing the serial number of the volume or indirectly by giving the name of a catalogued data set residing on the required volume.
16. The first time the Initiator assigns a volume to a nonspecific request, the volume can thereafter be referenced (in the same job) by providing the Initiator with the name of the EXEC statement and/or the name of the DD statement for which the nonspecific request was granted.
17. Space on a direct-access storage device may be requested by number of cylinders, number of tracks, and number of blocks. The keyword is SPACE.
18. Conditional space for future use can be requested when the initial amount of space is requested.
19. If space for a partitioned data set is being requested, one must specify the amount of space required for the directory.
20. Excess space can be returned for further allocation by supplying the parameter RLSE.
21. Contiguous space can be requested by supplying the parameter CONTIG.
22. Large data sets can be split into smaller, parallel data sets by using the keyword SPLIT.
23. To ensure that several data sets are recorded in sequential order, one can request total allocation for the first data set and suballocation for subsequent data sets.
24. The keyword SEP can be used to request different channel assignments for data sets needed concurrently.
25. The keyword LABEL is used to tell the operating system what kinds of labels a tape volume has, which data set on a tape volume is requested, and whether the data set is protected.
26. The DCB keyword is used to supply the Access Methods with data set attributes and buffer requirements.

27. DCB information for a new data set may be obtained from the DSCB of an old, mounted, and catalogued data set.
28. The conditioning of the printer's printing mechanism can be accomplished with the keyword UCS and the keyword that corresponds to the printing mechanism's character set.
29. When programs are kept in a private library, the request to allocate the private library must be in a DD card preceding the EXEC card.

SUGGESTED READING ASSIGNMENT

IBM System/360 Operating System
Job Control Language (C28-6539)

Section 1: Job Control Statements

(The material in this publication is rather detailed. Rather than read it word-for-word, just become familiar with its organization and contents.)

11 PROCEDURES AND THEIR USE

REVIEW

Whenever a job step or a related series of job steps is executed frequently, it is a good idea to name each collection of steps and place the named collection into the partitioned data set library called SYS1.PROCLIB. When the series of steps is to be executed, one places the name of the procedure in an EXEC card. The reader task, upon recognizing the name as referring to a procedure, retrieves from PROCLIB the steps of the procedure. These entries from PROCLIB are then regarded as though they had been supplied in the job stream.

SIZE OF PROCLIB

It is not unusual for an installation to have 50 or more standard procedures. That many procedures would require rather few cylinders of a DASD. Some installations, however, require as many as 200 basic procedures with 10 or 15 variations of each. Such a requirement could use up a considerable portion of a disk pack. (Each variation would be a procedure in itself requiring space and its own unique name.) To implement variations to standard procedures without the overhead of including each variation in PROCLIB, IBM has developed two kinds of override techniques. These techniques are the use of symbolic parameters and the override.

SYMBOLIC PARAMETERS

The first order of business is to determine which keywords may have variable parameters. Let's consider the following DD card (required for some compilers) that is in a procedure named PROC23:

//SYSUT1 DD UNIT=2311,SPACE=(1700,(400,50)).

The value most subject to variation is the number of records (400) required. For example, if the source program consists of a small number of cards, the space required may not exceed 200 records; on the other hand, if the number of source cards is large, the space required may consist of 750 or 1000 or even 1200 records. Therefore, instead of writing an actual value for the number of records, one must supply a symbolic value.

RULES FOR SYMBOLIC NAMES

1. The symbolic name chosen must start with an ampersand.
2. The rest of the symbolic name follows the rules of all other kinds of names used in OS.

Example

Let's say that the symbolic name for amount of space is &NUMRECS. The above DD card in the procedure would then appear as

//SYSUT1 DD UNIT=2311,SPACE=(1700,(&NUMRECS,50))

SUBSTITUTING THE ACTUAL VALUE FOR THE SYMBOLIC VALUE

The symbolic value &NUMRECS would get no space allocated at all. An actual value must be supplied. It is supplied in the execute card which calls the procedure. (Remember, the above DD card is in a procedure called PROC23.)

The execute card calling that procedure would contain

//CALLPROC EXEC PROC=PROC23,NUMRECS=590

The Initiator recognizes NUMRECS as a symbolic value and realizes that the actual value equated to it must be used to replace a symbolic value in the procedure.

When the named procedure (PROC23) is called in, *any* symbolic parameter named &NUMRECS is replaced by the actual value *590.*

DEFAULTS FOR ACTUAL VALUES

As insurance against someone forgetting to provide the actual value in the execute card which calls the procedure, one must provide a default value. This value must appear in the first line of the procedure. The first line of the procedure must contain the term PROC. The PROC entry in the procedure must be included if symbolic parameters are to be used.

To state a default value of 400 requires the following PROC statement for the procedure named PROC23:

```
//PROC23 PROC NUMRECS=400
```

Now if someone forgets to equate NUMRECS in the execute card which calls the procedure, there won't be an immediate catastrophe. Rather, the Initiator, recognizing that no actual parameter had been provided, will use the default value from the PROC statement.

THE OVERRIDE TECHNIQUE

What action can you take if you have to change an actual parameter in a procedure (i.e., a nonsymbolic one)? First, you must determine what the keyword is. Next you'll have to know whether the parameter is in the procedure's EXEC statement or one of its DD statements. If the parameter is in the EXEC statement you must determine the name of the EXEC statement. If it is in a DD statement you must determine the names of both the EXEC and DD statements in the procedure. Let us suppose that the procedure's EXEC statement is named ROTE and that the DD statement is named BARON. In the DD statement is the keyword/parameter UNIT=SYSSQ; you want to change this to UNIT=TAPE. Here is what you must place into your overriding DD statement:

```
//ROTE.BARON DD UNIT=TAPE
```

None of the other keywords/parameters in the procedure will be affected. (One note of caution: If you are overriding parameters in several DD statements of a procedure be sure to place the overriding statements in the same order as the ones to be overridden.)

READER AND WRITER PROCEDURES

The Reader program, you should recall, places

1. JCL information into the data set called SYS1.SYSJOBQE.
2. input stream data into a temporary data set on disk.

The output writer is primarily concerned with taking data from a direct-access storage device and recording it on an output device. (A problem program usually places its output on direct access rather than placing its output on the printer or punch.)

In both MFT-II and MVT there are a number of Reader programs and Output Writer programs that can be in core storage at one time. That is, there can be several Reader programs and 36 Output Writers in core storage at one time. Of course, to support 36 simultaneous Output Writers one would need 36 different output devices and lots of core storage to contain 36 copies of the Output Writer.

Calling the Reader or Writer Procedure

Reader and Writer procedures are invoked by the operator issuing the START command together with the name of the Reader or Writer procedure. (In contrast, most other procedures are invoked by placing the name of the procedure in the EXEC card of a job stream.)

Number of Reader Procedures

As you already know, a procedure consists of EXEC statements and related DD statements. The EXEC statement names the program and the DD statements specify such items as data sets required, amount of direct-access space needed, serial number of the volume, and type of unit information for allocation. Hence, if one wanted to have the same program with various specifications for data sets, volumes, units, and space, he could either have each variation as a separate procedure or have just one procedure and then provide overrides when something has to be changed. Since the Reader and Writer procedures are invoked by commands (issued via a keyboard), the override technique would be rather inefficient. Therefore, most installations have for each important variation a separate reader procedure. (Certain information in Reader and Writer procedures can be overriden with information supplied by the START command.) What are some of these important variations? One of the most important concerns the blocking of the 80-character input-stream data records. Performance studies have shown that when input-stream data is blocked (before writing it into a temporary data set), it takes much less time to read the input stream than when each input-stream data record is written in unblocked form.

Another important variation concerns the way to request space for the temporary input-stream data set. One could make a nonspecific request or a specific request. That is, a unit could be requested (UNIT=190), a specific volume could be requested (VOLUME=SER=222222), a unit type could be specified (UNIT=2311), and so on. The variation chosen would, of course, depend upon the requirements.

Let us now look at six different procedures as used by one particular installation. These procedures are shown in Figs. 125 to 130. The first thing to notice are the names of the procedures: RDR, RDR2, RDR400, RDR3200, RDR190, and RDR192. These procedure names are what the operator must supply with the START command to initiate a Reader program.

Parameters in the EXEC Card for Reader Program

You may have been wondering about the significance of the characters between the single quotes of the PARM keyword in the EXEC card of each reader procedure. These characters are parameters required by the Reader/Interpreter program. There must always be 27 characters. Their general format is as follows:

PARM='bppttooommmiiicccrssssssss'

The meanings of these general characters are explained below.

b—A numeric character from 0 to 3 that indicates whether jobs read during this procedure must specify a programmer's name or an account number. The Reader/Interpreter, if b, is:

- 0—does not require a programmer's name or an account number.
- 1—ends all jobs that do not specify a programmer's name.
- 2—ends all jobs that do not specify an account number.
- 3—ends all jobs that do not specify a programmer's name *and* an account number.

pp—Two numeric characters from 00 to 14 indicating the default priority for jobs read from this input stream. When no priority is specified in the Job statement, this default priority is assigned to the job.

ttt—Three numeric characters indicating the default for the maximum time (in minutes) that each job step may run.

ooo—Three numeric characters indicating the default for the primary number of tracks assigned for SYSOUT data sets. This primary allocation should be made sufficient for most of your needs so that secondary allocation will not usually be needed.

mmm—Three numeric characters indicating the default for the secondary number of tracks assigned for SYSOUT data sets.

```
//IEFPROC   EXEC     PGM=IEFIRC,                     READER FIRST LOAD        ,03000000
//              REGION=40K,                        READER BASIC REGION      ,06000014
//              PARM='00103005001024905010SYSDA   '   DEFAULT OPTIONS      ,09000000
//              BPPTTTOOOMMMIIICCCRLSSSSSSSS      PARM FIELDS DEFINED     ,12000000
//              PROGRAMMER NAME AND                         B              ,15000000
//              ACCOUNT NUMBER       NOT NEEDED                            ,18000000
//              PRIORITY=01                                   PP           ,21000000
//              JOB STEP INTERVAL=30 MINUTES                  TTT          ,24000000
//              PRIMARY SYSOUT SPACE=50 TRACKS                000          ,27000000
//              SECONDARY SYSOUT SPACE=10 TRACKS              MMM          ,30000000
//              READER/INTERPRETER DISPATCHING PRIORITY=249 III          ,33000000
//              JOB STEP DEFAULT REGION=50K                   CCC          ,36000000
//              DISPLAY AND EXECUTE COMMANDS=1                R            ,39000000
//              BYPASS LABEL OPTION=0                         L            ,42000000
//              SYSOUT UNIT NAME=SYSDA                        SSSSSSSS      45000000
IEFRDER  DD  UNIT=00C,                                                     X
//              LABEL=(,NL),                      UNLABELED                ,51000000
//              VOLUME=SER=SYSIN,                 VOLUME NAME              ,54000000
//              DCB=(BLKSIZE=80,RECFM=F,BUFL=80,BUFNO=1)
//IEFPDSI       DD  DSNAME=SYS1.PROCLIB,          PROCEDURE LIBRARY        ,60000000
//              DISP=OLD                                                    63000000
//IEFDATA  DD  UNIT=(2311,2),                                              X
//              VOLUME=SER=(222222,333333),                                X
//              SPACE=(80,(500,500),RLSE,CONTIG),     AMOUNT               ,69000000
//              DCB=(BUFNO=2,LRECL=80,BLKSIZE=80,RECFM=F,BUFL=80)           72000000
```

Fig. 125 Reader procedure RDR.

```
//IEFPROC   EXEC     PGM=IEFIRC,                     READER FIRST LOAD        ,03000000
//              REGION=40K,                        READER BASIC REGION      ,06000014
//              PARM='00103005001024905010SYSDA   '   DEFAULT OPTIONS      ,09000000
//              BPPTTTOOOMMMIIICCCRLSSSSSSSS      PARM FIELDS DEFINED      12000000
//IEFRDER  DD  UNIT=00C,                                                   X
//              LABEL=(,NL),                      UNLABELED                ,51000000
//              VOLUME=SER=SYSIN,                 VOLUME NAME              ,54000000
//              DCB=(BLKSIZE=80,RECFM=F,BUFL=80,BUFNO=5)
//IEFPDSI    DD  DSNAME=TEST.PROCLIB,DISP=OLD,VOLUME=SER=222222,           X
//              UNIT=2311
//             DD DSNAME=SYS1.PROCLIB,DISP=OLD
//IEFDATA  DD  UNIT=(2311,2),                                              X
//              VOLUME=SER=(222222,333333),                                X
//              SPACE=(80,(500,500),RLSE,CONTIG),     AMOUNT               ,69000000
//              DCB=(BUFNO=2,LRECL=80,BLKSIZE=80,RECFM=F,BUFL=80)           72000000
```

Fig. 126 Reader procedure RDR2.

```
//IEFPROC   EXEC     PGM=IEFIRC,                     READER FIRST LOAD        ,03000000
//              REGION=42K,                        READER BASIC REGION      ,06000014
//              PARM='80103005001024905010SYSDA   '   DEFAULT OPTIONS      ,09000014
//              BPPTTTOOOMMMIIICCCRLSSSSSSSS      PARM FIELDS DEFINED     ,12000000
//              PROGRAMMER NAME AND                         B              ,15000000
//              ACCOUNT NUMBER       NOT NEEDED                            ,18000000
//              PROGRAM CAN BE ROLLED OUT                                  ,19000014
//              PRIORITY=01                                   PP           ,21000000
//              JOB STEP INTERVAL=30 MINUTES                  TTT          ,24000000
//              PRIMARY SYSOUT SPACE=50 TRACKS                000          ,27000000
//              SECONDARY SYSOUT SPACE=10 TRACKS              MMM          ,30000000
//              READER/INTERPRETER DISPATCHING PRIORITY=249 III          ,33000000
//              JOB STEP DEFAULT REGION=50K          000                   ,36000000
//              DISPLAY AND EXECUTE COMMANDS=1                R            ,39000000
//              BYPASS LABEL OPTION=0                         L            ,42000000
//              SYSOUT UNIT NAME=SYSDA                        SSSSSSSS      45000000
//IEFRDER   DD  UNIT=2400,                        9 TRK TAPE               ,48000000
//              LABEL=(,NL),                      UNLABELED                ,51000000
//              VOLUME=SER=SYSIN,                 VOLUME NAME              ,54000000
//              DCB=(BLKSIZE=80,RECFM=F,BUFL=80,BUFNO=1)                    57000000
//IEFPDSI   DD  DSNAME=SYS1.PROCLIB,              PROCEDURE LIBRARY        ,60000000
//              DISP=OLD                                                    63000000
//IEFDATA   DD    UNIT=SYSDA,                     SPOOL DEVICE             ,66000000
//              SPACE=(80,(500,100),RLSE,CONTIG),     AMOUNT               ,69000000
//              DCB=(BUFNO=2,LRECL=80,BLKSIZE=400,RECFM=FB,BUFL=400)        72000000
```

Fig. 127 Reader procedure RDR400.

```
//IEFPROC   EXEC      PGM=IEFIRC,                    READER FIRST LOAD         ,03000000
//             REGION=44K                          READER BASIC REGION          ,06000014
//             PARM='80103005001024905010SYSDA     '   DEFAULT OPTIONS          ,09000014
//             BPPTTTOOOMMMIIICCCRLSSSSSSSS        PARM FIELDS DEFINED          ,12000000
//             PROGRAMMER NAME AND                          B                   ,15000000
//             ACCOUNT NUMBER        NOT NEEDED                                 ,18000000
//             PROGRAM CAN BE ROLLED OUT                                        ,19000014
//             PRIORITY=01                                     PP               ,21000000
//             JOB STEP INTERVAL=30 MINUTES                    TTT              ,24000000
//             PRIMARY SYSOUT SPACE=50 TRACKS                  000              ,27000000
//             SECONDARY SYSOUT SPACE=10 TRACKS                MMM              ,30000000
//             READER/INTERPRETER DISPATCHING PRIORITY=249     III              ,33000000
//             JOB STEP DEFAULT REGION=50K          000                         ,36000000
//             DISPLAY AND EXECUTE COMMANDS=1                  R                ,39000000
//             BYPASS LABEL OPTION=0                           L                ,42000000
//             SYSOUT UNIT NAME=SYSDA                          SSSSSSSS          45000000
//IEFRDER    DD  UNIT=2400,                        9 TRK TAPE                   ,48000000
//             LABEL=(,NL),                        UNLABELED                    ,51000000
//             VOLUME=SER=SYSIN,                   VOLUME NAME                  ,54000000
//             DCB=(BLKSIZE=80,RECFM=F,BUFL=80,BUFNO=1)                          57000000
//IEFPDSI   DD  DSNAME=SYS1.PROCLIB,               PROCEDURE LIBRARY            ,60000000
//             DISP=OLD                                                          63000000
//IEFDATA   DD    UNIT=SYSDA,                      SPOOL DEVICE                 ,66000000
//             SPACE=(80,(500,012),RLSE,CONTIG),      AMOUNT                    ,69000000
//             DCB=(BUFNO=1,LRECL=80,BLKSIZE=3200,RECFM=FB,BUFL=3200)            72000000
```

Fig. 128 Reader procedure RDR3200.

```
//IEFPROC   EXEC      PGM=IEFIRC,                    READER FIRST LOAD         ,03000000
//             REGION=40K,                         READER BASIC REGION          ,06000014
//             PARM='00103005001024905010SYSDA     '   DEFAULT OPTIONS          ,09000014
//             BPPTTTOOOMMMIIICCCRLSSSSSSSS        PARM FIELDS DEFINED          ,12000000
//             PROGRAMMER NAME AND                          B                   ,15000000
//             ACCOUNT NUMBER        NOT NEEDED                                 ,18000000
//             PROGRAM CAN BE ROLLED OUT                                        ,19000014
//             PRIORITY=01                                     PP               ,21000000
//             JOB STEP INTERVAL=30 MINUTES                    TTT              ,24000000
//             PRIMARY SYSOUT SPACE=50 TRACKS                  000              ,27000000
//             SECONDARY SYSOUT SPACE=10 TRACKS                MMM              ,30000000
//             READER/INTERPRETER DISPATCHING PRIORITY=249     III              ,33000000
//             JOB STEP DEFAULT REGION=50K          000                         ,36000000
//             DISPLAY AND EXECUTE COMMANDS=1                  R                ,39000000
//             BYPASS LABEL OPTION=0                           L                ,42000000
//             SYSOUT UNIT NAME=SYSDA                          SSSSSSSS          45000000
//IEFRDER    DD  UNIT=00C,                                                      X
//             LABEL=(,NL),                        UNLABELED                    ,51000000
//             VOLUME=SER=SYSIN,                   VOLUME NAME                  ,54000000
//             DCB=(BLKSIZE=80,RECFM=F,BUFL=80,BUFNO=5)
//IEFPDSI   DD  DSNAME=SYS1.PROCLIB,               PROCEDURE LIBRARY            ,60000000
//             DISP=OLD                                                          63000000
//IEFDATA   DD  UNIT=190,                                                       X
//             SPACE=(80,(500,500),RLSE,CONTIG),      AMOUNT                    ,69000000
//             DCB=(BUFNO=2,LRECL=80,BLKSIZE=80,RECFM=F,BUFL=80)                 72000000
```

Fig. 129 Reader procedure RDR190.

```
//IEFPROC   EXEC      PGM=IEFIRC,                    READER FIRST LOAD         ,03000000
//             REGION=40K,                         READER BASIC REGION          ,06000014
//             PARM='00103005001024905010SYSDA     '   DEFAULT OPTIONS          ,09000014
//             BPPTTTOOOMMMIIICCCRLSSSSSSSS        PARM FIELDS DEFINED          ,12000000
//             PROGRAMMER NAME AND                          B                   ,15000000
//             ACCOUNT NUMBER        NOT NEEDED                                 ,18000000
//             PRIORITY=01                                     PP               ,21000000
//             JOB STEP INTERVAL=30 MINUTES                    TTT              ,24000000
//             PRIMARY SYSOUT SPACE=50 TRACKS                  000              ,27000000
//             SECONDARY SYSOUT SPACE=10 TRACKS                MMM              ,30000000
//             READER/INTERPRETER DISPATCHING PRIORITY=249     III              ,33000000
//             JOB STEP DEFAULT REGION=50K          000                         ,36000000
//             DISPLAY AND EXECUTE COMMANDS=1                  R                ,39000000
//             BYPASS LABEL OPTION=0                           L                ,42000000
//             SYSOUT UNIT NAME=SYSDA                          SSSSSSSS          45000000
//IEFRDER   DD  UNIT=2400,                         9TRK TAPE                    ,48000000
//             LABEL=(,NL),                        UNLABELED                    ,51000000
//             VOLUME=SER=SYSIN,                   VOLUME NAME                  ,54000000
//             DCB=(BLKSIZE=80,RECFM=F,BUFL=80,BUFNO=5)
//IEFPDSI   DD  DSNAME=SYS1.PROCLIB,               PROCEDURE LIBRARY            ,60000000
//             DISP=OLD                                                          63000000
//IEFDATA   DD  UNIT=192,                                                       X
//             SPACE=(80,(500,500),RLSE,CONTIG),      AMOUNT                    ,69000000
//             DCB=(BUFNO=2,LRECL=80,BLKSIZE=80,RECFM=F,BUFL=80)                 72000000
```

Fig. 130 Reader procedure RDR192.

iii—Three numeric characters indicating the priority of this reader during the period while it is processing JCL statements.

ccc—Three numeric characters indicating the default for the region size (specified as a number of 1,024-byte blocks) assigned to job steps read from this input stream.

r—A numeric character from 0 to 3 that specifies the disposition of commands read from this input stream (the operator may punch certain commands into cards as an alternative to typing them). The Reader/Interpreter

if r is 0, executes the command.

if r is 1, displays the command and executes it.

if r is 2, displays the command but does not execute it until advised by the operator.

if r is 3, ignores the command (treated as no operation).

ssssssss—Eight alphameric characters specifying the default device for SYSOUT. This becomes the UNIT subparameter in the DD statement that defines SYSOUT (if the UNIT field is omitted from the DD statement).

SAMPLE CATALOGUED PROCEDURES

When an installation orders its operating system kit from IBM, one of the modules it receives is a "standard" PROCLIB. In the PROCLIB there usually are three procedures for each of the compilers. The first of these three procedures consists of one step: the compilation. The second procedure consists of two steps: the compilation and the linkage edit. The third procedure consists of three steps: the compilation, the linkage edit, and the execution of the program produced by the first two steps.

The procedures that will be shown here are those consisting of three steps. They are

1. ASMFCLG—The procedure to use the Assembler F Compiler, the Linkage Editor, and the program produced by steps 1 and 2.
2. COBFCLG—The procedure to use the COBOL F Compiler, the Linkage Editor, and program produced by the first two steps.
3. FORTGCLG—The procedure to use the FORTRAN G Compiler, the Linkage Editor, and the program produced by the first two steps.
4. PL1LFCLG—The procedure to use the PL/1 F Compiler, the Linkage Editor, and the program produced by the first two steps.
5. RPGECLG—The procedure to use the RPG E Compiler, the Linkage Editor, and the program produced.

The letters CLG are in each of the procedure names used in the above five examples. The significance of these is as follows:

C—Compile
L—Link Edit
G—Go (meaning "Go with the program produced in the first two steps")

Procedure ASMFCLG

Figure 131 shows the ASMFCLG (compile with Assembler F, Link Edit, and Execute) procedure as it might appear in an installation's PROCLIB. The first 10 lines concern the requirements of compilation, the next eight lines show the requirements of the Linkage Editor, and the last line refers to the program produced by the Compiler and Linkage Editor.

Let us now look at the EXEC and DD cards. ASM, LKED, and GO are names of the Execute statements for each of the three steps. In the ASM Execute card, PARM=LOAD tells the Assembler F Compiler that its output is to be placed on the device specified in the SYSGO DD statement (line 9). IEUASM is the name of the Assembler F Compiler. The amount of main storage space required by IEUASM is 50,000 bytes.

In the LKED Execute statement, IEWL is the name of the Linkage Editor program. The parameters given with the keyword PARM are used by the Linkage Editor to print several lists for the programmer (XREF,LIST), to mark the output as executable even though errors are detected (LET), and to eliminate searching in subroutine libraries (NCAL). The main storage requirements are 96,000 bytes. The COND keyword parameters say, "If 8 is less than the return code in register 15 (placed there by the program specified in the execute card named ASM), terminate the job."

In the GO Execute statement, the asterisk states that the program to be executed can be determined by looking at other information available in the EXEC and DD steps of this job. The .LKED states that the step to be referred to is named LKED and the .SYSLMOD states that the DD statement is named SYSLMOD. In the SYSLMOD DD card is the name of the partitioned data set GOSET and its

```
//ASM       EXEC  PGM=IEUASM,PARM=LOAD,REGION=50K                       00020000
//SYSLIB    DD    DSNAME=SYS1.MACLIB,DISP=SHR                           00040000
//SYSUT1    DD    UNIT=SYSSQ,SPACE=(1700,(400,50))                      00060000
//SYSUT2    DD    UNIT=SYSSQ,SPACE=(1700,(400,50))                      00080000
//SYSUT3    DD    UNIT=(SYSSQ,SEP=(SYSUT2,SYSUT1,SYSLIB)),             X00100000
//                SPACE=(1700,(400,50))                                 00120000
//SYSPRINT  DD    SYSOUT=A                                              00140000
//SYSPUNCH  DD    SYSOUT=B                                              00160000
//SYSGO     DD    DSNAME=&LOADSET,UNIT=SYSSQ,SPACE=(80,(100,50)),      X00180000
//                DISP=(MOD,PASS)                                       00200000
//LKED      EXEC  PGM=IEWL,PARM=(XREF,LET,LIST,NCAL),REGION=96K,        C00220000
//                COND=(8,LT,ASM)                                       00240000
//SYSLIN    DD    DSNAME=&LOADSET,DISP=(OLD,DELETE)                     00260000
//          DD    DDNAME=SYSIN                                          00280000
//SYSLMOD   DD    DSNAME=&GOSET(GO),UNIT=SYSDA,SPACE=(1024,(50,20,1)), X00300000
//                DISP=(MOD,PASS)                                       00320000
//SYSUT1    DD    UNIT=(SYSDA,SEP=(SYSLIN,SYSLMOD)),SPACE=(1024,(50,20)) 00340000
//SYSPRINT  DD    SYSOUT=A,DCB=(,BLKSIZE=121)                           00360000
//GO        EXEC  PGM=*.LKED.SYSLMOD,COND=((8,LT,ASM),(4,LT,LKED))       00380000
```

Fig. 131 Procedure ASMFCLG.

member (GO) from which the program will be retrieved. (One knows that GOSET is a partitioned data set because the request for SPACE included a request for a directory.) The COND keyword parameters say, "If 8 is less than the return code from the program named in the ASM execute card, or if 4 is less than the return code from the program named in the LKED execute card, terminate the job" (i.e., do not execute the *.LKED.SYSLMOD program).

SYSLIB is the name of the DD card that is used to request the allocation of MACLIB.

SYSUT1, SYSUT2, and SYSUT3 are the names of the DD cards that are used to request temporary data sets for the intermediate results of compilation. The amount of primary space requested for each of these temporary data sets is four hundred blocks of 1,700 bytes each. The conditional space is fifty blocks of 1,700 bytes each. Since there is no disposition keyword (DISP), the default is assumed (i.e., NEW,DELETE,DELETE). The device to be used for satisfying the request for the temporary data sets will be chosen from the list (SYSSQ) that is available to the Initiator. SYSSQ would probably contain the physical addresses of tape and disk units. In the SYSUT3 DD card, a request is made to allocate the SYSUT3 data set on a volume separate from the other temporary data sets and MACLIB.

SYSPRINT and SYSPUNCH DD cards specify that output writers are to prepare the output.

The SYSGO DD card is used to allocate a unit from the SYSSQ list. The *standard* temporary data set name is &LOADSET (only one ampersand is used because no symbolic parameters are used in this procedure). This temporary data set will record the output of the compiler. The DISP keyword specifies MOD,PASS. PASS is used because the output data set is to be passed to the next step. Space is requested because the Initiator may choose a disk unit from the SYSSQ list.

The SYSLIN DD card specifies the data set name that is to be input to the Linkage Editor program.

The unnamed DD card following SYSLIN is used to concatenate any input that may be in the input stream for the Linkage Editor with the input from SYSLIN.

The SYSLMOD DD card names the output data set (a temporary one) produced by the Linkage Editor, &GOSET(GO).

The SYSPRINT DD card contains a DCB subkeyword which specifies the blocksize of the printed output as 121 bytes.

Procedure COBFCLG

The general structure of the COBFCLG (compile with COBOL F, Link Edit, and Execute) procedure (Fig. 132) is very similar to the ASMFCLG procedure. There are some different names, however. Most significant is the name of the compiler (IEQCBL00), the need for four temporary data sets for intermediate results, and the request for SYSLIB (line 15) during linkage editing rather than during compilation. (In an assembly, the macros are in symbolic form and therefore must

```
//COB     EXEC      PGM=IEQCBL00,REGION=86K                                00020000
//SYSPRINT  DD SYSOUT=A                                                    00040000
//SYSUT1   DD    UNIT=SYSDA,SPACE=(460,(700,100))                          00060000
//SYSUT2   DD    UNIT=SYSDA,SPACE=(460,(700,100))                          00080000
//SYSUT3   DD    UNIT=SYSDA,SPACE=(460,(700,100))                          00100000
//SYSUT4   DD    UNIT=SYSDA,SPACE=(460,(700,100))                          00120000
//SYSLIN   DD    DSNAME=&LOADSET,DISP=(MOD,PASS),UNIT=SYSDA,              X00140000
//               SPACE=(80,(500,100))                                      00160000
//LKED    EXEC   PGM=IEWL,PARM=(XREF,LIST,LET),COND=(5,LT,COB),           X00180000
//               REGION=96K                                                00200000
//SYSLIN   DD    DSNAME=&LOADSET,DISP=(OLD,DELETE)                         00220000
//        DD     DDNAME=SYSIN                                              00240000
//SYSLMOD    DD DSNAME=&GODATA(RUN),DISP=(NEW,PASS),                      X00260000
//               UNIT=SYSDA,SPACE=(1024,(50,20,1))                         00280000
//SYSLIB   DD    DSNAME=SYS1.COBLIB,DISP=SHR                               00300000
//SYSUT1   DD    UNIT=(SYSDA,SEP=(SYSLIN,SYSLMOD)),                       X00320000
//               SPACE=(1024,(50,20))                                      00340000
//SYSPRINT  DD SYSOUT=A                                                    00360000
//GO      EXEC   PGM=*.LKED.SYSLMOD,COND=((5,LT,COB),(5,LT,LKED))          00380000
//SYSABEND  DD SYSOUT=A                                                    00400000
```

Fig. 132 Procedure COBFCLG.

be compiled. In the high-level languages, many of the subroutines are already in machine language code and don't have to be compiled.)

Another new item is the last line, the SYSABEND DD card. This DD card allocates a device on which will be written the contents of storage if the program requested in the GO EXEC statement fails during execution.

Procedure FORTGCLG

The main difference between the FORTGCLG (Compile with FORTRAN G, Link Edit, and Execute) procedure (Fig. 133) and the previous two is the intentional omission of DD cards for requesting compiler work space. The Fortran G compiler is called an "in-core" compiler (i.e., all the intermediate results are kept in main storage).

Procedure PL1LFCLG

The PL1LFCLG (Compile with PL/1 F, Link Edit, and Execute) procedure (Fig. 134) is somewhat unusual in that there is no SYSUT2 DD card, even though there are SYSUT1 and SYSUT3 DD statements.

Procedure RPGECLG

The RPGECLG (Compile with RPG E, Link Edit, and Execute) is a procedure (Fig. 135) with symbolic parameters. You should recall that when a procedure expects the actual value, it must come either from the PARM keyword of the Execute statement calling the procedure or from the PROC statement in the procedure; if they come from the latter they are called default values.

```
//FORT    EXEC    PGM=IEYFORT,REGION=100K                                        00200000
//SYSPRINT  DD SYSOUT=A                                                          00040000
//SYSPUNCH DD  SYSOUT=B                                                          00060000
//SYSLIN   DD  DSNAME=&LOADSET,DISP=(MOD,PASS),UNIT=SYSSQ,                      X00080000
//             SPACE=(80,(200,100),RLSE),DCB=BLKSIZE=80                          00100014
//LKED  EXEC  PGM=IEWL,REGION=96K,PARM=(XREF,LET,LIST),COND=(4,LT,FORT)          00120000
//SYSLIB   DD  DSNAME=SYS1.FORTLIB,DISP=SHR                                      00140000
//SYSLMOD  DD  DSNAME=&GOSET(MAIN),DISP=(NEW,PASS),UNIT=SYSDA,                  X00160000
//             SPACE=(1024,(20,10,1),RLSE),DCB=BLKSIZE=1024                      00180000
//SYSPRINT DD  SYSOUT=A                                                          00200000
//SYSUT1   DD  UNIT=SYSDA,SPACE=(1024,(20,10),RLSE),DCB=BLKSIZE=1024             00220014
//SYSLIN   DD  DSNAME=&LOADSET,DISP=(OLD,DELETE)                                 00240000
//       DD    DDNAME=SYSIN                                                      00260000
//GO   EXEC    PGM=*.LKED.SYSLMOD,COND=((4,LT,FORT),(4,LT,LKED))                 00280000
//FT05F001  DD DDNAME=SYSIN                                                      00300000
//FT06F001  DD SYSOUT=A                                                          00320000
//FT07F001  DD SYSOUT=B                                                          00340000
```

Fig. 133 Procedure FORTGCLG.

```
//PL1L     EXEC  PGM=IEMAA,PARM='LOAD,NODECK',REGION=52K                         04000017
//SYSPRINT  DD SYSOUT=A                                                          08000017
//SYSLIN    DD DSNAME=&&LOADSET,DISP=(MOD,PASS),UNIT=SYSSQ,                     *12000017
//             SPACE=(80,(250,100)),DCB=BLKSIZE=80                               16000017
//SYSUT3   DD  UNIT=SYSSQ,SPACE=(80,(250,250)),SEP=SYSPRINT,                    *20000017
//             DCB=BLKSIZE=80                                                    24000017
//SYSUT1    DD UNIT=SYSDA,SPACE=(1024,(60,60),,CONTIG),                         *28000017
//             SEP=(SYSUT3,SYSPRINT,SYSLIN),DCB=BLKSIZE=1024                     32000017
//LKED    EXEC PGM=IEWL,PARM='XREF,LIST'COND=(16,EQ,PL1L),                      *36000017
//             REGION=96K                                                        40000017
//SYSLIB    DD DSNAME=SYS1.PL1LIB,DISP=SHR                                       44000017
//SYSLMOD   DD DSNAME=&&GOSET(GO),DISP=(MOD,PASS),                              *48000017
//             UNIT=SYSDA,SPACE=(1024,(50,20,1),RLSE)                            52000017
//SYSUT1    DD UNIT=SYSDA,SEP=(SYSLMOD,SYSLIB),SPACE=(1024,(200,20))             56000017
//SYSPRINT DD  SYSOUT=A                                                          60000017
//SYSLIN    DD DSNAME=&&LOADSET,DISP=(OLD,DELETE)                                64000017
//       DD    DDNAME=SYSIN                                                      68000017
//GO      EXEC PGM=*.LKED.SYSLMOD,COND=((9,LT,LKED),(11,LT,PL1L))                72000017
//SYSPRINT  DD SYSOUT=A                                                          76000017
```

Fig. 134 Procedure PL1LFCLG.

```
//DEFAULT PROC RGREGN=52K,RGPARM='NODECK,LOAD,LIST,NOSEQN',                     104000016
//             RGU3SPC='(600,(100,20))',RGU2SPC='(600,(100,20))',               208000016
//             RGU1SPC='(600,(100,20))',RGGOSPC='(80,(200,50))',                312000016
//             LKREGN=100K,LKPARM='XREF,LIST,LET',                              416000016
//             LKMDSPC='(1024,(50,20,1))',LKU1SPC='(1024,(50,20))',             520000016
//             GOCOND='((9,LT,RPG),(5,LT,LKED))',GOPARM='DATE=000000'            24000016
//RPG     EXEC PGM=IESRPG,REGION=&RGREGN,PARM=(&RGPARM)                          28000016
//SYSPRINT DD  SYSOUT=A                                                          32000016
//SYSPUNCH DD  SYSOUT=B                                                          36000016
//SYSUT3   DD  UNIT=SYSSQ,SPACE=&RGU3SPC                                         40000016
//SYSUT2   DD  UNIT=SYSSQ,SPACE=&RGU2SPC                                         44000016
//SYSUT1   DD  SPACE=&RGU1SPC,UNIT=(SYSSQ,SEP=(SYSUT2,SYSUT3))                   48000016
//SYSGO   DD   DSNAME=&&GO,UNIT=(SYSSQ,SEP=SYSPUNCH),                           152000016
//             DISP=(MOD,PASS,DELETE),SPACE=&RGGOSPC                             56000016
//LKED   EXEC  PGM=IEWL,REGION=&LKREGN,PARM=(&LKPARM)                            60000016
//SYSLIN   DD  DSNAME=&&GO,DISP=(OLD,DELETE)                                     64000016
//         DD  DDNAME=SYSIN                                                      68000016
//SYSLMOD  DD  DSNAME=&&GOSET(RPG),UNIT=SYSDA,DISP=(NEW,PASS,DELETE),           172000016
//             SPACE=&LKMDSPC                                                    76000016
//SYSUT1   DD  SPACE=&LKU1SPC,                                                  180000016
//             UNIT=(SYSDA,SEP=(SYSLIN,SYSLMOD))                                 84000016
//SYSPRINT DD  SYSOUT=A                                                          88000016
//GO     EXEC  PGM=*.LKED.SYSLMOD,COND=&GOCOND,PARM='&GOPARM'                    93000017
```

Fig. 135 Procedure RPGECLG.

Providing Source Statements to CLG Procedures

Before the procedures in Fig. 131 through 135 can be executed, one must prepare a Job statement and an Execute statement in which is placed the name of the appropriate procedure. Other important ingredients are the source statements to be compiled. To identify these cards as source statements one must create a //SYSIN DD * card.

When the collection of JOB, EXEC, SYSIN DD *, and source statements are read by the Reader program, the statements from the procedure will be merged into their proper place. Then the Reader program will record the job information on the JOBQE and the source statements in a temporary disk data set.

SUMMARY

1. A procedure consists of one or more EXEC statements and their associated DD statements.
2. Each procedure is named and recorded in a partitioned data set named SYS1.PROCLIB.
3. When the reader task recognizes that an EXEC statement in the input stream refers to a procedure, the procedure is retrieved from PROCLIB and augmented with job control information from the input stream.
4. Information in a procedure may be overriden with information from the input stream.
5. When symbolic parameters are used in procedures, the symbolic parameters must be replaced by actual values. The actual values are supplied by the EXEC statement in the input stream.
6. The Reader and Writer procedures are requested by an operator command, not with an EXEC statement.
7. Each installation may have as many Reader and Writer procedures as it requires.
8. The parameters in the EXEC statement of the Reader procedure
   a. indicate whether jobs statements read by this Reader require a programmer's name or an account number.
   b. indicate the default priority when none is in the Job statement.
   c. the maximum amount of time the job may use the system.
   d. the region size if none is provided in the input stream.
   e. the amount of space assigned to SYSOUT data sets.

SUGGESTED READING ASSIGNMENT

IBM System/360 Operating System
Job Control Language (C28-6539)

Section 2: A Guide to Using Job Control Language

(The same advice given for reading Section 1 applies to this section; become familiar with the contents and organization rather than reading it word-for-word.)

This concludes the main portion of the text. For those of you who wish to pursue the use of OS/360 JCL for specific data-processing jobs, the following publications will be helpful (contact IBM for availability and purchase price).

IBM S/360 OS	Assembler F Guide	C26-3756
IBM S/360 OS	FORTRAN IV (G) Guide	C28-6639
IBM S/360 OS	PL/1 (G) Guide	C28-6594
IBM S/360 OS	COBOL (F) Guide	C28-6380
IBM S/360 OS	RPG Language	C24-3337
IBM S/360 OS	Job Control Language	C28-6539
IBM S/360 OS	Sort/Merge	C28-6543

APPENDIX

I DEFINITION OF A PROGRAM

One of the modern dictionaries describes a program as a plan or schedule to be followed. Many of the programs to which we respond as either participants, audience, or observers are static and rigid. That is, the schedule (program) tells us about step 1 first, then step 2, and so on, until we get to the last step in the schedule. When the last step has been executed, the program is over—the participants and observers "go home." The steps of a static and rigid program are always carried out in the same sequence. (If the step sequence is changed, it's a different program.) Some examples of this type of program are the order of a church service, the sequence of musical selections at performance of a symphony orchestra, the baking of a cake, and the checkout sequence for a passenger plane's departure.

There are some programs that are not static or rigid. That is, the sequence of the steps varies depending upon certain influences and conditions. One such program is required by people using the long form for reporting their income tax. After completing certain steps in the process of calculating the income tax data, the taxpayer must evaluate his intermediate results. For example, if the condition of the results is not of one type, his next series of calculation steps may come from page 3, line 1; if the condition of his results is of another type, his next series of calculation steps may be on page 4, line 9. In computerese (i.e., computer terminology) we would say that the programmed taxpayer *branches* to one set of instructions on condition A, and to a different set of instructions on condition B.

To illustrate the concept of such a flexible, yet controlled program, let us review a game played by coffee drinkers (for determining who buys the coffee). One of the gamblers chooses a number within a certain range and writes the number on a piece of paper (to prevent mind changing). The rest of the gamblers take turns trying to guess what the number is. The person who guesses it wins the privilege of buying coffee for the others.

If the range of numbers is large (say 1 to 1,024) and all the gamblers have no plan for asking questions, it is conceivable that 1,023 questions would have to be asked before the number is guessed. (With no plan, they'd average about 512 questions.) Such a lengthy exercise in question asking would discourage them from playing the game again.

A mathematical technique can be used to *discover* the chosen number (in the range 1 to 1,024) with 10 questions. The technique narrows the *range* of numbers from one question to the next. For example, the first player asks, "Is it 512 or less?" No matter what the answer to this question is, the *range* has been reduced in half—if the answer is yes, the range is 1 to 512; if the answer is no, the range is 513 to 1,024. If the answer had been no (513 to 1,024), the second player would ask, "Is it 768 or more?" A yes answer narrows the range to 768 to 1,024; a no answer narrows it to 513 to 767. Thus you see that by asking one question, the range is reduced by a factor of 2; by asking a second question the range is reduced by a factor of 4. The third question will reduce the range to one eighth of its original size, the fourth question will reduce it to one sixteenth of its original size, and so on. By the time the tenth question is asked, the number will have been discovered by the lucky coffee buyer. (Of course, the game is seldom played this way, for if it were, the element of chance no longer exists. To provide for some excitement the players usually vary from the mathematically logical choice by plus or minus 20 percent.)

One word of caution: Although the minimum number of questions that *will be* asked is 10, there are 1,024 minus 1 questions from which to choose (one question less than all the possible values).

This technique is really a program! *A program* for determining, in 10 questions, the value chosen from the range of numbers 1 to 1,024. Understanding the philosophy of how the program works is one thing. Writing it down is a task of another dimension. (You would have to write down 1,023 questions together with the number of the next question to ask.) To illustrate the dimension of this task, we would like you to look at Fig. A1, which shows the program for determining, with 5 questions, the chosen value in the short range 1 to 32.

The program for asking questions shown in Fig. A1 is mighty cumbersome. Think of what it would be like for a range of 1,024; one would require over 31 sheets of paper (even though only 10 questions would be asked). There are several things we can do to reduce the amount of writing required. First, we can say that whenever the answer is *no* to the question, "Is it x or less?", one will automatically go to the next sequential question (as sort of an unwritten law).

Another attack is to examine the sequence of questions and determine if there is anything common about all the questions being asked. One of the common

A program for determining any number between 1 – 32 by asking five questions or less. (Although there are thirty two questions, five at most will be asked)

01	Is it 16 or less? Yes, ask Q 17; No, ask Q 2	(Y; 1-16) (N; 17-32)
02	Is it 24 or less? Yes, ask Q 10; No, ask Q 3	(Y; 17-24) (N; 25-32)
03	Is it 28 or less? Yes, ask Q 7; No, ask Q 4	(Y; 25-28) (N; 29-32)
04	Is it 30 or less? Yes, ask Q 6; No, ask Q 5	(Y; 29-30) (N; 31-32)
05	Is it 32? Yes, it is 32; No, it is 31	(Y; 32) (N; 31)
06	Is it 30? Yes, it is 30; No, it is 29	(Y; 30) (N; 29)
07	Is it 26 or less? Yes, ask Q 9; No, ask Q 8	(Y; 25-26) (N; 27-28)
08	Is it 28? Yes, it is 28; No, it is 27	(Y; 28) (N; 27)
09	Is it 26? Yes, it is 26; No, it is 25	(Y; 26) (N; 25)
10	Is it 20 or less? Yes, ask Q 14; No, ask Q 11	(Y; 17-20) (N; 21-24)
11	Is it 22 or less? Yes, ask Q 13; No, ask Q 12	(Y; 21-22) (N; 23-24)
12	Is it 24? Yes, it is 24; No, it is 23	(Y; 24) (N; 23)
13	Is it 22? Yes, it is 22; No, it is 21	(Y; 22) (N; 21)
14	Is it 18 or less? Yes, ask Q 16; No, ask Q 15	(Y; 17-18) (N; 19-20)
15	Is it 20? Yes, it is 20; No, it is 19	(Y; 20) (N; 19)
16	Is it 18? Yes, it is 18; No, it is 17	(Y; 18) (N; 17)
17	Is it 8 or less? Yes, ask Q 25; No, ask Q18	(Y; 1-8) (N; 9-16)
18	Is it 12 or less? Yes, ask Q22; No, ask Q 19	(Y; 9-12) (N; 13-16)
19	Is it 14 or less? Yes, ask Q 21; No, ask Q 20	(Y; 13-14) (N; 15-16)
20	Is it 16? Yes, it is 16; No, it is 15	(Y; 16) (N; 15)
21	Is it 14? Yes, it is 14; No, it is 13	(Y; 14) (N; 13)
22	Is it 10 or less? Yes, ask Q 24; No, ask Q 23	(Y; 9-10) (N; 11-12)
23	Is it 12? Yes, it is 12; No, it is 11	(Y; 12) (N; 11)
24	Is it 10? Yes, it is 10; No, it is 9	(Y; 10) (N; 9)
25	Is it 4 or less? Yes, ask Q 29; No, ask Q 26	(Y; 1-4) (N; 5-8)
26	Is it 6 or less? Yes, ask Q 28; No, ask Q 27	(Y; 5-6) (N; 7-8)
27	Is it 8; Yes, it is 8; No, it is 7	(Y; 8) (N; 7)
28	Is it 6? Yes, it is 6; No, it is 5	(Y; 6) (N; 5)
29	Is it 2 or less? Yes, ask Q 31; No, ask Q 30	(Y; 1-2) (N; 3-4)
30	Is it 4? Yes, it is 4; No, it is 3	(Y; 4) (N; 3)
31	Is it 2? Yes, it is 2; No, it is 1	(Y; 2) (N; 1)

Fig. A1 A 32-question program.

items that can be "discovered" is the relationship between successively *asked* questions. That is, the current question asked concerns a value that was obtained either by adding one half of the previous range to the range value or by subtracting one half of the previous range from the range value. For example, if the range value in question 1 is 16, the next question to be asked is either question 2 (no) or question 17 (yes); the range value of question 2 is 24 $(16 + 8)$ and the range value of question 17 is 8 $(16 - 8)$.

Another "discovery" is that the *answer* has been automatically determined when the range value has been reduced to 1. (When the range value is 4, there are still four numbers to choose from; when the range value is 1, there is no "choice"; the mystery number has been discovered.)

Figure A2 shows a program for determining any value whose range is a multiple of 2 (2,4,8,...,512, 1024,...,8192, etc.). When programs for doing things are presented in the form shown in Fig. A2, they are referred to as flow charts or block diagrams. Let's look at Fig. A2 more closely. The first (rectangular) block says to find a quotient by dividing the range (e.g., 32) by 2 ($32 \div 2 = 16$). The second (rectangular) block says to set x and y equal to the quotient ($x = 16$, $y = 16$). The third (diamond-shaped) block asks a question to which the answer is either no or yes. When the answer is no, the fourth block says to divide y (still 16) by 2 ($16 \div 2 = 8$). The new value of y is now 8 (i.e., it has replaced the old value of 16). The next block asks a question, "Is N greater than or equal to ($\geqslant$) x? (N is the mystery number.) A no answer directs us to execute the instruction in block F1, "Make the new value of x equal to the difference between the old value of x and the value of y." A yes answer in block E1 directs us to execute the instruction in block E2, "Make the new value of x equal to the sum of the old value of x and the value of y."

The block diagram in Fig. A2 is an intermediate step in the development of the program we want to write. Figure A3 shows a "program" of 11 statements which can be used to determine any value in a range of almost any size.

TYPES OF INSTRUCTIONS IN FIGURE A3

The first two statements in Fig. A3 belong to a class called *processing instructions.* That is, these instructions perform some kind of process; in the first the process is division; in the second the process is *setting* two variables equal to a third. The third statement is called a conditional branch instruction. That is, on the *condition* that $y = 1$, go to statement 10. If the condition $y = 1$ does not exist, one must go to statement 4 automatically.

Statement 7 is an unconditional branch instruction. No matter what kind of condition exists, one goes to statement 3 after executing statement 7. Since no conditions have been specified, statement 7 is an example of an *unconditional* branch instruction.

DATA AND CONSTANTS

If statements 01 to 11 are instructions, what are statements 12 to 17? Statement 12 represents the upper limit of the range (which might vary each time the game is played). This upper limit is the data to be processed by the instructions. Statements 13 and 17 are true constants; that is, each time the program is "executed," the

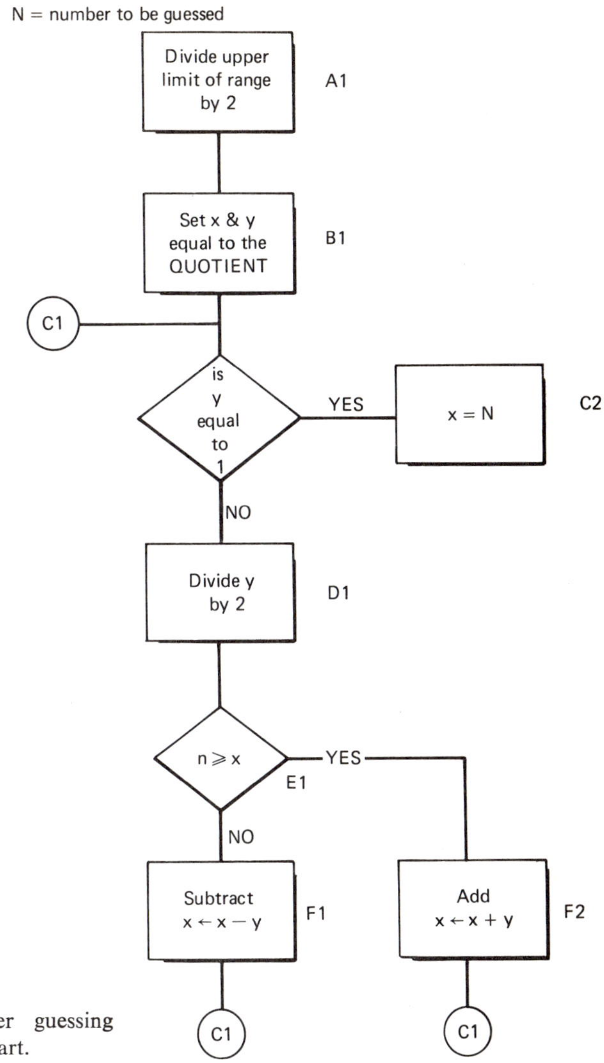

Fig. A2 Number guessing flowchart.

value of statements 13 and 17 remains the same. Statements 14, 15, and 16 are also regarded as constants, but only because they are neither instructions nor original data. It might have been a good idea for data-processing people to have come up with a term such as "elderkins" to distinguish these values from both the true constants and original data. But they didn't, so we'll have to remember them as a variety of constant.

```
01  Divide upper limit of range by 2
02  set x and y equal to quotient.
03  Is y equal to the value of 1? If yes, go to statement 10.
04  Divide value of Y by 2
05  Is N equal to or greater than x? If yes, go to statement 8.
06  Subtract Y from X
07  Go to statement number 3
08  Add Y to X
09  Go to statement number 3
10  Print the value of x (it equals the value of n)
11  Buy coffee
12  Upper limit of range
13  2
14  x
15  y
16  n
17  1
```

Fig. A3 Number guessing: symbolic program.

DEBUGGING

After a person has written a program, he puts it to the test with sample data (to make sure there are no errors). The discovery and correction of errors in a program is called debugging.

ENCODED INSTRUCTIONS

The programs shown in Fig. A3 reads very much like a series of interrogative and imperative English sentences. One of the first recommendations a program efficiency expert would make is, "Encode the instructions so they won't be so long." If he had his way, the expert would rewrite the program as shown in Fig. A4. The expert might also say that to play the coffee-buying game (i.e., to execute the instructions) the participants *must* use the encoded version. We will say that the encoded version is in the *execution language* form.

The ordinary instruction writer (the person who wrote the program in Fig. A3) rarely writes programs in the execution language form (Fig. A4). Rather, he writes his instructions in a language conducive to programming (as opposed to being conducive to execution). This form is called a *programming language;* sometimes it is called a symbolic language. The program written in symbolic form is often referred to as a symbolic program.

The process of transforming the symbolic program from the form in Fig. A3 (programming language) to the form in Fig. A4 (execution language) is called

	Encoded Instructions	Explanation of Encoded Instructions
01	D1213	(Divide "D" the contents of statement 12 by statement 13) Quotient will be in Stmt. 12)
02	T141512	(Set "T", the contents of statements 14 and 15 with the contents of Stmt. 12.)
03	B1015E17	(Branch "B" to Stmt. 10 if contents of Stmt. 15 equals contents of Stmt. 17)
04	D1513	(Divide "D" contents of stmt 15 by contents of stmt 13. Quotient will be in stmt 15)
05	B0816J14	(Branch "B" to stmt 08 if contents of stmt 16 equal or greater than (J) to contents of stmt 14)
06	S1514	(Subtract "S" contents of stmt 15 from contents of stmt 14)
07	B03	(Branch "B" to stmt 03)
08	A1514	(Add "A" contents to stmt 15 to contents of stmt 14)
09	B03	(Branch "B" to stmt 03)
10	P14	(Print the contents of stmt 14)
11	C	(Buy coffee "C")
12	'1024'	(The decimal value 1024)
13	'2'	(The decimal value 2)
14	'xxxx'	(Four positions for the value of x)
15	'yyy'	(Three positions for the value of y)
16	'nnnn'	(Four positions for the value of n)
17	'1'	(The value 1)

Fig. A4 Number guessing: execution program.

compilation. Whoever or whatever does this compilation process must also follow a series of instructions. This series of instructions is called a compilation program (*compiler* for short). Naturally, the compiler will exist in the form of the *execution* language.

NUMBER OF PROGRAMMING LANGUAGES

You will often hear the question why there are so many programming languages to choose from (IBM provides the FORTRAN, COBOL, PL/1, RPG, and Assembly programming languages.) Wouldn't it be better, one might ask, if there were just one programming system—for then the creators and developers of the language could produce a truly superior product—it would also make it much easier for all users to share each other's programming experiences. Although the two conclusions just proposed are relatively true, they disregard the historical development of the progamming languages.

For example, FORTRAN was developed in the mid-1950s primarily for engineering and science.* As the years progressed, FORTRAN's capabilities were incorporated by IBM. No matter how much FORTRAN improved, however, it was primarily a language for scientists and engineers and *not* for accountants, auditors, and the general, commercial data-processing people. These people were writing most of their programs using the Assembly language, which basically, is equivalent to writing programs in machine language. Hence the COBOL programming language was developed in the early 1960s and it has been continually improved in subsequent years.†

Although the rules and grammar of the COBOL language are not too difficult to learn, it takes a fair amount of programming talent and training to write a COBOL program. There are a substantial number of people who do have access to a computer but don't have the programming training necessary to write the COBOL program needed to produce the desired report. Should these people be denied the privilege of using the computer? Definitely not—but then someone (e.g., IBM) had better develop a programming language the main objective of which is to write reports from a simple description of data in cards or on tape or on disk. IBM did develop the report program generator (RPG) to meet this objective.

With the advent of S/360 it became evident to many computer users and IBM that a new programming language (combining the best features of COBOL and FORTRAN with new features present in neither) was needed. This new programming language is PL/1 (pronounced pea-ell-one; it means programming language one). It meets the need for all scientific, engineering, and commercial programming requirements.

You may be wondering why some people are still using FORTRAN and COBOL if PL/1 is such a cure-all for programming needs. The answer is fairly simple: Installations that have been using FORTRAN and COBOL for years feel comfortable and secure when programming with these languages. It is, so to speak, their programming blanket. It will take several years before they have the same

---

* The term FORTRAN comes from the words *formula translation.* Scientists and engineers apply mathematical *formulas* in doing their work. The equivalent of a *formula* can be expressed in a programming language. To be executed, the *for*mula must be *tran*slated into machine language—hence the term FORTRAN.

† COBOL means common business oriented language, that is, a programming language designed by people engaged in common, ordinary, everyday business. The language is made up of words, symbols for representing arithmetic operations, and a set of punctuation and syntax rules for composing data-processing *sentences* (referred to as *statements*).

feeling of comfort and security with PL/1. Until they attain this feeling, these installations will continue to write most of their programs with the language they're most familiar with. For these reasons, therefore, COBOL and FORTRAN are still provided by IBM.*

The people who write programs for solving the problems of everyday business, engineering, and science are called *problem programmers*; the output of their programming efforts are called *problem programs.*

CLASSIFYING PROGRAMMING LANGUAGE LEVELS

The collection of programming languages, like so many other collections of similar objects, eventually becomes subjected to a classification system. One of the ways a programming language is classified is by level. So far there are only two levels: high and low. What qualifies a language to be called high level or low level? A programming language is said to be low level when the statements of the language are similar in format to the machine language (execution language) instructions of the computer for which the statements are written. For example, the S/360 Assembly language statements are the symbolic equivalent of the S/360's machine language instructions. The Assembly language statements of the IBM 1401 (one of the S/360's predecessors) are the symbolic equivalent of the 1401's machine language instructions. In contrast, the format of statements for a high-level language program remains consistent regardless of the computer's machine language format. That is, the format of a FORTRAN statement can be just as valid for IBM's 7094, 1410, or S/360.

Advantages/Disadvantages of High/Low Levels

Let's consider some of the high-level language's advantages first. For the most part, the high-level language programmer does not have to know anything about machine language instructions. As a matter of fact, he may not even know the name or manufacturer of the computer on which his program is to eventually run. This minimizes the programmer's education requirements in that he doesn't have to study each new computer that comes into his installation.

---

* Stating a preference for a programming language is akin to having a preference for a conversational language. Many families when they leave their homeland and become foreigners find that the language of the new country is *inflexible* (they don't know the words), *difficult* (they haven't learned the grammar and syntax rules), and *incomprehensible* (they think in the old language and mentally translate before speaking). Hence they are very apt to continue to use the old language.

On the other hand, the low-level (Assembly) language programmer must know a *considerable* amount about a computer's machine language instructions. That is, he must know in great detail what each operation can do. In general, it takes a great deal longer to become proficient at Assembly language programming than it does for programming in COBOL, FORTRAN, or PL/1. The reason is that the rules for writing high-level language programs are much simpler and fewer than are the rules for writing Assembly language programs. Of couse, the more complex rules you have, the easier it is to make mistakes. You are probably wondering why anyone would use the Assembly language in preference to any of the high-level languages. One reason is quite simple: The machine language program compiled from instructions written in the Assembly language has the potential of being more efficient (in terms of execution time and storage requirements) than the machine language program compiled from a high-level language. Observe that we used the phrase "has the *potential* of being." This is because the Assembly language program also has the potential of being *less* efficient. That is, unless the Assembly language programmer has had a great deal of training and has the talent for working with small details, it is possible that his program will be less efficient than if it had been written with a high-level language. Even when a data-processing installation has an ample supply of programmers with these characteristics, it is less economical to write programs in the Assembly language. That is, no matter how much more efficient the end product will be, it won't be useful unless it is produced in time. For example, if a program has to be written by, say, tomorrow afternoon and the only way to meet this schedule is to write it in FORTRAN (even though the execution program might be 100 times more efficient if it were to be written by next week in the Assembly language), it is written in FORTRAN.

THE LINKAGE EDITOR

Regardless of which of the five symbolic languages is used, the symbolic programs must be translated into machine language before the computer can execute the program. Thus we say that the source language statements are input data to a program called a Compiler whose output is machine language instructions. Now, even though the symbolic statements have been translated into a machine language program, the machine language program is not executable (i.e., the computer cannot yet execute the program). To make it executable the output of a compiler must be processed by a program called the Linkage Editor. Figure A5 illustrates the relationship between the programs for (1) compiling the symbolic language statements and (2) link editing the Compiler output.

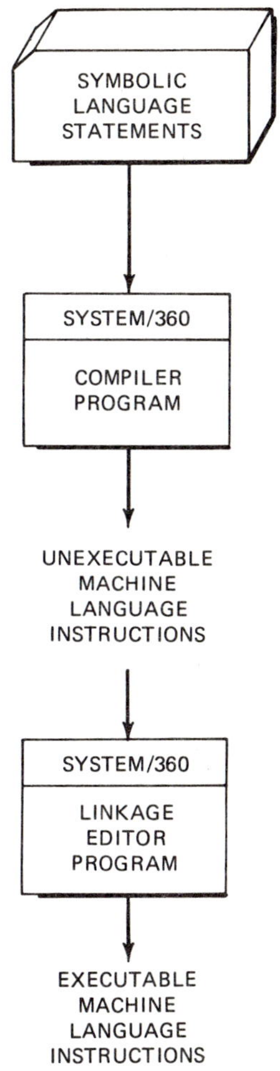

Fig. A5 Steps to produce machine language instructions.

APPENDIX

II *NUMBERING & COUNTING SYSTEMS*

The arithmetic of today would not have been possible had it not been for the development of a simple numbering system. A numbering system is another term for a counting system. What is a counting system? It is basically a technique for remembering how many of a certain item exists. Counting systems most people are familiar with are the Roman numeral counting system and the decimal counting system.

In early civilizations mankind did not count at all. For example, if a shepherd were asked how many sheep he had, he couldn't answer. As a matter of fact, he didn't know from one day to the next whether his flock increased, decreased, or remained the same (unless it was very, very small). Eventually, one smart shepherd developed a technique to help him "remember" how many sheep he had: He put one stone in a pouch for each sheep in his charge. Then each time he was asked if he had all his sheep, he'd pair off each sheep with a stone. When the flock of sheep became large, the bags got quite heavy and it was difficult to carry the bag. It also took a long time to pair off stones and sheep. Another precocious shepherd discovered that a scratch (called a tally) was just as effective as a stone. With a pound of tablets he could keep track of as many sheep as with 50 pounds of stones (see Fig. A6). However, with large quantities even the tally marks became hard to use. Whenever the shepherd was asked how many sheep he had, all he could do was show the tablets with the tally marks on them.

A Roman who visited the sheep-raising countries suggested the use of symbols for various quantities of tallies.

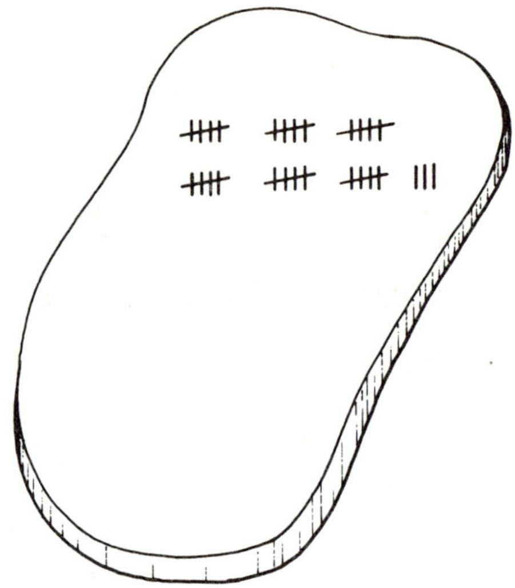

This stone tablet contains 33 tallies that have been scratched on with a harder stone. Even today many people use the tally technique. For example, people who count traffic (vehicular, super market, movie theater, etc.) often record one tally for each item of traffic.

Fig. A6 Stone tablet for tallies.

For 5 tally marks he used a V, for 10 tally marks he suggested an X, for 50 tally marks he chose an L, for 100 tally marks he suggested a C, and for 1,000 tally marks he used an M (see Fig. A7). Relatively large quantities could be represented by combining a few symbols. It was then a fairly simple matter to compare several symbol strings to determine which string represented the largest quantity (or smallest quantity, whichever the case might be). For example, one found it not too difficult to state that MCMLXX represented a greater quantity than MCMLXVI.

Using Roman numerals to perform arithmetic operations was something else. Although some people could perform arithmetic with Roman numerals, it was difficult and slow—there are no simple rules (or algorithms) to follow for dividing even such small values as DLXXV by XXIII. The difficulty of discovering simple rules for Roman numeral arithmetic is probably what spurred the development of a positional number system. A positional number (or counting) system has at least three advantageous characteristics:

1. There can be relatively few symbols.
2. Each symbol can (depending upon its position relative to other symbols in the number) represent many values (e.g., each 5 in 555 has a different value than the other two).
3. If a position in a number has no value, the absence of a symbol is designated with a special character—0 (zero). A zero is necessary whether the positional counting system has just one other symbol or 25. (If there were

Tally Marks	Symbol	Tally Marks	Symbol
I	I	one hundred tally marks	C
II	II	⋮	
III	III	one hundred forty-nine tally marks	CXLIX
IIII	IV	⋮	
𝍸	V	five hundred tally marks	D
𝍸 I	VI	⋮	
𝍸 II	VII	one thousand tally marks	M
𝍸 III	VIII		
𝍸 IIII	IX		
𝍸 𝍸	X		
⋮			
𝍸 𝍸 𝍸 IIII	XIX		
𝍸 𝍸 𝍸 𝍸	XX		
⋮	⋮		
𝍸 𝍸 𝍸 𝍸 𝍸 𝍸 𝍸 𝍸	XL		
⋮			
𝍸 𝍸 𝍸 𝍸 𝍸 𝍸 𝍸 𝍸 𝍸 𝍸	L		

Fig. A7 Relationship between tallies and roman numerals.

no zero, the string 3 8 could mean three hundred eight, or three hundred eighty, or thirty-eight, or three thousand eight, or three thousand eight hundred, etc.)

NUMBER SYSTEM BASE

Let us say that the base of a numbering system means the number of symbols. That is, since the decimal counting system uses 10 symbols we say it has a base of 10. The binary counting system has 2 symbols and therefore a base of 2. The hexadecimal system has a base of 16 and hence consists of 16 different symbols.

Let's now look at some numbers in the decimal counting system, where the position of each symbol in a number has a special name (see Fig. A8). Figure A9 is a variation of Fig. A8. The nonsignificant zeros have been left out, and terms such as millions and hundred thousands have been replaced by their equivalent exponent form [i.e., 1 million is equal to $10 \times 10 \times 10 \times 10 \times 10 \times 10$ (six tens) and can be written 10^6; one hundred thousand is equivalent to $10 \times 10 \times 10 \times 10 \times 10$ (five tens) and can be written 10^5].

Figure A10 illustrates how counting systems with different numbers of symbols compare when representing the same quantity. Note how many dots represent a "one zero" in each of the four numbering systems. What should we call the one

Each of the sample numbers shown consists of seven digits. Examples 3, 4, 5, 6, 8, 9, and 10 have non-significant zeros (i.e., zeros which if they had been left out would not change the value of the number). All examples (except number 4) have significant zeros (i.e., if the position they occupy were left blank, the entire value of the number could change (e.g., Example 6 might be mistaken for 123). The zero in the thousands position of example 3 is significant whereas the zero in the thousands position of examples 4 and 5 is non-significant.

Position Values →	Millions Position	Hundred Thousand Position	Ten Thousands Position	Thousands Position	Hundreds Position	Tens Position	Ones or Units Position
1.	2	0	7	3	9	1	4
2.	7	9	0	8	0	0	6
3.	0	0	3	0	7	0	9
4.	0	0	0	0	0	0	8
5.	0	0	0	0	3	1	0
6.	0	1	0	2	0	3	0
7.	9	0	0	0	0	0	0
8.	0	0	1	4	0	9	9
9.	0	0	1	4	1	0	0
10.	0	0	0	8	0	1	7

Fig. A8 Conventional position values.

POSITION VALUES Shown in Exponent Form →	10^6	10^5	10^4	10^3	10^2	10^1	10^0
1.	2	0	7	3	9	1	4
2.	7	9	0	8	0	0	6
3.			3	0	7	0	9
4.							8
5.					3	1	0
6.		1	0	2	0	3	0
7.	9	0	0	0	0	0	0
8.			1	4	0	9	9
9.			1	4	1	0	0
10.				8	0	1	7

Fig. A9 Exponential position values.

zero in each of the four cases? The answer is easy for decimal—it is ten. The string of one zero in the other number systems has no agreed-upon names. The most common way of overcoming the vocabulary problem in number systems is to first say the name of the number system and then say the number as though it were decimal. For example, we would say either binary ten, or senary ten, or hex ten when talking about the string "one zero" in the respective numbering system.

Objects To Be Counted	Decimal 0,1,2,3,4,5,6,7,8,9	Hexadecimal 0,1,2,3,4,5,6,7,8,9 A,B,C,D,E,F	Senary 0, 1, 2, 3, 4, 5	Binary 0, 1
	Number Counting Systems			
	0	0	0	0
.	1	1	1	1
:	2	2	2	10
:.	3	3	3	11
::	4	4	4	100
::.	5	5	5	101
:::	6	6	10	110
:::.	7	7	11	111
::::	8	8	12	1000
::::.	9	9	13	1001
:::::	10	A	14	1010
:::::.	11	B	15	1011
::::::	12	C	20	1100
::::::.	13	D	21	1101
:::::::	14	E	22	1110
:::::::.	15	F	23	1111
::::::::	16	10	24	10000
::::::::.	17	11	25	10001
:::::::::	18	12	30	10010
:::::::::.	19	13	31	10011
::::::::::	20	14	32	10100
::::::::::.	21	15	33	10101
:::::::::::	22	16	34	10110
:::::::::::.	23	17	35	10111
::::::::::::	24	18	40	11000
::::::::::::.	25	19	41	11001
:::::::::::::	26	1A	42	11010
:::::::::::::.	27	1B	43	11011
::::::::::::::	28	1C	44	11100
::::::::::::::.	29	1D	45	11101
:::::::::::::::	30	1E	50	11110
:::::::::::::::.	31	1F	51	11111
::::::::::::::::	32	20	52	100000
::::::::::::::::.	33	21	53	100001
:::::::::::::::::	34	22	54	100010
:::::::::::::::::.	35	23	55	100011
::::::::::::::::::	36	24	100	100100

Fig. A10 Counting objects with different numbering systems.

CONVERTING FROM ONE NUMBERING SYSTEM TO ANOTHER

There will be opportunities in your career as a data-processing expert to convert values from one numbering system to another.

Converting from Decimal to Hexadecimal

For this topic, refer to Fig. A11. Note that there are six columns of figures. The bottom of the table shows that the columns are numbered 6, 5, 4, 3, 2, and 1 from left to right. Each of the columns stands for one position in a hexadecimal number. The table can therefore be used to convert as many as six places (the decimal number from which the conversion takes place can have up to eight places). When a decimal number is given the table can be used to develop the hexadecimal string from left to right. Let's look at an example: Convert 50,000 to hex.

The first operation with the table is to find either

1. the largest number that is less than the number we wish to convert (i.e., 50,000), or
2. the decimal number that is equal (which would be the case if we wanted to convert, e.g., 20,480).

Is 50,000 a value in the table? If it is, you have the wrong figure. The closest value to 50,000 is in column 4 and the number is 49,152.

This first operation tells us two things:

HEX	DEC	HEX	DEC	HEX	DEC	HEX	DEC	HEX	DEC	HEX	DEC
0	0	0	0	0	0	0	0	0	0	0	0
1	1,048,576	1	65,536	1	4,096	1	256	1	16	1	1
2	2,097,152	2	131,072	2	8,192	2	512	2	32	2	2
3	3,145,728	3	196,608	3	12,288	3	768	3	48	3	3
4	4,194,304	4	262,144	4	16,384	4	1,024	4	64	4	4
5	5,242,880	5	327,680	5	20,480	5	1,280	5	80	5	5
6	6,291,456	6	393,216	6	24,576	6	1,536	6	96	6	6
7	7,340,032	7	458,752	7	28,672	7	1,792	7	112	7	7
8	8,388,608	8	524,288	8	32,768	8	2,048	8	128	8	8
9	9,437,184	9	589,824	9	36,864	9	2,304	9	144	9	9
A	10,485,760	A	655,360	A	40,960	A	2,560	A	160	A	10
B	11,534,336	B	720,896	B	45,056	B	2,816	B	176	B	11
C	12,582,912	C	786,432	C	49,152	C	3,072	C	192	C	12
D	13,631,488	D	851,968	C	53,248	D	3,328	D	208	D	13
E	14,680,064	E	917,504	D	57,344	E	3,584	E	224	E	14
F	15,728,640	F	983,040	E	61,440	F	3,840	F	240	F	15
6		5		4		3		2		1	

HEXADECIMAL AND DECIMAL CONVERSION

To find the decimal number, locate the Hex number and its decimal equivalent for each position. Add these to obtain the decimal number. To find the Hex number, locate the next lower decimal number and its Hex equivalent. Each difference is used to obtain the next Hex number until the entire number is developed.

Fig. A11 Hexadecimal and decimal conversion chart.

1. The hex number will have four positions (we started in column 4).
2. The leftmost position (high-order position) of the hex number will contain the symbol opposite 49,152. This is the symbol C.

Of the original 50,000 we have taken care of 49,152 with the hexadecimal symbol C (in fourth position).

There is still a difference of 848 (50,000 — 49,152 = 848) to be accounted for. We go to the next column (column 3) and repeat the operation for 848. The closest lower value is 768. The hex symbol that stands for 768 is 3—this 3 will occupy the third position of the hex number.

So far we have filled two positions of the four position hex number as follows:

C	3	?	?

We still have a difference of 80 (848 — 768 = 80) to account for. Column 2 shows that the decimal value of 80 can be shown with the hex symbol 5 (in the second position). Now we have filled three positions of the four position hex number as follows:

C	3	5	?

We now have a difference of zero (80 — 80 = 0). As column 1 shows, a decimal 0 is equivalent to a hex 0. We can now complete the hex equivalent of 50,000. It is

C	3	5	0

Let's look at another example. Convert decimal 2317 to its hex equivalent.

Since the nearest lesser value is in column 3 we know we'll have a three-digit hex string: The appropriate hex value is a 9 (opposite the 2304). Up to this point we have

9	?	?

The amount still to be accounted for is 13 (2317 — 2304 = 13). Column 2 shows us that the hex symbol necesary for representing a decimal 13 is zero (0). We now have

9	0	?

Of course, the difference is still 13 but now we have to look at the next column (which is column 1). There we find that the equivalent of decimal 13 is the hex symbol D. We now have the equivalent of decimal 2317. It is

9	0	D

Convert the following decimal numbers to their hex equivalent using the conversion chart (Fig. A11):

1. 72,501
2. 36,879
3. 2,986
4. 61,455
5. 4,096
6. 4,095
7. 12,245,761
8. 11,537,390
9. 61,904
10. 12,648,430
11. 524,287
12. 12,698,464

Converting from Decimal to Binary

The direct conversion of a decimal number to a binary number is a fairly lengthy procedure. Therefore, we shall use an indirect method!!! What we are really saying is that conversion of decimal to binary can be accomplished most efficiently by first converting from decimal to hex.

There is a very simple relationship between a hex symbol (regardless of its position in the number) and its four-position binary equivalent. For example, the four-position binary equivalent of the hex symbol 0 is 0000; the four-position binary equivalent of the hex symbol 7 is 0111; the four-position binary equivalent of the hex symbol E is 1110. The following table summarizes the four-position binary equivalents of the 16 hex symbols.

Hex Symbol	Binary Equivalent
0	0000
1	0001
2	0010
3	0011
4	0100
5	0101
6	0110
7	0111
8	1000
9	1001
A	1010
B	1011
C	1100
D	1101
E	1110
F	1111

Let's look at a couple of equivalences. Note that regardless of the position which the hex symbol occupies, its four-position binary equivalent is the same as the above table indicates.

A 1 B 2 C 3

1010 0001 1011 0010 1100 0011

F O F O F O

1111 0000 1111 0000 1111 0000

Convert each of the following decimal values to its binary equivalent:

1. 8,190	5. 1,000
2. 514	6. 2,000
3. 1,536	7. 255
4. 131,000	8. 7,531

Converting from Hex to Decimal

Not only must you be able to "translate" a decimal number into a hex number, you must be able to convert a hexadecimal value to its decimal equivalent. The conversion of hex to decimal is quite easy with the chart in Fig. A10. You simply add together the decimal numbers that correspond to each of the symbols (by position) in the given hex number. For example, B3D7 converts as follows:

```
B     = 45056
 3    =   768
  D   =   208
   7  =     7
-----   -----
B3D7  = 46039
```

Convert each of the following hex values to its decimal equivalent:

1. 0DD	5. 301E
2. 1,000	6. ABCD
3. DDDD	7. DCBA
4. F00D	8. F03

Converting from Binary to Decimal

There will be occasions when the information that is in the S/360 is only available to you in binary form. The easiest way to convert from binary to decimal is to perform the intermediate operation of converting from binary to hex. The technique for doing this is quite simple. The first thing to do is record the binary value on a piece of paper, e.g.,

0000 1111 0000 0011

The next thing to do is to surround each collection of four binary digits with a box. (You can perform this mentally or actually draw lines.) Always start with the right side of the binary number:

0000	1111	0000	0011

Next, determine the hex symbol for each collection of four binary digits:

0 F 0 3

Convert each of the examples from binary to hexadecimal. (If the quantity of binary positions is not evenly divisible by 4, place binary zeros at the left of the binary string to make the number of positions evenly divisible by 4.)

1. 1100101011111110
2. 11010000000011011110
3. 11111000011001110
4. 0010010001101000
5. 111111000000000111
6. 1011001011100111010

COMPLETING THE CONVERSION

The next step is to convert the hex value into its decimal equivalent. (You can do this quite easily by using the hex and decimal conversion chart in Fig. A11.) All that you have to do is find the decimal equivalent of each hex value (make sure to use the proper column) and add the values together. Let's consider the hex value 360.

A hex 3 in column 3 is equivalent to a decimal	768
A hex 6 in column 2 is equivalent to a decimal	96
A hex 0 in column 1 is equivalent to a decimal	0
	864

Hence the decimal equivalent of hex 360 is 864.

Convert the hex values that you obtained in the previous review exercise into their decimal equivalents.

ADDING AND SUBTRACTING HEX NUMBERS

One of the skills required of you will be the addition and subtraction of hexadecimal numbers. There are several ways of obtaining the sum or difference of two hex numbers. One technique is to convert the hex number to a decimal value, then perform the arithmetic, and then convert its answer back to hex. Although this three-step operation may at first seem simpler than hex arithmetic, you will, with practice, be able to add and subtract hex numbers as easily as decimal values. Figure A12 is an addition/subtraction table for hex arithmetic (read the rules once and then study the following examples).

Examples

1. (9 + 9)—The intersection of 9 + 9 is in the shaded area signifying a carry. The sum digit is a 2.

2. (7 + 8)—The intersection of 7 + 8 is not in the shaded area and hence there is no carry. The sum digit is F.

3. (A − 7)—Here we subtract 7 from A. We find the 7 in the leftmost vertical line; then we find the A in the horizontal line next to the 7. Next we look at the digit on the top row (directly above A) to find the difference; it is 3. Since A is not in the shaded area, there is no borrow.

Y \ X	0	1	2	3	4	5	6	7	8	9	A	B	C	D	E	F
0	0	1	2	3	4	5	6	7	8	9	A	B	C	D	E	F
1	1	2	3	4	5	6	7	8	9	A	B	C	D	E	F	0
2	2	3	4	5	6	7	8	9	A	B	C	D	E	F	0	1
3	3	4	5	6	7	8	9	A	B	C	D	E	F	0	1	2
4	4	5	6	7	8	9	A	B	C	D	E	F	0	1	2	3
5	5	6	7	8	9	A	B	C	D	E	F	0	1	2	3	4
6	6	7	8	9	A	B	C	D	E	F	0	1	2	3	4	5
7	7	8	9	A	B	C	D	E	F	0	1	2	3	4	5	6
8	8	9	A	B	C	D	E	F	0	1	2	3	4	5	6	7
9	9	A	B	C	D	E	F	0	1	2	3	4	5	6	7	8
A	A	B	C	D	E	F	0	1	2	3	4	5	6	7	8	9
B	B	C	D	E	F	0	1	2	3	4	5	6	7	8	9	A
C	C	D	E	F	0	1	2	3	4	5	6	7	8	9	A	B
D	D	E	F	0	1	2	3	4	5	6	7	8	9	A	B	C
E	E	F	0	1	2	3	4	5	6	7	8	9	A	B	C	D
F	F	0	1	2	3	4	5	6	7	8	9	A	B	C	D	E

Addition Rules (X + Y)

1. Find the lines of intersection of the two hex digits to be added. The intersection is the sum digit.
2. If the sum is
   a. Not in the shaded area there is no carry.
   b. In the shaded area there is a carry of 1.

Subtraction Rules (X − Y)

1. Find Y in the vertical line.
2. Find X in the horizontal line which corresponds to the Y value.
3. The difference is the digit in the top row which is directly above X.
4. If X is
   a. Not in the shaded area there is no borrow.
   b. In the shaded area there is a borrow.

Fig. A12 Hex addition and subtraction chart.

4. (9 − D)—Subtract D from 9. Find D in the leftmost vertical column, then locate the 9 in the horizontal line next to the D. (It is in the shaded area, signifying a borrow.) The digit in the top row directly above the 9 is a C.
5. Add the following values. Use the chart in Fig. A12 as often as you wish.

a.		d.		g.	
	28 + 96		41C + 287		4D3F + 1FFF
b.	12 + 18	e.	64B + 38C	h.	ABCD + DCBA
c.	164 + 23A	f.	9BB + 2C0		

6. Find the difference of the following hex numbers:

a.	1999 – 888	d.	FACE – CAD0	g.	51D7 – 10EA
b.	19AA – 777	e.	3927 – 419	h.	3A80 – FFF
c.	2CF9 – 14A9	f.	4162 – 30B		

INDEX

A

Access arm, 67
Access mechanism, 67, 68
Access Methods:
  definition, 129
  relationship to I/O Supervisor, 129, 170
  varieties, 170
Access time, 73
Addresses (*see* Main storage)
Address marker, disk, 73
ATTACH macro, 155

B

Base address (*see* Instruction components)
Basic access method, 170
Batch processing, 89, 112
Binary system, 287
Bit, definition, 11
Buffers, 180
Byte:
  combinations of cores within, 11
  definition, 11
  relationship to graphic symbol, 14, 15

C

Called and calling modules, 146
Catalog, 171
Cataloging, 171
CCW (channel command word), 41
Channel address word, 60
Channel allocation, 248–249
Channel status word, 60
Channels:
  multiplexor, 41
  selector, 58, 67, 71
Checkpoint restart, 213
COBLIB, 132
Code:
  card, 35
  definition, 12
  EBCDIC, 13
Compilers:
  examples of different types, 110
  I/O requirements, 111
Compiling a source program, 110, 111
Computer dialing, 94
Conditional branch, 276
Contents Supervisor, 153
Control units, 36, 37, 38, 41, 49, 60, 71, 83, 91, 101
Conversational programming, 114, 115
Core storage (*see* Main storage)
CPU:
  definition, 5
  master over channel, 44, 59
  operations, 6, 7
  program, 8
Cylinder concept, 72

D

DASDI, 179
Data Control Block, 179, 182
  specifying DCB information in DD statement, 251
Data factory, 1, 2, 3, 4, 44, 119
Data-processing applications, 108–110
Data set:
  characteristics, 192
  general definition, 45
  integrity, 198
  requests, 193
  temporary, 135, 193
Data set control block (DSCB), 174–179

Data set names, 231–233
DD statement, 135, 161, 181, 227
Debugging, 278
Deferred mounting, 191
Device independence, 182
Direct organization, 79–80
Directory, 130
Disk I/O operations, 83–84
Disk track format, 74
Displacement (*see* Instruction components)
Disposition of data sets, 227–230
Double word, definition, 16
Dynamic area of storage, 149

E

EBCDIC:
  definition, 12, 14
  graphic symbols represented, 13
EXEC statement, 135, 161, 217
  accounting information, 221
  conditional bypassing/execution, 223
  naming procedure, 219
  naming program, 219
  parameter passing, 220
  region size, 222
  restart, 224
  rollout/rollin, 224
  time limit, 222
Execution language:
  definition, 278
  understood by CPU, 8, 9

F

Field, definition, 45
Fixed area of storage, 149
FORTLIB, 132

G

Generation data groups, 183–189
GETMAIN macro, 159

H

Half-byte, definition, 14
Half-word, definition, 16
Hardware buffer, 40
Hexadecimal system:
  adding and subtracting, 294–296
  conversion to decimal, 16
  definition, 287
  operand of instruction, 19
  operation code of instruction, 19
  relationship to byte, 14
Hierarchy of main storage (*see* Main storage)

I

Indexed sequential organization, 75–78
Initiator, 134, 143, 155, 171
Input/Output commands, issued by channel, 41
Input/Output devices:
  card punch, 37, 42
  card reader, 36, 42
  data cell, 81–83
  disk drive, 69
  drums, 80–81
  magnetic tape drive, 47, 50, 51
  printer, 38, 42
  sketch pad, 98
  terminals, 91–96
  typewriter, 33
Input stream (*see* Job stream)
Inquiry processing, 90
Instruction components:
  base address, 19
  displacement, 19
  length, 23
  index value, 24
  operands, 19
  operation code, 19
Instruction types:
  register-to-register, 25
  storage-to-register, 24
  storage-to-storage, 23
Interrecord gap, 51
Interruptions:
  events causing, 27
  input/output, 60
  masking, 27
  programs for handling, 28, 60, 125, 128, 152
  SVC, 155
I/O device address, 103
I/O Supervisor, 128, 152
IPL, 157, 196

J

Job, 138
Job class, 141, 210
Job control, 161
JOBQE, 134, 143
JOB statement, 139, 161, 203
  accounting parameters, 205
  checkpoint/restart, 213
  class, 210
  message device, 211
  message display, 207
  prevent initiation, 212
  priority, 210
  programmer name, 207
  region size, 211
  rollout/rollin, 212
  termination conditions, 209
Job step, 138
  accounting, 221
Job stream, 140, 152

K

Key, disk, 74
Keypunch (card punch), 36

L

Library (*see* Partitioned data set)
Linkage Editor, 139, 193, 282
LINKLIB, 129
Link Pack Area, 160
LOGREC, 128

M

Machine language (*see* Execution language)
MACLIB, 132
Magnetic ink character recognition, 102
Magnetic tape:
  capacity, 49
  description, 47
  interrecord gap, 51
  nine track, 48
  seven track, 48
Magnetism:
  bar, 9, 11
  core, 9, 11
Main storage:
  addresses, 17
  core combinations, 10
  definition, 8
  hierarchy, 18
  relationship to CPU, 9, 18
  size, 9
Main Storage Supervisor, 153
Mask, definition, 27
Message switching, 97
MFT, 150
Microsecond, definition, 4
Millisecond, definition, 4
Modular programming, 145
Multidrop line, 94
Multiplexor channel (*see* Channels)
MVT, 150

N

Nanosecond, definition, 4
Nonreusable program, 156
Number system conversion, 289–294

O

Operating system, definition, 120
Optical character recognition, 102
Output classes, 144
Output data set queue, 144
Output writer, 144
Overriding procedures, 261

P

Parameters:
  definition, 23
  use in EXEC statement, 220
Parity bit, 47
Partitioned data set (library), 130
Partitions, 150
Passwords, 189–191
PCP, 148, 151
Picosecond, definition, 5
PLILIB, 132
Priority of job, 210
Priority Scheduler, 152
Private library, 254–255
Problem program, 281

Problem state, 28
Procedure examples, 264, 265, 267, 269, 270
Procedures, 162, 259
PROCLIB, 162, 219, 259
Program fetch, 129
Programming languages, 278–281
Program status word:
  function of, 26, 27
  interrupt mask, 27
  I/O PSW, 60
  new, current, old PSW's, 126
  problem state, 28
  protection key, 28
  restoring PSW's, 127

Q

Qualified names, 172
Queue, 153, 154
Queued access method, 170

R

Reader (program), 135
Reader/Interpreter, 135
Reader procedures, 262
Real-time processing, 97
Record:
  blocked, 54
  definition, 44
  fixed length, 55
  logical, 54
  physical, 54
  unblocked, 53
  variable length, 55
Record identification, 46
Reentrant programs, 156–159, 160
Regions, 150, 211, 222
Register (general):
  definition, 20
  number of, 20
  use of, 23
Request block (RB), 154, 155
Resident SVC's, 160
Resources, definition, 153
Return code, 209, 223, 224
RETURN macro, 148
Reusable programs, 156–158
Rollout/Rollin, 212, 224
Rotational delay, 73

S

SAVE macro, 147
Searching for disk record, 75
Selector channel (*see* Channels)
Sequential organization, 46
Sequential processing:
  definition, 57
  frequency of, 56, 59
Sequential Scheduler, 151
Sketch pad (electronic), 98
SORTLIB, 132
Space requests, 242-248
START command, 143, 144
STOP command, 143
Storage (*see* Main storage)
Storage protection, 28
Subroutine libraries, 131
Subtasking, 151
Supervisor, 121
SVCLIB, 160
Symbolic parameters, PROCLIB, 260
System generation, 121
System tasks, 135, 155

T

Tape label types, 249–250
Task Control Block (TCB), 153, 154
Task Dispatcher, 153
Tasks, general definition, 134
Task Supervisor, 153
Terminal device, 91, 94
Terminator, 153, 156, 187
Timer, 29
Time Supervisor, 153
Track index, 76
Transient area, 160

U

Unconditional branch, 276
Unit requests, 234–239

V

Volume allocation, 192
Volume identification, 239–242

Volumes:
availability, 195
definition, 132
informing OS about characteristics, 196
mount characteristics, 194–195
sharing, 196
VTOC (Volume Table of Contents), 133
VTOC (*Cont.*)
relationship to catalog, 172
relationship to label, 133

W

Word, definition, 16